Teaching and Understanding Pneumatology & Spiritual Gifts

Teaching and Understanding Pneumatology & Spiritual Gifts

Exegetes and Apologetes
Emphatically on Leadership and
Ministry, An Interdisciplinary Text

Elijah Eddie Dunbar

Copyright © 2009 by Elijah Eddie Dunbar.

ISBN: Softcover   978-1-4415-2930-5

All rights reserved. No part of this book may be reproduced or transmitted in any form or by any means, electronic or mechanical, including photocopying, recording, or by any information storage and retrieval system, without permission in writing from the copyright owner.

Most of the biblical references and quotations used in this book are taken from the King James Version of the Holy Bible. Other versions, references, and quotations are noted in the text as well.

This book was printed in the United States of America.

To order additional copies of this book, contact:
Xlibris Corporation
1-888-795-4274
www.Xlibris.com
Orders@Xlibris.com
61381

TABLE OF CONTENTS

INTRODUCTION   13

CHAPTER ONE   19

PNEUMATOLOGY AS A THEOLOGICAL DISCIPLINE   20

The Evolvement and Transition of Pneumatology 20
The Manifestation Holy Spirit 22
Pneumatology and Systematic Theology 24
Contemporary Perspective on Pneumatology 25
Biblical Perspectives on the Spirit 25
Spirit Featured in the Old Testament 26
The Spirit During the Intertestament Period 27
Spirit Featured in the New Testament 27
Spirit Featured in the Gospels 27
Spirit Featured in the Acts of the Apostles 28
Spirit Featured in the Pauline Letters 28
Summary 28
Assessment 29
Perspectives 29

CHAPTER TWO   31

APOLOGIES   32

Apology of Barnabas Lindars on the Holy Spirit 32
Apology of Philip Edgcumbe Hughes on Hebrews 6:4; 8:3 32
Apology of C. E. B. Cranfield on Romans 12:3-8 32
Apology of John Calvin on I Timothy 4:14-15 33
Apology of Robert Mounce on Romans 12:3-8 34
Peake's Apology on I Corinthians 12 34
Apologies from the Wycliffe Bible on I Corinthians 12 35

Summary 35
Assessment 35
Perspectives 36

CHAPTER THREE   37

KNOWING YOUR GIFT   38

I Corinthians 12: 7-11, 28-30 38
Exegesis of Gordon Fee on I Corinthians 12:7-8; 28-31 42
Summary 50
Assessment 51
Perspectives 52

CHAPTER FOUR   53

NINE GIFTS OF I CORINTHIANS 12   54

Word of Wisdom 55
The Word of Wisdom in the Ministry of Jesus 56
The Word of Wisdom in the Early Church 56
Word of Knowledge 57
The Word of Knowledge in the Ministry of Jesus 57
The Word of Knowledge in the Early Church 57
Discerning of Spirits 58
Scriptural Examples of the Discerning of the Holy Spirit 59
Scriptural Examples of the Discerning of Faithful Angels 59
Scriptural Examples of the Discerning of Human Spirits 59
Scriptural Examples of the Discerning of Evil Spirits 59
The Gift of Faith 60
New Testament Examples of Faith in Action 61
The Gift of Healings 61
Works Through Physical Contact 62
Works Through a Point of Contact 62
Scriptural Examples of Healings 62
Minister With Your Eyes Open 63
Summary 64
Assessment 65
Perspectives 65

CHAPTER FIVE   66

EXEGESES   67

Exegesis of Allen Hunt on I Corinthians 12 67
Exegesis of Simon J. Kistemaker on I Corinthians 12:7-11 68
Exergesis of Philipp Melanchthon on 1 Corinthisn 12 69
Exegesis of Victor Paul Furnish on I Corinthians 12 71
Dale B. Martin's Apology on the Cultural Background
    of the Corithian Church 73
Exegeses from the New International Greek Testament
    Commentary on I Corinthians 12 74
Summary 77
Assessment 78
Perspectives 79

CHAPTER SIX   80

INDIVIDUAL GIFTS   81

Faith as a Gift and Gifts Of Healing (12:9) 81
The Deeds of Power or Working of Miracles/ Power (I Corinthians12:10a). 82
Hellenistic Background of the Word "Prophecy" 83
Apocalyptic Background of the Word "Prophecy" 83
Prophecy as Pastoral Preaching 84
Discerning What is of the Spirit (12:10b) 84
Divers kinds or Species of Tongues and Their Intelligible
    Utterances (12:10c) 85
Tongues as the Miraculous Power to Speak Other Languages 86
Tongues as "Ecstatic" Speech 86
Summary 87
Assessment 87
Perspectives 87

CHAPTER SEVEN   89

PROPPOSED MODIFICATION FROM THEISSEN: CONSCIOUS, UNCONSCIOUS, AND A RELEASE (CF. ROMANS 8:26)   90

Summary 94
Assessment 95
Perspectives 95

CHAPTER EIGHT 97

EXEGETES AND APOLOGETES 98

Exegesis of Stowers on Romans 12:3-6 98
Apology of Origen on Ephesians 98
Apology of Jerome on Ephesians 99
Exegesis of Margaret Macdonald on Ephesians 4:4-16 99
Exegesis of John R. W. Stott on Ephesians 4:1-16 100
Exegesis from the Anchor Bible on Ephesians 4:4 100
Exegesis of Markus Barth on Ephesians 4:12-16 100
Exegesis of John Calvin on Ephesians 4:4-16 101
Summary 101
Assessment 102
Perspectives 102

CHAPTER NINE 103

THE FOUR-FOLD MINISTRY 104

The Nature of God's Leaders 106
Accepting God's Leader as an Eagle 106
What to do When the Bottom Falls Out? 107
Accepting God's Leader as an Ox 108
God's Leader as a Lion 110
God's Leader as a Man 112
Summary 114
Assessment 114
Perspectives 115

CHAPTER TEN 116

THE VALUE OF YOUR GIFT/ CALLING 117

Exegesis on Romans 12:3-8 122
Exegesis of David K. Bernard 124
Exegesis of Christopher Bryan on Romans 12:3-8 125
Exegeses of Robert Jewett et al on Romans 12:3-8 126
Exegesis of Theodore De Bruyn on Romans 12:3-8 127
Exegesis of Joseph A. Fitzmyer, S.J. on Romans 12:3-8 127
Apology of Alexander Maclaren on Romans 12:3-8 129
Exegesis of F. F. Bruce 129
Summary 135

Assessment 136
Perspectives 137

CHAPTER ELEVEN   138

LEADERSHIP IN MINISTRY   139

Summary 151
Assessment 151
Perspectives 152

CHAPTER TWELVE   153

GOD'S OVERVIEW OF YOUR GIFT/ CALLING   154

Exegesis of Ernest Best on Ephesians 4:4 155
Exegesis from the Anchor Bible on Ephesians 4:4 156
Exegeses of Kuhn and Other Exegetes 156
Exegesis of Origen on Ephesians 4:3 157
Exegesis of Jerome on Ephesians 4:3-4 158
Tyndale New Testament Commentaries on Ephesians 4:3-6 158
Diversity in Unity (Ephesians 4:7-16) 159
Exegesis on James 1:17 160
Exegesis of H. Greeven 161
Summary 167
Assessment 168
Perspectives 168

CHAPTER THIRTEEN   169

EDUCATION MINISTRY   170

Summary 178
Assessment 178
Perspectives 179

CHAPTER FOURTEEN   180

THE PURPOSE OF YOUR GIFT   181

Exegeses from the Interpreter's Bible 183
Exegesis on Ephesians 4:4-6 From the Interpreter's Bible 187
Exegesis of Ernest Best on Ephesians 4:12-16 188

Exegesis of S. Wibbing 188
Exegesis of Origen on Ephesians 4:11-16 189
Exegesis of Jerome on Ephesians 4:11-16 190
Exegesis of Wayne A. Gruedem on I Peter 4:10-11 191
Summary 198
Assessment 198
Perspectives 199

CHAPTER FIFTEEN   200

THE PREMISE OF YOUR GIFT/ CALLING   201

Exegesis of William Temple on John 4:10 201
Preparing to Deliver 206
The Curriculum 212
Learning Objectives 212
Summary 230
Assessment 230
Perspectives 230

CHAPTER SIXTEEN   231

THE EXTENT OF YOUR GIFT/ CALLING   232

Exegesis on Romans 12:9-21 236
Exegesis of David K. Bernard 239
Exegesis of F. F. Bruce 241
Exegesis of Robert B. Hughes 242
Practical Observations on the Operation of the Gifts 250
A Revelation May be Seen 251
A Revelation May be Heard 251
The Revelation to Occur May be Felt 252
The Four-Pronged Key to Success in Ministry 252
Summary 253
Assessment 254
Perspectives 254
Essential Vocabulary 256
Bibliography 261
Quotations 272
Appendix A 275
Appendix B 278

Appendix C	279
Appendix D	281
Appendix E	283
Notes	285
Name Index	297
General Index	305

INTRODUCTION

GREEK ETYMA

Birth—Genēsis (γέννησις) begetting, a birth

Bishop—Episkopos (ἐπίσκοπος) an overseer

Body—Sōma (σώμα) the instrument of life, of a physical nature

Breath—Pnoē (πνοή) to blow, signifies the breath of life, wind;

Cloud—Nephelē (νεφος) besides the physical element, the cloud with cover the children of Israel in the Red Sea.

Pneuma (πνεύμα) spirit, breath, ghost, life, wind

Reason—Logos (λόγς) a word, the significance of the inward thought

Talent—Talanton (τάλαντον) gift, ability

Teacher—Didaskalos (διδάσκαλος) teachers of the truth in the churches; Kalodidaskalos (καλοδιδάσκαλος) teacher of what is good.

Understand—Sunesis (σύνεσις) to set together, to understand, reflective thought

"And he gave some, apostles; and some, prophets; and some, evangelists; and some, pastors and teachers" **Ephesians 4:11.**

Faith is not merely praying upon our knees at night; faith is not merely straying through darkness into light; faith is not merely waiting for glory that may be. Faith is the brave endeavor, the splendid enterprise, the strength to serve, whatever conditions may arise (Anonymous)

The Hebrew root word for gift "nata" means "to give" which also means "gratuity." The Greek word "charismata," in its plural form signifies "gifts of grace" while "charisma" in its singular form signifies "a gift of grace." Interestingly, the word "charisma" is frequently used to describe the uniqueness, enthusiasm, and magic or magnetic appeal of a person with great leadership skills. The charisma of a person reveals that he or she is very special or talented. The "gift of grace" relates to God as being the donor to humanity in the person of Jesus Christ who was the "sacrifice" or "gift" to redeem the world. The "gift of grace" is the semblance of Gods' unmerited gift to an undeserving people (Romans 5:15, 16; 6:23; 11:29).

The Apostle Paul's usage of "gifts," refers to extraordinary powers given to certain Christians that distinguish them from others and enable them to be operational in the church (Romans 12:6-8; I Corinthians 12:1-31; I Corinthians 7:7). Barclay and Hendry join me in authenticating the significance of the presence of the Spirit in the church as God's instrument to spiritually liberate the church as thus: "The church needs the power of the Holy Spirit to confront the challenge and to grasp the opportunity. The church cannot do without the things which only the Holy Spirit can bring. Without the Holy Spirit the church cannot have a message. It was through the Holy Spirit that the gospel was first preached, and it is through the Holy Spirit that the gospel must continue to be preached" (Barclay, 105).[1]

Emphasizing more on the importance of the Holy Spirit's presence in the church, George Hendry adds the following: "The Holy Spirit is the soul of the church in the same service as our souls are the souls of our bodies. The church is primarily the succession of Christ; the presence and power of the Holy Spirit are regarded as the endowments bequeathed by Christ to the church to enable it to discharge its supernatural role. The Holy Spirit is regarded as the source or principle of the Church's power" (Hendry, 55).[2]

Ministerial leadership is not an idea of human origin. It is the gift to the Church from the Lord Jesus Christ. 'Jesus is the bearer and sender of the Spirit. The Spirit is the earthly presence of the exalted Lord. The Spirit is the builder of the Church and edifier of the faithful. The Spirit is the soul of the church. The Holy Spirit is individualized and institutionalized. The Holy Spirit is the builder of the church as

---

[1] William Barclay, The Promise of the Spirit. Philadelphia: The Westminster Press, 1960.

[2] George Hendry, The Holy Spirit in Christian Theology. Philadelphia: The Westminster Press, 1952.

a body, as a communion. The movement of the Holy Spirit is the movement of One to the man, of the *pars* to the *totum*' (Berkhof, 63).[3]

The effects of the Spirit in the church are worth noting. Yocom, Rena, Barr, and William R. share their views in this regard:

> "The Holy Spirit bestows on the community diverse and complimentary gifts. They are for the common good of the whole people and are manifested in acts of service within the community and to the world. All members are called to discourse, with the help of the community, the gifts they have received and to use them for the building up of the church and for service of the world to which the church is sent. The Spirit pours out an abundance of charisms. These charisms are for the building up of the church and for service in the world through teaching, prophecy, healing, miracles, tongues, and discernment of spirits" (Yocom, 112).[4]

Ministering under the anointing will mean the total ministry will be more effective. If a call of God to the work of the ministry has come upon a man's heart, he should earnestly enter into preparation for his life's work. Any effort to minimize the importance of these servants of the Lord is an affront to the Son of God. "Spiritual gifts always bring someone closer to God. Spiritual gifts come in limitless varieties. Spiritual gifts need to be exercised decently and in order. God gifted some in order to extend grace to all" (Haberer, 52).[5]

Pastors who may be wondering how important their role is in God's plan should proudly ahere to these informative notes from scholars as spelled out in this manner:

> If pastors are to have effective ministries, they must be leaders. They must have the inner conviction that they are doing what Christ would have them do. People who are called of God sometimes have handicaps which in the natural seem to disqualify them for the work of God. Moses pleaded to be excused on the basis of the unbelief of Israel and a speech problem he had (Exodus 4:1-13). The pastor will be effective only as he recognizes that the pastoral office is created by Christ, that the individual call and guidance come from Christ, and that he is ultimately accountable to Christ (Pastoral Theology In Action, 1,3,15,158).[6]

---

[3] Hendrikus Berkhof, The Doctrine of the Holy Spirit: The Annie Kinkead Warfield Lectures, 1963-1964. Richmond: John Knox Press, 1967

[4] Rena Yocom and Barr, and William R., The Church in the Movement of the Spirit. Grand Rapids: William Eerdmans Publishing Company, 1994.

[5] Jack Haberer, Living the Presence of the Holy Spirit. Louisville, Geneva Press, 2001.

[6] Thomas E. Zimmerman, Carlson, G. Raymond, Bicket, Zenas J., And He Gave Pastors. Sprinfield: Gospel Publishing House, 1995.

Teaching in my own words is the art and science of building and translating symbols, and giving instructions reflecting on the significance and usage of those symbols. A teacher is one who imparts knowledge or instructs by precepts (commands or principles intended as a general rule of action). The Greek word "didaskalos" describes a teacher as one who lectures and entertains questions. "Teach" originates from the Hebrew word "lama" and the Greek "didasko." In the East, it was common to see a Jewish Rabbi or teacher, Pharisee or Greek scholar conducting private or public lectures. This was the principle used to impart knowledge relating to a variety of topics, such as history, governments, politics, law, religion and culture.

These individuals were not paid, although they received voluntary gifts, they did not idly allow their talents to be ruined or kept their knowledge to themselves. They found a means to share their knowledge with others. This was a kind of service or gesture that satiated them because of the passion they had for their respective professions. The Apostle Paul, a great teacher and writer is noted for his lecturing ability in synagogues and public arenas. One of the outstanding examples was when he was in Athens on Mars' Hill where he met Greek scholars (Stoicks and Epicureans) also lecturing in public. As an experienced scholar, Paul used that occasion to lecture on an inscription he saw on an altar that read "To The Unknown God." Many were touched by the Apostle's lecture and asked to hear from him again (Acts 17:22-34).

God needs anointed teachers who are able to impart His divine knowledge to His people; He needs people who are capable of instructing His precepts in a compassionate and loving manner. Just as Israel was a repository in the Old Testament for the plan and representation of God, it is just how the church in this dispensation, is set aside as a repository for God and His redemptive plan through Christ:

> "God ordains the church to be the vanguard of His kingdom. To be filled with Christ is to be filled with obedience. God has purposed to manifest His authority to the world through the church. God's authority can be seen in the coordination of the various members of the body of Christ. For authority to be expressed there must be subjection. If there is to be subjection, self needs to be excluded; but according to one's self-life, subjection is not possible. This is only possible when one lives in the Spirit. It is the highest expression of God's will" (Spiritual Authority, 13,47,55).[7]

God used great instructors like Moses, Aaron and Joshua to help in forming the commonwealth of Israel. Teaching is a vital part of the ministry and the church. In fact, it is an important component of the great commission given by Christ (Mark 15:16; Matthew 28:19-20). Teaching is a divine gift. Teachers are mentioned in scriptures

---

[7] Watchman Nee, Spiritual Authority. New York: Christian Fellowship Publishers, Inc., 1972

as recipients of God's divine gifts (Ephesians 4:11-12; I Corinthians 12:28). This is a delicate office for a committed person.

Your gift was transferred to you by your Maker without any merits or reciprocal bargains, therefore it is reasonable for you to be willing to transfer your gift to those with whom you share knowledge. The gift is being backed by the "spirit" of God or the "Holy Spirit." *The term "spirit" translates Hebrew (ruach) and Greek (pneuma) words denoting "wind," "breath," and, by extension, a life-giving element. With the adjective "holy," the reference is to the divine spirit, i.e., the Spirit of God* (HarperCollins Dictionary, 432).[8] "*Ruach* is used to speak of God as present and active in the world and in particular among human beings" (Heron, 7).[9]

Paul Achtemeier and associates splendidly point out the various implications and applications of the terminology "spirit" in both the Old and New Testaments as thus:

> *Emphasis in the OT*: In the OT, three major emphases may be identified, the first of which is the Holy Spirit as an agent in creation. This is almost an impersonal representation of the Spirit by which the awesome power of God is depicted (e.g., Genesis 1:2; Psalm 33:6; Ezekiel 37:1-10. The second is the Holy Spirit as a source of inspiration and power. The Holy Spirit becomes the vehicle of God's revelation and activity. Israel's leaders - from Moses to Joshua, to the judges, to David and Solomon, to the enigmatic "Servant of God" of Isaiah 42 - all receive their wisdom, courage, and power as gifts resulting from the possession of God's Spirit. The Spirit can be conveyed from one person to another, as with Moses and Joshua, Saul and David, Elijah and Elisha. The third emphasis is the Holy Spirit as God's presence in the covenantal community. To some degree connected to the eschatological hope and expectations of the sanctification of Israel. *In the NT*: In the NT, a more diverse range of meaning for this term is to be seen. Although the earlier usage continues (it is the Spirit of God that endows Jesus with power as the Messiah [Matthew 3:13-17; Mark 1:9-11; Luke 3:21-22; Matthew 12:28; Luke 4:16-21] and that empowers the church for its mission [Acts 2]), the close relationship of Jesus to God (the incarnation) expands and significantly transforms the understanding of the Holy Spirit in Christianity (cf. the related expressions, "Spirit of Christ," "Spirit of the Lord," "Spirit of Jesus," and especially passages such as Galatians 4:6, where God sends "the Spirit of his Son" to the followers of Jesus). In God's economy, the distribution of one's gift is imperatively crucial to the expanding His

---

[8] Paul J. Achtemeire, The HarperCollins Bible Dictionary. San Francisco: Harper Collins Publishers, 1996

[9] Alasdair C. Heron, The Holy Spirit. Philadelphia: The Westminster Press, 1983.

kingdom and work on earth. I label "gift" with three important words: *Power, Act,* and *Right*; the "PAR phenomenon" if you will. A gifted teacher has the *power* or ability to act or produce an effect on what he teaches and those who he teaches and others with whom he has company. The state of real existence rather than possibility which is the *act,* tends to be the norm in terms of evaluating the performance of a gifted teacher in and out of the classroom. The *right* to exercise freely one's God-given talent beyond and above to get the best result is a noble undertaking in itself. The "par phenomenon" is a way of accessing the value and expectancy of a gifted person. Not every teacher exercises his or her *PAR*. Some teachers are afraid to operate in this manner because it is out of their comfort zone. Only in gifted teachers will you find *PAR* to be vividly seen and demonstrated as essential elements in their tutelage and mentoring (The Harper Collins Dictionary, 1062).[10]

---

[10] Paul J. Achtemeire, The HarperCollins Bible Dictionary. San Francisco: Harper Collins Publishers, 1996

CHAPTER ONE

GREEK ETYMA

Comforter—Paraklēsis (παράκλησις) calling to one's side; Paraklētos (παράκλητος) called to one's aid, as Christ was to His disciples, as the holy ghost or holy spirit would to the believers

Divide—diamerismos (διαμερισμός) parting, dissension, discord, breaking up as of family ties; dichostasia (διχοστασία) a standing apart; schima (σχίσμα) a cleft, to cleave.

Life—Zōē (ζή) life in the absolute sense, life as God has it; Bios (βίος), duration of life, zōē is life intensive, and Bios is life extensive; Psuchē (ψυχή) life in two respects: the breath of life which is natural life, and the seat of personality

Likeness—Homoiōma (ὁμοίωμα) that which is made like something, the image, a resemblance, the glory of the incorruptible God

Message—Angelia (ἀγγελία) angellō to bring a message, proclaim, news,

Tabernacle—Skēnē (σκηνή) a tent, dwellings, where the people of God are called to meet, metaphorically of His people, the eternal abodes of the saints

Tongue—Glossa (γλῶσσα) tongues like as fire which appeared on the day of Pentecost, tongue as an organ of speech, supernatural gift of speaking in another language; Dialektos (διάλεκτος) language, dialect, tongue.

PNEUMATOLOGY AS A THEOLOGICAL DISCIPLINE

The Evolvement and Transition of Pneumatology

Many scholars never thought that the study of the Holy Spirit would have gotten more attention as other theological disciplines in Divinity and Theology. They were all proven to be wrong because the subject of the Holy Spirit which happens to be the core of Christianity and the church has surfaced on the chart to be the most appealing of all disciplines in Seminaries and Bible colleges. The Holy Spirit is that substance that gives life to the Christian community and ministry. Over the years there have been many works and studies done on the Holy Spirit. However, interestingly the Holy Spirit is not a new subject. The Holy Spirit existed long time ago even before the creation of the universe and humanity, but somehow humanity happens to place the subject of the Holy Spirit on the backburner. Therefore, approaching the matter of discussing the Holy Spirit in this century will make it look like we have made a new discovery about the Holy Spirit which is not true. However, humanity's reluctance to share light on the subject matter has made the topic appear to be archaic and outdated or alienated. Scholars believe that this transition in the study of the Holy Spirit is *pneumatological renaissance* which is the doctrine of the spirituality of the Holy Spirit. The emergence of other movements and orientations introduce a new approach to analyzing and synthesizing the nature and function of the Holy Spirit as the *green pneumatology* or *liberation pneumatology*. The Catholic Theologian Elizabeth Dryer shares this renewed revelation of Pneumatology: *Renewed interest in the Holy Spirit is visible in at least 3 contexts: individual Christians who hunger for a deeper connection with God that is inclusive of all life as well as the needs of the world; the church that seeks to renew itself through life-given disciplines and a return to sources; and the formal inquiring of academic philosophy and theology. In effect, one can hear the petition, 'come Creator Spirit' on many lips these days* (Elizabeth A. Dryer, "Resources for a Renewed Life in the Spirit and Pneumatology: Medieval Mystics and Saints," in Advent of the Spirit: Orientations in Pneumatology, Conference Papers from Symposium at Marquette university, 17-19 April 1998, unpublished, 1).[11]

The doctrine of the Holy Spirit has always played a significant role in Orthodox Theology. The Holy Spirit was the bedrock of the organization. Works of Athanasius, Cyril of Alexandria, and Basil the Great bear record to this fact. It is noted that the

---

[11] Veli-Matti Kärkkäinen, Pneumatology: The Holy Spirit in Ecumenical, International and Contextual Perspective. Grand Rapids: Baker Academic, 2002.

eastern church as opposed to the western, embraced the concept of pneumatology as an integral part of the church while the west focused on Christology as the foundation of the church. "Eastern foundation pays more attention to the Holy Spirit both in the doctrine of salvation and in ecclesiology" (Pneumatology, 12).[12]

Even today, this observation stills proves true. It still exists. Referring to the Holy Ghost as the "Cinderella of Theology," Kärkkäinen attests that before the division of the church in 1054 A. D., eastern theologians accused their western counterparts of "forgetfulness" of the Spirit" (Kärkkäinen, 2002).[13]

The eastern churches were not the only promulgators of the doctrine of the Holy Spirit as being the source of power and pillar in the church or Christian community. There were a handful of other churches in the west that were realizing the absence of this truth in the Christian community. They believed that the significance of the Holy Spirit or the talk of the Holy Spirit had been concealed and quieted by the west. How hard it is for the truth to be hidden? Jesus gives the parable that the city upon the hilltop cannot be hidden (Matthew 5:14). It is that light in the city positioned on the top of the hill that is visible to all. Likewise, Jesus gives another parable about how believers are the light of the world, and their light cannot be hidden or placed under a bushel with the intent of hiding it from others (Matthew 5:14-16). It is very difficult to stop a light from being visible. When light shines, darkness has to disappear. Therefore, light overpowers darkness and all other environmental intricacies. In the aforementioned analogy, "light" is a representation of the "truth" as revealing the importance of the Holy Spirit in Christendom. The church cannot exist without the Holy Spirit. The astronomical increase and expansion of the Pentecostal and other Charismatic movements in the world have alarmingly drawn the attention of many Christians. It is a given attestation.

Many Christians now than before are recognizing the significance of the Holy Sprit in the church. In its December 23rd release in 2006, The Economist Magazine revealed some interesting facts on the Pentecostal movements in the west and America:

> A century after its birth Pentecostalism is redrawing the religious map of the world and undermining the notion that modernity is secular. The great secular ideologies of the 19th and early 20th centuries from Marxism to Feudalism have faded while the spirit-filled version of Christianity has flourished. Pentecostal denominations have prospered, and Pentecostalism has infused traditional denominations through the wildly popular charismatic movement. Today there are more than 500 million "revivalists" in the world (i.e., members of Pentecostal denominations plus "charismatics"

---

[12] Ibid., 12.
[13] Veli-Matti Kärkkäinen, Pneumatology: The Holy Spirit in Ecumenical, International and Contextual Perspective. Grand Rapids: Baker Academic, 2002.

in traditional denominations). In a recent survey of Pentecostalism, the Pew Forum on Religion and Public Life argues that "renewalist movements" are the world's fastest-growing religious movement: the World Christian Database shows that renewalists now make up about a quarter of the world's Christian population compared with just 6% 30 years ago. The evidence can be seen every where in America and the world. They believe not only that the Last Days are coming, but also that the Spirit can enter ordinary mortals and give them extraordinary powers. From studies done on ten countries, The Pew Forum discovered that vast majority of the Pentecostals interviewed, said they had experienced or witnessed divine healing. Even in predominated Catholic countries in South America and other parts of the world are impacted from the widespread of the Pentecostals and or charismatic movement.

In 1998 Pope John Paul II assigned that year as the year of the Holy Spirit. In 1991 the World Council of Churches under the theme, "Come Holy Spirit, Renew the Creation," devoted their time on the theological reflection on various aspects of the doctrine of the Holy Spirit as it relates to the church, ecumenism, and creation.

The Manifestation Holy Spirit

Many scholars in the theological realm believed that the manifestation and discussion of the Holy Spirit was an outdated subject. They believe that the Spirit was only manifested to the disciples or apostles by Christ in the early days of the church and does not exist anymore. Many scholars today do not believe in divine healing or miracles, less much to mention the power of the Holy Spirit. Many scholars do not believe that today's church has access to the divine intervention of God. They do not believe that God's gifts are existing in the church at all. Some may ask out of curiosity, then why was Christ resurrected? Why do we still preach Christ? As Paul puts it, if Christ is not resurrected than his preaching is in vain (I Corinthians 15:14). The church has no power without the divine intervention of God. God's Spirit is alive and is manifested in individuals to carry out His divine mission. "Many faithful desire to encounter a Holy Spirit who brings new life to their spirits in the concrete circumstances of their lives and who renews the face of the earth . . . " (Pneumatology, 14).[14]

Catholic theologian John R Sachs shares his observations as thus: An incredible interest today in the Spirit and spirituality reveals that people are paying attention to the spiritual dimension of their lives and often seem to be experiencing the Spirit in ways and places that often challenge traditional theologies and church structures,

---

[14] Veli-Matti Kärkkäinen, Pneumatology: The Holy Spirit in Ecumenical, International and Contextual Perspective. Grand Rapids: Baker Academic, 2002.

and structures have little connection with traditional religious practice. The Spirit is present and active beyond the official structures and ordained ministries of the church (John R. Sachs, 'Do Not Stifle the Spirit: Karl Rahner, The Legacy of Vatican II, and its Urgency for Theology Today," in Catholic Theological Society Proceedings, ed. E. Dreyer, 51 (1996):15).[15]

The conception of *pneuma* or the Spirit is a major element in Paul's theology. In order to understand the contextual usage of the word *pneuma* in Paul's theology, Cooper shows the etymological descriptions of the word and how it is defined and used in two ways. Referring to one category of the term as *pneuma* A and the other *pneuma* B, Cooper gives the meanings or usages of the word distinctly in the aforementioned categories. *Pneuma* A (sprit) is used in some parts of the Bible to refer to the human spirit and *pneuma* B refers to the Spirit of God. An illustrative usage of *pneuma* A is seen in Philemon 25: "The grace of our Lord Jesus Christ be with your spirit." Another example is I Thessalonians 5:23: "… and your spirit and soul and body be kept sound." The usage is analogous to the Old Testament word *nephesh* for soul, life, or self which is also analogous to *ruah* or spirit. Usage of *pneuma* A is a minor part of Paul's treatment of the term *Pneuma*.

Note that Paul uses psyche (vitality or life) to refer to "the human spirit." In contrast, Paul uses *pneuma* B (God's divine Spirit) predominantly (I Thessalonians 1:5-6; 4:8).

Veli-Matti Kärkkäinen shares Augustine's views on spirituality and pneumatology as follows: linguistically the Spirit, "pneuma" and spirituality belong together. Augustine speaks of this revelation in three ways: 1. The Spirit cannot be based on pure theory but must touch on experienced reality 2. Experience alone does not suffice. It must be tested and tried so that one's own spirit does not take the place of the Holy Spirit. 3. The originality of an individual theologian has to be replaced by the communal discernment of the whole church which is guided by the very same Spirit (Kärkkäinen, 2002).[16]

Paul's distinguishes the two in Romans 8:16 and in I Corinthians 2:1. This ambiguous usage of *pneuma* requires that we carefully understand the context of Paul's usage of the word in his writings. Rudolf Bultmann classifies pneuma as used in an "animistic" and a "dynamistic" fashion. Bultmann points out the inconsistency of Paul's reference to Divine Spirit as "Holy Spirit," "the Spirit of God," and "the Spirit of Christ." According to Bultmann, Paul's basic idea in referring to the Divine is clear. *Pneuma* does not mean spirit in the Platonic, idealistic sense, i.e., it does not mean "mind" in contrast to body (regarded as the sensuous life), or in contrast to nature. "Mind" in this sense, the active subject in mental or spiritual life, is called

---

[15] Veli-Matti Kärkkäinen, Pneumatology: The Holy Spirit in Ecumenical, International and Contextual Perspective. Grand Rapids: Baker Academic, 2002.

[16] Veli-Matti Kärkkäinen, Pneumatology: The Holy Spirit in Ecumenical, International and Contextual Perspective. Grand Rapids: Baker Academic, 2002.

in Greek *nous* or *psyche* or *logos*. Rather *pneuma* B is the divine power that stands in absolute contrast to all that is human.

From the fact that Paul uses *Pneuma* in a dual sense, it is reasonable to conclude that there is an analogy between the spirit of humans and the Spirit of God. The spirit is the dimension of creativity in humanity, and therefore it seems a fitting symbol for dimension creativity in God. Man spirit is dependent upon the Spirit of the Divine. Man's spirit alone is ineffectual and powerless. God's Spirit is self-sufficient and powerful. Thus *Pneuma* B serves a term both of contrast and of analogy. The experience of *Pneuma* B is at once a point of contact between humanity and God and the reason why humanity needs contact with the Divine. The Spirit Pneuma B is also connected with the revealing activity of God. It is in the dimension of the Spirit, in the encounter of one's spirit with the Divine's Spirit that man becomes aware of God and of God's demand upon his life (The Spiritual Presence of Theology of Paul Tillich, 4-7).[17]

In Congar's view on *The Anthropology of the Mystical Body Theology*, he affirms that: "God not only created humankind in the divine image with the capacities for knowledge, love, and freedom but also destined humanity to communion in the divine life. We are created to become sons and daughters of God, a divine plan that is fulfilled through the incarnation of the Word and the gift of the Spirit" (Congar's Theology, 117).[18]

The Spirit of God makes God's power knowable. The Spirit reveals the power of God in and on human beings . . . The Spirit shows that human beings cannot bear abundance, vitality, richness, freedom, and the divine vocation to reflect God's glory. The powerful action of the Spirit, that which is characteristic of this 'power by which God accomplishes the divine will' comes to expression through the pouring out of the Spirit. "It is in fact all believers, the whole people of God as the body of Christ with the indwelling of the Holy Spirit, who preserve the tradition of the Apostolic faith" (Chapman, 81).[19] The Spirit comes upon individual persons and groups of people to influence both their proximate and distant environments (God the Spirit, 2, 228).[20]

Pneumatology and Systematic Theology

Systematic Theology is a part of theological studies that concentrates on the summarizing of the traditions of religion or Christianity from the present day's religious perspective. It is evident that pneumatological topics are often times

---

[17] John Charles Cooper, The Spiritual Presence in the Theology of Paul Tillich. Macon: Mercer University Press, 1997.

[18] Elizabeth Teresa Groppe, Yves Congar's Theology of the Holy Spirit. Oxford: Oxford University Press, 2004.

[19] Geoffrey Chapman, The World and the Spirit. San Francisco: Harper & Row Publishers, 1984.

[20] Michael Welker, God the Spirit. Minneapolis: Fortress Press, 1994.

infused with salvation (soteriology) and the doctrine of the church. An excerpt from *traditio apostolic of Hippolytus* proves this phenomenon as such: From the [Nicene-Costantinopolitan] creed itself should be clear that ecclesiology can only be understood in connection with and is a consequence of Pneumatology.

The church cannot be grasped apart from the Holy Spirit, and can only be grasped as the work of the Holy Spirit. Only after Pentecost, that is, after the sending of the Spirit through the risen One (Pneumatology, 19).[21]

Contemporary Perspective on Pneumatology

Like every discipline, whether secular or non-secular, there are always conservative, moderate, and liberal views from scholars on the subject matter. As being no different in this regard, Theologians freely share their views on pneumatology. To name a few, Jürgen Moltmann, in his literary piece, "Spirit of Life," looks at pneumatology in a holistic sense. He proffers that the doctrine of the Spirit is associated with a type of pneumatology that relates to the nature of the human body and the earth. If you will, it is a type of pneumatology he views as being anthropological and geological. Michael Welker in his work, "God the Spirit," clearly bases his perspective on pneumatology on the canon or scripture despite his philosophy and theology background. At least Mr. Welker did not get carried away with his secular knowledge to modify the scriptures as most of his contemporaries. Clark Pinnock telescopically views pneumatology from a systematically theological approach. His brand was a mixture of theology. He defines pneumatology through a traditional and modern perspective.

He shares a moderate view, one that accommodates a conservative and liberal view on the subject matter. Liberation Theologian, Joseph Comblin views the Holy Spirit as a liberator, one that brings spiritual freedom to the individual and the church. This he believes aids in fostering community development. Elizabeth Johnson, from a Roman Catholic tradition discusses pneumatology from a feminist perspective. Of course, the Bible does not support gender biasness when it comes to salvation and the doctrine of the Spirit. Although Elizabeth may have a traditional Catholic view, the Bible shows that even Mary, the mother of Jesus was in the upper room in Jerusalem and was a recipient of the Holy Spirit on the Day of Pentecost. Therefore, women are not excluded or exempt from God's salvation plan. The Spirit extends to all, irrespective of race, gender, or religiosity.

Biblical Perspectives on the Spirit

Contextually addressing the nature of the Spirit in the Bible, one can look at a few images in the Bible that relate and describe the nature of the Holy Spirit. Some of these

---

[21] Veli-Matti Kärkkäinen, Pneumatology: The Holy Spirit in Ecumenical, International and Contextual Perspective. Grand Rapids: Baker Academic, 2002.

biblical images that reflect on the Spirit are: (a) *Life-breath* in Genesis 2:7. This verse relates to the Hebrew word, "ruach" which means *breath, wind,* and *spirit,* or *life-breath* in Genesis 6:17; Ezekiel 37:5; John 20:22; Psalm 104:29-30; 104:2; (b) *Wind,* as referenced in Genesis 8:1; Numbers 11:31; Isaiah 27:8; Exodus 15:8,10; John 3; (c) *Fire,* Isaiah 4:4; 31:11; Matthew 3:11-12; Luke 3:16-17; 12:49; Acts 2:3; (c) *Water,* Isaiah 32:15; 44:3; John 4:10; 7:38-39; Revelation 22:1-2; (d) *Cloud,* Exodus 24:15-18; 33:9-10: 40:36-38; I King 8:10-12; 40:33; Luke 1:35; (e) Dove, at Jesus's baptism, this became visible and verbal to John the Baptist. The Greek words "paraclete" and "paraklètos" define dove symbolically as the Spirit of God descending upon Jesus John 14:16; I John 2:1.

Spirit Featured in the Old Testament

The Greek terminology "pneuma" which is "Spirit" is tentamont to the Hebrew terminology "ruach." "Ruach" is used about 264 times in the Old Testament and "pneuma" 377 times, and in each of those instances "ruach" is translated as "pneuma" or "Spirit." Another Greek word "anemos" which means "wind" is used about 49 times in the Old Testament. The connotation of "ruach" emphasizes on the extraordinary persuasion that air should move; "blowing". Another interesting Greek word "pnoē" means also "to blow" or "a blowing" as referenced in the book of Acts on the Day of Pentecost (Acts 2:2). The Old Testament "ruach" and New Testament "pneuma" both are capable of being understood in two or more ways. They represent multiple meanings, such as but not limited to "breath," "air," "wind," "soul," There are other terms and phrases used in the Bible that are representative of the "Spirit." The term "Spirit of God" is used about 100 times in the Old Testament as mentioned in Genesis 1:2, and the phrase "The Spirit of the Lord" as mentioned in Isaiah 11:2. However, theologians dispute the passage in Genesis 1:2. They question whether the Hebrew word "ruach" "elohim" should be translated as "a mighty wind that swept over the waters" (NAB) or as "the Spirit of God that was moving over the face of the waters" (RVS). However, the meaning of "ruach" still remains the same in the passage irrespective of its revised usages. There are three categorical usages of the word ":ruach" (1) wind or breath of air; (2) the principle of life, in other words, the force that endows life in human beings; and (3) the life of God Himself both at the physical and spiritual level. The usage of the word in this context proffers no opposition attraction to the body. When the "Spirit" is opposed to "flesh" it reminds us of the power of God interacting with humanity which is a mundane reality. "Ruach" also relates to "life-force" as in Judges 15:19; Numbers 16:22; Psalms 33:6; 31:5; Isaiah 11:4; 42:5. As a charismatic power, "ruach" does come upon human being as a mighty force Judges 14:6; Isaiah 16:13. "Clothe" (equip) may be used in a biblical passage to describe "ruach" as in Judges 6:34. The same Spirit enables humans to perform the impossible or supernatural power; Judges 3:10; 6:34; Ezekiel 3:12; 8:3; 11:1; 31:3; Daniel 6:3; Isaiah 11:1-8; 42:1-4; 49:1-6; 32:15-20; Ezekiel 11:19; 18:31; 36:36; 37:1-14; Joel 2:28-32; Proverbs 8:22-31.

The Spirit During the Intertestament Period

The intertestament period in Biblical history is the period between the Old Testament and New Testament eras. That time featured the captivity of the Children of Isreal by the Babylonians, Assyrians, and Persians. That was the era of the Jews warfare interations with the Romans, the birth of the Hellensic or Grecian Civilization under Alexander III or Alexander the Great, and the birth of Christ. During that period Aramaic and Hebrew were the prominent spoken languages existing. Most literary and formal works were done in Greek. According to Kärkkäinen during this period Palestine Judaism emphasized that the Spirit was created by God alone, suggesting a distinction between the Creator and creature. In the intertestament literature, the expression "Spirit of God," "divine Spirit," and "Holy Spirit" sometimes meant the God-given spirit of humans.

In some cases these terms referred to the spiritual reality that performed Gods's work on earth (Kärkkäinen, 2002).[22]

Spirit Featured in the New Testament

The terminology "penuma" is dominantly used in the New Testament as opposed to the Hebrew "ruach." However, they both carry the homologous ambiguity. Both terms still ascribe to "air" and "breathing." It is noted that some ancient civilizations considered the air breathed as the "bearer of life." Pneuma is used about 40 times in the New Testament. Interestingly, pneuma in some instances in the New Testament is used in reference to the human spirit but sorely subscribes to the spiritual realm. "The spirit of human beings is that aspect of a man or woman through which God most immediately encounters him or her" (Kärkkäiren, 2002).[23] Scripture refereces in support of this thought are as follows: Romans 8:16; 1:9; 8:15; 11:8; Galatians 6:18; Philippians 4:23; Hebrews 4:12; Matthew 5:3' Luke 1:47; I Corinthians 4:21; I Peter 3:4.

Spirit Featured in the Gospels

There are a host of references in the gospels that touch on the "Spirit." Some of those passages are: Matthew 3:7-12; 12:28; 10:20; 1:18-25; 3:16-17; 1:10-11; 4:1; Mark 1:12; 1:10-11; 13:11; Luke 4:1; 3:22; 4:18-19. Some Old Testament scriptures are the book of Malachi, Deuterbonomy 18:15; Isaiah 61:1.

---

[22] Veli-Matti Kärkkäinen, Pneumatology: The Holy Spirit in Ecumenical, International and Contextual Perspective. Grand Rapids: Baker Academic, 2002.

[23] Ibid., 28.

Spirit Featured in Acts and the Early Church

From the promise of the Holy Ghost to the outpouring of the Spirit upon humanity through out the history of the church, Acts is being noted as the book of action of the life of the followers of Christ. Passages that mentioned the Spirit are: Acts 1:8; 2:38; 4:31; 8:15-19; 10:44-47; 19:6; 19:11; 9:17; 11:15-18; 15:8; 19:1-17; 1:16; 3:18; 4:25; 28:25: 4:8, 13, 29-31; 13:9; 5:32; 6:10; 18:25.

Spirit Featured in the Pauline Letters

As a great writer and one used as a chosen vessel for God to reach out primarily to the Gentile world, Paul wrote extensively on the Spirit. Some referred passages are: Romans 3:24; 8: 4-6, 9,14, 16, 15-17; 12:3, 6-8; I Corinthians 12:1, 3; 15:45; 12:13; 6:11; 15:10; 1:4-7; 6:9-11; 12:14-26; 12:8-11; 12:28; 14:1-5, 13-19; 2:12-14; 15:42-50II Corinthians 2:10-12; 3:14-17; 1:22; 5:5; Galatians 1:15; 3: 5, 14; 4:6-7; 5:16; Ephesians 1:13-14; 4:3, 11-16; Philippians 1:27; 2;1; I Thesssalonians 1:6; 5:19-22.

SUMMARY

Pneumatology as any other topic or discipline is an interesting an appealing subject that needs to be studied passionately. The Holy Spirit is that substance that gives live to the Christian community and ministry. The study of the Spirit is *pneumatology* and *Pneumatological renaissance* refers *to the* doctrine of the spirituality of the Holy Spirit. The doctrine of the Holy Spirit has always played a significant role in Orthodox Theology. The Holy Spirit was the bedrock of the organization. The concept of pneumatology as an integral part of the church while the west focused on Christology as the foundation of the church. "Eastern foundation pays more attention to the Holy Spirit both in the doctrine of salvation and in ecclesiology. Charismatic movements in the world have alarmingly drawn the attention of many Christians. Many scholars in the theological realm believed that the manifestation and discussion of the Holy Spirit was an outdated subject. The conception of *pneuma* or the Spirit can be defined and used in two ways: *Pneuma* A (sprit) is used in some parts of the Bible to refer to the human spirit and *pneuma* B refers to the Spirit of God. The church cannot be grasped apart from the Holy Spirit, and can only be grasped as the work of the Holy Spirit.

The doctrine of the Spirit is associated with a type of pneumatology that relates to the nature of the human body and the earth. One can look at a few images in the Bible that relate and describe the nature of the Holy Spirit. Some of these biblical images that reflect on the Spirit are: (a) *Life-breath* in Genesis 2:7. This verse relates to the Hebrew word, "ruach" which means *breath, wind,* and *spirit,* or *life-breath*. The Greek terminology "pneuma" which is "Spirit" is tantamount to the Hebrew terminology "ruach." "Ruach" is used about 264 times in the

Old Testament and "pneuma" 377 times. The intertestament period in Biblical history is the period between the Old Testament and New Testament eras. The terminology "penuma" is dominantly used in the New Testament as opposed to the Hebrew "ruach."

"However, they both carry the homologous ambiguity. There are a host of references in the gospels that touch on the "Spirit." From the promise of the Holy Ghost to the outpouring of the Spirit upon humanity through out the history of the church Paul wrote extensively on the Spirit.

ASSESSMENT

1. What is pneumatology?

2. Could one's quest for in-depth knowledge on pneumatology be satisfied in the Occideontal or Oriental hemisphere, why or why not?

3. Is pneumatology a renaissance doctrine to the East as it is to the West, why so?

4. What is the Greek equivalent of Holy Spirit and what are some descriptions of the word in the Bible?

5. Is the Hebrew term "Ruach" equivalent to the Greek term "pneuma"? Are there any dissimilarities?

PERSPECTIVES

In his book on "objectivism (20th century ethical theory that moral good or precepts are real or valid)," Dr. Leonard Peikoff shares philosopher Ayn Rand's view on "reality" in this light: According to Dr. Peikoff, Philosophy is the power from which no human can abstain. He adds that human by nature is conceptual and cannot function without some form of philosophy. Ayn Rands says that without abstract ideas one will not be able to deal with concrete real-life problems. She believes that one at some point must be able to conceptually integrate one's observations, experiences, and knowledge into abstract ideas in order to be normal or able to survive. Emphasizing on the role of Metaphysics (a branch of philosophy concerned with the fundamental nature of reality and existence that includes ontology; a theory about the nature of being or the kinds of things that have existence, cosmology; a theory dealing with the nature of the universe, and epistemology; the theory of the nature and grounds of knowledge) in society, Ayn Rand terms metaphysics as the "absolute" based on "human facts," not superstition or preternaturalism. From the rules of conduct to the existence of the universe, Ayn believes that there are only man-made laws that govern the human race.

Regarding her take on "creation," Ayn Rand notes that creation means "the power to bring into existence an arrangement (or combination or integration) of natural elements that had not existed before. . . . metaphysically given facts are reality not subject to anyone's apprassal and must be accepted without evaluation. . . . the idea of the supernatural is an assault on everything man knows about reality" (Peikoff, 25, 31).[24]

What views do you have in reponse to the aforementioned philosophies of Dr. Peikoff's and Ayn Rand, heretical, apologetic, or liberalistic? Could you scripturally support your position?

---

[24] Leonard Peikoff, Objectivism: The Philosophy of Ayn Rand. New York, Penguin Books, 1991.

CHAPTER TWO

GREEK ETYMA

Acknowledge—Epiginōskō (ἐπιγινώσκω) to know thoroughly, to recognize a thing to be what it really is; Epignōsis—(N) (ἐπίγνωσις) full, thorough knowledge, discernment.

Author—Aitios (αίιος) the which causes something

Baptism—Baptisma (βάπτισμα) immersion, submersion and emergence (from baptō to dip)

Benevolence—Eunoi (εύοια) good will

Divine—Theios (τείος) from theos, God

Prayer—Proseuchē (προσευχή) prayer to God; Deēsis (δέησις) an asking, entreaty, supplication; Enteuzis (ἐντευξις) intercession

Truth—Alētheia (ἀλήθεια) objectively signifying the reality lyingat the basis of an appearance, the veritable essence of a matter, the truth og God, the truth of the gospel

Utterance—Logos (λόγος)

Wisdom—Sophia (σοΦία) spiritual wisdom, human wisdom,

APOLOGIES

Lack of faith in God is the result of most of society's troubles (Albert E. Ribourg)

Apology of Barnabas Lindars on the Holy Spirit

'Spirit' (ruah) in the Old Testament is one of those words which, when applied to God, refers to an attribute of God (in this case His power). In scripture, the 'Spirit of grace" refers to the Spirt as the giver of gifts which flow from the grace of God. In the New Testament times the Holy Spirit is frequently referred to as the source of prophetic inspiration (The Theology of Hebrew, 56-57).[25]

Apology of Philip Edgcumbe Hughes on Hebrews 6:4; 8:3

Touching on "heavenly gifts" and "enlightenment," Hughes equates the heavenly gifts with the Holy Spirit. He argues that the Holy Spirit endows power upon the believers to perform a series of spiritual tasks. These powers referred to in verse six of chapter four he says can be identified with signs, wonders, and miracles as accompaniments of the preaching of the gospel. He claims that they are the dynamic evidence of the activity of the Holy Spirit within the community of believers (Christ Superior to Aaron, 210-211).[26]

Apology of C. E. B. Cranfield on Romans 12:3-8

Paul speaks solemnly in command by virtue of grace, the undeserved favor of God to humanity. He speaks directly to every member of the church. instead of thinking of himself more highly than he ought, is to think of himself as to think soberly, measuring himself by the standard which forces him to concentrate on the things which precisely puts him on the same level with his fellow-Christians rather than those things which may make him appear to superior or inferior to his fellow believers. This type of standard represents dependence and commitment to Jesus Christ. Christians who behave otherwise are ignorant. They display their lack of

---

[25] Barnabas Lindars,The Theology of the Letter to the Hebrews. Cambridge: Cambridge University Press, 1991.

[26] Philip Edgcumbe Hughes, A Commentary on the Epistle to the Hebrews. Grand Rapids: William B. Eerdmans Publishing Company, 1977.

understanding (cf. II Corinthians 10:12), and are sure to have too high (or else too low) an opinion of themselves, but, when they measure themselves by the standard which God has given them in their faith, they then, and only then, achieve a sober and true estimate of themselves as equally with their fellows. The Christian faith is the individual's free personal response (made in the freedom which is restored by God's gift of His Spirit) to God's action in Christ, it must always be remembered that the most important and, indeed, the controlling, determinative element in faith is not the believing subject but the object believed in, and to estimate oneself according to the standard which consists of one's faith in Christ is really to recognize that Christ Himself in whom God's judgment and meanings are revealed is the one by whom alone one must measure himself and also one's fellow-men. Those who do measure themselves by the standard which God has given them in their faith will realize that they do not live for themselves but for their fellow-Christian, whether their gifts are more, or less impressive than others, they are equally members of one body, Christ's church.

The figure of the body as a unit made up of various members is one that occurs frequently in ancient literature. The wide variety of the gifts is grounded in the one grace shown to all. The gifts are given for the fulfillment of different functions (Commentary on Romans, 611-319).[27]

Apology of John Calvin on I Timothy 4:14-15

According to John Calvin, the gift (charisma) which Timothy must not neglect appears to be the spiritual equipment received at the time of ordination. God's gift, like the talent, must never be left unused. The methods by which the gift may be nurtured are to be shown in diligence and care. Moral and spiritual rectitude is an indispensable preliminary to doctrinal orthodoxy (Tyndale New Testament Commentaries, 110).[28] To teach is *to cause to know something; to cause to know how; to accustom to some action or attitude; to cause to know disagreeable consequences of some action; to make known and accepted; to conduct instruction regularly in; to impart knowledge of; to guide the studies of and to provide instruction* (Merriam - Webster's Collegiate Dictionary, 11th ed.).

To cause to know something is the manner in which teaching is able to make someone who had prior knowledge of nothing to know something. In other words, the doctrine of primitivism which promotes non-civilization or unsophisticated beliefs and lifestyles, would be a prime example if converted or taught and are able

---

[27] C. E. B. Cranfield, A Critical and Exegetical Commentary in the Epistle to the Romans. Edinburgh: T & T Clark, 1979.

[28] John Calvin, Commentaries on The Epistles of Paul to the Galatians and Ephesians. Grand Rapids: Baker Book House, 1981.

to modernize their way of thinking and behaving, it then can be said that knowledge has been attained. To enable non-industrialized societies to embrace the values and norms of industrialized societies, we say teaching has taken place. Teaching causes not only the acquiring of knowledge to take place, it involves the acquiring of skills as well

Any means by which information or skills are transferred to others can be said that teaching has taken place. To have a rebel sit at the table to negotiate peace illustrates that a lesson has been taught and learned. To instruct is the same as teaching. Instructions give a methodological or former picture for imparting knowledge. To train is another form of inputting information by drills and instructions. To discipline is a routine manner in which a learned behavior shapes or molds a person's way of thinking and doing things. School is the institution through which discipline, principles, and instructions are learned.

Apology of Robert Mounce on Romans 12:3-8

Paul cautions the Christians at Rome not to think of themselves more highly than they ought, and reminds them that they are all members of the one body. They are encouraged to utilize their individual gifts for the benefit of the entire church. Paul offers the instructions in virtue of the office he himself held. His appointment as an apostle was a special act of divine favor. He calls on his readers not to entertain an inflated view of their own importance. Rather, they should model the humility that places the rights and welfare of others above their own (The New American Commentary, 233).[29]

Peake's Apology on I Corinthians 12

Paul considers the value of some of the gifts which appears functioning, not distinct offices of members of the church. The Spirit is the donor in each instance and each gift contributes to the corporate life of the body of Christ, the church. The one Spirit, Lord or God, is at work in the body. The Spirit enables each independent member to function, whether his gift be a word of wisdom (moral teaching?) or a word of knowledge (of God), or a deep faith in God, or a gift of healing or of the ability to work miracles or to preach or to discern spirits or to talk in tongues or to interpret them.

All gifts are given in proportion to the Spirit's will and are all grace-gifts, freely confirmed (Peake's Commentary on the Bible, 961-962).[30]

---

[29] Robert H. Mounce et al, The New American Commentary. Broadman & Holman Publishers, 1995.
[30] Matthew Black, Peake's Commentary on the Bible. London, Routledge, 1962.

Apologies from the Wycliffe Bible on I Corinthians 12

Gifts, Gk charismatōn, connects to the word "charis" (grace), rendered "grace-gifts." The word is used in its technical sense as spiritual gifts, administrating gifts, services, operations to the assembly. The "word of wisdom" probably a tempoaray gift like apostleship, had to do with the communication of the spiritual wisdom. The "word of knowledge" had to do with the truth of a more practical character. "Faith" not to be confused with saving faith, this is the faith that manifests itself in unusual deeds of trust.

"Gifts of healing," the gift of healing provided restoration of that which is beyond the power of the socalled divine healers of today. Prophecy, the gift of foretelling and forthtelling new revelation from God was also temporary. Discerning of spirits is done by the Spirit through the word.

Tongues and interpretation were also temporary, having to do with known languages rather than with ecstatic utterances, although the question of speaking in tongues is a moot one. The Spirit is the sovereign dispenser of the gifts (The Wycliffe Bible Commentary, 1249-1250).[31]

SUMMARY

'Spirit' (ruah) in the Old Testament is one of those words which, when applied to God, refers to an attribute of God [(in this case His power) (The Theology of Hebrew, 56-57)]. The Holy Spirit endows power upon the believers to perform a series of spiritual tasks. Paul speaks solemnly in command by virtue of grace, the undeserved favor of God to humanity. God's gift, like the talent, must never be left unused. Paul cautions the Christians at Rome not to think of themselves more highly than they ought, and reminds them that they are all members of the one body. The Spirit is the donor in each instance and each gift contributes to the corporate life of the body of Christ, the church. The Spirit enables each independent member to function. Gifts, Gk charismatōn, connects to the word "charis" (grace), rendered "grace-gifts." The word is used in its technical sense as spiritual gifts, administrating gifts, services, operations to the assembly.

ASSESSMENT

1. What is the purpose of the Holy Spirit in the life of a believer?

2. What is grace?

---

[31] Charles F. Pfeiffer et al, The Wycliffe Bible Commentary. Chicago: Moody Press, 1962.

3. Is God's gift the same as one's talent?

4. How does each gift contribute to the corporate life of the body of Christ?

5. What are the Greek equivalents of "grace-gifts?"

PERSPECTIVES

Epistemology, that branch of Philosophy that deals with knowledge or human cognitivity, reflects the following views: (a) Platonic realism, (b) Aristolian realism, (c) normalism, (d) objectivism, and (e) subjectivism. Platonic realism asserts that if one were given a proper intellectual and moral preparation, the memories of these entities which men knew in previous life will gradually return. Aristolian realism which assets that one is able to group thoughts together under a single concept, and there is another factor that gives uniqueness to memory that makes only specific thoughts repeatable based on the circumstance warranted. Normalism asserts that there is no objectively right or wrong way to form concepts. It is to the discretion of a person to choose what would subjectively suit his or her ideas. Normalists believe that knowledge is the grasp of an object through passive absorption of revelations. According to these realists, conception is construed on perception, and perception is drawn from an external table we need exposure to (whether in heaven or physical tables). Subjectivists believe that knowledge is the creation of an object through the active inner processes of the object. The Intrinsicists believe that although knowledge requires conformitive to rules of reality, there is no way one could attain such conformity.

The intrinsicists believe that external factors of all scopes impact the attainment of knowledge. Intrinsicists describe human's mental faculty as "intuition," a "sixth sense," "extra-sensory perception, "reminiscence," and "divine revelations." However, objectivists say knowledge is the grasp of an object through an active, reality based process chosen by the subject (The Philosophy of Ayn Rand, 124-145).[32]

What views could you share in reponse to the aforementioned philosophies of each school of thought as presented by Dr. Peikoff, heretical, apologetic, or liberalistic? Could you scripturally support your position?

---

[32] Leonard Peikoff, Objectivism: The Philosophy of Ayn Rand. New York, Penguin Books, 1991.

CHAPTER THREE

GREEK ETYMA

Duty—Opheilō (ὀΦείλω) to owe, to be indebted, it was our duty, we owe it.

Faithful—Pistos (πιστός) to be trusted, reliable

Grace—Charis (χάρις) divine favor

Shepherd—Poimēn (ποιμήν) metaphorically of Christ, and pastors in the churches.

Spirit—Pneuma (πνεύμα) denotes the wind, to breathe, blow, breath, immaterial, the invisible part of man, the Holy Spirit, the Holy ghost, the Spirit of Christ; Pneumatikos (πνευματικός) spiritual, invisibility and of power, the angelic host, things that have their origin with God,

Strength—Ischus (ἰσχύς) ability, might; Kratos (κράτος) force, might, power,

Teach—Didasko (διδάσκω) to give instruction; Didaktikos (διδακτικός) skilled in teaching, apt to teach

Knowing Your Gift

"For the gift and calling of God are without repentance" **Romans 11:29**
We need abounding faith that will cut all the "ts" off all the "cants" and make them into "cans" (Anonymous)

I Corinthians 12: 7-11, 28-30

7   But the manifestation of the Spirit is given to every man to profit withal

8   For to one is given by the Spirit the word of wisdom; to another the word of knowledge by the same Spirit;

9   To another faith by the same Spirit; to another the gifts of healing by the same Spirit;

10 To another the working of miracles; to another prophecy; to another discerning of spirits; to another divers kinds of tongues; to another the interpretation of tongues;

11 But all these worketh that one and the selfsame Spirit, dividing to every man severally as he will.

28 And God hath set some in the church, first apostles, secondary prophets, thirdly teachers, after that miracles, then the gifts of healings, helps, governments, diversities of tongues.

29 Are all apostles? Are all prophets? Are all teachers? Are all workers of miracles?

30 Have all the gifts of healing? Do all speak with tongues? Do all interpret? KJV

In verse seven Paul is bringing the Christian at Corinth back to the good of the community, not the personal whims of the individual. Individual Christians are intended to demonstrate that they have the Spirit of God within them in a boasting manner. Tom Smail has written that "the Spirit must be spiritualized." The Spirit operates in the body to produce the glory of God. It is important to appreciate that the rich variety of such operation by the Holy Spirit in the body of Christ is completely unrelated either to Christian maturity or to personal deserts.

The Christian community should be the community of the Spirit of God. The real gifts of the Spirit are only those which are manifestly supra-natural. A person natural talent cannot be translated into a spiritual gift. Dealing with the *utterance of wisdom* in verse eight, the literal Greek is *logos sophias* (a word of wisdom). Such a gift could well be revealed by a thoroughly wise Christian (a pastor or teacher) who has learnt consistently to fear the Lord, and does not lean towards or upon his own understanding, so that he clearly is a wise person, both in counsel and behavior. The *utterance of knowledge*, in the Greek, *logos gnōseōs* literally means "a word of knowledge." The Holy Spirit is concerned to "equip" the body of Christ with knowledge. Jesus Himself clearly demonstrated such knowledge. Peter for an example, had the gift of knowledge in revealing the hypocrisy of Ananias and Sapphira, and for revealing the revelation of God pouring out His Spirit upon all flesh in the last days on the day of Pentecost. Concerning the gift of *faith*, it is neither credulity, gullibility, optimism, nor easy believing. *Faith* looks at God's character and stands firmly on God's promises. This gift of faith looks through the immediacy of the situation to Him who is invisible and brings the confidence that God will move in apparently impossible situations. This gift often seems linked with miracles and gifts of healing.

The gallery of heroes of faith in Hebrews eleven certainly lends reality to this gift as seen consistently in the lives of men and women of God. The gifts of healing, *charismata iamaiōn*, i.e., both are in the plural form. Paul is not talking about the gift of healing or the healing ministry. He is encouraging the Corinthians to expect many different ways in which God in His sheer grace gives healing of all kinds to different people, relationships, even situations. For example, James urges that if any members of the church were sick they should call for the elders to pray in faith for their healing. The *working of miracles*, "in-workings of powers" (energēmata dynameōn): Paul has in view the power of working all sorts of miracles other than simple cures, corresponding to different situations, such as raising the dead, driving out demons, inflicting of judgments on unfaithful Christians, and deliverance from poison intakes, diseases, and snakebites as Paul experienced on the Island of Malta.

The ability to distinguish between spirits, *discerning of spirits, diakriseis pneumatōn*: In the context of the above discussion, this could refer very specifically to the ability to discern the presence of evil spirits in a person, place, or situation. More widely, it probably means an ability to recognize from what source any purported spiritual manifestation comes. Of such the Bible seems to identify three: *Holy Spirit, human spirit,* and *evil spirits.* Verse eleven, the desire to make these gifts available by God for the service of others comes from God alone; it cannot be produced by purely exhortation or pressure.

Verses twelve and thirteen show Paul affirming both the rich variety and deep unity in Christ himself. In all this Christians share as members of the one body through the one Spirit. In verses twenty-eight through thirty Christ appointed *apostles (those sent out)* to plant churches to give them authoritative teaching. *Teachers* enable Christians to grow towards maturity. Without such teaching ministry new life simply dries up. Those called and gifted in this area need to concentrate fully on it, because it requires single-minded application. Ephesians 4:11 has both teacher and pastor listed but they are not totally interpreted as the same. Although pastor needs to be apt to teach, his ministry calls for more than just teaching. All pastors are not good teachers and vice versa. One must be called by God. *Helpers*, in essence demonstrate a Christian ministry geared towards the helping of the weak. The Greek word *antilēpseis*, refers to the gift, not the person. It reflects on practical assistance at all times. Administrators, Greek, *kybernēseis*, (pilotings). The reference is to the helmsman of the ship, the person with the responsibility of steering the vessel, keeping it on course, avoiding changes, recognizing changes in weather and adjusting accordingly. The helmsman knows well the capabilities both of his craft and crew. He knows which expertise to call on at which moment. Paul urges the saints to be zealous but having a spiritual gift because it is essential for the church, not self (Concerning Spiritual Gifts, 197-224).[33]

Exegeses on I Corinthians 12:7-30

According to Ambrosiaster, in verse seven, each person receives a gift so that by governing his life by divine constraints he may be useful both to himself and to others while presenting an example of good behavior. According to Chrysostom, whatever measure of the Spirit has been given you, it is for your benefit, so there is no reason to complain of what seems like a small gift. Basil says, since no one has the capacity to receive all spiritual gifts, but the grace of the Spirit is given proportionately to the faith of each, when one is living in commune with others, the same privacy bestowed on each individual becomes the common possession of the others . . . One who receives any of these gifts does not possess it for his own sake but rather for the sake of others. Verse eight, *Wisdom and knowledge*. According to Ambrosiaster, one is given knowledge not by book learning but by the enlightenment of the Holy Spirit. Augustine refers *wisdom* to the knowledge of *a divine thing*, and *knowledge* to *human science*. Regarding the utterance of wisdom, Severian Gabala says *wisdom* means understanding what God has said through the prophets and evangelists and communicating this to those who are listening.

The *utterance of knowledge* according to Gabala is the revelation of things which have been forgotten, which someone learns for the first time and then shares with others. Verse nine: the gifts of *faith* and *healing*, Cyril of Jerusalem says faith which is given by the Spirit as a grace is not just doctrinal faith but faith which empowers activities surpassing human nature, a faith which moves mountains . . . For just as a grain of mustard seed is of little bulk but of explosive energy, taking a trifling space for its planting and their seeding out great branches all around, so that when it is grown, it can give shelters to the birds. Ambrosiaster says Paul was

---

[33] David Prior, The Message of I Corinthians: Life in the Local Church. Downers Grove: InterVarsity Press, 1985.

encouraging concerned persons to suppress his shyness and receive the ability to profess and lay claim to faith. Augustine says without the Spirit of faith no one will rightly believe. Theodoret of Cyr says faith mentioned here is not the kind given to every believer but the kind which can move mountains. Concerning *prophecy* in verse ten, Ambrosiaster says prophecy is possible only through the Holy Spirit. In reference to *tongues* and *interpretation*, Ambrosiaster says to interpret is to interpret faithfully by God's gift the sayings of those who speak in tongues or in writing. Chrysostom says the Corinthians boasted of their speaking in tongues, which is only last on Paul's list of gifts. Verse eleven: inspired by the same Spirit, according to Augustine, it means that there are so many spirits, but in all things are one and the same Spirit works, who apportions to each one individually as he wills. Cyril of Jerusalem says the Spirit has authored the scriptures. He has spoken of Himself all that he wished, or all that we could grasp. Let us confine ourselves to what he has said, for it is reckless to do otherwise. According to Chrysostom, the universal medicine of his consolation stems from the same root, from the same treasure, the same stream. Therefore Paul occasionally dwells on this expression so as to level out apparent inequalities and console them. Ambrosister says the Spirit spoke also to the Patriarchs and prophets, and finally the apostles then began to be more perfect after they had received the Holy Spirit. Thus, there is no separation of the divine power and grace, for although there are varieties of gifts, yet there is the same Spirit. Theodoret suggests that Paul is comforting those who received the lesser gifts, pointing out that they too come from the Holy Spirit.

Ambrose says it belongs to God's justice that He divides and to His power that He divides according to His will and because He wishes to give to each one what He knows will be of profit. Jerome notes that Paul does not say according to the will of each and every member but according to the will of the Spirit. Augustine adds that not everyone has all the gifts, but some have these and others those, although each has the gift himself by whom the things proper to each one are divided, namely the Holy Spirit. Concerning verse twenty-eight, Ambrosiaster agrees that Paul has placed the *apostles* at the head of the church. They may be identified with bishops, as Peter. There are two types of *prophets, those who predict the future* and *those who interpret the scriptures*. The apostles are also prophets because the top rank has all the others subordinated to it. *Teachers are those who instruct boys in the synagogues*, a practice which has come down to us as well. Regarding the listing of tongue last, Chrysostom mentions that the order of going from higher to lower, and quite deliberately, because the Corinthians were in the habit of putting speaking in tongues of the top of the list. Ambrosiasters suggests that the church has only one bishop, and prophesying is not given to everybody. Chrysostom notes that even as God did not grant the greater gifts to everyone, so also did he give lesser gifts to some and not to others. He did this in order to obtain the maximum of harmony and love. Since each one would see his need of the others and therefore be brought closer to them. Ambrosiasters concludes that the graces of the Lord which are seen in persons do not relate to the merit of the individual but to the honoring of God (Ancient Christian Commentary on Scripture, 121-129).[34]

While the church at Corinth had many problems, they did not come behind in any gift (see I Corinthians 1:7). The gifts of the Spirit operated profusely in the Corinthian church. There were, however, abuses of the gifts, and Paul wrote to correct them in I Corinthians 12:14. The carnality of the Corinthians (I Cor. 3:3-4) did not prevent the gifts from operating. The reason for this is that the gifts of the Spirit are just that: *gifts*. They are not the evidence of spiritual maturity. They do not indicate that the person operating them has achieved advanced spiritual power. This is the difference between gifts and fruit. The fruit of the Spirit (Galatians 5:22-23) gives evidence of spiritual maturity. The fruit tells us something about the person's character and spirituality. But the gifts tell us nothing about the person's character of spirituality. Instead, they tell us about the nature of the giver, who is God Himself. "It is in and through the Spirit that Christ takes possession of us. We are utterly dependent on the Spirit for apprehension of spiritual truth . . . can only be parted to us by the Spirit of God. The spirit inspires, guides, and bestows freedom on the believer. The Spirit constitutes the life and efficiency of the church. It is this indwelling of the Spirit that gives the church its existence. Without the experience of the indwelling Spirit there could be no such thing as the Christian church" (The Work of the Holy Spirit, 103,106,119,131).[35]

Exegesis of Gordon Fee on I Corinthians 12:7-8; 28-31

Verse seven: Paul proceeds to articulate that diversity is worked out in the life of the church. Paul's emphasis is to be found in holding together in these leading ideas: First, "each one," standing in the emphatic first position as it does, is his way of stressing diversity. This pronoun is the distributive (stressing the individualized instances) of the immediately preceding collective (in all people) which emphasizes on men who make up the community as a whole. Second, what "each one" is given in this case is not a "gift," but a "manifestation of the Spirit." Paul's own emphasis through these chapters, which is on the Spirit himself, not on the "gifts" as such. Thus each "gift" is a manifestation," a disclosure of the Spirit's activity in their midst. Paul's urgency, as vv. 8-10 make clear, it is not that each person is "gifted," but that the Spirit is manifested in a great variety of ways. His way of saying that is, "to each is given the manifestation of the Spirit." Third, probably to give a proper balance to "each one," he concludes with the reason for this great diversity: "for the common good." Verses 8-10: Paul proceeds to offer a sizeable list of ways in which the Spirit is manifested in the Christian assembly.

---

[34] Gerald Bray and Thomas C. Oden, Ancient Christian Commentary on Scripture: New Testament VII 1-2 Corinthians. Downers Grove: InterVarsity Press, 1999.

[35] Walter Thomas Conner, The Work of the Holy Spirit. Nashville: Broadman Press, 1940

Paul attempts to classify that several items are numerous and varied. Some have suggested that they reflect a descending order of value. A popular grouping is (1) gifts of instruction (*wisdom* and *knowledge*); (2) gifts of supernatural power (*faith, healings, miracles*); and (3) gifts of inspired utterance (*prophecy, discerning of prophecies, tongues, interpretations of tongues*). The seventh item) discerning of spirit) tends to give trouble to most of these arguments. The first two gifts are chosen for very specific ad hoc purposes, "wisdom" and "knowledge" held high count in Corinth. He then adds a random list of five items that have as their common denominator a supernatural endowment of some kind, and concludes with the "problem child" and its companion, tongues and interpretation. What distinguishes this listing is the concretely visible nature of these items, especially of the last seven. These, after all, are not only "gifts," they are above all manifestations of the Spirit's presence in their midst, most likely chosen because they are extraordinary phenomena. (1) The message (logos) of *wisdom* (Sophia); a message/ utterance full of wisdom or "an utterance characterized by wisdom." The word of wisdom is revealed by the Spirit, is not some special understanding of "deeper things" or "mysteries" of God. Rather, it is the recognition that the message of Christ crucified is God's true wisdom. The utterance of wisdom comes "through the Spirit." (2) The message (*logos*) of *knowledge* (gnōsis). Some suggest that Paul had in mind a supernatural endowment of knowledge, factual information that could not otherwise have been known without the Spirit's aid. Others see it as referring to something more akin to inspire teaching, perhaps related to receiving Christian insight into the meaning of the Scripture. The two, words of wisdom and words of knowledge should be considered as parallel in some way. (3) *Faith.* What Paul has in mind is the supernatural gift of faith that can move mountains. It probably refers to a supernatural conviction that God will reveal his power or mercy in a special way in a specific instance. Faith that moves mountains can rightly be called the "*working of miracles.*" (4) *Gift of Healings.* This expectation was bound in part on the Old Testament promises that in the messianic age God would "heal" His people. Such healings accompanied Paul's ministry, and Paul himself probably referred to them in "the signs of the apostle" in II Corinthians 12:12. Only among intellectuals and in a "scientific age" is it thought to be too hard for God to heal the sick. What is interesting here is the language, "gift of healing," itself suggests that the "manifestation" is given not to the person who is healed, but to the person God uses for the healing of another. The plural *charismata* probably suggests not a permanent gift as it were, but that each occurrence is a "gift" in its own right. (5) Miraculous power (lit. "workings of miracles"). Although Paul wanted to probably include gift of healings under "working of miracles," this manifestation most likely covers all other kinds of supernatural activities beyond the healing of the sick.

The word translated "miracles" is the ordinary one for "power" and associated in Jewish antiquity with the Spirit of God. The current context suggests that it would cover a broad range of supernatural events that ordinary parlance would call miracles. (6) Prophecy. This phenomenon was widely understood in the religions of antiquity. The prophet was a person who spoke to God's people under the inspiration of the Spirit. The "inspired" utterance come by revelation and announced judgment (usually) or salvation. With the outpouring of the Spirit at the end of the age, the early Christians understood the prophecy of Joel 2:28-30 to have been fulfilled, so that "prophecy" not only became a renewed phenomenon, but was available to all, since all now possessed the Spirit in fullness (cf. Acts 2:17-18). This consisted of a spontaneous, Spirit-inspired, intelligible messages, orally delivered in a gathered assembly intended for the edification or encouragement of the people. (7) Distinguishing between spirits (lit. "discernment of spirits"). The ability to discern what is truly of the Spirit of God and what comes from other spirits. (8) Different kinds of tongues. Spirit-inspired utterances, utterances that are self-controlled. Speakers must speak in turn and they must remain silent if there is no one to interpret. It is speech intelligible both to the speakers and hearers (14:14, 16). It is speech directed toward God (14:1-2, 14-15, 28); one may assume, therefore, that what is "interpreted" is not speech directed toward others, but the "mysteries" spoken to God. Paul's argument is predicated on the unintelligibility of the language to both the speaker and hearer. He does not think that it is an earthly language because there is no analogy sharing such. He wants to agree that it relates to an unknown language as noted in 13:1 to be the "language of angels." (9) The interpretation of tongues. This is the obvious companion of tongues precisely because of the unintelligibility of the latter. Although in translation it means "translation," it could also mean "to put into words." In this context it means to articulate for the benefit of the community what the tongue-speaker has said. This also would be a spirit-inspired gift of utterance given either to tongues-speakers or another.

In verse eleven, Paul sums it up by emphasizing that the diversity is the product of the one God, who by His Spirit works in these manners. In verse 28, Paul reasserts that God is responsible for the diversity that makes up the one body (cf. vv. 4-6, 11, 18, 24b). Paul illustrates by presenting another list of persons: (1) (apostles, prophets, teachers); (2) miracles, and gifts of healings; (3) helps and guidance. (1) Apostles functional and positional or official term; (2) Prophets, suggests that all "Spirit people" were potential prophets in a sense that they could prophesy or preach. (3) Teachers: (inspiring utterance of instruction) The emphasis is on the function, not their office. (4) Miracles: gifts of healings, the emphasis is not on the people who have these gifts, but simply on the presence of the gifts themselves in the community. (6) Helpful deeds (service, giving to the needs of others, doing acts of mercy. Ministering to the physical and spiritual needs of others in the community. (7) Gift of administration, acts of guidance. (8) Different kinds of tongues, a gift of utterances. Verses 29, 30, 31: Paul emphasizes on the importance of unity amidst diversity in terms of gifts in the community. He mentions tongues as being the least among the gifts and encourages the believers to seek other gifts, most especially, prophecy (The First Epistle to the Corinthians, 588-599, 618-623).[36]

Many are confused at this point. Since they think the gifts of the Spirit could operate only in the life of one who is spiritually mature, of sterling character, and perfect in every way, they reject any apparent operation of a gift through anyone who does not measure up to these qualifications. When, in their view, genuine gifts do operate through a person, they tend to idolize that individual as one who is far advanced spiritually. They seem to think spiritual gifts can operate only through those who are exceptional; they have little hope they could ever reach the place in God where He could trust them with these gifts. But all of this is in error. The Corinthians are themselves proof that the possession of gifts is not to be equated with maturity or perfection. A gift tells us nothing about the character of the recipient; it reveals only the character of the giver. A gift is not merited or earned, or it would not be a gift.

The validity of a gift is not so much determined by an examination of the life of the person through whom it operates. It is determined by comparing its message with the word of God and its fruit with the criteria of edification, exhortation, and comfort (I Corithians 14:3, 12, 29). By virtue of your membership in the body of Christ, you have at least one spiritual gift: "But the manifestation of the Spirit is given to every man to profit withal . . . But all these worketh that one and the selfsame Spirit, dividing to every man severally as he will. For as the body is one, and hath many members, and all the members of that one body, being many, are one body: so also is Christ. For by one Spirit are we all baptized into one body, whether we be Jews or Gentiles, whether we be bond or free; and have been all made to drink into one Spirit . . . But now hath God set the members every one of them in the body, as it hath pleased him . . . Now ye are the body of Christ, and members in particular: (I Corinthians 12:7,11-13,18,27). The context of the granting of the spiritual gifts is membership in the body of Christ. In other words, it is your spiritual gift, in this context, which gives you your place in the body of Christ, or the church. By virtue of being a member of the body of Christ, you have been given at least one spiritual gift to give you your place and function in the body.

There is no member of your physical body without a specific gift and function; there is no member of the body of Christ without a specific gift and function. This is an important point, for many do not realize or believe they have a spiritual gift. This unbelief prevents them from ever operating the gift they have been given. An illustration of the fact that those who are baptized by the Spirit into the body of Christ are immediately, by virtue of their membership in the body, given spiritual gifts, occura in Acts 19:1-6. When Paul met the disciples of John the Baptist, he

---

[36] Gordon D. Fee, The First Epistle to the Corinthians. Grand Rapids: William B. Eerdmann Publishing Company, 1987.

taught them about Jesus and baptized them in the name Lord Jesus, he laid his hands on them and the Holy Ghost came on them, "And they spake with tongues, and prophesied" (Acts 19:6). The speaking with tongues was the initial evidence of the baptism of the Holy Ghost. (see also Acts 2:4; 10:44-46). But immediately following their speaking with tongues, these men began to prophesy. *Prophecy is not the initial evidence of the baptism of the Holy Ghost; it is one of the nine spiritual gifts* (I Corinthians 12:10; 14:1,3,5,6,24,25,29-32). These men moved immediately from the initial evidence of the Holy Ghost baptism to the operation of a spiritual gift. And just moments before this, they did not even realize Jesus was the promise Messiah! This illustrates that gifts are not earned by seniority. They are given immediately to those who are baptized with the Holy Ghost.

Peter also addressees this point: "As every man hath received the gift, even so minister the same one to another, as good stewards of the manifold grace of God" (I Peter 4:10). The implication is that there is no man who has not received a gift, so as to be unable to minister to another. All are to be good stewards of the grace of God, that is. They are to properly handle the gifts given them by God.

In discussion of the *seven motivational gifts*, Paul also revealed that they are given universally to all who are members of the body of Christ: "For I say through the grace given unto me, to every man that is among you, not to think of himself more highly than he ought to think; but to think soberly, according as God hath dealt to every man the measure of faith. For as we have many members in one body, and all members have not the same office: so we, being many, are one body in Christ, and every one members of another" (Romans 12:3-5). So every member of the body of Christ has a motivational gift which serves as his primary vehicle for ministry, and he has at least one spiritual gift which ordinarily compliments that motivational gift. That is, the motivational gift will often be expressed through and/or assisted by the spiritual gift.

Jesus talked about an "evil eye" (Matthew 6:23). But again, the physical eye is simply a purveyor of information. Behind it and beneath it is a spiritual eye which is used as "looking unto Jesus the author and finisher of our faith" (Hebrews 12:2). While God, as a Spirit, does not have a body with physical senses, He said, "I will not smell in your solemn assemblies (Amos 5:21). It seems at least possible, then, that there is a spiritual sense of smell. This would seem to be born out by Paul's statement, "But I have all, and abound: I am full, having received of Epaphroditus the things which were sent from you, an odour of a sweet smell, a sacrifice acceptable, well-pleasing to God" (Philippians 4:18).That there is a spiritual sense of feeling is indicated in Ephesians 4:19: "Who being past feeling have given themselves over unto lasciviousness, to work all uncleanness with greediness." The people spoken of here doubtless still had the physical sense of feeling, or touch, but they were past feeling in a spiritual sense. The ideal that God had in the beginning was that there would be perfect union between the visible and the invisible realms. The visible realm was to reflect the spiritual or invisible realm. He wished for there to be no division between the two.

Man himself was made in the image of God (Genesis 1:26). Adam was the figure of him who was to come (Romans 5:14). There was a tree of life in the Garden (Genesis 2:9). It is seen again in the eternal state (Revelation 22:2). Because of the perfect unity which existed between the visible and invisible realms before the fall of man, Adam and Eve could hear the voice of God walking in the garden in the cool of the day (Genesis 3:8). But sin drove a wedge between man and God, a wedge which hides God's face from man and man's voice from God (Isaiah 59:1-2). But even under the Law of Moses, visible things on earth represented things in the invisible realm: "Who serve unto the example and shadow of heavenly things, as Moses was admonished of God when he was about to make the tabernacle: for see, saith he, that thou make all things according to the pattern shewed to thee in the mount (Hebrews 8:5). "For Christ is not entered into the holy places made with hands, which are the figures of the true; but into heaven itself, now to appear in the presence of God for us (Hebrews 9:24). The sin which drove the wedge between man and God was the work of the devil. The Son of God was manifested to destroyed the works of the devil (I John 3:8), and this included a restoration of the relationship between the natural and the spiritual for those who would come through the blood of Christ.

"Having therefore, brethren, boldness to enter into the holiest by the blood of Jesus, By a new and living way, which he hath consecrated for us, through the veil, that is to say, his flesh (Hebrews 10:19-20). This "holiest" is not a physical building or room; it is a spiritual place of relationship to God. In the invisible realm of the Holy Spirit, there is no sickness, disease, bondage, lack, depression, and so forth. All of the woes which have come upon man are the result of sin.

Jesus said, "The thief commeth not, but for to steal, and to kill, and to destroy: I am come that they might have life, and that they might have it more abundantly" (John 10:10). Success in ministry will come when we are sufficiently sensitive to the Holy Spirit to bring over into the natural realm those things available in the realm of the Spirit. The key to the success of Jesus' ministry was that he attempted nothing by the power of the flesh. Instead, he was so spiritually sensitive that he looked over into the realm of the Spirit and did only what his father showed him.

"But Jesus answered them, My Father worketh hitherto, and I work . . . Verily, verily, I say unto you, the son can do nothing of himself, but what he seeth the father do: for what things soever he doeth, these also doeth the son likewise. For the father loveth the son, and sheweth him all things that himself doeth: and he will shew him greater works than these that ye may marvel (John 5:17-20). The unity between the visible and the invisible realms found perfect expression in the ministry of Jesus. He did only what, with the eye of the Spirit, he saw his father do. Indeed, this harmony was so intimate and perfect that Jesus could truthfully say that the Father showed him all things that He did. These works, which Jesus saw occurring in the realm of the Spirit, he acted on in the natural, visible realm. He simply carried out in the physical and natural realm what God was doing in the Spirit realm. "I can of mine own self do nothing: as I hear, I judge: and my judgment is just; because I seek not mine own will, but the will of the Father which hath sent me . . . the works which the Father hath given me to finish, the same works that I do, bear witness of me, that the Father hath sent me (John 5:30,36).

Since he moved in perfect harmony with the Spirit, Jesus' ministry never failed. When he said to the man at the pool of Bethesda, "take up thy bed, and walk" (John 5:8), he was not speaking merely on impulse or by optimism, hoping it could be God's will to heal the man at that time.

Instead, he saw that that moment was God's time to loose the infirmity of 38 years, and he merely acted on what was going on in the Spirit realm. This explains why none others lying about the pool on the five porches (John 5:2-3) were healed. In the sovereign timing of God, it was time for only one of them to be healed. This is the answer to those who doubt healing is for our day. They sometimes protest, "But if you believe in healing, why don't you go to the hospitals and empty them out?" The pool of Bethesda was a sort of hospital of its time. There were many sick folks there at all times. But Jesus healed only one. We may not understand why it was not God's time for any of the others, but we cannot question God. The point is, success in ministry comes when we are so perfectly in tune with what God is doing in the spiritual realm, not what we attempt to do in the visible, natural realm. Any attempt to go beyond Him to do something we want to do in our flesh will be doomed to failure.

There have been others through out the Scripture who were able to see over into the realm of the spirit and to translate those invisible realities into the visible world: Even Moses, under the limitations of the Old Covenant, endured not until seeing Him who is invisible with his natural eyes (Hebrews 11:27); Elisha could see the horses and chariots of fire his servant could not see (II Kings 6:17); Stephen saw the heavens opened and Jesus standing on the right hand of God (Acts 7:55-56); Twice Peter saw angels which delivered him from prison, going so far as to open literal doors (Acts 5:19;12:7-11);Saul saw a bright light from heaven and heard an audible voice (Acts 9:3-6); Ananias saw the Lord in a vision and was given Saul's name and address (Acts 9:10-11); Cornelius in a vision saw and talked with the angel of the Lord who gave him Peter's name and address (Acts 10:3-4); Peter saw a vision from heaven and talked with the Lord (Acts 10:10-16); Paul was caught up into Paradise where he heard unspeakable words (II Corinthians 12:2-4); The Lord appeared to Paul in a vision and spoke encouraging words to him (Acts 27:22-24); The church began with a visible glimpse into the realm of the Spirit when cloven tongues like as of fire were seen resting upon each believer (Acts 2:3); Stephen did great wonders and miracles (Acts 6:8); Phillip performed miracles which could be seen and heard, including the casting out of evil spirits and healing of palsy and lameness (Acts 8:7,13); Phillip took a 20 mile S.R.T.T. (Spiritual Rapid Transit Trip (Acts 8:39-40); Ananias saw visions (Acts 9:10); Peter healed Aeneas, who had been bedridden 8 years with palsy (Acts 9:32-35), which resulted in the conversion of all in Lydda and Saron; Peter raised Dorcus from the dead (Acts 9:36-42), which resulted in many believing); Peter saw a vision (Acts 10:9-16) giving specific direction, which resulted in the conversion of a whole household of Gentiles; Agabus prophesied of a great famine, which came to pass (Acts 11:27-28);

Paul pronounced blindness on an evil socerer (Acts 13:9-12), which resulted in the salvation of the deputy, Sergius Paulus; Paul and Barnabas performed signs and wonders (Acts 14:3); Paul healed a man of Lystra crippled from birth (Acts 14:8-10); Paul had a vision which gave him specific ministry direction to Macedonia (Acts 16:9-10); Paul cast the evil spirit out of the fortune-telling damsel in Thyatira (Acts 16:14-18); Paul and Silas sang a jailhouse opened, converting the jailor and his entire family (Acts 16:25-34); Paul had a vision giving him ministry direction (Acts 18:9-10); Special miracles were done as hankerchiefs and aprons ahich had been on Paul's body were placed on the sick and demon possessed (Acts 19:11-12); Paul raised Eutychus to life after he had gone to sleep during Paul's sermon and fell out a third story window (Acts 20:9); The Lord appeared to Paul giving him specific ministry direction (Acts 23:11); Paul predicted no loss of life on the ship to Rome, regardless of the storm (Acts 27:21-26), and he was right; Paul handled a viper with no harm (Acts 28:1-6); Paul healed Publius' father of a fever and hermorrhage (Acts 28:7-10); Paul healed others on the island (Acts 28:9-10).

It would seem that, just as Jesus said, even greater works were done by his followers after his ascension than he did while on earth! Of course, it was not really his followers doing the works themselves; they were merely doing it in the natural, visible realm what they saw him do in the realm of the Spirit. The exalted Jesus was actually doing the work, through his disciples, just as the Father had done His work through Jesus, when he was on earth in a physical body. This helps us understand the significance of this statement: "And whatsoever ye shall ask in my name, that will I do, that the Father may be glorified in the Son. If ye shall ask any thing in my name, I will do it (John 14:13-14). This does not refer to an indiscriminate use of the name of Jesus as a kind of magic talisman, where we just tack the words "in Jesus' name" onto our request, but they refer to asking by his authority in the same sense that Jesus came in his Father's name (John 5:43) doing the specific works the father gave him to do (John 5:36). In other words, we ask in his name when we look over into the spirit realm, see what he is doing, and acts as his legal representative by doing that same work in the visible realm, in the same sense that Jesus said, "My Father worketh hitherto, and I work" (John 5:17). This is further illustrated by the following references: "Even the Spirit of truth; whom the world cannot receive, because it seeth him not, neither knoweth him: but ye know him; for he dwelleth with you, and shall be in you" (John 14:17); "Yet a little while, and the world seeth me no more; but ye see me; because I live, ye shall live also" (John 14:19);

"At that day ye shall know that I am in my Father, and ye in me, and I in you" (John 14:20); "He that hath my commandments, and keepeth them, he it is that loveth me: and he that loveth me shall be loved of my Father, and I will love him, and will manifest myself to him (John 14:21); "But the comforter, which is the Holy Ghost, whom the Father will send in my name, he shall teach you all things, and bring all things to your remembrance, whatsoever I have said unto you (John 14:26); If ye abide in me, and my words abide in you, ye shall ask what ye shall, and it shall be done unto you (John 15:7); Henceforth I call you not servants; for the servant knoweth not what his Lord doeth: but I have called you friends; for all things that I have heard of my father I have made known unto you (John 15:15); Ye have not chose me, but I have chosen you, and ordained you, that ye should go and bring forth fruit, and that your fruit should remain: that whatsoever ye shall ask of the father in my name he may give it you (John 15:16). I john 5:14-15 seems to be a further explanation of the principle seen in John 14:12-14: "And this is the confidence that we have in him, that, if we ask anything according to his will he heareth us: And if we know that he hear us, whatsoever we ask, we know that we have the petitions that we desired of him. This is a marvelous promise, much like the promise of Jesus in John 14:13-14. But how do we know the will of God? We know His will in general from His written word, the Bible.

Anything the Bible promises to the New Testament believers will without question be granted if the conditions are met. But how do we know His specific will in situations not addressed in Scripture? How do we see over into the realm of the Spirit? Jesus did nothing but what he saw the father do. He said that following his ascension, believers would do what he does. But how do we know what he is doing? We know the specific will of God or what He is doing in the Spirit realm by means of the gift of the Spirit: Through the word of wisdom, God gives us direction; through the word of knowledge, God gives us information; through the discernment of spirits, God allows us to see what spirit is at work in a given situation; through the working of miracles, God allows us to transcend natural laws; through the gifts of healing, God reverses the progress of sickness and disease; through the gift of faith, God allows us to envision what He sees as possible; through the gifts of divers kinds of tongues, interpretation of tongues, and prophesy.

We hear the Lord speaking for edification, exhortation, and comfort; through the gifts of the Spirit, we see over into the Spirit realm; it is not us, but Jesus at work. This explains Mark 16:17-20: "And these sign shall follow them that believe; in my name shall they cast out devils; they shall speak with new tongues; they shall take up serpents; and if they drink any deadly thing, it shall not hurt them; they shall lay hands on the sick, and they shall recover . . . And they went forth, and preached every where, the Lord working with them and confirming the word with signs following." Amen. All of these miracles are done "in his name," as we act on his authority. This is seen in the phrase, "The Lord working with them, confirming the word with signs following." When believers actually enter into this type of ministry, it will be like the ministry of Jesus being multiplied over hundreds of thousands of times. The world's impact will be staggering.

SUMMARY

The Spirit operates in the body to produce the glory of God. A person natural talent cannot be translated into a spiritual gift. The *utterance of wisdom* in verse eight, the literal Greek is *logos sophias* (a word of wisdom). The *utterance of knowledge*, in the Greek, *logos gnōseōs* literally means "a word of knowledge." The Holy Spirit is concerned to "equip" the body of Christ with knowledge. Spirit as a grace is not just doctrinal faith but faith which empowers activities surpassing human nature, a faith which moves mountains . . . For just as a grain of mustard seed is of little bulk but of explosive energy, taking a trifling space for its planting and their seeding out great branches all around. "Gift of healing," itself suggests that the "manifestation" is given not to the person who is healed, but to the person God uses for the healing of another. Miraculous power (lit. "workings of miracles"). Although Paul wanted to probably include gift of healings under "working of miracles," this manifestation most likely covers all other kinds of supernatural activities beyond the healing of the sick. The prophet was a person who spoke to God's people under the inspiration of the Spirit. The ability to discern what is truly of the Spirit of God and what comes from other spirits. Spirit-inspired utterances, utterances that are self-controlled. Speakers must speak in turn and they must remain silent if there is no one to interpret. The validity of a gift is not so much determined by one's eloquence or spirituality. There is no member of your physical body without a specific gift and function; there is no member of the body of Christ without a specific gift and function. It is an examination of the life of the person through whom it operates. All are to be good stewards of the grace of God, that is. They are to properly handle the gifts given them by God. We know the specific will of God or what He is doing in the Spirit realm by means of the gift of the Spirit: Through the word of wisdom, God gives us direction; through the word of knowledge, God gives us information; through the discernment of spirits, God allows us to see what spirit is at work in a given situation; through the working of miracles, God allows us to transcend natural laws; through the gifts of healing, God reverses the progress of sickness and disease; through the gift of faith, God allows us to envision what He sees as possible; through the gifts of divers kinds of tongues, interpretation of tongues, and prophesy, we hear the Lord speaking for edification, exhortation, and comfort; through the gifts of the Spirit, we see over into the Spirit realm; it is not us, but Jesus at work.

ASSESSMENT

1. The teleology of the Spirit in operation is to do what?

2. What is the difference between logos sophias and logos gnōseōs?

3. Are Spirit-inspired utterances and self-controlled utterances homologous? If yes, why, or if no, why not?

4. Are the duties or functions of the Old Testament prophets similar to that of the New Testament and modern-day prophets? If not, what are the dissimilarities?

5. What does God give and allow through wisdom, knowledge, discernment of Spirit, working of miracles, gifts of healing, divers kinds of tongues, interpretation of tongues, and prophecy?

PERSPECTIVES

"What is man that thou art mindful of him" (Psalm 8:4)?

Scholars from various disciplines have eagerly sought to answer this question. After a thorough observation of man, these observers decided that they can fully define the nature of man. The Greek philosopher, Aristotle defines man as a "rational being." Plato and medieval thinkers view man as "other-worldly soul trapped in a bodily prison." Shakespeare dramatized man as "an aspiring but foolish mortal defeated by a tragic flaw." Thomas Hobbes describes man as a "mechanistic brute." Kant views man as a "blind chunk of unreality in hock to the unknowable." Hegel pictures man has a "half real fragment of the state." Victor Hugo sees man as a "passionate individualist undercut by an inimical (unfriendly) universe." (Peikoff, 187, 200, 202).[37]

What views could you share in reponse to the aforementioned thought about "man" as presented by Dr. Peikoff, heretical, apologetic, or liberalistic? Could you scripturally support your position?

---

[37] Leonard Peikoff, Objectivism: The Philosophy of Ayn Rand. New York, Penguine Books, 1991.

CHAPTER FOUR

GREEK ETYMA

Charisma (χάρισμα) a gift of grace, a gift involving grace on the part of the giver or donor, God, of His endowments upon believers by the operation of the Holy Spirit in the churches.

Earth—Gē (γή) the world, a place characterized by mutability and weakness,

Gift—Dōron (δῶρον) to give, of salvation by grace, as the gift of God; Dōrea (δωρεά) a free gift, of a spiritual or supernatural gift, the gifts of the Holy Ghost; Dosis (δόσις) the act of giving;

Messenger—Angelos (ἄγγελος) one sent; Apostolos (ἀπόστολος) an apostle, messenger of the church

Obedient—Hupakoē (ὑπακοή) Hupakouō (ὑπακούω) to listen, to submit; Peitharcheō (πείθρχέω) to obey one in authority

Office—Praxis (πράξις) a doing, deed, practice

Useful—Euchrēstos—useful, servicesble, meet for use, profitable,

NINE GIFTS OF I CORINTHIANS 12

"For to one is given by the Spirit the word of wisdom; to another the faith by the same Spirit; to another the gifts of healing by the same Spirit; to another the working of miracles; to another prophecy; to another discerning of Spirits; to another divers kinds of tongues; to another the interpretation of tongues" (I Corinthians 12:8-10).

For the sake of identification, these spiritual gifts are often divided into three groups of three:

The Revelation Gifts

    Word of wisdom

    Word of knowledge

    Discernment of spirits

The Power Gifts

    Faith

    Gifts of Healing

    Working of Miracles

The Vocal Gifts

    Tongues

    Interpretation

    Prophecy

While this organization of the spiritual gifts is helpful in identifying something of the nature of each gift and in remembering what they are, it is also somewhat artificial. The person who begins to operate in the spiritual gifts soon discover that in practical operation, most of the gifts will work together to accomplish common purposes. For example, one operating with the gifts of healing may discover that the word of knowledge works in conjunction with that gift, giving him information about the sick person's condition. After healing has been ministered, he may find the word of wisdom in operation to give the healed individual direction as to how to stay healed.

If we remember that the gifts of the Spirit are given to those who are members of the body of Christ to give them their specific function in the body, and how this is compared to a human body, it will be readily seen that all of the gifts must operate together, complementing each other. It would be of little use to be able to identify the eye, or the ear, or the arm, or the leg, or the hand, or the foot, if all of these members were severed from one another and if there were no cooperation among them. There is a great deal of difference in the abilities of a dissect corpse and a living human being. For there to be spiritual life, and for the body of Christ to accomplish his purposes, the spiritual gifts must operate in harmony, just as the members of the human body operate to mutual advantage.

As we discuss the gifts, we will use illustrations, as appropriate, from the Old Testament, from the ministry of Jesus, and from the early church. We understand there could be some debate as to whether various events in the Old Testament or in the ministry of Jesus were actually the operation of the spiritual gifts, but we should remember that it was at least the same Holy Spirit in operation in that specific situation as in the New Testament church. We understand there is a debate as to whether Jesus ministered as God Himself or as an anointed man. We know there were many times in His life on earth in the flesh when he did indeed act as a man. It is our belief that even in his ministry, he willingly limited himself to that which could be accomplished by an anointed man fully yielded to the Spirit of God (see John 5:19-20). This does not at all, of course, detract from his full deity. It was simply his choice as to how he would minister. But let us not allow differences here to prevent us from grasping the larger picture: Whatever supernatural work was performed by men of God of old, or by Jesus himself, was done by the power of the same Holy Spirit which dwells in us. We can therefore learn a great deal about the operation of the Spirit, and the gifts of the Spirit, by observing His work in the lives of others. Now let us consider each of the nine spiritual gifts.

Word of Wisdom

The first thing we should note is that this is the gift of the *word of wisdom*. It is not the "gift of wisdom." Indeed, there is no such gift as the "gift of wisdom." Any believer may apply himself to the pursuit of wisdom and gain this valuable quality (Proverbs 3:13-20; 4:5-13). He may pray and ask God for wisdom (James 1:5). But this is not the supernatural gift of wisdom. The gift of the word of wisdom may be defined as "a small portion (a word) of God's total wisdom supernaturally imparted by the Holy Spirit."

We must distinguish between "wisdom" and "knowledge." Knowledge is information. Wisdom is knowing what to do with that information. "If the iron be blunt, and he do not whet the edge, then must he put to more strength: but wisdom is profitable to direct (Ecclesiastes 10:10). *Wisdom is profitable to direct:* if the axe is blunt, the workman may still be able to chop down the tree, but it will be a slower process and it will require more strength and effort. If the axe is sharp, the task can be accomplished much more quickly, cleanly, and easily. Likewise, it may be possible to accomplish a spiritual task without wisdom, but it will be a much more difficult process, requiring more effort, and having the possibility of more damage. But the supernatural gift of the word of wisdom will tend to get the job done quickly, smoothly, with a minimum of fleshly effort, and with the smallest possible amount of damage. Wisdom and knowledge depend upon each other. Wisdom needs knowledge to work with; knowledge must be directed by wisdom. It is, after all, possible to use knowledge unwisely (Proverbs 15:2).

The Word of Wisdom in the Ministry of Jesus

There are several examples of the word of wisdom at work in the ministry of Jesus. These would include: (1) directions as to where and when to fish (Luke 5:4-10). This results in the conviction of the fishermen. (2) Directions as to where to find the ass and the colt (Matthew 21:1-7). This worked in conjunction with the knowledge of Scripture.

The Word of Wisdom in the Early Church

The word of wisdom was greatly needed in the days of the early church, and it was supplied by the Holy Spirit: (1) Recognition of the need and direction for the method of appointing men to serve the widow's needs (Acts 6:1-7). This resulted in unanimity and progress. (2) Direction for Philip's ministry (Acts 8:26-29). This resulted in an open heart on the part of the Eunuch. (3) Direction for Peter's ministry (Acts 10:9-16). This resulted in an open door to Cornelius, a Gentile. (4) Direction for solution of the problem relating to Gentile converts (Acts 15:13-29). This was based on knowledge of Scripture and resulted in unanimity and progress. (5) Direction for the ministry of Paul and Silas (Acts 16:6-10). This resulted in an open door. The word of wisdom seems many times to be associated with knowledge of the Scripture. It tends to produce conviction, unanimity, progress, open hearts, and open doors. The word of wisdom is the supernatural revelation by the Holy Spirit of divine purpose. It is the supernatural declaration of the mind and will of God. It is the supernatural unfolding of His plans and purposes concerning things, places, and people. By virtue of this gift being the word of wisdom, it will most often operate by means of the spoken word. In this sense it has some similarity to the word of knowledge, to prophecy, and to the interpretation of tongues.

How will a person know that God is moving him to speak a word of wisdom? While there are differences in the way the gifts are administered and operated (I Corinthians 12:5-6), most people report that the vocal gifts usually originate in an impression or in thoughts or words which spring unbidden into the mind. Many people do not receive the complete message in advance, but as they speak what they do have, the Holy Spirit supplies more of the message until it is complete. Some report seeing the words as if they were on a scroll, or a screen in their mind. Some see a visual picture, which they then describe in their own words. It is important to remember that there must be endless variety in the manner in which the Holy Spirit can impart His messages. He may deal with two people in entirely different ways. One thing for certain is that none of the gifts are forced upon a person. God will not override a person's freedom of choice. The person who waits until God forces him to operate in the spiritual gifts will never be used in this ministry. At some points, the believer must take what the Holy Ghost has given him and give expression to it.

The Word of Knowledge

Like the gift of the word of wisdom, this is the gift of the word of knowledge. It is not the "gift of knowledge." An individual can gain knowledge by study and research. He can gain great knowledge of the Scriptures. But this he can achieve largely by his own determination and efforts, as God gives him the strength and ability. But this is not the supernatural gift of the word of knowledge.

The word of knowledge is information about which the believer has no personal knowledge which is imparted to him by the Holy Ghost. It is not suspicion or guesswork. *The word of knowledge is a small portion of the total knowledge of God supernaturally imparted by the Holy Spirit.* God does not impart the sum total of His knowledge to any man. No man is equipped to handle such knowledge. But, as it befits His purposes, God does communicate small portion of His knowledge to His people so they, in turn, can minister to others.

The Word of Knowledge in the Ministry of Jesus

Jesus revealed that He saw Nathanael under the fig tree before He saw him with his natural eye (John 1:47-49). This resulted in conviction. (2) Jesus knew about the Samaritan woman's five husbands (John 4:16-19). This resulted in the conviction of the Samaritan woman, making it seems that her whole life was an open book before Jesus, and in the conversion of many in that town.

The Word of Knowledge in the Early Church

Peter knew of the deception attempted by Ananias and Sapphira (Acts 5:1-11). This resulted in the deaths of these two and conviction coming on the whole church.

(2) Ananias knew Saul's name and address as well as additional information about his future ministry (Acts 9:11-12). The result was that Saul had an open heart to receive the message from Ananias. (3) Peter knew about the three messengers from Cornelius (Acts 10:19-20). This was a confirmation of the message of the angel to Cornelius. (4) Paul was warned of the things which awaited him in Jerusalem (Acts 20:22-23; 21:10-11). This enabled him to prepare for those events. It seems, then, that the word of knowledge produces *conviction, confirmation,* and *preparation.* Daniel Segraves shares his testimony in this light. We have experienced the word of knowledge in the form of names of individuals who had a specific need. In one case, the name "Frederick" came to mind. It was asked if that name meant anything specifically to anyone in the room. One of the ladies present said she had come that night especially to have prayer for a sick little baby in a distant state. The baby's name was Frederick. We were then able to pray intelligently and with faith for the child. Within a couple of weeks we had a picture of the child and a testimony as to how God had touched the baby.

On another occasion, the name "Gilbert" came to mind. We asked if the name had any special significance to anyone in the room. A husband and wife immediately raised their hands. They said they had a backslidden friend named Gilbert who had resisted all their efforts to win him back to the Lord. He had drifted far from his relationship with God. We told them to tell Gilbert that God had his number, and that he had to get right with God immediately. The next week, Gilbert attended the meeting with them and prayed through to the baptism of the Holy Ghost. That has been tears ago, and he is still walking with God today.

As in the case of the word of wisdom, the word of knowledge often comes as an impression, thought, or as words unbidden to the mind. It can also take the form of a visual picture on the "screen" of one's mind, wherein a person sees someone engaged in some activity, and he then describes what he sees. A person ministering healing to another may "feel" the other's pain in his own body, or he may "see" the affected portion of the body in some way as to understand that it is deceased.

Discerning of Spirits

This gift is sometimes mistakenly identified as the gift of "discernment." It seems that those who so identify it have it confused with the gift of the word of knowledge. There is no gift of the Spirit called the gift of "discernment." It is the discerning of Spirits. The word "discern" means "to recognize and distinguish between." The person being used in this gift will discerner or recognize what spirits are at work in a given situation. It is helpful to recognize that there are several categories of spirits in existence:

The Holy Spirit

Faithful angels (Hebrews 1:14)

Fallen angels

Demons, or evil spirits

Human spirits

Scriptural Examples of the Discerning of the Holy Spirit

John the Baptist discerned the Holy Spirit upon Jesus in the form of a dove (John 1:32-33). This was a confirmation to John that Jesus was the Messiah. (2) The believers in the upper room discerned the Holy Spirit upon them like cloven tongues of fire (Acts 2:3). This may have signified to them the beginning of a new dispensation.

Scriptural Examples of the Discerning of Faithful Angels

An angel appeared to Jesus as he prayed (Luke 22:43).
Mary saw two angels at the sepulcher (John 20:11-13).
An angel appeared to Paul on board a ship (Acts 27:23-24).

Scriptural Examples of the Discerning of Human Spirits

Jesus discerned the guileless spirit of Nathanael (John 1:47).
Peter discerned the wrong motives of Simon (Acts 8:20-24).
Paul discerned a "spirit of faith" in a lame man (Acts 14:8-10).

Scriptural Examples of the Discerning of Evil Spirits

A dumb spirit (Matthew 9:33-34).

A spirit of blindness and dumbness (Matthew 12:22-24).

A dumb and deaf spirit (Mark 9:17-27).

A spirit of infirmity (Luke 13:11-17).

A spirit of divination (Acts 16:16-18).

Those who are used in this gift often report that the discernment is in the form of a "vision," where spirits are seen in the form of animal creation. For example, the Holy Spirit has been seen as a dove (John 1:32), and unclean spirits have been seen as frogs (Revelation 16:13). *Sometimes the discernment takes the from of seeing people as they are spiritually: crooked, unclean, with Satanic features, etc.* More commonly, however, it seems that this gift operates simply as s spiritual interpretation of what the natural senses show.

Many people have reported seeing angels. This was a recognized possibility in both Old and New Testaments, and it occurs frequently today. One night my son-in-law awakened to see a silver haired man standing beside the bed, gazing at my daughter and son-in-law. My son-in-law was fully awake, and could see other features in the room by by the light of the street lamp. At first he thought the man was an intruder, bent on harm. He thought about how he could leap up from the bed and strike him before he had a chance to move. But the man obviously had no evil intentions; he just looked on as if he were watching over the couple on the bed. Then, before my son-in-law's eyes, the man vanished. Later, as he considered this unusual occurrence, he was reminded that he prayed nightly that God would allow His angels to watch over them through the night.

But while many are used in this gift by "seeing" visible representations of the spirit world, others do not see, they simply know what spirit is at work. In other words, they know there is an angel in the room, or what spirit is at work in the life of another, or the nature of the evil spirit troubling a person who needs deliverance. We should remember that, when God allows us to have information supernaturally, it is so we can do something about it. Often as we step out on the basis of the on formation we have, the Holy Spirit will continue to supply additional information or direction until we have accomplished His purposes in that particular situation.

The Gift of Faith

It may at first seem strange to think about a "gift of faith," since faith has such a predominate role throughout Scripture. All men are required to have faith to come to God (Hebrews 11:6), so what is the difference between this and the "gift of faith"? There are three different kinds of faith referred to in the New Testament. They are: The faith that comes by hearing the word of God (Romans 10:17). This faith is essential to salvation (Ephesians 2:8; Romans 4:5; Hebrews 11:6). Every believer is given a measure of this kind of faith (Romans 12:3).

The faith that is a part of the fruit of the Holy Spirit (Galatians 5:22). There is, of course, a great difference between fruit and gift. Fruit is a natural outgrowth, due to the nature of the tree. It is cultivated by care and labor (II Timothy 2:6). A gift, on the other hand, is not something that grows over a period of time, but something that is given, intact, freely. Fruit reveals a great deal about a person's character; a gift says nothing about the character of the receiver, but it does reveal something about the character of the giver. The faith that is the fruit of the Holy Spirit could perhaps be described as "continuing quiet trust."

The gift of faith which is given by the Holy Ghost. The gift of faith is a small portion of the total faith of God which is a gift of the Holy Spirit. It can be operated only under God's control. There are two ways this faith can be exercised: 1. You can speak words to God on behalf of a person, object, or situation. Elijah's word controlled the rain and dew (I King 17:1; 18:41-45; James 5:16-18). 2. You can speak words to a person, object, or situation on behalf of God. Joshua spoke to the sun and moon (Joshua 10:12-14). Jesus spoke to a tree (Mark 11:12-14,20-24). He said that we could speak to a mountain (Matthew 17:20). In fact, Paul seemed to identify faith as "mountain-moving" gift (I Corinthians 13:2).

New Testament Examples of Faith in Action

Jesus calmed the storm (Mark 4:39-41).

Jesus raised the widow's son (Luke 7:12-15).

Jesus raised the daughter of Jairus (Luke 8:54-55).

Jesus called Lazarus out of the tomb (John 11:43-44)

Peter raised Dorcus (Acts 9:40).

Paul pronounced judgment upon Elymas (Acts 13:9-12).

Paul commanded a spirit of divination to leave (Acts 13:9-12)

Those who are used in this gift testify that a sudden dramatic assurance will come upon them that some miraculous thing can indeed occur. There is suddenly no doubt, only confidence and conviction. Along with this may come even a physical sensation of well-being and joyous abandon. Often the gift is operated by short, even one word commands: "Rise!" "Walk!" "Be Healed!" Jesus said loudly, "Lazarus, come forth!" (John 11:43). Peter said, "Look on us!" (Acts 3:4).

The Gift of Healings

While there are similarities between healings and miracles in many cases, there are also important differences. A healing many times occurs gradually, almost imperceptibly, relieving the body of disease. A miracle, on the other hand, is almost instantaneous, usually perceptible, and may go beyond healing. For example, a leg may be lengthened, a missing eyeball created, or internal organs replaced, even when they have previously been removed by surgery.

This spiritual gift is actually the gifts (plural) of healings (plural). This is important to recognize, for there may be different gifts for various diseases. Some seem uniquely gifted in the healing of specific problems, for example, deafness, blindness, back problems, etc. It is possible that a person with a gift in one area would have less success in another area.

Works Through Physical Contact

The little woman who touched Jesus' clothes was healed (Mark 5:30).

A whole multitude sought to touch him, for all who touched him were healed (Luke 6:19).

Works Through a Point of Contact

Many were healed as Peter's shadow passed over them (Acts 5:15).

Scriptural Examples of Healings

Jesus laid his hands on every one and healed them (Luke 4:40).

Jesus touched and healed a leper (Matthew 8:1-3).

Jesus healed a man of deafness and a speech impediment (Mark 7:32-35).

Jesus healed a man of blindness, in two stages (Mark 8:22-26).

Paul healed the father of Publius (Acts 28:8).

While all believers have the promise that they may lay hands on the sick and see them recover (Mark16:18), the gifts of healings go beyond that, somewhat in the same way that the gift of divers kinds of tongues goes beyond the speaking with tongues which occurs as the initial evidence of the baptism of the Holy Ghost. In other words, the phenomenon is similar, but it is different as to purpose and function. Again, the person with this gift may be uniquely gifted to pray for specific types of diseases. He may find a certain methodology works best for him in his exercise of the gift. In our experience, we have found the following to be valuable insights: *As far as possible, lay hands specifically on the area of the body that is affected.* Nothing in the Scripture indicates that we should always lay hands on the afflicted person's head. While we must practice modesty and decorum, we have found it best many times to place our hand precisely over the troubled area. If this is not possible, ask the sick person to place his or her own hand over the place, then touch his or her hand as you minister healing. Or you may have another person of the same sex as the afflicted person to place his or her hands directly over the afflicted area. We may not understand why this works better, but Jesus many times touched the specific afflicted area, whether it was the eyes, tongue, or whatever.

Minister With Your Eyes Open

Nothing in the Scripture indicates that you must pray for the sick with your eyes closed. Indeed, if you do that, you will often miss seeing the way the Holy Spirit is moving on the afflicted person. As you observe the moving of the Spirit on the person to whom you are ministering, you will often gain further insight as to minister. Remember, Peter told the lame man, "Loon on us!" Think of Your Ministry as Ministering Healing not "Praying for the Sick." Jesus did not say, "You shall pray for the sick, and they shall recover." He said we would lay hands on the sick. There is without question a place for praying over the sick (James 5:14-16), but this seems to be in the case of a sinning brother or sister whose sin has caused their sickness. But ordinarily, men of faith in the New Testament did not pray for the sick; they minister healing to the sick. Jesus did not so much pray for the sick; he healed the sick. The apostle and disciples in the Book of Acts did not so much pray for the sick; they healed the sick. Indeed, Jesus told has twelve disciples to "heal the sick, cleanse the lepers, raise the dead, cast out devils . . . " (Matthew 10:8). The power to heal is not, of course, inherent in any believer, and he has commanded us to do his work.

It is thus important for us, as we were moved in this gift, to pronounce healing rather than to pray for healing:

"Rise up and walk!" (Acts 3:6).

"Tabitha, arise!" (Acts 9:40).

"Thou shalt be blind, not seeing the sun for a season" (Acts 13:11

"Stand upright on thy feet!" (Acts 14:10).

"Trouble not yourselves; for his life is in him" (Acts 20:10).

". . . Paul entered in, and prayed, and laid his hands on him, and healed him" (Acts 28:8). Make no mistakes; there is a time and place for prayer. But often prayers for the sick, if we are not careful, degenerate into subtitutes for faith. Sometimes we are tempted to make up for our lack of results by praying even more loudly and longer.

As a rule, when going to minister healing, we should, like Paul, pray in order to enter into the presence of God and to invite Him to come and confirm His word with signs and following, then we should place our hand upon the afflicted part of the body and command sickness and disease to go and healing to come. We have found that the more specific the prayer, the greater the result. It is helpful to speak directly to the afflicted part of the body and command sickness and disease to go and healing to come. We have found that the more specific the prayer, the greater the result. It is helpful to speak directly to the afflicted part of the body and to command it to be made whole. If you are praying for someone with back problems, it is helpful to place your hand precisely where the pain is, and to command the vertebrae, the disks, the spinal cord, the muscles, the ligaments, the tendons and the skeletal structure to be healed. It is also important to speak to the pelvis and sacrum to command them to be healed, if you are praying for someone with diabetes, it is useful to speak directly to the pancreas to command it to be healed. While there is no need to try to master the anatomy at level of a medical doctor, it is helpful to know basic things about the anatomical structure so as to pray more intelligently and specifically. It is also helpful to ask the afflicted person where the pain is and what the problem is. Ask if he or she has been to the doctor for diagnosis or treatment. If so, ask what the doctor said. All of this will give you additional information to help you pray more intelligently.

SUMMARY

Spiritual gifts are often divided into three groups of three; The Revelation Gifts: Word of wisdom, Word of wisdom, Discernment of spirits; The Power Gifts: Faith, Gifts of Healing, and Working of Miracles; The Vocal Gifts: Tongues, Interpretation, and Prophecy. The gifts of the Spirit are given to those who are members of the body of Christ to give them their specific function in the body, and how this is compared to a human body, it will be readily seen that all of the gifts must operate together, complementing each other. The gift of the word of wisdom may be defined as "a small portion (a word) of God's total wisdom supernaturally imparted by the Holy Spirit." Knowledge is information. Wisdom is knowing what to do with that information. There are several examples of the word of wisdom at work in the ministry of Jesus. One of them is: (1) directions as to where and when to fish (Luke 5:4-10). The word of wisdom was greatly needed in the days of the early church, and it was supplied by the Holy Spirit: (1) Recognition of the need and direction for the method of appointing men to serve the widow's needs (Acts 6:1-7). The word of knowledge is a small portion of the total knowledge of God supernaturally imparted by the Holy Spirit. An example of the "word of knowledge" gift used in Jesus' ministry is when Jesus revealed that He saw Nathanael under the fig tree before He saw him with his natural eye (John 1:47-49). An example of the "word of knowledge" used in the early church is Peter's knowledge of the deception attempted by Ananias and Sapphira (Acts 5:1-11). There is no gift of the Spirit called the gift of "discernment." It is the discerning of Spirits. The person being used in this gift will discerner or recognize what spirits are at work in a given situation there are several categories of spirits in existence: The Holy Spirit, Faithful angels, Fallen angels, demons or evil spirits, and human spirits. A scriptural example of the gift is John the Baptist discerning the Holy Spirit upon Jesus in the form of a dove (John 1:32-33). Scriptural examples of the discerning of "faithful angels are: Mary saw two angels at the sepulcher (John

Teaching and Understanding Pneumatology & Spiritual Gifts 65

20:11-13) and an angel appeared to Paul on board a ship (Acts 27:23-24). Examples of discerning human spirits are: Jesus discerned the guileless spirit of Nathanael (John 1:47). Peter discerned the wrong motives of Simon (Acts 8:20-24). Examples of the discernment of evil spirits are as follows: A dumb spirit (Matthew 9:33-34). A spirit of blindness and dumbness (Matthew 12:22-24). A dumb and deaf spirit (Mark 9:17-27). The gift of faith is a small portion of the total faith of God which is a gift of the Holy Spirit. It can be operated only under God's control. There are similarities between healings and miracles in many cases, there are also important differences. A healing many times occurs gradually, almost imperceptibly, relieving the body of disease.

ASSESSMENT

1. Group Spiritual gifts into three groups.

2. The gifts of the Spirit are only confined to believers or non-believers as well? Please support your answer.

3. Give as many scripture references relating to the word of wisdom, word of knowledge, and discernment.

4. Name some categories of spirits relating to discernemtn of spirits.

5. What are the similarities and dissimilarities between healings and miracles?

PERSPECTIVES

Philo of Alexandria, an early Christian Thinker, says 'man is created by God, first as a form in the mind or "logos" of God, and next as a corporeal being possessed of an incorporeal soul' (Stokes, 35).[38]

What are your thoughts about the aforementioned thought, heretical, apologetic, or liberalistic? Could you scripturally support your position?

---

[38] Philip Stokes, Philosophy: 100 Essential Thinkers. New York: Enchanted Lion Books, 2003.

CHAPTER FIVE

GREEK ETYMA

Disciple—Mathētēs (ματētές) a learner (from manthanō, to learn, from a root math, indicating thought accompanied by endeavorour) in contrast to Didaskalos, teacher, one who follows one's teaching. A disciple was not only a pupil, but an adherent; a disciple is spoken of as an imitator of his or her master.

Interpret—Hermēneuō (ἑρμηνεύω) to explain; Diermēneuō (διερμηνεύω) a strengthened form, to expound; Methermēneuō (μεθερμηνεύω) to change or translate from one language to another; Hermēneia (ἑρμηνία) as in I Corinthians 12:10;14:26

Preacher—Kērux (κήρυξ) preacher of the gospel, preacher of righteousness

Prophet—Prophētēs (προΦήτης) A proclaimer of a divine message

Word—Logos ((λόγος) the expression of thought, a saying or statement, a message; Rhēma, that which is spoken,

EXEGESES

Unless there is within that which is above us, we shall soon yield to that which is about us (Peter Taylor Forsyth)

When Spirit soars, my body falls on its knees (George Christoph Lichtenberg)

Exegesis of Allen Hunt on I Corinthians 12

Hunt, in his apology entitled "The Inspired Body," compares the input of Paul in I Corinthians Chapter 2:6-16 relating to the incomparability of the wisdom and power of God to anything. The author points out how God willingly decides to grace the body of Christ, the church, with His secret treasures to be a blessing to humanity. In his own words, Allen Hunt categorically talks about the issue of "inspired speech" versus uninspired speech. Inspired speech according to Hunt is one that is expected of all Christians under the power of the spirit. Not an ordinary speech spoken merely by anyone without any divine authorization. Allen lays out two points: First, he says all Christians are inspired by virtue of their reception of the Holy Spirit at the initial stage of baptism because at this juncture, it is the Holy Spirit at work according to I Corinthians 12:3. Second, he says that the empowerment of the spirit upon of a believer, makes that person eligible to utter inspired speeches, such as the "utterance of wisdom," (12:8), "utterance of knowledge" (12:8), and "utterance of tongue-speaking" (12:10). Allen speaks of the endowment of God's varied gifts to the individual Christians as a symbol of "communal inspiration" whereby not only is a Christian blessed with a gift, that Christian has been given that gift as a spiritual investment from above to be a blessing to the community. He says God intends it to be this way so that both the community and the church or Christians can share the same inspiration of God, and these gifts are to be used for the common good. Allen Hunt believes in the unity of the Spirit and the church by affirming that the same Spirit that imbues the variety of gifts is the same Spirit that inspires. Avoiding the presence of pluralism, he points out that there shows the singleness of one body, one Spirit, one baptism but many believers and many gifts in the church. Allen concurs with other exegetes and lexical depictions that the premise of Apostle Paul's concern during this discourse regarded the creeping in of factionalism and dissention among the believers in Corinth. Paul had to make it clear to the church that the issuing of these gifts was not intended to divide the church but unite the church to the common good of winning souls for Christ. Moreover, in I Corinthians 14:1-12 Paul addresses the issues of factionalism and dissention but Allen says that the assessment an valuation of inspired speech is for edification and up-building of the community. He says that believers are the beneficiaries and objects of inspired speech and the community is both the locus and focus of inspiration. (Allen Rhea Hunt, 109, 111, 112, 123).[39]

Exegesis of Simon J. Kistemaker on I Corinthians 12:7-11

Verse seven: Too often ministers of the gospel, evangelists, and missionaries are considered to be the only recipients of special gifts. Too often, a distinction is made between sacred and secular occupations. Kingdom service is frequently understood to be performed by those people who have been ordained to serve the Lord in special ministries. Paul notes that the manifestation of the Spirit is given to each believer. That is, the Holy Spirit dwells on every believer (6:18) and this makes his presence known with some indication of gifts. The phrase "the manifestation of the Spirit" can be either objective or subjective. Objectively it signifies an action that reveals the presence of the Spirit, subjectively, it reveals an action which the Spirit generates. The evidence of the Spirit's presence in the life of the believer serves the common good of the entire community.

The intent here is to promote the common good and to prohibit any one from using a gift for personal profit. Verse eight: Paul lists 9 gifts (vv 8-10). Scholars attempt to make a distinction between the gifts that are either temporal or permanent, verbal or non-verbal, and important or less important. An attractive threefold division of the gifts follows: **1.** Pedagogical: wisdom and knowledge. **2.** Supernatural: faith, healings, miracles. **3.** Communicative: prophecy, spirit discernment, tongues, interpretation of tongues. Among the gift, only "healing" is specifically called a gift (v.9). "Word of wisdom," or "utterance of wisdom," is the ability to speak divine wisdom which believers receive through the Holy Spirit. Divine wisdom is contrasted from human wisdom. Isaiah prophecy that the Spirit of wisdom would rest on the Messiah (11:2) was fulfilled in Jesus, who increased in wisdom (Luke 2:52). Jesus promised his disciples divine wisdom, Stephen in Acts 6:10 was known to be filled with divine wisdom and the Spirit. James talks a lot about wisdom and how if any lacks it he or she should ask God, who gives it generously (James 1:5). The *word of knowledge*, the second pedagogical gift is essentially the intimate personal knowledge of god which depends, not upon intellect but on love, and on God's knowledge of or acquaintance with . . . man. The term denotes affinity and signifies a personal relationship that exists between God and the redeemed person in Christ. Thus knowledge comes to expression in knowing, understanding, and explaining to his people God's revelation in the scripture and creation. Verse nine: The gift of *faith*, together with miracles and healings, it is part of the category of supernatural gifts. Jesus told his disciples of faith being as small as a mustard seed can move mountains (Matthew 17:20; I Corinthians 13:2) and the

---

[39] Allen Rhea Hunt, The Inspired Body: Paul, the Corinthians, and Divine Inspiration. Macon: Mercer University Press, 1996.

apostles did exhibit such faith. The book of Hebrews presents a list of Old Testament heroes of faith. The *gift of healing*, faith and the gifts of healing are closely related. James offers that the prayer of faith can heal the sick (James 5:14-15). Two cautionary remarks regarding this: **1.** The elders should not expect that they have received a permanent gift to heal every member of the church who is ill, **2.** In spite of fervent prayer offered in faith, God may choose not to restore someone to normal health and strength. Not only apostles but deacons received the ability to perform miracles of healing in the early church. Verse ten: *working of miracles*, the third gift in the sequence of supernatural gifts. If healing of the sick is a temporary gift so is the gift of miracles. In the scripture, miracles are supernatural acts that occur contrary to the laws of nature. God temporarily intervenes in nature by performing the miracle.

The Old Testament teaches that God performed miracles through Moses prior to and during the exodus from Egypt. 4 observations: **1.** Paul writes that miracle is among the supernatural gifts. **2.** He does not say that every believer receives the power to work miracles. Instead he notes that the gift was distinctive mark of an apostle. **3.** Miracles of healing and miraculous powers seen to overlap now and then in the New Testament, although a distinction should be made between miracles in nature and those that relate to the human body. **4.** According to Kistemaker, during the apostolic era, miracles in nature appears to have come to an end. *Prophecy*, a communicative gift, is that person who occasionally serves as God's mouthpiece either to utter predictions or more often to interpret God's will to the church (Ephesians 4:11). *Discerning of spirits*, the 2nd communicative gift, is linked to the preceding of prophecy. Some believers have received the gift to distinguish spirits. In other passages, he urges that prophetic utterances should be examined and evaluated but these 2 passages do not convey the same message. The power and influence of spirits can be discerned by their word, deed, and appearance. Verse eleven: *The one and same Spirit*. The genuine confession of Jesus' Lordship can come only by the Holy Spirit. Every one of the 9 gifts has its origin in the Holy Spirit. The same Spirit works all these things. Both gifts and power energize and believe to originate with the Holy Spirit.

No one in the Christian community is receiving all the gifts and no one is without a gift. Verse ten: As he adds, the Spirit exercises his prerogative to determine and distribution individual gifts to the believes (Kistemaker, 416).[40]

Exergesis of Philipp Melanchthon on 1 Corinthisn 12

Philipp Melanchthon (1497-1560), was an influential Theologian and contemporary professor with Martin Luther in Germany at the University of Wittenberg where he taught Greek. His love for Greek, Philosophy, Scholastic

---

[40] Simon J. Kistemaker, New Testament Commentary: Exposition of the 1st Epistle to the Corinthians. Grand Rapids: BakerBooks, 1993.

Theology [(the combination of Theology and Scholasticism. *Scholasticism in Latin and Greek means that which belongs to the school or academics.* It has to do with reconciling the philosophy of ancient classical philosophers such as Aristotle, Plato, and Boethius with Medieval Christian Theology, a theology of the middle ages about the 13th century that attempts to show that Greek philosophy and Christian faith were in fact compatible methods for arriving at divine truths. Scholasticism is not a philosophy or theology in itself, but a tool and method for learning which puts emphasis on dialectic reasoning which entails exchanging arguments and counter-arguments respectively to advocate propositions or theses. The primary purpose of Scholasticism was to find the answer to a question or resolve a contradiction.

Early Scholastics were Anselm of Cantebury (1033-1109) "father of Scholasticism", Anselm of Laon (died in 1117), Hugh of St Victor (1078-1151), Bernard of Clairvaux (1090-1153), Hildegard of Binger (1098-1179), Peter Lombard (1100-1160), Alain de Lille (1128-1202), Joachim of Fiore (1135-1202). High Scholastics were Thomas Aquinas (1225-1274, Saint Dominic (1170-1221), Alexander of Hales (died in 1245), and Roger Bacon (1214-1294). Late Scholastics were William Ockham (1285-1349) and John Wycliffe (1320-1284).

(www.encyclopedia.thefreedictionary.com/scholastictheology).], and especially Aristotelian Philosophy (the philosophical ideologies of Aristotle), made him change his German family last name (Schwartzerd) to the Greek name (Melanchthon). He obtained his Master's degree at age 16 and appointed first professor at Wittenberg. Philipp published his first work *loci communes* at age 24. He taught and wrote synthetic theology which was admired by Luther. Synthetic Theology is the reflection and action that requires living faith in Christ who is Himself the word made flesh. It has to do with the discerning sensitivity to the person and activity of Christ and to the many ways He reveals Himself in both word and world (*www.enrichmentjournal.ag.org*). Synthetic Theology somewhat aligns with practical theology which implies that the sufferings, trials, tribulations experienced by Christians are common features that empower Christians and make them real disciples of Christ. Obviously, "it is the truth of God revealed in His word, spoken in our hearts by His Spirit" (*www.bible.org/page*). Philipp is accredited for composing the Lutheran Augsburg Confession and contributed immensely to the foundation and consolidation of Lutheranism, including Luther's ninety-five theses in October of 1517. Interestingly while being a professor of Greek and the humanities, Philipp enrolled at seminary to study Theology simultaneously. Philipp wrote many Greek Grammar, Philosophy, and Neo-Scholastic Theology textbooks. His renowned work *Annotationes in Epistolam priorem ad Corinthios* appealed greatly to Luther and other exegetes. His annotations (a series of lecture notes on specific verses in First Corinthians) of the Apostle Paul to the Corinthian Saints, highlight some supporting points. In his commentary on the epistle, he gives several views on faith, hope, charity and the gifts of the spirit. First, he believes that faith assents to the whole word and promise of God. Second, he says human cognition by nature is not faith because human cognition or knowledge is gathered from the causes of nature. Among men, he says, the divine word has no cause according to nature because the unspiritual man does not perceive the things of the Spirit. Third, faith is truly believing God from the heart, Fourth, faith cannot be found in the wicked or damned. Philipp emphasizes how the gifts are the efficacy and work of the Holy Spirit in the heart of the believers. Philipp, however, says that the gifts are given to the just only. This position I dispute because the gift of God is not based on one's merits and good works. God's gift is freely given to whomever He decides to give it to. Another point of refutation is that Philipp believes that the Holy Spirit does speak through demons. Although he was trying to make a point of distinguishing the power of the devil in creating a counterfeit or false spirit to that of God's, he does not make himself clear. I do agree that there are demonic spirits but in no form or fashion the manifestation of the demonic spirit is the same as the Holy Spirit. However, the Spirit of God enters an unsaved person to become saved and delivered from the bondage of sin. But the Spiritual gifts spoken about by the Apostle Paul in Corinthians have no reference to the power of darkness. These gifts are for the edification of the church and to be used to win more souls to Christ. The demons are not recipients of God's spiritual gifts. They must be delivered first. The demons speak under the influence of the devil. Philipp and I agree that dissensions and jealousies existed in the church at Corinth which led to Paul's writing of the epistle to address them particularly. Philipp believes that the manifestation of the Spirit was warranted so that the faithful have the pledge and guarantee of God's favor. (Philipp Melanchthon, 129-150).[41]

Exegesis of Victor Paul Furnish on I Corinthians 12

Furnish believes that the unity of the church or the body of Christ is evident only by the Spirit. According to him being baptized in the Spirit, is the initial stage at which God begins to unite the church for a specific mission. Furnish believes that in order for a person to be used by God for any mission, one has to be baptized in the Spirit. In his own words, Furnish says, "the Lord's claim is established at baptism when the believer becomes "one spirit with Him. Baptism is also the occasion for God's giving of the Holy Spirit through whose working the believer's body becomes the temple in which the Spirit dwells" (Holding to the Center, 59).[42] Furnish acknowledges that the Apostle Paul lays down the Theological groundwork for membership in the body of Christ through the portrayal of the gifts of the Spirit, which gifts he believes are only the reflection of Christ's love for the church and humanity. Furnish lays out

---

[41] Philipp Melanchthon, Annotations on First Corinthians. Milwaukee: Marquette University Press, 1995.

[42] Victor Paul Furnish, New Testament Theology: The Theology of the First Letter to the Corinthians. Cambridge: Cambridge University Church, 1999.

two major ways in which Paul attaches importance to the operation of the Spirit in the Corinthian church. *First*, the Spirit was the *founding and initial formation* of a believing community. By this Furnish means only the Spirit can search out and reveal the *wisdom* of God. The Spirit serves in the capacity of a mediator between the church and Christ, between man and God, earth and heaven. The Spirit is associated with conversion in the declaration that believers have been washed, sanctified, and rectified in the Spirit. The Spirit is thus instrumental in establishing the wholeness as well as the holiness of believing community.

Second, the Spirit role is to uplift and build up the believing community. It is at this end the Christ has chosen to grace believers individually with varied gifts that the body and all believers might function as god intends. Furnish gives a panoramic perception of Paul's first letter as addressing four important areas: *Christology, soteriology, eschatology,* and *ecclesiology*. In first Corinthians the Christological veiw of the Apostle Paul emphasizes on the image of Christ being identified with God's saving power with the cross. Christ is being identified as the *first fruits (aparchē)* of those who are died. Christ's resurrection inaugurates the resurrection of the dead. Christ is also portrays as the last Adam, the second man, the man from heaven as opposed to Adam, the first man with flaws, the man of the mundane sphere. *Soteriology* is a theology that deals with salvation as affected by Christ. Therefore, Furnish views Christ as the sacrifice for humanity's transgressions. Christ is our "righteousness," "sanctification," and "redemption" served the initial purpose of death on the cross to save fallen humanity. "Paul's exposition of the cross as exposing the wisdom and power of God in the context of *being saved* means deliverance from the folly that attends humanity's ultimately futile and self-destructive attempt to know God through its own finite wisdom" (The Significance of I Corinthians, 127, 128).[43]

Eschatology deals with the Second Coming, the resurrection of the dead, or the Last Judgment. The liberation accorded the church or humanity by Christ sacrificial redemptive role entitles humanity or believers to the eternal rule of Christ someday as a reward for their labor with and for Christ. Death is being defeated by Christ and the dead in Christ shall be changed in a new body or form to eternally reign with Christ. *Ecclesiology* is a theological doctrine relating to the church. Furnish views the church as the image of the believing community as "one body" with many members (12:12-30). He views the church as diversity-within-unity. Furnish urges that the diversity of spiritual gifts represented among the believers is not to be exploited or abused. He asserts that it is the affirmation and celebration of God's provision for the spiritual needs of the body. Furnish emphasizes that unity in Christ is representative of each member being equally important to one another.

---

[43] Victor Paul Furnish, New Testament Theology: The Theology of the First Letter to the Corinthians. Cambridge: Cambridge University Church, 1999.

Dale B. Martin's Apology on the Cultural Background of the Corithian Church

Unlike most orthodox Christians who spend a great deal of their time on only compiling religious data to validate their orthodox beliefs and views, Dale Martin brings to the discussion a lot on the Greco-Roman society that existed during the days of Paul and other Christian apologists. Martin shares the ways in which ancient literary societies unlike modern societies addressed the components of the human body in terms of the *body* and *soul*, and *spiritual* and *physical*. Properly addressing these dichotomies and material/ immaterial dualism, Martin turns to the views of one of humanities elite philosophers of the ancient world with Western conceptualization, René Descartes, a devout Catholic, sought a scientific methodology to analyze the material/ immaterial dualism of the human body or spiritual and physical without threatening the church's views. He invented the category of nature as a self-contained system. He however acknowledges that the world beyond the physical could not be analyzed by nature. He says, "to the nonphysical realm belong all those aspects of reality that exercise volition and true freedom: *God, the soul or mind, the I of human self.* There could be no ontological relation, therefore, between the *I* and the material world" (Hierarchy, 5).[44] The ontological argument argues the existence of God based on the fact of God as being God). Ontology is a branch of metaphysics that deals with the nature of being or the kinds of things that have existence.

According to Descartes: I thence concluded that I was a substance whose whole essence or nature consists only in thinking, and which, that I, that is to say, the mind by which I am what I am, is wholly distinct from the body and is even more easily known than the latter, and is such, that although the latter were not, it would still continue to be all that it is (The body in Greco-Roman Culture, 5).[45] It is wildly said however that Descartes's dichotomy has misled many who spent most of their time trying to make sense of ancient literary works. Biblical scholars such as Paul and others perhaps, had to distinguish Platonism (philosophical concept of Plato that actual things are copies of transcendent ideas) from Biblical concepts in terms of defining the *body* (sōma), *psychē* (soul), and *physis* (nature). Aristotle along with Greek and Roman thinkers did believe that the human *soul*, the basis of animated life and is part of nature. Another Greek philosopher, Democritus, refers to the soul as fire and heat. Leucippus says the *soul* composes spherical atoms that move easily through things. Pythagoreans (associates of the Greek philosopher, Pythagoras) identify the soul with the particles in the air. Another group of philosophers, *Epicureans* held the concept that "nothing that lacks body can act or be acted upon, nor can anything except void and emptiness provide place. Thus, all entities that act or acted upon are

---

[44] Dale B Martin, The Corinthian Body. New Haven: Yale University Press, 1995.
[45] Dale B Martin, The Corinthian Body. New Haven: Yale University Press, 1995.

bodies. Mind and soul are corporeal because they move the body" (Hierarchy, 9).[46] Putting in his two-cent explanation, Lucretius believes the mind strikes the human spirit, the spirit strikes the body, enabling the body to walk and move. Another group of philosophers, *Stoics* believe that nature includes both things that exist and things that do not exist. They call the things that exist corporeal and things that do not exist incorporeal. Philo of Alexandria, an apologist, agrees with Democritus that the soul was equivalent to fire. Modern apologists use the Greek word *pneuma* to define the *spirit*. It is from this Greco-Roman background the Apostle came. He was well versed and trained in Greek. Most of his writings portray most of these concepts. That is why Paul spent a lot of time and wrote a lot to explain and distinguish these so-called philosophies from Theology. Because Paul was educated, many of his converts were scholars as well, therefore, he faced a lot of challenges in addressing the issues of grace, the gifts of the spirit, and other Biblical concepts to his educated church congregants, most of whom were Greeks.

Exegeses from the New International Greek Testament Commentary on I Corinthians 12

In comprehending the grammatical correlations of Greek etymologies in terms of translation and interpretation, one will notice that certain words or phrases elaborated on by these exegetes may very well bring gender into play. There may be instances when a gender (forms of words that designate sex) may project femininity, masculinity, or a neuter stance. There may be a genitive plurality and singularity in either of the aforementioned gender cases. Take for instance the phrase "spiritual gifts" in verse one of I Corinthians is taken by some exegetes to refer to "spiritual persons." However, most interpreters, including Tertullian, Novatian, and Cyril of Jerusalem, believe that the phrase denotes literally "spiritual gifts" or "gifts of the Spirit." In this case, it is conventionally concurred that the Greek gender applicable in this case is neither feminine nor masculine but neuter in meaning. *What criteria are we to apply for specific people or specific gifts to be considered genuinely "of the Holy Spirit"?* This is what vv 2 and 3 explicate in terms of a *Christomorphic criterion* (NIGTC, 910).[47] The Apostle Paul attempts to clarify to the church what counts as *people or gifts of the Spirit*. He informs the saints that it is expedient that they understand the spiritual things of God well because the people of God should not be ignorant concerning spiritual matters. Paul then takes on the subject of diversity versus unity in the operation of varied gifts from verses 4 through 7. Dale Martin, Harrington, and Lategan argue convincingly that the Apostle is mainly emphasizing on unity amidst diversity.

---

[46] Ibid., 5

[47] Anthony S Thiselton, The First Epistle to the Corinthians: A Commentary on the Greek Text. Grand Rapids: William B. Eerdmans Publishing Company, 2000.

With regards to the apostle's positions, the scholars jointly believe that unity is taking precedent over diversity not in a divisive manner but believe the apostle is saying that God is concerned about the faith community being united even if cultural differences or and varied gifts are present in the community. Martin observes, "Thus in 12:4-11 Paul continually stresses unity in diversity in order to overcome divisiveness owing to different valuations being assigned to different gifts, with tongues as the implied higher-status gift" (NIGTC, 928).[48] Lategan argues that the body imagery which expresses a careful balance between unity and diversity here undergoes revision and qualification in the light of the same *Spirit... the same Lord...the same God* (vv.4-6) in order to stress that the diversity is secondary to the unity (NIGTC, 928).[49] Harrington argues that the cohesive bestowal of the gifts ensures their fundamental unity. Thus both contextually and theologically the unity constitutes the major emphasis in vv. 4-11, since "building" provides the cohesive goal and purpose of the gifts, whatever their variety (NIGTC, 928).

It can conclusively be drawn from the three arguments that unity is the premise of the Apostle exegesis to the Corinthian saints. Harrington argues on the unity of source whereas Lategan stresses on the unity of goal and Martin underlines the unity of community. The one source is not only the one Spirit (12:1-3), but one God as giver of grace through Christ and the Spirit. Conzelmann's argument about "spiritual gifts" is that these gifts were also termed gifts of grace, which implies that God out of generosity apportions different gifts freely to different recipients. "Grace" used by Conzelmann implies that God does not give out gifts as a reward for one's service or labor for the kingdom of God. Instead, God's gifts are priceless and unmerited. God's apportionment of His gifts is for the amelioration of His kingdom. God's gifts are apportioned to save and edify the church, not of works.

Zodhiates observes: "The most striking element of these statements [i.e., in vv. 4-6] is the one recurring word 'the same.' . . . No one is to say that he has more of the Holy Spirit because he has more gifts. The same Spirit distributes the small or the large gift, not because He favors one Christian less or more than another, but because of His sovereign purposes. . . . The Giver, not Gift, is what accomplishes anything" (Commentary on 12:4-5, 930).[51] Believers are called or chosen to serve in a variety of ways but in harmony with God through His gifts. Regarding 12:8-11 of I Corinthians, Weiss and Allo are among those who perceive a triad of triads here, while Collins argues for a 2 + 5 + 2 chiasmus. Bengel and Meyer divide the list into three: (a) gifts which relate

---

[48] Anthony S Thiselton, The First Epistle to the Corinthians: A Commentary on the Greek Text. Grand Rapids: William B. Eerdmans Publishing Company, 2000.
[49] Ibid., 928.
[50] Ibid.
[51] Anthony S Thiselton, The First Epistle to the Corinthians: A Commentary on the Greek Text. Grand Rapids: William B. Eerdmans Publishing Company, 2000.

to "intellectual power (v. 8), (b) those which depend on "special energy of faith (vv. 9-10a), and (c) "Charismata." Different "lists" of instantiations of gifts in Paul assume various shapes and sizes. Four lists occur in Romans 12:6-8; 12:27-28; and Ephesians 4:11. On this basis Dunn prefers to distinguish thematically between gifts which relate respectively to miracles, revelation, inspired utterance, and service, perceiving all of them to proceed from divine grace (NIGTC, 937)[52]. The NIGTC exegetes propose that the translation relating to "wisdom" reflects two points: First, a *subjective genitive* (articulate utterance) derived from God's wisdom, or *objective genitive* (articulate utterance) about God's wisdom. Second, σοφία or *Sophia* relating to divine wisdom which is used sixteen times in this epistle, out of only four major epistles, Romans 11:33 and II Corinthians 1:12; six instances in Colossians [1:9, 28; 2:3, 23; 3:16; and 4:5]; and three in Ephesians including the following passages:1:17, 19, 20, 21, 22, 24, 30; 2:1, 4, 5, 6, 7, 13: 3 ;19. The background which controls the exegesis, therefore, derives from the contrast between the pretentiousness and competitive status-seeking of human wisdom (1:17-22; 2:1-5; 3:19) and the gift of divine wisdom (1:24-31; 2:6-13).

Since the emphasis in 12:8 falls entirely on gift, clearly *divine wisdom* as a gift of the Spirit lies in view here. Kistemaker offers an exegesis which coheres with factors: "The gift is the ability to speak divine wisdom which believers receive through the Holy Spirit (cf. 2:6-7). Divine wisdom is contrasted with human wisdom (1:17, 20, 25). Similarly, Zodhiates defines this gift as "an intelligent utterance of God's wisdom. Wisdom, in this context, becomes an evaluation of realities in the light of God's grace and the cross of Christ (NIGTC, 939).[53] Some other interpretations and scholars give a more pragmatic and individualistic view on wisdom as one that reflects intelligible communication of the purposes of God to man. Other writers like Chrysostom believes that "spiritual gifts" happened once or amongst the saints of the early church era and do not happen anymore. This interpretation somehow sends the message that Christ is not alive but dead because if you can say that spiritual gifts exist no more then you mean that Christ exist no more. We know that before Christ ascended to heaven He told the disciples to go to Jerusalem and wait in the upper room until they were filled with power from on high. He told them he would send them the comforter which is Himself in the Spirit that shall live in them and reveal all things to them. Therefore, if Chrysostom can pose in his writings that Spiritual gifs do not exist anymore, then I believe he is speaking as an infidel.

However, Tertullian, the great Christian writer, in a Christological perspective poses that the utterance which relates to "the Spirit of wisdom" which Isaiah alludes to in his messianic proclamation (Isaiah 11:1-3), views that "wisdom" and "knowledge" a gospel because they profess Christology. Clement of Alexandria addresses on the unity and diversity of the gifts.

---

[52] Ibid., 937.

[53] Anthony S Thiselton, The First Epistle to the Corinthians: A Commentary on the Greek Text. Grand Rapids: William B. Eerdmans Publishing Company, 2000.

He did not go into details but said that the gifts were "apostolic" in nature. He said that the mention of gifts reflect on *knowledge, preaching, life, righteousness, purity*, and *prophecy* of the apostles, concerning faith in Christ and the knowledge of the gospel.

It is not clear as to whether or not Clement was posing that the gifts of the spirit only related to the apostles and are not effective today. From reading through the lines, it shows some kind of neutrality. It however, sounds like he is supporting the views of Chrysostom, who believes that the gifts of the spirit only existed in the days of the apostles but are not real today. Other older modern writers recited lines from Thomas Aquinas as interpreting that wisdom is view as knowledge of salvation that is communicated to people. Some of these modern writers believe that "wisdom" traditionally relates to morality. It includes moral guidance for life. Yet in the light of James Davis's study of Jewish sapiential traditions, streses that this must not be understood to take us into the domain of "achievement" rather than of divine grace (Davis, wisdom and spirit, 113-37; cf. 16-27).[54] Hence, just as "wisdom" occurs in this epistle both in a pejorative sense of human status seeking and achievement and in a positive sense as the divine wisdom of the cross, so "knowledge" in a "proto-gnostic" or "standing-on-one's-rights frame means "the static, cognitive epistemology of the gnostics" and in a positive, relational, Christological frame "a dynamic affectional relationship from knowledge of God to being known by God (Khiok-khing Yeo, Rhetorical Interaction in I Cor 8 and 10, Biblnt 9. Leiden: Bill, 1995, 186-87).[55] Bengel assigns a more theoretical role to *articulate utterance relating* to "wisdom" and more practical role to the discourse relating to "knowledge"; for knowledge, he says it relates to things that are to be implemented as opposed to wisdom which relates to things eternal. One of the great scholars of all times, Augustine, acknowledges Paul's remarks to the Corinthians that in Christ are hidden al the treasurers of wisdom and knowledge (Colossians 2:3). According to Augustine, although wisdom may relate to "divine things" and "knowledge to human things," both are concerned with the believer's relationship to Christ which is activated through the Spirit. Augustine continues to say that wisdom relates to the intellectual understanding of eternal realities as knowledge relates to the "rational cognizance of temporal things" which come as gifts from the holy Spirit who is beyond the merely earthly (NIGTC, 942).[56]

SUMMARY

Allen Hunt categorically talks about the issue of "inspired speech" versus uninspired speech. Inspired speech according to Hunt is one that is expected of all Christians under the power of the spirit. Not an ordinary speech spoken merely by

---

[54] Anthony S Thiselton, The First Epistle to the Corinthians: A Commentary on the Greek Text. Grand Rapids: William B. Eerdmans Publishing Company, 2000.

[55] Ibid.

[56] Ibid., 942.

anyone without any divine authorization. Allen lays out two points: First, he says all Christians are inspired by virtue of their reception of the Holy Spirit at the initial stage of baptism because it this juncture, it is the Holy Spirit at work according to I Corinthians 12:3. Second, he says that the empowerment of the spirit upon of a believer, make that person eligible to utter inspired speeches, such as the "utterance of wisdom," (12:8, "utterance of knowledge" (12:8), and "utterance of tongue-speaking" (12:10). Allen speaks of the endowment of God's varied gifts to the individual Christians as a symbol of "communal inspiration" whereby not only is a Christian blessed with a gift, that Christian has been given that gift as a spiritual investment from above to be a blessing to the community. The Holy Spirit dwells on every believer (6:18) and this makes his presence known with some indication of gifts. The phrase "the manifestation of the Spirit" and be either objective or subjective. Objectively it signifies an action that reveals the presence of the Spirit, subjectively, it reveals an action which the Spirit generates. The gift of *faith*, together with miracles and healings, it is part of the category of supernatural gifts. The *gift of healing*, faith and the gifts of healing are closely related. *Prophecy*, a communicative gift, is that person who occasionally serves as God's mouthpiece either to utter predictions or more often to interpret God's will to the church (Ephesians 4:11). *Discerning of spirits*, the 2nd communicative gift, is linked to the preceding of prophecy. Some believers have received the gift to distinguish spirits. *Soteriology* is a theology that deals with salvation as affected by Christ. *Eschatology* deals with the Second Coming, the resurrection of the dead, or the Last Judgment. *Ecclesiology* is a theological doctrine relating to the church. "spiritual gifts" is that these gifts were also termed gifts of grace, which implies that God out of generosity apportions different gifts freely to different recipients. "Grace" used by Conzelmann implies that God does not give out gifts as a reward for one's service or labor for the kingdom of God. Instead, God's gifts are priceless and unmerited. God's apportionment of His gifts is for the amelioration of His kingdom. "Wisdom" reflects two points: First, a *subjective genitive* (articulate utterance) derived from God's wisdom, or *objective genitive* (articulate utterance) about God's wisdom.

ASSESSMENT

1. According to Hunt what is inspired speech?

2. What does Hunt mean by "communal inspiration?"

3. What are the objective and subjective descriptions of the phrase "the manifestation of the Spirit?

4. What is a communicative gift?

5. Define the following terms: Soteriology, Eschatology, and Ecclesiology

PERSPECTIVES

As a philosopher, scientist, and political theorist, Aristotle believes that the behavior of both the animate and inanimate is directed to a common purpose or "telos" (goal). He believes that everything in the universe has a natural function and strives toward fulfilling that function. From the school of the Cynics (a thought that rejects the complications and machination of civil society), Diogenes of Sinope believes that 'mastery of self, or self-sufficiency, leads to both happiness and freedom but requires constant practice and training in the face of adversity' (Stokes, 31).[57] From his work predicated on "correct living," Lucius Annaeus Seneca believes that only "good" is a virtue. He says that doing the right thing is important and one should display an attitude of indifference to others. Seneca also says, 'each and every one of us has a god within him guiding us along the path set for us by Providence' (Stokes, 37).[58]

What is your reponse to the aforementioned schools of thought, as presented by Philip Stokes, heretical, apologetic, or liberalistic? Could you scripturally support your position?

---

[57] Philip Stokes, Philosophy: 100 Essential Thinkers. New York: Enchanted Lion Books, 2003.
[58] Ibid., 37

CHAPTER SIX

GREEK ETYMA

Discern—(ἀνακρίνω) To separate out as to investigate (krinō) by looking through out (ana, intensive), to examine scrutinize, determining the excellence or defects of a person or thing; diakrisis (διάκριςις) discerning, judgments, discrimination between good and evil.

Heal—Sōzō (σώζω) to save, to make whole; Iama (ἰαμα) of divinely imparted gifts in the churches in the Apostolic times.

Holy—Hagios (ἅγιος) Concentrated to God, sanctified, holy ones, sacred; Hosios (ὅσιος) righteously right

Intent—Ennoia (ἔννοια) a thinking, idea consideration, purpose, design

Pastor—Poimēn (ποιμήν) a shepherd, one who tends herds, pastors guide and feed the flocks

INDIVIDUAL GIFTS

Faith is the eye that sees Him, the hand that clings to Him, the receiving power that appropriates him (Frederick James Woodbridge)

Orthodoxy can be learned from others; living faith must be a matter of personal experience (J. W. Buchsel)

Faith as a gift and gifts of healing (12:9)

The Greek word *pistis* (πίστις) primarily means a strong persuasion or conviction. However, the type of faith used by the Apostle Paul is different from the faith of conviction or persuasion. The verse asserts that the Lord will give this particular gift not to all believers but to certain believers or another as defined by the Greek word *heteros* (ἕτερος.) Therefore, the connotation of this particular type of faith is different from *pistis*. The type of faith is not saving faith. Bruce observes that it is not the saving faith which is basic to all Christian life, but special endowment of faith for a special service (cf. 13:2), while Collins calls it "something different from the faith that characterizes all believers" (NIGTC, 945).[59]

Conzelmann suggests that the type of faith the Apostle Paul alludes to is not saving faith rather it is one that can be equated or linked to the performance of miracles and healing (13:2) because it is beyond saving faith. Another exegete, Fee, refers to this type of faith as unique from that of saving faith, it is one that reveals the supernatural conviction of God in reflecting on His power or mercy in a very spectacular way in special instances. Bittlinger agrees with Conzelmann in his hypothesis and succinctly uses Hebrews chapter eleven to give a little distinction between the faith that the writer of the book of Hebrew, who many allude to being the Apostle Paul, where paradigms of faith in a general sense have been used. The writer to the Hebrew Christians suggests that *faith entails a willingness to act or to venture in the present on the basis of reality which has yet to be fully visible when it finally occurs* (NIGTC, 945).[60] Martin Luther defines faith as a living, daring confidence in God's grace, so sure and certain that a man would stake his life upon it a thousand times. This confidence in God's grace makes men glad and bold... (NIGTC, 945).[61] In verse 9 also Paul mentions the *gifts of healing* which shows a plurality. The Greek word *iama* (ἴαμα) denotes *various kinds of healing*. It is however noteworthy that various kinds of healing is not mentioned among the

---

[59] Anthony S Thiselton, The First Epistle to the Corinthians: A Commentary on the Greek Text. Grand Rapids: William B. Eerdmans Publishing Company, 2000.

[60] Ibid.

[61] bid., 945

gifts mentioned in Romans 12:3-8 and Ephesians 4:11. The Greek word *iama* appears only in verses nine, twenty-eight, and thirty of I Corinthians chapter 12. However the cognate verb *iaomai* appears nineteen times in the Gospels (including twelve times in Luke, four times in Acts, and once each in Hebrews, James, and I Peter).

One must understand that the gift of healing is a different office than the gift of faith. The healed does not have to have the gift of faith in order to receive healing or spiritual cure. The faith that the healed needs is as equivalent to that of saving faith. It is the healer or the person who is endowed with the gift of healing who exercises a special kind of faith or active faith (relying, trusting, and believing God to perform that which He promises without any doubtful reservations), not necessarily the gift of special faith. The word *kinds* denote variations. It may refer to a gradual, physical mental, psychosomatic, or mundane phenomenon but should not be stereotypical used as the sole premise of the word's meaning. Donald Gee, a Pentecostal says that *kinds of healing* should not preclude the merciful and manifold work of medical healing (NIGTC, 948).[62] Bengel also supports Gee as saying that the gifts in verse nine, although refer to the supernatural, the natural is included. Healers are given varied gifts at varied times for varied tasks, and we should not imposed a post-eighteenth century dualism of "natural" and "supernatural" upon the way in which God chooses to use, or not to use, regular physical means (NIGTC, 948).[63]

The Deeds of Power or Working of Miracles/ Power (I Corinthians 12:10a).

Whether subjective genitive, working of miracles, or objective genitive, power to work miracles, exegetes conclude categorically that the Apostle is referring to the supernatural phenomenon of God that performs beyond mundane domains. The resurrection from the dead is the premise of the issue which guarantees power to perform supernaturally. In Acts chapter one, Jesus directs His disciples to go to Jerusalem until they were endued with power from on high. This *power* Christ is referring to subjects both the natural and spiritual spheres to its authority.

This is a power that heals, casts out unclean spirits, and at the same time destroys sin. As an accommodation to tradition and Synoptic usage we translate *actively effective deeds of power* (i.e., mighty works); but this may already concede too much expectations of the spectacular (NIGTC, 955).[64] Similarly ἐνεργήματα δυνάμεων concerns *effective deeds* which *actively* operate with the *power*, whether rational or supranational, whether to overcome

---

[62] Anthony S Thiselton, The First Epistle to the Corinthians: A Commentary on the Greek Text. Grand Rapids: William B. Eerdmans Publishing Company, 2000.

[63] Ibid., 948.

[64] Anthony S Thiselton, The First Epistle to the Corinthians: A Commentary on the Greek Text. Grand Rapids: William B. Eerdmans Publishing Company, 2000.

spiritual or earthly forces of operations, and whether by means of self-sacrifice and the witness of an outstanding life or by some more spectacular and (in the modern sense) "miraculous" working. The victorious Christ, who was nevertheless crucified and raised, bestows through the Spirit a gift of victory which may draw its *power* both from the pattern and reality of the cross (with all its constraints and "weakness") and from the pattern and reality of the resurrection (NIGTC, 956).[65] In verse 10 of chapter 12 of First Corinthians, the phrase, "to another prophecy" is another gift attributive to the array of gifts Paul informs the saints of Corinth the church is blessed with from God. However, the Greek reads the phrase, "to another prophecy" as "to another, prophecy." If you notice, a comma is placed after the phrase, "to another," ἄλλῳ προφητεία. Prophecy in this context would mean not "foretelling, rather forth-telling in light of the present, past and the future. According to Bittlinger the address to a present situation retains an expected strand of continuity with prophet and prophecy in the Old Testament. Therefore, the New Testament as well as the Old Testament prophets often allude to past and future events and share light on the present. Revelation 1:3 refers to John's acopcalyptic discourse as "this prophecy" (cf. also Revelation 19:10; 22:10, 19; I Timothy 1:8; 4:14; II Peter 1:19; I Corinthians 13:2. The verb προφητεύει, occurs thirteen times in the Gospels and Acts, but mainly in reference to the Old Testament prophecies. Paul uses the verb about eleven times exclusively in this epistle (11:4, 5; 13:9; 14:1, 3, 4, 5, 24, 31, 35, 39. There are two references in Revelation 10:11 and 11:3, and two in I Peter and Jude [(I Peter 1:10; Jude 14) (NIGTC, 956)].[66]

a. Hellenistic Background of the word "prophecy"

According to Religious Greek texts, a prophet is one who speaks on behalf of a god, an announcer, or a spokesperson. However, in Hellenistic secularism, a prophet is an official of the cult who serves as a keeper of an oracle.

The prophet is also referred to as an oracle. An oracle is also referred to as a shrine or a ritual through which a deity reveals hidden knowledge or divine purpose through this person. The secular definition seems to give a vivid picture of the function of a prophet in essence. Although the afore-description projects a Hellenistic concept, it pretty much explains the religious role of a prophet but from a different source of authority. As opposed to the Hellenistic revelation of a prophet from a mundane source, "prophet" in the religious context as mentioned in the Bible, reflects on God as the divine source of the revelation.

b. Apocalyptic Background of the word "prophecy"

In the apocalyptic context prophecy is review in terms of a mystery. Prophecy is a revelation of mysteries to an intended person or people. Prophecy is an explanatory

---

[65] Ibid., 956.
[66] Ibid.

communication if you will, one with a message or purported knowledge or revelation. The spiritual and apocalyptic perspectives of prophecy synonymously reveal it as the revelation of hidden wisdom. According to Ulrich Müller the apocalyptic emphasis is on the oracles of judgment which embodies "teaching" as well as announcement or pronouncement on prophetic teaching of judgment and grace. The goal of prophetic speech is to challenge to repentance and to build up the community to salvation (NIGTC, 960).[67]

c. Prophecy as Pastoral Preaching

A prophet is a Spirit-endowed person whose teachings admonish and comfort the saints, whose message calls for repentance and promise, one who counsels as a pastor, and blames and praises people. Prophets preach grace and judgment, and their work may win the unbeliever (14:24) of First Corinthians chapter one as well as build the church. Prophecy is a word of divine revelation consisting spontaneously of Spirit-inspired, intelligible messages orally delivered in a gathered assembly. Prophecy, as a gift of the Spirit, combines pastoral insight into the needs of persons, communities, and situations with the ability to address these with God-given utterances or longer discourse (whether unprompted or prepared with judgment, decision, and rational reflection) leading to challenge or comfort, judgment, or consolation but ultimately building up the addressees (NIGTC, 961).[68]

Discerning What is of the Spirit (12:10b)

Some exegetes believe that the Apostle Paul was alluding to distinguishing evil spirits from that of the Holy Spirit. The verse says "to another discerning of spirits." The word spirit is pluralized with an "s" at its end. Therefore, some scholars believe that the Apostle is drawing a line between evil spirits and the Spirit of God. However, by and large as Robert Jewett and other theologians suggest that the plurality of the verse shares Paul's distinguishing views of the Spirit of God from the human spirit. The Gnostics and various philosophers or humanists in the Apostle's days venerated human intelligence instead of God. Therefore, the Apostle Paul is making this clear to the Corinthians saints that the discerning of spirits has to do with the ability of the Spirit of God to discern the true or divine Spirit than that of human influence. The gifts of discernment or discrimination include (a) a critical capacity to discern the genuine transcendent activity of the Spirit from merely human attempts to

---

[67] Anthony S Thiselton, The First Epistle to the Corinthians: A Commentary on the Greek Text. Grand Rapids: William B. Eerdmans Publishing Company, 2000, p 960

[68] Anthony S Thiselton, The First Epistle to the Corinthians: A Commentary on the Greek Text. Grand Rapids: William B. Eerdmans Publishing Company, 2000, p 961

replicate it; and (b) a pastoral discernment of the varied ways in which the Spirit of God is working, in such a way as to distinguish various consequences and patterns (NIGTC, 966).[69]

Only the Spirit of God is capable of discerning the things of God. A human spirit cannot discern the things of God. God's Spirit has the advantage of being able to discern both mundane and heavenly things. Therefore, the gift of discerning spirits is needed in the Christian community or the church to have the Spirit of God single out the false spirits that are trying to creep into the church to bring about division. The discerner of the spirit will be able to try or test the spirits to see whether they be of God or man. Chrysostom defines, "discerning of spirits" constructively as a starting point in his comment as mean "knowing who is spiritual, and who is not: who is a prophet, and who a deceiver, as mentioned to the Thessalonians by the Apostle Paul also (I Thessalonians 5:20), "respect prophesying, but test everything, hold fast to the good. Dunn adds that the gift concerns itself with "evaluating, testing, weighing of the prophetic utterance of the rest of the assembly or prophets (NIGTC, 968).[70]

Divers kinds or Species of Tongues and Their Intelligible Utterances (12:10c)

Species of tongues, and intelligible articulation of tongues-speech are two interactive gifts. They work together. Interpreting one will be interpreting the other. "Tongues" are being described as a form of inspired prayer and praise with praying and singing in the Spirit (I Corinthians 14:15). "Prophecy" denotes a speech-act from God to the church or the Christian community. "Tongues" are addressed from believers to God, not to human persons, 14:2). C Forbes categorizes "tongues" as "a sign" as another or "second view" of the same phenomenon rather than the manifestation of some different kind or "species of tongues" (NIGTC, 970).[71] However, a cluster of generic characteristics distinguishes "tongues" from "prophecy." "Tongues" are characterized to be unintelligible utterances which are mysterious and "prophecy" is characterized as being intelligible (I Corinthians 14:2b, 5, 7-9, 11, 19). In another context there is a contrast between addressed to God and to other human persons 14:2a; 14:15); in another context there seems to be a distinction of tongues as a communicative discourse associated with "angelic utterances" (13:1); in another context believers are made to feel as "strangers" not at home in the community of believers relative to tongue speaking (14:23a) and unbelievers are completely

---

[69] Anthony S Thiselton, The First Epistle to the Corinthians: A Commentary on the Greek Text. Grand Rapids: William B. Eerdmans Publishing Company, 2000.

[70] Ibd., 968

[71] Anthony S Thiselton, The First Epistle to the Corinthians: A Commentary on the Greek Text. Grand Rapids: William B. Eerdmans Publishing Company, 2000.

alienated (14:23b). On the other hand, one or more of the above characteristics or family traits give adequate grounds for the use of "tongues," provided they are "given" by the Holy Spirit and not self-induced (NIGTC, 971).[72]

Tongues as the Miraculous Power to Speak Other Languages

The most widespread pre-modern view held among the church Fathers, medieval writers, and Reformers perceived "tongues" as the "miraculous power to speak unlearned foreign languages. Among the Fathers, it is generally claimed that Origen, Chrysostom, Theodore, Cyril, and Thedorett held this view; among the medieval writers and Reformers, Thomas Aquinas, Pontius, Estius, and Calvin; among modern writers especially J. G. Davies, Robert Gundry, and Christopher Forbes. Chrysostom places a lot of emphasis on Acts 2 on the content of "wonderful things" spoken at Pentecost rather than "tongues" in any linguistic sense. Theodoret explains the purpose of "tongue" in I Corinthians 12:10 as for "evangelical mission." Thedoret further explains that these two gifts, "tongues" and "prophecy" serve the "kerygma" or "gospel" together because one person could speak one language with a message for another who understands that language. Hodge describes the gift of "tongues" as "the ability to speak in languages primarily unknown to the speakers." The nature of the gift is determined in Acts 2:4-11 (NIGTC, 975).[73]

Tongues as "Ecstatic" Speech

The word ecstatic comes from the Greek and Latin word "ecstasies" which is the English word "ecstasy," meaning emotional, or the state of being beyond reason and self-control. Tertuullian and other Montanists (2nd century Christian Sect that upheld ascetic discipline) coined the term "ecstasy" and "amentia" in the context of "madness" or "out of one's mind." However the treatise on Ecstasy did not last for long. Although Tertullian and the Montanists were trying to define the mystery of the gift of tongues but they could not because of the divine nature of the gift. No one can clearly explain the things of God except that person is used by God to do so. Only the Spirit can interpret the Spirit or spiritual things, not the flesh or human power. Although the mystery of speaking in tongues is done under the Spirit of God, it does not show that the speaker or possessor of the gift is mad or insane. The gift is displayed under the power of the Spirit, which transcends human understanding but does not show insanity. Of course, humans take the spiritual

---

[72] Ibid., 971
[73] Anthony S Thiselton, The First Epistle to the Corinthians: A Commentary on the Greek Text. Grand Rapids: William B. Eerdmans Publishing Company, 2000.

things of God to be foolish or insane because of their inability to comprehend the things of God.

SUMMARY

The Greek word *pistis* (πίστις) primarily means a strong persuasion or conviction. However, the type of faith used by the Apostle Paul is different from the faith of conviction or persuasion. The type of faith is not saving faith. Bruce observes that it is not the saving faith which is basic to all Christian life, but special endowment of faith for a special service. Conzelmann suggests that the type of faith the Apostle Paul alludes to is not saving faith rather it is one that can be equated or linked to the performance of miracles and healing because it is beyond saving faith. Regardind the power to work miracles, exegetes conclude categorically that the Apostle is referring to the supernatural phenomenon of God that performs beyond mundane domains. Prophecy, as a gift of the Spirit, combines pastoral insight into the needs of persons, communities, and situations with the ability to address these with God-given utterances or longer discourse "Prophet" in the religious context as mentioned in the Bible, reflects on God as the divine source of the revelation. Therefore, the gift of discerning spirits is needed in the Christian community or the church to have the Spirit of God single out the false spirits that are trying to creep into the church to bring about division. The discerner of the spirit will be able to try or test the spirits to see whether they be of God or man. Species of tongues, and intelligible articulation of tongues-speech are two interactive gifts. They work together. Interpreting one will be interpreting the other.

ASSESSMENT

1. What is your understanding about the type of faith Bruce is talking about, is it the same as saving faith?

2. Explain Conzelmann's suggestions.

3. What is your understanding of prophecy as spelled out in the text?

4. What are some benefits of the gift of discerning of spirits?

5. What are species of tongues?

PERSPECTIVES

Roman Emperor, Marcus Aurelius says that happiness of one's life depends on the quality of one's thoughts. Aurelius believes that 'divine providence has placed reason in man, and it was in the power of man to one with the the rational purpose of the universe' (Stokes, 39).[74] An African born of Algeria, one of the renowned writers of Catholicism, St Augustine of Hippo, believes that only through faith can wisdom be attained. He adds that rational thought is the servant of faith. Augustine uses reason to justify the doctrine of faith, a belief which was later embraced by John Calvin. Basing his argument on the "free will" of man and the concept of "determinism (the doctrine that emphasizes on the state of being determined), Boethius postulates that punishment is the right measure to correct the bad. He says only those who with good intentions and behavior gets "virtue." He belives that those who do bad suffer more if they are not caught, than those who are caught. Boethius further says, 'if God knows that you intend to do something before you even do it, you could hardly do otherwise. However, if you could not do otherwise, than it appears you do not have a free will' (Stokes, 47).[75] St. Anselm defines 'God" as something greater than which nothing can be thought of... the quality of perfection is an attribute only applicable to God' (Stokes, 49).[76]

What is your reponse to the aforementioned schools of thought, as presented by Philip Stokes, heretical, apologetic, or liberalistic? Could you scripturally support your position?

---

[74] Philip stokes, Philosophy: 100 Essential Thinkers. New York: Enchanted Lion Books, 2003.
[75] Ibid., 47.
[76] Ibid., 49.

CHAPTER SEVEN

GREEK ETYMA

Heresy—Hairesis (αίρεσις) a self-willed opinion which is substituted for submission to the power of truth.

Manifest—Phaneroō (Φανερόω) to make visible, the true meaning is uncovered; Phanerōsis (Φανέρωσις) manifestation, revelation.

Philosophy—Philosophos (ΦιλόσοΦος) loving wisdom; Philosophia (ΦιλοσοΦία) love and pursuit of wisdom.

Sanctification—Hagiasmos (γιασμός) separation to God, separation from evil ways and things

Tongue—Glossa (γλῶσσα) tongues like as fire which appeared on the day of Pentecost, tongue as an organ of speech, supernatural gift of speaking in another language; Dialektos (διάλεκτος) language, dialect, tongue.

Utter—Laleō (λαλέω) to speak; Phthengomai (Φθέγγομαι) to utter a sound or voice, translate

    A gift is as a precious stone in the eyes of him that hath it (OT: Pr 17:8)
    It is not faith and works; it is not faith or works; it is faith that works (Anonymous).

Proposed Modification From Theissen: Conscious, Unconscious, and a Release (Cf. Romans 8:26)

Gerd Theissen in an incisive and innovative treatment of tongues in his work *Psychological Aspects of Pauline Theology*, argues that tongues "are the language of the unconscious which is capable of consciousness through interpretation." Theissen also believes that tongues relate to ecstatic characteristics in certain ways. It is noted that Theissen worked with some noble scholars, namely Euripides, Virgil, Plato, and Philo, who elaborate extensively on tongues as relating to the unconscious and ecstasy. He also worked with apocalyptic studies and social psychology. Stendahl, another scholar, on his essay dealing with "glossolalia" or "tongues speaking," emphasized on the view of Pentecostal writer F. D. Macchia on :unspeakable groaning" or "Sighs Too Deep for Words" and "he who searches the hearts . . . the Spirit in Romans 8:26 and 27. According to Macchia and Stendahl, "groaning" relate to the eschatological expectancy of redemptive completion to take place via the Spirit through Christ as an authentic Christian Prayer. Theissen shares some meaning perspectives on the issue than any other writers. He notes (a) Paul and the Corinthians believe that tongues also have ["a personal value for the individual. One who speaks in tongues edifies oneself (I Corinthians 14:4)" NIGTC, 986].[77] "Feelings of happiness" or of relieve, intimacy with God, or other "positive inner consequences are then a motive for repetition of the behavior." (b) Tongues can become divisive for at least three reasons: First, they can become specific to a given group as an emotional bond with a tendency to make glossolalia as a criterion to belong to a group within the church (cf. do all *speak in tongues?* 12:30). That is a misusage and contradiction of the gift specifically when referring to I Corinthians 14:22 and 14:24-25.

Second, Theissen links this phenomenon with what J. P. Kildahl identifies as the "dependency syndrome": "I belong to Paul," "I belong to Apollos . . . " in a sociopolitical term. Hurd suggests that Paul himself may have more of this gift in his earlier ministry than he now wishes he had. E Best urges that to ignore possible affinities and aids to understanding would be to deprive the interpreter of a needed tool, provided the judicial care is retained. Third, Theissens argues that tongues had a social status significance according to the differing social stratification in Corinth at the time, especially in the church. The literate and upper

---

[77] Anthony S. Thiselton, The First Epistle to the Corinthians: A Commentary on the Greek Text. Grand Rapids: William B. Eerdmans Publishing Company, 2000.

class would rarely incline themselves to such devotional state as would the slaves or illiterate who would seek such heightened spiritual invocation of consciousness in tongues. "Tongues" may be viewed as "the language of the unconscious" because it is unintelligible (unless it is "interpreted") not only to others but the speaker. In 14:11 "foreign language" is unintelligible to the listener but intelligible to the speaker (NIGTC, 987-988).[78]

Paul then urges the speaker, not the listener to pray for power from on high to interpret or articulate the tongues spoken from the unconscious level to the cognitive or conscious. The term "glossolalia" does not appear in many English dictionaries. It is not that the word is archaic, it is somewhat esoteric in that it is not frequently used by linguists, less much to mention Theological scholars. *Glossolalia* originates from the Greek root word *glosso* which means *tongue*, and *lelein* which means to *speak*. Inspite of it esoteric feature, the term gains a dydadic relationship in the Theological and Psychopathological worlds. Although dydadic, the word is uniquely described differently in each disciplines. Some proffer that glossolalia is a "fabricated speech in a strange tongue" (English & English, 1985, 226)[79] as others define it as being synonymous to a mental illness. Lombard suggests that glossolalia was an automatism or automatic action induced by hypnosis which has no conscious control (Lombard, 1907).[80]

Additionally, Mackie says that glossolalia is a pathological ecstatic utterance in which language fragments are released from the subconscious mind (Mackie, 1921).[81] There has been a birage of research undertakings on glossolalia. And many exotic findings were uncovered. One finding bearing the emblem of a spiritist phenonmenon was revealed by researcher Flournoy in the 1900s after observing the performance of a spiritist Hélèn Smith, who claimed to speak in a Martian language. Another medium observational feedback comes from Psychiatrist, Carl Jung, who studied tongue speaking in an adolescent girl. He says the girl experienced visions, prophesied, did automatic writing. In his own words he describes the calmness she displayed in the state of mind: She spoke fluently, rapidly and with charm. It was possible to make out a few words, but not to memorize them because the language was so strange . . . the abosolute naturalness of the performance was amazing (Jung, 1902/ 1970, 28)[82]. Historically, the tradition and practice of glossolalia is being attributed to Islam and Christianity. Earliest records show that glossolalia was practiced by Christians since

---

[78] Anthony S. Thiselton, The First Epistle to the Corinthians: A Commentary on the Greek Text. Grand Rapids: William B. Eerdmans Publishing Company, 2000.

[79] H. Newton Mahony, Lovekin, A. Adams, Glossolalia. Oxford: Oxford University Press, 1985.

[80] Ibid., 1907.

[81] H. Newton Malony and A. Adams lovekin, Glossolalia: Behavioral Science Perspectives on Speaking in Tongues. Oxford: Oxford University Press, 1985.

[82] Ibid., 1921

the first century A.D. There are two primary references to glossolalia in the New Testament. The first account is recorded in the book of Acts when the disciples were praying in the upperroom in Jerusalem: suddenly a sound came from heaven like the rush of a mighty wind and it filled all the house where they were sitting, And there appeared to them tongues as of fire, distributed and resting on each one of them. And they were filled with the Holy Spirit and began to speak in other tongues as the Spirit gave them utterance (Acts 2:2-5, RSV). The assetion from this experience is that this was an example of intelligible utterances because apparently, the bystanders could understand the languages these disciples were speaking, although the disciples themselves did not know what they were speaking. In other words, although these spoken languages by the disciples were intellige to the hearers, the languages were unintellige to the speakers. Wasn't this a mystery?

The second account of glossolalia in the New Testament is found in I Corinthians chapters 12 through 14 as Paul talks about *spiritual gifts*. According to scholars, there are two differences between these two instances. The former is an example of intelligible utterances and the latter is one of unintelligible utterences. Its is believed that in ancient Corithn, the city of the church to which Paul addresses his letter, glossolalia as a ecstatic language, was commonly practiced as a norm for the Corinthians. Usaually according to scholars, interpreters were designated to interpret the Corinthian glossolalia. However, some proponents of this view did not specify whether the context or the pragmatics of this interpretation was carried out in a religious assemble or a secular gathering, or whether this was similar to a vanicular or pidgin (creole) commonly spoken by the Corinthians. Despite the ambiguity, Mills like a few scholars agree that the display of glossolalia in Corinth as mentioned in the First epistle to the Corinthians emphasizes on unintelligible utterances from a spiritual perspective were it was a faithful few chosen by God to give the gift of tongues to for a specific spiritual reason, not all believers as it was on the day of Pentecost. In the last three hundred years of Christian history, glossolalia has been the theological tradition for Jacobus Arminius, Wesleyan, and Holiness groups. According to Mills, the Wseleyan Rivival of the nineteenth century made this Arminian tradition popular through their theme, "growth in grace" and "scriptural holiness."

Believers emphatically reported themselves as being blessed by the "Holy Spirit" as on the day of Pentecost. Speaking in tongues became a sign of such blessing and norm (Mills, 5-6).[83] This movement expanded an took on a new meaning in a Pentecostal rival on Azuza Street in Los Angeles in 1906. That was a continuation of nineteenth century Pentecostal movement of *speaking in tongues* that started in Topeka, Kansas under the leadership of Charles Parham in 1901. According to an excerpt by Robin Johnstonin "Destination Texas" in the Petecostal Herald, a United

---

[83] Watson E. Mills, A Theological/ Exegetical Approach to Glossolalia. New York: University Press, 1985.

Pentecostal Magazine, he noted that the peak of the movement did not start until 1903 following an invitation by Mary Arthur, who had been healed of multiple diseases in a revival meeting in El Dorado Springs, inviting Charles Parham to run a revival meeting in Galena, Kansas.

At the close of this meeting, crowds of 2000 overflowed the building and experienced their "personal Pentecost." Parham went on staging revival meetings in Orchard, Texas in 1905. William J. Seymour was an African American Holiness preacher who was a student at Parham's Bible school in Houston Texas. Seymour left Texas and went to Los Angeles, California, where he shocked the religious and secular worlds with his amazing continuous hoiliness revival meetings where people experienced the infilling of the Holy Spirit and spoke in tongues. Sherrill gives an account of Agnes N. Ozman, as she explains her experience of speaking in tongues by the Holy Spirit ushering into the genesis of the Pentecostal movement in 1900, in Topeka Kansas. Agnes explains: . . . It was late at night. 'I wonder what would happen,' he (Charles Parham) said, 'if tomorrow we were all to pray together to receive the baptism in the same way it is described in the bible: with speaking in tongues?' The next morning, everyone, in Stone's Folly joined in prayer. They prayed through out the night ino the morning and into the afternoon. The atmosphere around the masion was charged with expectancy but the sun went down and still nothing unusual had occurred. Then at about seven o'clock that night . . . a young student named Agnes N. Ozman remembered something. Wasn't it true that many of the baptisms described in Acts were accompanied by an action, as well as prayer: didn't the person offering the prayer often put his hands on the one who wished to receive the baptism? . . . Miss Ozman went to find Charles Parham. She told him about her new thought. Would you pray for me in this way?" She asked. Parham hesitated just long enough to utter a short prayer about the rightness of what they were doing. Then gently he placed his two hands on Miss Ozman's head. Immediately, quietly, there came from her lips a flow of syllables which neither of them could understand (Sherill, 1964, 37-38).[84]

Later it was recorded that these syllables were Chinese (May, 1956)[85]. Other researchers record how a lady in her mid-30s became a glossolalic when she decided to let God pray through her as giving thanks for her husband's deliverance from surgery. Earlier her brother told her how he became a glossolalic at church service when he was blessed by the Holy Spirit. Many attested that they understood the French the young lady was speaking but the lady herself knew nothing about French (Malony, Zwaanstra, & Ramsay, 1972)[86].

---

[84] H. Newton Malony and A. Adams Lovekin, Glossolalia: Behavioral Science Perspectives on Speaking in Tongues. Oxford: Oxford University Press, 1985.

[85] Ibid.,

[86] Ibid.,

Boisen gives an account of an uneducated colored woman who addressed a meeting and under the power of the Holy Ghost she spoke in an unknown tongue, one that the intelligent observer could perceive was classic. When she stopped, she said, 'you know it wasn't me. I can't speak my own language right, much less a foreign one, that was the Holy Ghost.' Another sister rose and said she was not an interpreter but spoke the Spanish language. She attested to the fact that the lady was speaking Spanish, and the last phrase of the lady's speech was "glory to the precious name of Jesus" (Mills, 7-8).[87] Some researchers like Virginia Hine believe that glossolalia is a learned behavior that indicates loyalty to a religious group (Hine, 1969)[88]. Hutch believs that it is the means through which a person tries to seek "personality reorganization" (Hutch, 1980).[89] According to Sunden, glossolalia is the sign of the presence of God. Its function is both a private and public ritual in which human existence is lifted above the mundane. He says it is like taking a role in the divine/human drama through which life is given a purpose and meaning (Sunden, 1974).[90] Others deemed glossolalia to be an unsual and extraordinary behavior. It is an atypical behavior for either the individual or society at large (Alland, 1961; Paveisky, Hart, & Malony, 1975).[91]

SUMMARY

Pauline Theology, argues that tongues "are the language of the unconscious which is capable of consciousness through interpretation. "Tongues" may be viewed as "the language of the unconscious" because it is unintelligible (unless it is "interpreted") not only to others but the speaker. In I Corinthians 14:11 "foreign language" is unintelligible to the listener but intelligible to the speaker. Some researchers like Virginia Hine believe that glossolalia is a learned behavior that indicates loyalty to a religious group (Hine, 1969). Hutch believs that it is the means through which a person tries to seek "personality reorganization" (Hutch, 1980). According to Sunden, glossolalia is the sign of the presence of God. Its function is both a private and public ritual in which human existence is lifted above the mundane. He says it is like taking a role in the divine/ human drama through which life is given a purpose and meaning (Sunden, 1974). Others deemed glossolalia to be an unsual

---

[87] Watson E. Mills, A Theological/ Exegetical Approach to Glossolalia. New York: University Press, 1985.

[88] Ibid., 1969.

[89] Ibid., 1980.

[90] Ibid., 1974.

[91] H. Newton Malony and A. Adams Lovekin, Glossolalia: Behavioral Science Perspectives on Speaking in Tongues. Oxford: Oxford University Press, 1985.

and extraordinary behavior. It is an atypical behavior for either the individual or society at large.

ASSESSMENT

1. What theological argument some scholars profer about Pauling Theology regarding tongues?

2. What is your perception of I corithians 14:11? Do you agree or disagree with the general knowledge posed by scholars? Explain.

3. Whose argument is substantive on glossolalia, Hine's, Hutch's, or Sundane's? Why?

4. Do you believe that glossolalia is an unusual and extraordinary behavior?

5. Why would glossolalia be atypical for the individual and society?

PERSPECTIVES

Western thinkers coined the word "dualism" to define human nature as being composed of two parts, either *mind* and *matter, soul* and *body*, or *spirit* and *flesh*. This thought can be traced back to 427-347 BC when Greek philosopher, Plato divided reality into two parts: *mind* and *matter*. Plato suggests that the *mind* is higher and finer than matter and belongs to the celestial realm. He says matter is lower, cruder, and corruptible, belonging to the terrestrial realm. Plato notes that human nature was dualistic. The body as associated with matter or nature and the mind as associated with the immaterial or ideal form. He proffers that there is a constant internal struggle in humans between the body and mind or soul. Following Plato's theory of dualism comes the Christian Theology of *conflict dualism* which projects that human being consists of a soul that seeks God and a physical body that is tempted by the material world. The view of earthly life was a continued struggle between flesh and spirit (Lavenda and Schultz, 222).[92] Some Platonians and and many Christians believe that although humans have material bodies, their true nature is spiritual, and there continues to be a battle between the desires of the flesh and that of the spirit (Idealism). Cleavage to the desires of the flesh or body, and not spiritual liberation is *materialism*. *Determinism* (one single force causes complex events) now serves as the laboratory for closely observing materialism and idealism. Idealists believe that

---

[92] Robert H Lavenda. and Emily A. Shultz, Anthropology: What Doest it Mean to Be Human? Oxford: Oxford University Press, 2008.

"human nature is determined by the casual force of mind or spirit; materialists argue that human nature is determined by the causl force of physical nature" (Lavenda and Schultz, 223).[93]

What is your reponse to the aforementioned schools of thought, as presented by Robert H. Lavenda & Emily A. Schultz, heretical, apologetic, or liberalistic? Could you scripturally support your position?

---

[93] Ibid

CHAPTER EIGHT

GREEK ETYMA

Adorn—Kosmeō (V) (κοσμέω) to put in order, metaphorically, of adorning a doctrine.

Bless—Eulogeō (εύλογέω) to speak well of, to praise, to celebrate with praises.

Divers—Diaphoros (Adjective) (διαΦος) divers; polupoikilos, manifold; polutropōs, in many ways.

Revelation—Apokalupsis (ἀποκάλυψις) an uncovering, the purpose of God in this age, an expression of the mind of God for the instruction of the church.

Translate—Methistēmi or Methistano (μεθίστημι) to change, remove,

Worship—Proskuneō (προσκυνέω) to make obeisance, do reverence to, an act of homage,

EXEGETES AND APOLOGETES

Faith makes the discords of the present the harmonies of the future (Robert Collyer: Things New and Old)

Faith is the antiseptic of the soul (Walt Whitman: Leaves of Grass, Preface)

Exegesis of Stowers on Romans 12:3-6

Based on his grace as the apostle to the gentiles, Paul begs his readers 'not to think higher thoughts than one ought to think but to think with *sōphrosyne*, each person [to reach self-understanding] as God has measured him or her a measure of faithfulness [pistis].' Paul then goes on to use the metaphor of members as parts of a body, each having contributions, and to gifts as varied abilities to help others. Members sharing in faithfulness recalls the expression *ho ek pisteōs*, the one whose origin, life, or basis springs from or shares in Christ's faithfulness and the language that describes gentiles finding their new life by participating in Christ's life (A Rereading of Romans, 318).[94]

Apology of Origen on Ephesians

One of Christendom's renowned apologists of the early centuries of the church Fathers, Origen, highlights a few points in the Pauling epistle to the saints at Ephesus. In reference to Ephesians 3:5-7, Origen discusses the church in terms of its interrelationship or co-partnership with God in his Kingdom plan from the eons of creation to the present. Origen says the same manifestation or operation of God in the church era was not a disconnect from His dealings with the Law and Prophets of old. Origen attests that the old revelation, which relates to the Law and Prophets still exists in God's current plan for the church or the new covenant. Origen speaks of a unity that exits between the Law, Prophets, and the church through the apostles as being similarly the revelation of God. The new covenant or new revelation did not negate the old but modifies it to restore and effectively formulate a better relationship for God and humanity. Origen stresses that the only privilege enjoyed by the apostles over Moses and the prophets was that of being privileged to see in their lifetime the fulfillment of the promise made in the old revelation through Christ.

---

[94] Stanley K Stowers, A Rereading of Romans: Justice, Jews, and Gentiles. New Have: Yale University Press, 1994. 130 Chapter 8

Apology of Jerome on Ephesians

Eusebius Hieronymus, commonly known as Jerome, born about 345 A.D. in Dalmatia, Greece, schooled in Rome where he studied advanced Latin grammar, Greek, and Latin Classics, is credited for his translation of the Old Testament into Latin, or the Latin Vulgate. Jerome and Origen both share the same thoughts of the existence of unity of the old revelation and the new. However, unlike Origen, Jerome went deeply in his apology to talk about the gift of tongues or speaking in tongues, which he refers to as "ecstasy." He refers to ecstasy as a "quasi" language. According to Jerome: Those who want the prophets not to have understood what they said, and to have spoken in ecstasy, as it were an attempt to confirm their doctrine by dragging in, along with the present testimony, this, too, which is found in many manuscripts to the Romans, 'Now to him who is able to strengthen you according to my gospel and the preaching of Jesus Christ, according to the revelation of the mystery was not kept secret from eternal times but now revealed through the prophetic Scriptures and the advent of our Lord Jesus Christ' etc. [(Romans 16:25-26; I Timothy 6:14; II Timothy 1:10) (The Commentaries of Origen and Jerome on St. Paul's Epistle to the Ephesians, 61)].

Exegesis of Margaret Macdonald on Ephesians 4:4-16

"The body" is clearly a reference to the universal church. There are connections between 4:4 and the content of 2:11-22. 2:18 also refers to "one Spirit" who plays a fundamental role in the process of believers gaining access to God. The Spirit is central to the calling of believers into community. The confession of unity in vv 4-6 sets the stage for the treatment of the diversity of gifts and ministry in "one body" that begins here and continues to the end of v. 16. Christ as the giver of the gift (s). Nevertheless, the gifts mentioned in this section relate to those mentioned in Romans 12:5-8 and I Corinthians 12:27-28. It is interesting to note that God's gift or grace (charis) is clearly associated with Paul's unique role as an apostle. "Grace" itself implies the notion of "gift" (dōrea, cf. Acts 2:38; 8:20; 10:45; 11:17). Grace has been given according to the measure or proportion deemed appropriate for each of us. "Apostles" and "prophets" are listed together twice in Ephesians where they are presented as central witness and charismatic teachers of the early Christian movement (2:20) and 3:5. The fundamental role of prophets is spelled out in I Corinthians 12:28) apart from this theme is nothing revealed about their significance. The term "evangelist" (evanggelistēs) and "pastor" have no counterpart in the undisputed letter of Paul. However, in Acts 21:8 Philip is described as an evangelist. Timothy is also admonished to do the work of an evangelist (II Timothy 4:1-4). It is not clear why the definite article is missing before "teachers," apparently grouping "pastors" and "teachers" together. However, the role of "pastor" may also be connected to teaching. Christ's gifts are for the "equipping" of the saints, maturing, and unifying the church (McDonald, 287-294).[95]

Exegesis of John R. W. Stott on Ephesians 4:1-16

Christian unity depends on the charity of our conduct. Christian unity arises from the unity of our God. The one body is the church, the body of Christ comprises both Jews and Gentiles. Its unity and cohesion is due to the one Holy Spirit who dwells and animates it. Christian unity is enriched by the diversity of our gifts. Christian unity demands the maturity of our growth. God's new society is to display charity, unity, diversity and growing maturity. These are characteristics of a life worthy of the calling to which God has called us, and which the Apostle begs us to lead (Stott, 172).[96]

Exegesis from the Anchor Bible on Ephesians 4:4

Hope signifies the substance of hope rather than just the psychic disposition of hopefulness. The unity of the church is not constituted by something underneath or inside the church or her several members. Rather, it is eschatological: the reason for the church's hope for unity, and for commitment to unity is "deposited in heaven" [(Colossians 1:5) The Anchor Bible, 429].[97]

Exegesis of Markus Barth on Ephesians 4:12-16

In the clause "to equip the saints for the work of service for building the Messiah's body" (4:12, three elements can be distinguished: (1) the equipment of the saints; (2) the servant work; (3) the construction of Christ's body. These three concepts may denote three distinct purposes or they may be a triple definition of the one purpose that determines the "gift" of the ministries mentioned in vss. 7, 8, & 11. According to 4:14 the church order described in 4:11-13 is opposed to threatening disorder. 4:13 speaks of a movement in which all saints participate. They are depicted as people moving on a road toward a certain goal. As yet the church lacks fulfillment. She is dependent on that to which she is to come. The Greek verb *katantaē* (come to meet), is understanding the casual connection between the person met and the perfect quality acquired at the moment of meeting. In essence 4:1-16 describes a humble and loving church which is responsible and eager to reach her goal. Such a church

---

[95] Margaret McDonald, Colossians and Ephesians. Collegeville: The Liturgical Press, 2000.
[96] John R. W. Stott, The Message of Ephesians: God's New Society. Downers Grove: Inter-varsity Press, 1979.
[97] William F. and James Arthur Walter, The Anchor Bible: I Corinthians: A New Testament Translation. Garden City: Doubleday & Company, Inc., 1976.

is hard-working and dependent on God to achieve her goal of working in unity for a common good (Barth, 478-497).[98]

Exegesis of John Calvin on Ephesians 4:4-16

Christians ought to be united. The union ought to be such that we shall form one body and one soul. We ought to be united not in part only, but in body and one soul. We are called to one inheritance and one life. We cannot obtain eternal life without living in mutual harmony in this world (Calvin's Commentary Vol. XXI, 269).[99] In verse 12 Paul is talking about the adaptation of things possessing symmetry and proportion just as in the human body, the members are united in a proper and regular manner. Verse 13 is where Paul reminds the saints that the use of the ministry is not temporal, like that of school for children (Galatians 3:24), but constant so long as we remain in the world. Verse 14 shows the church as being charged by God to have sound doctrine as a distinction from the doctrines of the world. In verse 15, God's truth has to have a firm hold of us, that all the contrivances and attacks of Satan shall not draw us from our course. Verse 16 explains that no increase is advantageous, which does not bear a just proportion to the whole body (Calvin's Commentary Vol. XXI, 281-288).[100]

SUMMARY

Origen discusses the church in terms of its interrelationship or co-partnership with God in his Kingdom plan from the eons of creation to the present. However, unlike Origen, Jerome went deeply in his apology to talk about the gift of tongues or speaking in tongues, which he refers to as "ecstasy." He refers to ecstasy as a "quasi" language. "The body" is clearly a reference to the universal church. There are connections between 4:4 and the content of 2:11-22. 2:18 also refers to "one Spirit" who plays a fundamental role in the process of believers gaining access to God. The Spirit is central to the calling of believers into community. It is interesting to note that God's gift or grace (charis) is clearly associated with Paul's unique role as an apostle. "Grace" itself implies the notion of "gift" (dōrea, cf. Acts 2:38; 8:20; 10:45; 11:17). Grace has been given according to the measure or proportion deemed appropriate for each of us. Christian unity depends on the charity of our conduct. Christian unity arises from the unity of our God. The one body is the church, the body of Christ comprising both Jews and Gentiles. Its unity and cohesion is due to the one Holy Spirit who dwells and

---

[98] Markus Barth, The Anchor Bible, Ephesians. New York: Doubleday, 1960.
[99] John Calvin, Commentaries on The Epistles of Paul to the Galatians and Ephesians. Grand Rapids: Baker Book House, 1981.
[100] John Calvin, Commentaries on The Epistles of Paul to the Galatians and Ephesians. Grand Rapids: Baker Book House, 1981.

animates it. Christian unity is enriched by the diversity of our gifts. Christian unity demands the maturity of our growth. To equip the saints for the work of service for building the Messiah's body" (4:12, three elements can be distinguished: (1) the equipment of the saints; (2) the servant work; (3) the construction of Christ's body.

ASSESSMENT

1. Jerome's reference to tongues suggests that it is semblance of?

2. By what means believers gain access to God?

3. Explain "Christian unity depends on the charity of our conduct."

4. Explain "Christian unity is enriched by the diversity of our gifts."

5. What three elements have to be distinguished when discussing equipping the saints for service or building the body of Christ?

PERSPECTIVES

Philosopher and Theologian, Desiderius Erasmus, views religion as worship from the heart, not from offices and intermediaries. Erasmus say that true religion is simplistic and direct, not convoluted with 'unnecessary sophistication and dogmatic doctrine... religion is a confidence in huma reason to know and worship God' (Stokes, 61).[101] A philosopher and theologian, Nicolas Malebranche expresses that whenever we think we are doing something, it is God who is doing it for us, not ourselves (paraphrased). Malebranche says, 'individual minds are merely limitations of the one universal mind that is God' (Stokes, 77).[102] Benedict de Spinoza, a Jewish thinker, who was excommunicated from his community because of his philosophy, says, 'there is only one substance, and that substace we can conceive of as either Nature or God... Nature or God, is wholly self-contained, self-causing, and self-sufficient. Everything in the universe is part of God, and everything that happens is a necessary part or expression of the divine nature' (Stokes, 79).[103]

What is your reponse to the aforementioned schools of thought, as presented by Philip Stokes, heretical, apologetic, or liberalistic? Could you scripturally support your position?

---

[101] Philip Stokes, Philosophy: 100 Essential Thinkers. New York: Enchanted Lion Books, 2003.
[102] Ibid., 77.
[103] Ibid., 79.

CHAPTER NINE

GREEK ETYMA

Apostle—Apostolos (ἀπόστολος) One sent forth

Call—Kaleō (V) (καλέω) to call anyone, to summon, particularly of a divine call to partake of God's blessings of redemption; Proskaleō (προσκλέω) The divine call in entrusting men with the preaching of the gospel

Christ—Christos (χριστός) anointed

Gospel—Euangelion (εὐαγγέλιον) Good tidings of the kingdom of God and of salvation through Christ; Euangelizō (εὐαγγελίζω) to declare, to proclaim, to preach,

Minister—Diakonos (διάκονος), minster of the sanctuary; Hierourgeō (ἱερουργέω) to minister in priestly service; Parechō (παρέχω) to furnish, provide

Serve—Diakoneō (δικονέω) to minister

THE FOUR-FOLD MINISTRY

"And he gave some, apostles; and some prophets; and some, evangelists; and some, pastors and teachers; for the perfecting of the saints, for the work of the ministry, for the edifying of the body of Christ" Ephesians 4:11,12.

In the original Greek pastors and teachers are listed to be categorized as one, due to the fact that both offices are interdependent and co-related. Pastors are required to be "APT TO TEACH" as stated in II Timothy 2:24. In 20 different translations of the New Testament, these two positions are always combined. This therefore means that upon Christ's ascension to Heaven, His gift to the church was a four-fold ministry for the leadership of the church: (1) Apostles (2) Prophets (3) Evangelists (4) Pastors/ Teachers.

While we are not all pastors, evangelists, teachers or missionaries, we all are ministers unto the Lord: It is likely that we are also leaders by the way we live, how we speak, or the impact we have in leading people to God, or away from Him. Paul says the reason for the varied faceted ministry to the church is: "for the perfecting of the saints, for the work of the ministry, for the edifying of the body of Christ:" From the days of the tabernacle in the wilderness until the conclusion of the Bible: God refers to His leaders in a four-fold manner. Leadership of Israel in the wilderness was quadroplex in nature. The leadership consisted of Moses, Aaron, the Levites, and Elders. The encampment of the tribes as describes in Numbers chapter two was governed by four main tribes who pitched their banners to the compass points around the tabernacle: Judah to the East, Reuben to the South, Ephraim to the West, and Dan to the North. Their marching was in the same order of fours. Some theologians have suggested that these four tribe banners carried the drawn faces of the four-faced Cherubim of Ezekiel.

Ezekiel was a captive by the River Chebar and he saw visions of God: The first vision he saw was four living creatures that looked much like a man. They seemed to have four sides and had wings on all four sides, which were angels. "As for the likeness of their faces, they four had the face of a man, and the face of a lion, on the right side: and they had the face of an ox on the left side: they four also had the face of an eagle". These creatures are described as possessing four faces in four separate directions, and having a set of wings for each direction. In Ezekiel, chapter 10: He describes these living creatures again: This time calling them Cherubim (Angels). In the Bible there are seven ranks of angels listed: *Guardian Angels*: over little ones, *Ministering Angels*: concerned with the heirs of salvation, *Elected Angels*: responsibilities over the churches, *mighty Angels*: who are heaven's warriors, *Arch Angels*: concerned for the church in general, *Cherubim*: protectors of God's Holiness, and *Serephims*: who are concerned with man's sinfulness and God's redemption. The order here is arbitrary.

Ezekiel described the Cherubim in 10:14,22: Cherub, man, lion, eagle, "and every one had four faces: the first face was the face of a *cherub*, and the second face was the face of a *man*, the third face of a lion, and the fourth face of an eagle." "And the likeness of their faces was the same faces which I saw by the River of Chebar, their appearances and themselves; they went every one straight forward." He describes that these are the ones He saw before: **1.** Although he substitutes the word cherub for ox. **2.** Two visions of the same creatures: the first vision defines their number as four. And both visions describing their appearance as quadroplex with four separate faces: Man, lion, ox, and eagle. John the revelator was in exile too and he also was caught up in the heavens in a vision and he saw these same creatures:

Revelation 4:6-7 "And before the throne there was a sea of glass like unto crystal: And in the midst of the throne, and round about the throne, were four beasts full of eyes before and behind. And the first beast was like a lion, and the second beast like a calf, and the third beast had a face as a man, and the fourth beast was like a flying eagle." 2. John saw them in a stationary position. He described only the features that faced him: standing still. 3. He saw the fourfold nature of these high level angelic creatures who are certainly *God's leaders* in the heavens. So three times we are informed that at the high levels in the heavens God's leaders are quadruple in nature: 1. That is, they have four faces; 2. Four distinct natures by which they serve God. There are at least two *New Testament* examples of this principle: 1. The first is in the Gospels: Which says that the Spirit inspired the writings of four, not three or six gospels must have some significance: *Matthew*: was written to the Jews to present Jesus as their Messiah King, which is a fitting expressing of Christ's *Lion* like nature. For the lion as being called the king of the beasts. 2. Mark: shows Jesus as the *Ox* the servant of Jehovah: The key word is *straight way* signifying the constancy of Christ's labor. Jesus is depicted as a worker and a servant. 3. Luke: Reveals Jesus as the *Son of man*: It is the gospel of the *Humanity* of the Lord; where great attention is given to His manhood and the fact that He became . . . "a man of sarrows, and acquainted with grief." His ministry, in Luke's eyes was the ministry of a *Man*. 4 It is not until we get the Gospel of *John* that the divinity of Jesus is exalted: He is depicted as *the word robed in flesh*; the eagle who soars high into the heavens, untouched by the world beneath Him. Each Gospel writer saw a different face of Jesus Christ, just as John on Patmos saw four separate faces on the living creatures and as Ezekiel saw quadruple faces on the Cherubim. The second New Testament example of the fourfold ministry expected of God's leaders is found in the book of Ephesians' list of gifted men Christ generously gives to the church: Ephesians 4:11, 12 "And he gave some, apostles; and some, prophets; and some, evangelists; and some, pastors and teachers; for the perfecting of the saints, for the work of ministry, for the edifying of the body of Christ:" This list is popularly called: *the five-fold ministry*. In the original Greek however we must point out that the last two on the list are combined: Pastor and teacher: Since all pastors are required to be *apt to teach* as stated in II Timothy 2:24. In 20 different translations of the New Testament the final two positions are always combined. This means, then. That upon

His ascension into Heaven Christ's gift to the church was a four-fold ministry for the leadership of the church: Apostles, Prophets, Evangelists, and Pastors/ Teachers.

And these would correspond with the four-faced leaders in the Heavens: The *Apostles* may very well picture the *Lion*; daring to go out into the wild, new territory and roar the voice of God. The *Prophet*: may picture the *Eagle*, since the prophets always tend to be a bit unearthly soaring up above reality and seeing what others do not see. The *Evangelist*: is probably the old *ox* plowing the fields, turning the water wheels for irrigation, and treading out the grain as part of the threshing in harvest time. The Pastor/ Teacher: is best exemplified by the *man*. For he is deeply involved with people and his entire life is involved where the rubber meets the road. As a man, he ministers to men. Feels with them, understands their problems, and positions, and can relate to them intimately. So whether we are looking at: Living creatures of *Ezekiel chapter one*, the cherubim of Ezekiel *chapter ten*, the living creatures of *Revelation chapter four*, the standards of *Israel*, the *characterizations* of Jesus, or the *gifted persons* Christ gave to His church, they are all four-faced, and four-fold ministries: They are all seen as fulfilling multiple roles, possessing multiple character traits, and manifesting multiple dispositions. These roles are more a *contrast* one to the other than they are *similar*; For where would you find a greater contrast than: A man and a lion? Or an ox and an eagle? What have they in common? How could they possibly function harmoniously? Whatever conflict it may pose to us, we must admit it is God who chooses this unusual combination for His servants, and however awkward their appearance, their multiple attitude make them extremely valuable to the service of God.

The nature of God's leaders
Accepting God's leader as an Eagle

The eagle most graphically portrays the part of the leader that contacts God: For when we think of the eagle we have a mental image of the bird that flies the highest so effortlessly. In ancient times the symbols of eagles were used to represent courage, empires, and military prowess. The bald eagle is the official emblem or symbol of the United States. The eagle has a magnificent majesty in flight or flying. Its flight is majestic because it flies effortlessly, a few flaps of its wings can find an updraft where it relaxes and locks its wings, and then circles the columns of air. God yearns to teach His leaders to function with the nature of an *eagle*: to learn how to ascend into the rarefied atmosphere of heaven in a relaxed, effortless manner. In describing the clothing to be worn by the priest who ministered in the Holy courts; God declared: "They shall not gird themselves with anything that cause sweat" Ezekiel 44:18. Worshipping God is to be a *no sweat* operation for God's leaders. When it comes time to for personal worship, or for leading in worship, all of these activities are responsibilities of leadership. Leaders should teach their people how to *relax*. There should be enough flapping of the wings to find the upward *flow of the Holy Spirit* outstretched and locked in position: Soaring *higher and higher* into the presence of God, not by our *effort* but by God's provision that we can come into His presence. Isaiah 40:31 "But they that wait upon the Lord shall renew their strength: they shall mount up with wings as eagles: they shall run, and not be weary: and they shall walk, and not faint."

Deteronomy 32:9-12

"For the Lord's portion is His people: Jacob is the lot of His inheritance. He found Him in a desert land, and in the waste howling wilderness: he led him about, he instructed him, He kept him as the apple of His eye. As an eagle stirreth up abroad her wings, taketh them, beareth them on her wings: so the Lord alone did lead him, and there was no strange God with him."

What do you do when the bottom falls out?

God teaches us how to *fly spiritually*. It is God's provision that we move into the upward flow of His Spirit and ascend into His spiritual realms without great effort or activity. We do not come with extreme wing activity like a *hummingbird*, but with the immobile wings of the great Eagle. Some leaders put people through endless activities of *spiritual calisthenics*, in bringing them into the presence of God. One gets the feeling that they are more like a *sparrow* than an *eagle* in nature. They always seem to be fussing in the dirt with a lot of activity rather than flying on an updraft in a relaxed state of enjoyment. The concepts and conduct of these leaders who have never developed an eagle nature are very *earthbound*. Activities in a worship service, such as *everybody stand up!*, *everybody clap your hands!*, and everybody say hallelujah! Are all examples of calisthenics earthbound activities, like forcing people to worship God. In bird language it would be interpreted: Everybody flap your wings, everybody scratch in the dirt, or everybody run a little bit. All this energy is expanded by *fussing in the dirt* rather than *soaring in the spirit*. They seem never to get off the ground and they merely try the same thing more energetically the next time. Perhaps someone needs to tell them that they will never get a sparrow up to 10,000 feet no matter how hard they try. Sparrows are *low-flying* birds that are more interested in insects on the ground than an updraft into the Heavens as an eagle. Other leaders seem to be more of a *pigeon* nature than an *eagle* nature. Pigeons like to stand in groups on the ridge of a roof *preening* their feathers while gently cooing and sidestepping almost as if they were a dancing chorus line. These pigeons will continue their gentle cooing, apparently entranced by the sound of *their own voices*. But just let someone fire a gun, you will see an amazing flurry of feathers. Those pigeons will take to skillful flight leading us to believe that they are *actually going some place*. Only to make a wide circle and return to the same spot preening and cooing. They were stirred to a great *progress* but made no *progress*. They are beautiful birds but never go *anywhere*. God has not given His leaders the face of a sparrow or pigeon's, He had given them the faith and heart of the eagle. They cannot be content with fussing in earthbound activities, they will not satisfy themselves with mere outward show or equality in their peer group, the eagle's heart must *soar heavenward*. The eagle wants to get away from the flock in order to approach God on a one to one basis. The leader must view things from the top. When God calls for His eagle, when it is time to come into His presence, when it is worship time, let us learn to *relax* and *enjoy the Lord*. All the fervent activity while trying to come into God's presence shows great *immaturity*. Leaders must first learn to soar into God's presence as individuals. Until we know how to minister unto God, we cannot know how to minister God unto people. God would like to be ministered to His people, and only one who has been in His presence can minister God unto His people. Until God's leaders learn to soar like an eagle, they will never successfully teach another to rise on the currents of God's Spirit into the presence of God Himself. Flight cannot be taught from the ground. Both the instructor and student must fly together. If God's leader fussed in the dirt like a sparrow, so will his followers. If a leader made a fancy demonstration of outward correctness and proper words like a pigeon so will his followers. But if the leader can soar into God's presence His followers will develop a yearning for flight and soon will join him in his ascent into the presence of God. The image of a leader is passed on to his or her people.

Accepting God's Leader as an Ox

Mounting up on the wings of an eagle is exhilarating and relaxing but there is no *opportunity* to *minister* to people up there. Other soaring eagles seldom need *ministry*. God's apprehended leaders have not only the face of an eagle, they also have the face of an ox. The ox speaks of *work* not food or for the table. The ox was the tractor in Bible days and it is still used in the third world countries as tractors. II Corinthians 6:1 "we then, as workers together with Him, beseech you also that ye receive not the grace of God in vain." I Corinthians 3:9 "For we are laborers together with God: Ye are God's husbandry, ye are God's building." Leadership is *work*. We have not been called to hide but to be workers. The rule is that God's servants have an ox nature as a *balance* to their eagle nature. If while enjoying the presence of God as eagles and God states a need for ox service, we can fold our wings, extend our legs, and begin functioning as oxen. You can hitch such a leader to God's tools and that leader will bow his or her head and push strength against the yoke. Now the leadership is being *yoked* together with *Jesus* to start ministry on *earth*.

The New Testament speaks of three separate levels of ministry that have been entrusted to God's leaders: All of them are profitable and necessary, but we mature from one level to the next: he who as reached the highest level of service can always reach back to a lower level of ministry. But those at the first level must mature into the second level before they are capable of serving there. It is likely that all of God's leaders begin by learning to be *workers for God*. This is usually a response to a *precept*. We have seen a command in the word, and we set our wills to do as we have been,

Teaching and Understanding Pneumatology & Spiritual Gifts 109

instruct to do. This type of service is begun in obedience and usually is oriented to the needs of people. Example: "Go ye into all the world" (Mark 16:15-18), we then rise to obedience. This will raise the necessary funds, and it will motivate people to go. This will certainly get the job done and involve many individuals in service for God. But at best it is "*outer-court ministry*. It is a beginning place to learn to work, and it is genuine *service*.

There is a second level of service wherein we learn to minister *with God*. As Paul spoke of us in both of his letters to the church in Corinth, there is quite a difference in working for and with a person. One may be hired for a job, receive instructions, on what is to be done, and set about to fulfill by assignment, or can join the boss on the job and work along side of him. In the latter situation one gets to know *on the job training* that responsibility is primary his or hers. One will never be in doubt as to what to do, how to do it, and how long one should be involved in doing it. We may work for or with God. Jesus spoke to the weary and overworked of His day; Mathew 28:30 "Come unto me, all ye that labor and are heavy laden, and I will give you rest. Take my yoke upon you, and learn of me: for I am weak and lowly in heart; and ye shall find rest unto your soul, for my yoke is easy, and my burden islight." The message is as real today as it was then. God does not promise to let us out of work, but He offers to teach us how to work with Him, and or for Him. Christ's method of rest is not *inactivity* but *directed activity*. It is impossible to be in the same yoke with Christ without learning something about being an *ox*. If so, our ministry will not merely be a response to a precept or command, it will be a response to a *partner*.

The first lesson to learn is that the yoke is too big for us. It is His yoke, and He is in it too. We will find ourselves standing on tiptoes just to hold up our end of this yoke. We can never minister with God without standing on faith's tiptoes, because even when God stoops to be yoked with us He is still beyond every level of faith we have ever entered into. Example: A large ox with a smaller ox; "take my yoke upon you, and learn of me" (Matthew 11:28-30). The second lesson quickly learned is once we get yoked with Jesus, we get to move when He moves or the plow may come right up our backbone. What a victory it is when God's leaders learn to move when He chooses to move. Israel had to learn to move when the cloud moved, or they would have lost the cloud, forfeited their manna, water, and visitation privileges of God. It is better to move when He is moving for then everything around Him moves also. If we remained stationary when He is moving, we not only miss out on the benefits of the move, we endanger our very lives and the lives of others as well. What God is moving may be for our benefit. It may destroy us if we resisted or assist us if we moved along with God or at His command. The third lesson that a leader has to learn when being yoked together with Christ is that when Christ turns, the leader might as well turn with Christ or else that leader may have a bruised or even broken neck. Once we are yoked together with Christ, we lose the option of when we will move or when we will serve. The yoke offers only one option and that is to be a partner with God. The fourth lesson that a leader will learn when being yoked with Jesus is that when the lord eats and drinks, the leader better eat and drink. This will probably be the only time the yoke will be low enough for the leader to reach the grass or the water. This is not an easy lesson to learn, for it seems that He always feeds at the wrong time.

How often the Spirit makes the word come alive just as we are being beckoned into some other activity, or it is when we have already established a time for visitation or a friend's gathering, that the spirit beckons us to a season of earnest prayer. If we say, "I will later," we will discover that when we want to eat and drink, our partner has His head high and we cannot reach either the food or the water. Perhaps the greatest lesson is learning to keep *pace with Him*. We dare not get ahead of Him, and it is dangerous to be behind Him. In order for the yoking to work properly we must match Him step for step. This ministry with God is "Holy-place ministry," the place where the Old Testament priests fellowshipped with God. At the lamp stand, the table of showbread, and the golden altar. The third level of ministry available to the leader who has developed the Spirit of an ox is ministry *unto God*. If we ministered for God it will be in response to a precept. If we ministered with God it will be in response to a partner. But if we minister unto God we will develop a response to a *person*. The first level ministry will be outer-court ministry. The second level will be inner-court ministry, while the third level of ministry is strictly the servant and his God. Everything is done as an act of *worship*. All is done out of *love* motivation, and all will be done to meet His needs rather than the needs of the leader or the people led. It is the picture shared repeatedly throughout scripture of God's leaders being "Kings and Priests unto God" This level is in the "Holies of Holies."

God's Leader as a Lion

God's leader is sometimes a soaring eagle, at other times a sweating ox, and on some occasions a stalking lion. What does the eagle and lion have in common? How can we reconcile one person having both the docile dominated, domesticated nature of an ox to that of the fierce free, feline nature of the lion? The beauty of God's leaders is that God does not seek to blend these natures. He makes the leader *quadroplex* in nature. Each nature is separate and distinct. At times the leader God chooses to use has the unmistakable face of a *lion* which denotes that of a king, *authority, strength,* and *power*. There are times when God needs a man through whom He can *roar*. "The Lord roar from zion" (Amos 1:2). Isaiah, Jeremiah, Hosea, and Joel all speak of the Lord *roaring*. It is only when we loose sight of the holiness and sovereignty of God that we insist upon a perpetual "...still small voice." There are just some occasions when the gentle, loving voice of a shepherd is not sufficient to achieve the desired ends, and God must roar like a lion. When God roars, it terrorizes His enemies. Hosea 11:10 "They shall walk after the Lord; He shall roar like a lion; when He shall roar, then the children shall tremble from the west." When God roars He shakes the earth. Joel 3:8 "The Lord also shall roar out of zion, and utter His voice from Jerusalem; and the heavens and the earth shall shake but the Lord will be the hope of His people, and the strength of the children of Israel. When God roars, it wrecks havoc even of God's people. Amos 1:2 "And he said, the Lord will roar from zion; and utter His voice from Jerusalem; and the habitations of the shepherds shall mourn, and the top of Carmel shall wither."

Amazingly God chooses to roar through His leader. It is no secret that the screech of an eagle does not scare anyone nor does the lowing of oxen terrorizes a community. But when the lion roars, everything is immediately *terrorized*. There are times God needs His leaders to *roar like a lion*. Many denominational congregations of God's potential body are weak, sickly, and troubled because of a lack of strong leadership. The dilution of *humanism*, pollution of *sin*, profusion of *faith teaching*, confusion of *democracy in church government*, the conception of equality create such pandemonium that warrant only the great *roar* of the *lion* to restore proper order to few people. Sometimes an eagle, ox, or man will never get the attention or arrest the activity of these people. They need a lion-person who hears God's voice and has enough courage to stand and say: *thus saith the Lord*. But for any leader to get by this kind of roaring he must better never *fake* it. God will always back up anything that He says; but He is not responsible for our *speech*. Some leaders have treated the voice of God with such lightness that when they really do have a direct word from God no one would pay attention. Leaders must discern between a *quickening* from the Lord and a *quickening direct communication* from Him lest they claim that their words are literal words from Him. When it is direct communication from God, it is expressed with that authoritative roar of a lion. God does not approach His people like a lion very often, but when He does we should take *heed*. *Hosea 5:14* "For I will be unto Ephraim as a lion, and as a young lion to the house of Judah: I, even I, will tear and go away; I will take away, and none shall rescue him. The word of God put into the mouths of His servants not only becomes the roar of the lion, it also tears and rends like the powerful paws of the lion.

Those who will not heed the roar will need *renewing*. Hosea 6:1-2 "Come, and let us return unto he Lord: For He hath torn, and He will heal us; after two days will he revive us; in the third day he will raise us up, and we shall live in His sight." Those who will not hear must learn to heal for God's warnings are never idle *threats*. The lion speaks not only of threats; it speaks of strength, and how people in today's churches need that strength in their leaders. Every congregation needs a "king" if you will, someone who accept responsibility for the kingdom and manifests strength of character, purpose, and leadership. Such a leader is God's great gift to the church. Some leaders never exercise authority in their domains and, consequently, they allow almost anything to pass uncorrected. The people under them cannot help being *insecure* and unsure of themselves. All of us need someone to draw the line, *define the limits*, and describe what is right. Where nothing is judged, every man does that which is right in his own eyes, and *anarchy* soon reigns. There is strength when there is one lion who says, this is the way we are going, especially when that lion also has the faces of an eagle, ox, and man to *balance* him. Not suggesting dictatorship as the ultimate for leadership, but with the lack of definite direction in many churches, it is good to have a leader that is assertive and knows under the leadership of God's spirit where he is going. One of the titles of the Lord Jesus Christ in the New Testament is that He is *the lion of the tribe of Judah*. Knowing that Judah means praise, we can see that first this title suggests Christ strong leadership over *worshipers*. Would not then His appointed leaders also share in this lion-like authority in the midst of the saints?

God's Leader as a Man

If the contrast between the eagle and the ox seems startling, what is our reaction to the dissimilarity between the lion and the man? Yet God's leaders thought as: Apostles, Prophets, Evangelists, Pastors/ Teachers are infused with God with this four-fold nature and he than chooses which nature will serve in each situation. When the "three faces: are not functioning, they stand at attention waiting a call to action. Consistently the eagle, ox, and lion natures function only at the beckoning of God. Unless they are divinely energized they are impotent, and inactive, but the man nature is active at all times, since it is the foundation for all the other characteristics of leadership. Ezekiel reports that even the living creatures: the Cherubim has not only the face of a man but *has the likeness of a man*. At all times these highest level servants of God were more manlike than anything else. After the creation of man, God Himself walked in the garden with Adam, but Adam could not relate to God sufficiently enough to live above sin. Even God admitted: "it is not good that the man should be alone." Adam, like God needed someone to *love*.

Throughout the Old Testament almost every attempt God made to interact with man *failed*. The universal reaction of man to God's appearance was: fear, dread, and unbelief. Man could not handle direct or angelic revelation of God. God Himself had to become a man in order to reach humanity. Hebrews 1:1-2 "God, who at sundry times and in divers manners spake in time past unto us by his son, whom he hath appointed heir of all things, by whom also he made the world." Knowing that the separation between the human and the divine was too great for man to bridge, Christ emptied Himself of His divine prerogatives and became flesh, the man Christ Jesus. When God became man we heard Him, loved Him, were redeemed by Him, and related to Him. Man can associate comfortably with man, but he is very uncomfortable in an association with anything that is God-like or supernatural. In light of this fact, why then do we so earnestly endeavor to get rid of our *humanity* when we are called into the service of God? That is the most *valuable* part of us in our leadership of God's people. Jesus, the perfect leader, not only bore the quadroplex character, He actually had a dual *nature*. He was both God and man at all times, yet His man nature was so real that people desired to be *around Him*. Jesus never ceased being a "normal" man just because He was God. Jesus never forsook being the Lion of the tribe of Judah. (Matthew)He never ceased abandoned being God's ox working in the Father's field or Vine yard: (Mark) He never ceased being the eagle of divinity: (John). But the longest Gospel shows His *humanity*: (Mark). More is revealed about His humanity than

His divinity. We are able to relate to God through the face of God's flesh: *Jesus Christ*. It must become evident to God's leaders that at whatever point they get so caught up in their supernatural faces: Eagle, ox, and lion that they loose their natural face, *then people cannot relate to them*. We need to remind ourselves repeatedly that it is the will of God that we be people, that is what we were born as.

Nobody was born an *eagle*. God ordains a man, one of the *three main tools God uses*. It is nothing than a *cap-out* to hide behind the realization that our humanity is full of flaws and failures, but Jesus Christ came to *redeem* our humanity. He has rescued us from sin and has restored us to the position man held before Adam sinned. Paul tells us that Jesus was the *last Adam* and the *second Adam*. We need not to worry about our Adamic nature, it died with Christ. Christ began a whole new lineage. We are sons and daughters of God and as such we can *live, love, learn, be leaders with and for God*. As humans we have a great variety of roles to fill, and we must learn to adapt ourselves to these roles: some are very spiritual and others are quite natural. Sometimes the roles of our humanity intertwine with our leadership roles, making it difficult for us to differentiate between them. In the church we may be viewed as spiritual parents, in the home as natural parents. We function as the head of the church but also as the head of the home. We are lovers of God and lovers of our marriage partner. It is not surprising that of these four natures, God's leaders consistently have the most difficult time with the nature of a *man*. Somehow once God imparts the nature of an eagle, leaders try to be an *eagle* at all times, but as many leaders' spouses can attest, eagles are very difficult to sleep with, remember leader, your spouse did not marry a lion, ox, or an eagle. She married a man, It is the person we see in the mirror each morning when we shave or comb our hair that confuses us the most. We have but one mind and one set of emotions, and *Heaven, Earth,* and *Hell* all contribute impute to them. One reoccurring question that plaques the *man-face* side of our leadership characteristics is: "can this really be God or is it just me." The lion responds only to God, but the man responds to many *voices*. When God is not using His leader, he remains a man, and still a person. Man eats, sleeps, loves, etc. Yet many leaders find it very difficult to "be as other men." Some question whether a man of God can be a mere man at any time as a soldier on the alert.

Could not God's leaders live on an alert status? None who have entered into divine leadership would deny that all temptation comes to the man. The lion is never tempted to fly like the eagle, the eagle is never over tempted to plow, nor the ox is ever tempted to roar, but it is the man who undergoes constant temptation. When a leader is incapable of being a person, when he sets aside his humanity, he sets himself up for *self-destruction*. The enemy consistently destroys ministry in the area of the leader's *humanity*. Satan doesn't seem to have the ability to touch the flying eagle. The devil shuns getting too close to the ox that is yoked with Jesus. He does not have much capacity to come against the lion, who is Christ Jesus. The devil only roars like a lion but dare come near the Lion. Satan is a lying fake. When a leader is no longer soaring in the clouds, working in the yoke, or roaring in the jungle, that is the time *Satan* moves in for the *kill*. Many a good multi-faced leader has been destroyed by *sexuality, ruined marriages,* and *lust*. It is possible that God's leaders have been involved with eagle, ox, and lion ministries. They have abandoned and forgotten that *people, parents,* and *people roles* are also ministries. For instance the pastor's wife should not always have to take second place to "his ministry" nor should the children of leaders be always pushed to the background. Even outside the home some of God's leaders fail to let the human side of their nature show. "They keep their place." The basis of respect is that they need to see a man, as well as a man of God. We reach people only when we are *people*.

SUMMARY

Upon Christ's ascension to Heaven, His gift to the church was a four-fold ministry for the leadership of the church: (1) Apostles (2) Prophets (3) Evangelists (4) Pastors/ Teachers. Ezekiel was a captive by the River Chebar and he saw visions of God: The first vision he saw was four living creatures that looked much like a man. They seemed to have four sides and had wings on all four sides, which were angels. "As for the likeness of their faces, they four had the face of a man, and the face of a lion, on the right side: and they had the face of an ox on the left side: they four also had the face of an eagle". These creatures are described as possessing four faces in four separate directions, and having a set of wings for each direction. He saw the fourfold nature of these high level angelic creatures who are certainly *God's leaders* in the heavens. He saw the fourfold nature of these high level an God yearns to teach is leaders to function with the nature of an *eagle*: to learn how to ascend into the rarefied atmosphere of heaven in a relaxed, effortless manner. Angelic creatures who are certainly *God's leaders* in the heavens. God's apprehended leaders have not only the face of an eagle, they also have the face of an ox. The ox speaks of *work* not food or for the table. The ox was the tractor in Bible days and it is still used in the third world countries as tractors. At times the leader God chooses to use has the unmistakable face of a *lion* which denotes that of a king, *authority*, *strength*, and *power*. There are times when God needs a man through whom He can *roar*. God's leaders thought as: Apostles, Prophets, Evangelists, Pastors/ Teachers are infused with God with this four-fold nature and he than chooses which nature will serve in each situation. The Cherubim has not only the face of a man but *has the likeness of a man*.

ASSESSMENT

1. What is the four-fold ministry of the church?

2. Define the role of each of the four-fold ministry.

3. What was the vision Ezekiel saw at River Chebar?

4. How does the vision relate to the church?

PERSPECTIVES

German philosopher, Gottfried Wilhelm Von Leibniz, says, 'everything happens the way it does because it must, and it must because God has chosen to make actual the best of all possible worlds' (Stokes, 81).[104] Philosopher and Bishop of Cloyne, George Berkeley expresses that 'our perceptions are ideas produced for us by God. God perceives everything at all times, so the closed room still exists since it is perceived in the mind of God' (Stokes, 95).[105] Johann Christoph Schiller says 'fear only affects us as sensuous beings, and cannot hold sway over our will' (Stokes, 99).[106] Moritz Schlick argues that the soul survives after death, and deems God as being all-knowing and benevolent.

What is your reponse to the aforementioned schools of thought, as presented by Philip Stokes, heretical, apologetic, or liberalistic? Could you scripturally support your position?

---

[104] Philip Stokes, Philosophy: 100 Essential Thinkers. New York: Enchanted Lion Books, 2003.
[105] Ibid., 95.
[106] Ibid., 99.

CHAPTER TEN

GREEK ETYMA

Edification—Oikodomē (οἰκοδομή) the act of building, the promotion of spiritual growth,

Grow—Auxanō (αὐξάνω) to increase of the growth of that which lives naturally or spiritually; Ginomai (γίνομαι) of the development of apostolic work; Huperauxanō (ὑπεραυξάνω) to increase beyond measure.

Fellowship—Koinōnia (κοινωνία) sharing in common, communion; Metochē (μετοχή) partnership; koinōnos (κοινωνός) partaker or partner

Fulfil—Plēroō (πληόω) to preach fully, to complete the ministry of the gospel; Anaplēroō (ἀναπληρόω) of the status of a person in a church

Love—Agapaō (ἀγαπάω) and agapē God's love seen in the gift of his son, Christian love has God as for its primary object, love that seeks the welfare of all, without natural inclinations.

THE VALUE OF YOUR GIFT/ CALLING

A little faith will bring your soul to heaven, but a lot of faith will bring heaven to your soul (Dwight L. Moody)

KJV
Ephesians 3:7

7 Wherefore I was made a minister, according to the gift of the grace of God given unto me by the effectual working of his power.

NASB

... of which I was made a minister according to the gift of God's grace which was given to me according to the working of His power.

Here in the aforementioned verse of both the King James Version and New American Standard Bible, the context reflects the identical concept. Other than seeing the NASB beginning the verse with the proposition word "of," it still maintains the same idea. The apostle is addressing a company of Jews and Gentiles in the church of Ephesus. He is admonishing them of their role in the church, and having them understand that their calling or spiritual status in the church or community was not something they merited, rather it was bestowed upon them by the grace of God through Christ. In this discussion, the apostle puts himself in the picture to let the members know that he embraces his calling and appreciates it, so he wants them to do the same. Paul reveals that role of Christ in their lives as a mystery that had not been revealed by God to past generations but has now revealed it through a new covenant with Christ. Paul tells them to acknowledge that this is the power of God to embrace a people (Gentiles) who were not a part of the commonwealth of Israel before but are now a part. Also to the Jews, Paul says they should be grateful that even though, Christ was crucified and betrayed by his brethren, through grace, God still accepts them in His arms but this time it is through a covenant that embraces both Jews and Gentiles. This is the covenant that sees and treats everyone the same. Before the eyes of Christ, both Jews and Gentiles are the same creatures in the sight of God. *According to the gift of God's grace . . . by the working of his power.* "Paul's ministry in the gospel was not self-chosen, but was the gift of God's grace:

its efficacy was dependent not on his own natural capacities, but on the working of God's power (TIB, 668-69).[107]

You are the creation of God, shaped in His image. You are the representation of God, the express image of His person. God gives you dominion to rule over His creation. He endows you with wisdom, knowledge, and understanding. He empowers you to use these gifts wisely. You are a child of God by birth in the Lord Jesus Christ; a new creation designed by God for a divine purpose. All things work together for good to them that love God, and for those who are called according to His purpose.

Those He foreknew, He predestinated, and those He predestinated, He also called, and those He called, He justified (Romans 8:28-30). The purpose of Christ's coming into the world was to liberate humanity from bondage. Your role as a Christian is to carryout the mission of Christ which is to reach out to humanity. According to Harper Collins Lexicon, the word *"call" is a common word that acquires theological significance when God or Christ is the one who calls, it implies divine election or commission. Sometimes individuals are called to special vocations in God's plan of salvation: God called Moses (Exodus 3:4), the judges (Judges 3:9), the prophets (Jeremiah 1:5), and Jesus (Matthew 2:15), and Jesus called the disciples (Matthew 4:21) and the Apostles (Romans 1:1;8:28 - 30; II Timothy 1:9; II Peter 1:10; I Corinthians 1:26).*

When the call is a general summons to repentance and salvation, every Israelite or Christian is viewed as its recipient and hence Israel and the church are collectively designated God's "called" or "elect" (Isaiah 41:9; Hebrews 3:1). To accomplish this mission, the Lord has blessed the church with diverse kinds of gifts so that individuals can be used for this purpose (Ephesians 4:11-12). Nevertheless, although the gifts are free to everyone, not everyone makes himself or herself available for them. Only a few have what it takes to accomplish this mission and these are the chosen ones. It is one thing to be born again and another to know that you are gifted. It is your gift that makes you special and lifts you above others. You have a unique way of releasing your passion and connecting to others. While the majority is doing the ordinary, you find yourself doing the extraordinary. If you realize that there is something special about you then it is time for you to *pray about it, work on your confidence, prepare yourself,* and *take on the task.* God wants you to acknowledge Him and be grateful for the gift He has given you. You have to thank Him for it and ask Him to show you how to use it effectively. In all your ways you should acknowledge Him and He will direct your path (Proverbs 3:6). Lack of confidence brings about weariness and fear. The only way you can build on your confidence is when you put your trust in the Lord and be joyful about your gift. You should never try to rationalize the calling of God. Trust the Lord with all

---

[107] George Asthur Buttrick, Bowie, Walter Russell, Paul Scherer, John Knox, Samuel Terrien, The Interpreter's Bible: The Holy Scriptures in the king James and Revised Standard Versions With General Articles and Introduction, Exegesis, Exposition for each Book of the Bible. Nashville: Abingdon Press, 1983.

your heart and lean not unto your own understanding (Proverbs 3:5). Make yourself a vessel ready to be used by the master. Prepare yourself by undergoing training in that area or affiliating with an experienced person who has the same gift. You have to study to show yourself approved unto God (II Timothy 2:15). When you know that you are ready to take on the task, do not hesitate because the Lord has already commissioned you to do so. You should therefore go and teach all nations... teaching them to observe all things whatsoever the Lord commands you,

He promises not to forsake you but to be with you always even to the end of the world (Matthew 28:19-20). You should be able to know that you are called by God not appointed by man.

The call of God has no mandatory obligations attached to it but the appointment of man does. God's calling is not based on a merit system, favoritism, nepotism, social status, or fame. I guess if it were so, only the rich and famous would be called and Heaven would be pre-owned by Hollywood, but thank God it is not so. The call of God is extended to all. When the Lord calls you, He will allow your will to align with His will. It comes with complete liberty. But man's appointing is contractual and has mandatory obligations attached to it. You do not have any freedom; you work under pressure and within restricted guidelines. If you can feel the hand of the Lord upon you as you perform, then that should let you know that you are special in the sight of the Lord. The Lord called David the "apple of His eye" because David was special in His sight. David also knew that He was special in the Lord's sight. He had prayed to the Lord about his calling, and knew that someday it will come to fruition. He built up his confidence and became strong in the Lord. David was not only a shepherd-boy, he was a great hunter and musician but in spite of all that he was very humble. He stands out in history as the Jewish boy who challenged the great Philistine giant, Goliath. While King Saul and the rest of the army stood afraid of Goliath, David walked before all Israel with a sling gun and told Goliath that he has come in the name of the Lord to destroy him. Saul and his men tried to talk David into wearing a protective outfit to fight Goliath but David refused. David did not need the endorsement of Saul and the army. He already had God's endorsement. In fact, those armors were too heavy for David. They would have limited his ability to exercise his gift freely. Had he used their armor, probably God would not have given him the victory because that would have meant that he depended on the armor of Saul. Once again, if you try to get man's approval and support before you exercise your gift, you will wait for a long time. You might probably end up losing the gift because when God gives you His gift, He expects you to exercise it. If you don't, He will pass it on to someone else. Do not wait for anyone to tell you when to use your gift. It is very easy for others to envy you when they realize that you are talented. They may act like they are mentoring you but what they are doing is sabotaging you from exercising your gift. Saul was giving David a battlefield advice but after David slain Goliath, he got jealous and envious and sought to kill David. Once again, David knew that Saul was against him, yet he had great respect for him as a king.

David waited for the appointed time of the Lord. David could have killed Saul if he wanted to but did not because his trust was in the Lord. When the appointed time came, David assumed the leadership of being Israel's king. The only way to distinguish a gifted person from a non-gifted one is to see which one performs with the anointing. The persona, charisma, heart and soul of that person can be vividly seen in what he or she does.

Another Old Testament example of having the spirit of the Lord being upon someone to carryout a specific task is found in the book of Judges. Judges 3:10 shows how the Children of Israel forgot God and intermarried with the heathens, worship the gods of the heathens, and did abominable things in the sight of God. They committed immoral and despicable acts before God. Therefore, God made them to become enslaved into the hands of heathen kings for eight years until the Children of Israel came to their senses. After the Children of Israel realized their abominable encounters, they decided to cry unto the Lord for help. The Lord had to raise up a deliverer to let the Children of Israel know what their abominations were, and they were told to repent in order to regain fellowship with God. God will always raise up someone in a leadership role to inform and educate His people when there is a need. God raised up Othniel, Caleb's younger brother to impart divine knowledge to the Children of Israel. If you can remember the story of Moses how when he sent men over to view the land of Canaan to spy, Caleb and Joshua were the two men who came back with encouraging news for Moses. The other men said there were giants in the land and they did not think that the land could be habitable for the Children of Israel. A family that devotes itself to the things of God can possibly be the habitat of spiritually bred and nurtured people of God, a setting where the presence of the Lord will always be. When a need arises where the Lord needs a leader to implement a task, He will look into that home to select a God-fearing person to carryout His mission. Do you want to be a vessel ready to be used by God and also want to pass your anointing on to another member of your family who could be found worthy also in the sight of God to be chosen by God? The third chapter of Judges narrates in length the story of Othniel and His gift of leadership. Verse ten shows how the "spirit of the Lord" came upon Othniel and he judged Israel and took them to war and he conquered. So long you are graced with the spirit of the Lord, the blessing of the Lord will always be upon you, and whatsoever you undertake in the name of the Lord will be blessed. The key is to have God's approval or God's anointing in your service for Him. It is not strange to see a gifted teacher or person be gifted and successful in other areas as well. With God on your side, you can do greater things and the extent of your service would be unlimited.

Another Old Testament example of the Lord putting His spirit on people to work in His service is recorded in the book of Numbers chapter eleven. In this chapter, we see how the constant complaints of the Children of Israel to Moses for food and other needs frustrated Moses. Moses in his frustration also complained unto God about the complaints of the Children of Israel. The Lord finally tells Moses to gather unto Him seventy men of the elders and He will pass unto them a portion of the same "spirit" or "anointing" that Moses has.

> "And the Lord said unto Moses, gather unto me seventy men of the elders of Israel, whom thou knowest to be the elders of the people, and officers over them; and bring them unto the tabernacle of the congregation, that they may stand there with thee. And I will come down and talk with thee there: and I will take of the spirit which is upon thee, and will put it upon them; and they shall bear the burden of the people with thee, that thou bear it not thyself alone. And the Lord came down in a cloud, and spake unto him, and took of the spirit that was upon him, and gave it unto the seventy elders: and it came to pass, that, when the spirit rested upon them, they prophesied, and did not ceased. But there remained two of the men in the camp, the name of the one was Eldad, and the name of the other Medad: and the spirit rested upon them; and they were of them that were written, but went not out unto the tabernacle: and they prophesied in the camp. And there ran a young man and told Moses, and said, Eldad and Medad do prophesy in the camp. And Joshua the son of Nun, the servant of Moses, one of his young men, answered and said, My lord Moses, forbid them. And Moses said unto him, enviest thou for my sake? Would God that all the Lord's people were prophets, and that he would put His spirit upon them! And Moses gat him into the camp, he and the elders of Israel" (Numbers 11:16,17,25 - 30).

There is a lesson to learn in verse 16 of chapter 11 of the book of numbers. Because God was using Moses, as a human leader to appoint seventy men, God told Moses that his selection must not be bias, he is to select 70 men out of the experienced and wise, and men who are already leaders of the people who are favored by the majority. There will come a time when pastors or church leaders are to designate or train certain laypeople to take on certain roles in the church. These leaders must present these names unto the Lord, make appointments that are not bias, and select people who exhibit leadership roles and are favored by the majority in the church but not compromising the truth. Another lesson learned is from verse 26 of chapter 11. Two men of the 70, Eldad and Medad, did not make it to the tabernacle in time for the ordination ceremony but while they were in the camp, the spirit of the Lord came upon them and they began to prophesy.

No matter who you are or where you are when the Lord decides to use you for His purpose, you will be used. You do not necessarily have to be biblically astute or theologically inclined, when God selects you for the job, you will get it because God says so. Joshua even got concerned and confused and asked Moses how could this be because these men were not at the tabernacle? Moses responded by saying, it is the Lord's doing which he could not question. That is just how it is in the economy of

God. There is no formal attachment or pre-requisite to God's appointment. Whenever there is an appointment that baffles man's expectations, one can rest assure that that appointment is divine and God-approved. The education department or the ministry of teaching is vital in the church. Growth in Christ is only possible by studying and knowing the word of God. Jesus confirms this by saying that man shall not live by bread alone but by every word that proceeds out of the mouth of God (Matthew 4:4). It is expedient to say that the destiny of the church relies in the able hands of gifted teachers like you. Paul wrote to the believers in Ephesus informing them about the importance of the gifts and callings of God in the church, "and He gave some, apostles; and some, prophets; and some, evangelists; and some, pastors and teachers; for the perfecting of the saints, for the work of the ministry, for the edifying of the body of Christ: till we all come in the unity of the faith, and of the knowledge of the Son of God, unto a perfect man, unto the measure of the stature of the fullness of Christ" (Ephesians 4:11-13). Paul was letting the believers know that although one may be gifted with a different gift from others, his role is as important as others.

Everyone is vital to the survival of the church. No one should go looking over someone's shoulder in trying to envy the other person's gift. There is a phenomenal beauty arranged by God for the church only if God's people are prayerfully in-tune to Him. In other words, instead of trying to figure out who has what among yourselves, one needs to get down on his knees and ask God to bless him with a gift. Believers have to be able to discern the movement of the spirit as it utilizes God's leadership role amongst God's people. Biblically speaking, each believer plays a unique role in every local assembly. There is no need for believers to shove and push each other because God has designated each believer to play a role that serves as one of the other bricks in the body as the cornerstone, the stronghold of the church.

Exegesis on Romans 12:3-8

KJV

Romans 12:3 - 8

3   For I say, through the grace given unto me, to every man that is among you, not to think soberly, according as God hath dealt to every man the measure of faith.

4   For as we have many members in one body, and all members have not the same office:

5   So we, being many, are one body in Christ, and every one members one of another.

6   Having then gifts differing according to the grace that is given to us, whether prophecy, let us prophesy according to the proportion of faith;

7   Or ministry, let us wait on our ministering: or he that teacheth, on teaching;

8   Or he that exhorted, on exhortation: he that giveth, let him do it with simplicity; he that ruleth, with diligence; he that sheweth mercy with cheerfulness.

Verse three, the apostle is admonishing the believers of Rome not to be puffed up or extremely exalt themselves but thank God for the gifts bestowed upon them. There were some believers in the church who thought that they had special favor with God to have been given their gifts. Paul is trying to let them know that the gift of God is an unmerited one. Humility is encouraged by Paul to the gift recipients. It is given by grace through Christ not because of any special favor from God. In the verse also Paul lets them know that there are levels of faith in the economy of God. God grants people gifts based on the level of their faith. One with a "doubting-Thomas" type faith will not expect the gift of miracle or healing from God. (cf. Heb 11:6) God wants us to have faith in Him. It is essential for Christian growth and the Christian community as well. Also the lesson to learn in verse three is that everyone cannot have the same gifts. God is the author of the gifts, He is the chief executive officer of the church, if you will, therefore, He will make sure that there exists a fortitude of division of labor in His ruling economy to be certain that kingdom growth and spiritual productivity can be ascertained. Therefore, Paul is telling the saints not to look down on others who may have or not have certain gifts, to think that they are inferior and worth nothing in the community. God is the giver of the gifts and He gives it to everyone as he sees fit. God allots gifts to bring a spiritual balance in the Christian community.

Verse four, the apostle is drawing an analogy of the division of spiritual gifts in the community by God with that of the human body. Just like how the human body has cells, tissues, organs, and systems that have different functions but work for the well-being of the same body, so is it with God's gifts to the church. God gives out different gifts for the functioning of different offices in the church, all for the spiritual well-being of the body of Christ. Irrespective of one's gift, no one's gift is better or important than the other. Every gift is as important as the other. Take for example, the human body, one cannot say that the circulatory system is not important to the human body as the respiratory system is. The circulatory system is responsible for circulating blood in all parts of the body. The heart, brain and other parts of the body depend on the supply of blood to sustain life. Likewise the respiratory system is responsible for inhaling and exhaling air which the brain and other parts of the body need. Without adequate oxygen to the brain and other parts of the body, there will be no life in the body. Therefore every gift is importantly given by God to sustain the church, God does this for life to remain in the community (I Cor 12:12:20; Eph 4:4, 16).

Verse five, Paul is reaffirming and reiterating his thesis in the preceding verse about the importance of every individual gift in the church. Each gift is dependent on the other. Paul tells them that is just how the church should live. Everyone is important as the other in the church and so is the gift. The effectiveness of one gift is possible because of the operation of the other. In and through Christ the Christian community becomes a body comprising one family. This thought give reasons to agree with the scripture that says believers must not forsake the assembling of themselves together because the presence of one completes the whole (cf. Heb 10:25 [I Cor 10:17, 33; 12:20,27; Eph 4:12]).

Verses six through eight, now the apostle feels he has accomplished something from the exclusive sessions of explaining the importance of the gifts in the church, he encourages them to now go ahead and utilize the gifts apportioned to them by God and used them wisely for the betterment of the church, not themselves. He encourages them to embrace their individual gifts, cherish them, and be proficient in their respective offices.

Exegesis of David K. Bernard

Romans 12:3-8

Verse 3. Paul spoke by the grace given to him, namely, in virtue of his given calling as an apostle (1:5; 15:15). In doing so he himself became an example of his message. His inspired message to each individual believer: we must be humble, recognizing that God is the source of everything we achieve. We must not value ourselves too highly, but we must think with sober judgment. Humility does not mean disparaging ourselves or thinking we are worse than anyone else and that we all need God. We have to make this sober estimate in accordance with the faith God has given us. We have no cause for esteeming ourselves higher than others when we realize that God is the source of our faith and that God has given faith to every one of us. *Verse 4*, to illustrate this point, verse 4 uses the human body as an analogy. The human body has many parts, but not all these members have the same function. There is one body, but many members-one body, but different functions. *Verse 5* describes the church as the body of Christ, much as in I Corinthians 12:12-27. Christians are all members of the one body of Christ. Thus each one is part of the others; all are mutually dependent on one another. *Verse 6*. The different members of the church have different offices and gifts, just as the bodily parts have different functions. For this reason we dare not compare ourselves among ourselves (II Corinthians 10:12). We must seek to identify our particular gifts and exercise them to the best of our ability for the benefit of the body as a whole. The Greek word for gifts is *charismata*, the same word used of the nine spiritual gifts in I Corinthians 12:4-11. This passage lists seven gifts: *Prophecy* - divinely inspired utterance, speaking to edify others. This does not necessarily involve predictions of the future. The word can specifically mean a supernatural public message in the language of the audience (I Corinthians 14:29-31), but here it probably has the more general meaning of anointed proclamation or preaching (I Corinthians 14:3; Revelation 19:10). If someone has this gift he should exercise it in proportion to his faith as much as his measure of faith will enable him. *Verse 7*. *Ministry* - service to others, service in the church. The Greek word is *diakonia*, which specifically includes the office of a deacon. *Teaching* - instruction. *Verse 8. Exhortation* - encouragement or comfort. *Giving* - sharing material blessings with others and with the church. The KJV says to do this with "simplicity." Most commentators understand the underlying Greek word to mean "liberality or generosity," but it also can mean "singleness of heart, sincere concern." *Leading or ruling* - leadership role in the church. (Another possible meaning of the Greek word here is "to give aid.") Leaders are to exercise their role with diligence, carefulness, and earnestness. God has ordained rulers or leaders in His church. It is important to submit to human authority in the church (Hebrews 13:17), as long as human leaders exercise their authority under God according to the guidelines of His Word. These leaders are not to be dictators but are to be examples and servants to all (Mark 10:42-45); I Peter 5:1-3). Even leaders must submit to higher leaders, and the highest leaders must submit to one another and to the collective body. See Acts 11:1-4; 15:29; 21:18-29; Galatians 2:1-14). *Showing mercy* - being merciful and kind to others. This includes visiting the sick, helping the poor, assisting widows and orphans (Matthew 25:31-46; Galatians 2:10; James 1:27; 2:15-17). The person who exercises this office should do it cheerfully, not in a begrudging, mournful, or patronizing way. To summarize, each Christian has a particular gift, office, or function in the church)or possibly several of them). What ever God has given him to do he should exercise it to his full capacity, but always with humility.

Exegesis of Christopher Bryan on Romans 12:3-8

In verse three Paul begins with an exhortation and acknowledges that he depends on the goodwill of a sovereign God who graces him with His love and compassion, not that he is different from anyone else. Paul's usage of the phrase "each one" (Gk. hekastos) exemplifies a personal appeal to each member of the church at Rome to listen keenly to what he has to say. The apostle cautions the believers not think of too higly of themselves (Gk. huperphronein) than they ought to think (phronein) but to think with moderation (Gk. sōphrosunē) as God has assigned to each person the measure of faith (12:3). The believers are members one of another. They are united with each other in Christ. Their particular gifts (charismata) are rooted in the one gift that matters, God's grace (charis) given to them in Jesus Christ. Paul regards all such gifts (1) as mediated by the Holy Spirit (so much so that on another occasion he can use simply the adjective "pneumatikos" (spiritual) to speak of them. (I Corithians 14:1), (2) as particular ways in which individual Christians share in God's grace, which grace is, of course, finally and essentially the same for all, and (3) as given by God to individual members for the benefit of all. There are varieties of gifts but the same Spirit who gives them "for the common good" (I Corinthians 14:4, 7). Chrysostom, another exegete, understood Paul to be saying that the ability to prophesy was proportional to the capacity of the prophet's own faith in 12:6b). Bultmann, another exegete, connects 12:6 with 12:3 to conclude that prophets are to prophesy in accordance with the standard set by the gospel, which is the faithfulness of God in Jesus Christ, and the faithfulness to which they are summoned in response. Regarding ministry (diakonia) in verse seven, an alternate interpretation refers specifically to the practical service of the needy in the congregation (compare Matthew 25:44-45; Acts 6:1; Romans 15:25). It is believed that such service seems to be covered in the final three of five other "charisms" mentions in verses seven and eight, such as teaching, exhorting, giving, ruling, and showing of mercy (Listening to Romans, 197-199)[108]

Exegeses of Robert Jewett et al on Romans 12:3-8

Verse three: The issue here is one of communal discernment of God's will, which involves the exercise of the charismatic renewed mind of the Christian community. "sober-mindedness" was the virtue of mature civility and submission to laws while it s opposite, pride or high-mindedness, was the vice of tyrants. The philosophical treatment of sober-mindedness was shaped decisively by Plato and Aristotle. Plato says it is a cardinal virtue. Plato associated sober-mindedness with the divine. In the laws sobriety makes a person similar to God, says Plato. "God would be for us the measure of all things . . . and the one who would be dear to God must become like God, so far as possible." Aristotle adds by insisting that humans should make themselves immortal through the exercise of reason. The stoics during the Greco-Roman period picked this thought up by saying that the sobriety of God is equated to being sober-minded which expresses divine kinship.

Paul is suggesting that if one's self-image depends on one's own faith, then one would be entitled to think of oneself highly than others who have less faith, which would be fundamentally at variance with the argument. However, Paul means that the norm that each person is provided in the appropriation of the grace of God, although faith in its proper sense is the relationship of holding fast to the grace of God, it includes a measuring rod that allows for differentiation. Verses four and five: The metaphor of the "body" is used to describe the body of Christ or the church or community as an organism with component parts unified with one purpose in mind which is to edify one another and exalt Christ. This was a horizontal unity and relationship contrary to the divisive forces with and between the Roman houses and tenement churches and the refugees returning from the exile of the Edict of Claudius.This expression stresses the solidarity between Christian groups as a single body in Christ. Paul stresses that each Christian actually an independent "member" along with all others. Every single Christian has received God's "grace," of which the particular charismatic gifts are congregationally useful (Romans, 740-744).[109]

---

[108] Christopher Bryan, A Preface to Romans: Notes on the Epistle in Its Literary and Cultural Setting. Oxford: Oxford University Press, 2000.

[109] De Bruyn, Theodore, Pelagius's Commentary on St Paul's Epistle to the Romans. Oxford, Clarendon press, 1993.

Exegesis of Theodore De Bruyn on Romans 12:3-8

Paul disallows human wisdom in the picture by saying that he speaks not of his own mind, but the authority of a spiritual gift. "to all among you" who are priests and teachers, whose example the rest follow, not to be wiser than one ought, but to be wise with sober judgment. A *measure of faith* is a charismatic power apportioned to the faithful by God. In verse four Paul exhorts the saints in Rome to live in harmony by comparing them with the body, in case they are not roused at least by the fact that they have received different gifts. For they could not as individuals each have all the gifts because they would become proud knowing that they lack none. As they learn to serve one another in this regards, love may grow stronger and stronger. The gift depends not on us but the one who gives it. The person who has a heart so pure that he deserves it receives even in this present life the charismatic power to serve (Pelagius's Commentary on Romans, 132-133).[110]

Exegesis of Joseph A. Fitzmyer, S.J. on Romans 12:3-8

Paul, in verse three addresses the Christians of Rome as a commissioned apostle, called by the grace of God. He motivates them to live a proper Christian life. One made up of humility and the likeness of Christ. "One not to think overmuch of oneself but to be sober-minded, not only in one's self-esteem, but in the sense also of leading a righteous, godly, and sober life. God apportions His Spirit according to the weight of one's faith, the measure of one's spiritual responsibility" (Black, 152).[111] In verses four and five the apostle admonishes the likely divided Christian community in Rome to learn how to live in harmony, although diverse in other aspects of life, in Christ they are all one. Through the Spirit they are made to function through Christ, therefore, they must learn how to unite for the common good of the church. In Christ Christians are interrelated, and no one stands in isolation; so all their service must be in terms of the body as a unit. In verse six, Paul plays with the words *charismata*, "gifts, *charisma*" and *charis*, "grace." The *charisms* are the specific participation of individual Christians in grace, they are "the concretion and individuation of the Spirit" (Käsemann, Commentary, 335).[112] Such participation is rooted in the *gift of God*. Christ is the prime factor when it comes to charisms. Christians are endowed with, and other charisms which are indications of the measure of their faith. These are

---

[110] Theodore De Bruyn, Pelagius's Commentary on St Paul's Epistle to the Romans. Oxford, Clarendon press, 1993.

[111] Matthew Black, Peake's Commentary on the Bible. London, Routledge, 1962.

[112] Raymond E. Brown, Fitzmyer, Joseph A., Murphy Roland E., The New Jerome Biblical Commentary. Englewood Ckifts: Prentice Hall, Inc., 1990, p 863

called in theology "gratiae gratis datae," grace freely bestowed," in view of a function to be carried out in the community.

The different gifts of grace that Christians receive from the Spirit as a result of faith are destined for the benefit of the whole body. Each member must realize the social the social character of the God-given talent and make use of them for the common good without envy or jealousy of the gifts given to other members. Paul enumerates seven such charisms: *Prophecy*, the first gift is inspired Christian preaching, as in I Corinthians 12:10,28; 13:2; 14:1, 3-6, 24, 39; I Timothy 4:14. It is given in primacy of place among the *charismata*, clearly said to be a gift of the Spirit in I Corinthians 12:10-11. It denotes not one who predicts the future, but one who speaks in God's name and probes the secrets of hearts (I Corinthians 14:24-25). *Let it be used in proportion to one's faith.* "according to the analogy of faith." *Analogia* means "right relationship, proportion" (BAGD, 56).[113] Paul's caution is to curb the charismatics and their enthusiasm; all inspired preaching must be in accord with Christian faith. Faith thus serves as a norm. The second gift is *ministry, diakonia or service.* Paul may be using a generic term to mean to be of assistance administratively in the church or community. *Teaching*, Paul shifts now to mention the gifted person, the third category of gifts. *Ho didaskōn* is the one who instructs, either in catechesis (I Corinthians 14:19; Galatians 6:6) or in the interpretation of Scripture. In either case it has to do with the communication of God's will, a task seen as distinct from preaching and service. See I Corinthians 12:28; cf. Ephesians 4:11; I Timothy 4:13. An exhorter, i.e., the "spiritual father of the community, who by his consolation, encouragement, and admonition he guides the members in their communal life; he possesses the fourth kind of charisms. *Contributor to charity*, i.e., on who *shares* private wealth, a philanthropist, an almsgiver, the fifth kind of God-given charism. Some scholars believe that this gift refers to one who dispenses both spiritual gifts and material goods. Spiritual gifts would mean communication of the riches of the gospel with *haplotēs* or simplicity without self-exaltation. A philanthropist's giving should be characterized by haplotēs, i.e., lacking duplicity or secondary, ulterior motivation and should be done without thinking twice about it. A *leader*, the sixth charism belongs to *proistamenos*, "one standing at the head," "the one who presides, directs, or rules." See I Thessalonians 5:12; I Timothy 5:17 (presiders in the church); I Timothy 3:4, 5, 12 (preside over a household). Diligence should characterize the leader's oversight. The seventh gift, *one who does works of mercy*. Illustratively, a Christian social worker, the Good Samaritan." The seventh gift entails empathy, compassion, kindness and concern. This person is to render servise in a cheerful manner (The Anchor Bible, 645-649).[114]

---

[113] Ibid., 863.

[114] William F. and Arthur Walter, The Anchor Bible: I Corinthians: A New Testament Translation. Garden City: Doubleday & Company, Inc., 1976.

Apology of Alexander Maclaren on Romans 12:3-8

Paul wishes to invite the Roman Christians to an estimate of themselves based upon the recognition of God as the Giver of all capacities and graces, leading to a faithful use for the general good of the gifts differing according to the grace given to us. Faith is the measure we have to estimate ourselves. The strength of a Christian man's faith determines his whole Christian character. Concerning unity and spiritual gifts, many are one, because they are each in Christ, and the individual relationship and derivation of life from Him makes them whilst continuing to be many (Epistle to the Romans, 240).[115]

Exegesis of F. F. Bruce

Romans 12;3-8

Diversity, not uniformity, is the mark of God's handiwork. It is so in nature; it is equally so in grace, and nowhere more so than in the Christian community. Here are many men and women with the most diverse kinds of parentage, environment, temperament and capacity. Not only so, but since they became Christians they have been endowed by God with a wide variety of spiritual gifts as well. Yet because and by means of that diversity, all can co-operate for the good of the whole. Whatever form of service is to be rendered in the church, let it be rendered heartedly and faithfully by those divinely qualified to render it, whether it be prophesying, teaching, admonishing, administering, making material gifts, sick-visiting, or the performance of any other ministry.

To illustrate what he means, Paul uses the figure of a human body, as he had already done in I Corinthians 12:12-27. Each part of the body has its own distinctive work to do, yet in a healthy body all parts function harmoniously and interdependently for the good of the whole body. So should it be in the church, which is the body of Christ.

3. *By the grace given to me.* That is, the 'grace' or spiritual gift of apostleship (cf. 1:5;15:15). According to verse 6, each member of the church has received a special 'grace' in the sense, which is to be exercised for the good of all. *The measure of faith.* 'Faith' here has a rather different sense from that which it bears in the earlier part of the letter; here it denotes the spiritual power given to each Christian for the discharge of his or her special responsibility (cf. verse 6, 'in proportion to our faith').

5 One body in Christ. Compare I Corinthians 12:27, 'you are the body of Christ.' In I Corinthians and Romans the human body is used as an illustration of corporate life of Christians, but in Colossian and Ephesus the idea is carried farther. In these

---

[115] Alexander Maclaren, Expositions of Holy Scripture. Grand Rapids: Baker Book House

documents emphasis is laid on the relation the church, as the body, bears to Christ as the head. In them there is no possibility of an ordinary member of the being compared to the head, or to part of the head (as is done in I Cor 12:16-17, 21); in them, too, the body ceases to be used as a mere simile and becomes rather the most effective term which the apostle can find to express the vital bond which unites the life of believers with the risen life of Christ.

8. *In liberality.* NEB, 'with all your heart.' *He who gives aid.* Greek ho *proïstamenos,* understood in a similar sense to the related noun *prostatis,* 'helper', in 16:2. NEB 'if you are a leader' understands the participle in the sense which it bears in I Thessalonians 5:12 ('those who . . . are over you'). *He who does acts of mercy.* NEB 'if you are helping others in distress.'

"Having then gifts differing according to the grace that is given to us, whether prophecy, let us prophesy according to the proportion of faith" Romans 12:6. Gift differing according to the grace (ability, power, anointing, and/ or potential given to us by God. The importance of our gift is to display our God-given ability and potential effectuating Christ and the Good News with simplicity and conviction to the world. Christ has given us power to be able to fully and forcefully proclaim the truth with confidence and fearlessness to our fellowmen and the dying world. The power Christ has given us overcomes all other powers or obstacles both natural and spiritual that may try to hinder us from fulfilling our commission. The power Christ has give us is that which makes us unique upon delivering the Gospel. It is the anointing that makes us special and different from other teachers. E. Ellis gives his views on Spiritual gifts as mentioned in chapter twelve of the book of Romans as thus:

Verse 6, *we have gifts*: The different gifts of grace that Christians receive from the Spirit as a result of faith are destined for the community's benefit. Each one must realize the social character of their God-given talents or gifts and make use of them for the common good without envy or jealousy. Paul enumerates seven of them, at first in abstract terms, then later in names for persons. *Inspired Preaching*: Lit., "prophecy," understood in the NT sense (I Corinthians 12:10; 13:2; 14:3-6, 24; I Thessalonians 5:20). *In proportion to (our) faith: Gk analogia* means "right relationship, proportion" and creates little problem here. The word *pistis* is more problematic. It is understood here as *fides quae,* the body of Christian belief. Verse seven, *service*. The second gift is *diakonia,* which refers to administration of material aid or the distribution of alms of the community (I Corinthians 16:15; Acts 6:1). Nothing in this context relates it to a distinct class of persons ("deacons"). *If one is a teacher*: The third gift is the teaching of Christian doctrine, a task distinct from preaching and service previously mentioned (I Cor 12:28; cf. Ephe 4:11). Verse eight, *if one exhorts*: The fourth gift is possessed by the "spiritual father" of the community. *If one contributes*: The fifth gift is possessed by the one who "shares" private wealth by way of alms; such a philanthropist is expected to exercise it "with a generous simplicity" (II Cor 9:11, 13) and comment on II Cor 8:2). *If one is a leader*: The sixth gift belongs to *ho proistamenos,* "the one who is at the head" of the community, an official or administrator (I Thess 5:12). If the order of the gifts be significant, the "leader's" place in the list is note worthy. Another translation is sometimes used, "the one who contributes" (RSV; cf. BAGD 707)[116]; but then it is difficult to distinguish this gift from the second or fifth. *With diligence.* Diligent attention should characterize the leader's governance. *A merciful helper.* The seventh gift belongs to the person who performs acts of mercy; such one is expected to do them cheerfully. The spirit in which they are done is more important than the acts. (6) The anointing assures you that the Lord's hand is upon you and that you are called by God. Before David became King of Israel, he knew that he was special in the sight of God. He knew he was anointed and had the hand of the Lord upon him. Therefore, he was not afraid to walk up to challenge Goliath. David had the confidence in himself because he knew God was on his side. When God is on your side, you have nothing to be afraid of. You can count yourself a winner.

We are more than conquerors through Him who loves us (Romans 8:37). It was the same assurance David had when Saul, the first King of Israel tried to take his life after Saul realizes the perculiarity of David as a special person in the sight of God. Saul became inferior to David because he saw the anointing and talent of David. Not only could David be a general at battle, Saul saw David display his musical talent by playing and singing under the anointing of God. All this made Saul envious. The more Saul became envious, the more insecure he made himself. The proportion of our faith as emphasized in verse six of Romans 12,shows that we have different levels of faith in God, that does not make us less of a Christian or powerless. This is just the reflection of the magnitude of our perception in God and His authority. The level of faith that brings us to Christ to obtain salvation enables us to repent or change our ways and accept Christ as Lord and Savior but it does not stop there. With spiritual growth and nurturing, one is able to explore another dimension in Christ. Christ is not limited to only provide salvation, He can heal the sick, raise the dead and do anything we want Him to do. Sometimes it is easier said than done, but how many Christians today exercise the measure of faith that Christ expects them to exercise? Are you preaching Christ as He should be preached and teaching Him as He should be taught with a conviction that He still performs miracles, or you just say things to motivate your listeners? It is the measure of your faith in Christ that determines your expectations. It is the fraction of your belief in Christ that shapes your perception of how you see Christ and what you believe He is capable of doing. Ephesians 4:7 - 8 give more light on this thought. I advise that you read these verses.

On their part, George Arthur Butler and others share views reflecting the variety of gifts mentioned in I Corinthians 12. *Varieties of gifts and services*: The Apostle repeats the word *varieties* (διαιρέσεις) three times (RSV), thought the KJV obscures this. All are gifts; yet at the same time they are activities involving effort on the part

---

[116] Raymond E. Brown, Joseph A. Fitzmyer, Murphy Roland E., The New Jerome Biblical Commentary. Englewood Ckifts: Prentice Hall, Inc., 1990, p 863.

of those receiving them. Paul's procedure here is that not all gifts possess the same value. Some are more helpful to others. But there are certain aspects common to them all. God is the source of them and they are given to serve the common good of the community or the church. Nine different gifts of the Spirit are enumerated to emphasize with almost monotonous repetition the fact that they are from the same spirit. The first two: *knowledge* and *wisdom* two indistinguishable gifts from one another. V 8, *to one is given through the Spirit the utterance of wisdom, and to another the utterance of knowledge according to the same Spirit*. Broadly speaking, in our own time one may distinguish between knowledge and wisdom by saying that wisdom is the deeper insight which can turn knowledge to the best advantage. It is doubtful that Paul had such distinction in mind.

One finds it difficult to resist the inference that the apostle himself had his convictions about the same relative value of different gifts, and he may have recognized a difference of degree between knowledge and wisdom. Or perhaps he meant that some members of the community were able to state the facts of the gospel to their brethren, while others were better able to expound the significance of the facts in their bearing upon the spiritual development of the church and its mission in the world. V 9, *the gift of faith*: It is striking that Paul calls *faith* a gift (cf. Rom 12:3). Certainly the apostle does not conceive of the faith that justifies as a human work; it is the product of divine grace. Yet here Paul is speaking of a gift which only certain members of the community receive, so that *faith* cannot be understood as the common faith involved in the reception of salvation, but as faith of a particular kind (cf. 13:2; it is the wonder-working faith that lead to healings (Mark 5:34; 10:52). There are degrees of faith. The faith of some is stronger, more robust, more contagious and inspiring than that of others. The faith of few, varying circumstances, has more than once been the living spring which has nourished the morale of the many. V 9, *the gift of healing*: This great gift should be taken as a special instance of the working and power of Christian faith. In the gospel it is made well plain that the salvation which the Master proclaimed involved the well-being of the whole man, body, soul, and spirit. It is true that the deeper need was spiritual. It is also true that he healed the sick and mentally deranged where he found men and women whose faith in him and whose spirit of expectancy gave him an opportunity to perform a healing work. His message was for the whole of the human personality, both physically and spiritually. Healing took place in the Christian church through faith and prayer. Certain members of the church were endowed with gifts of healing. Some are so endowed to this day, and services of faith healing, which are meant to supplement and not to dispense with orthodox medical aid, are frequently held in churches. V 10, *the working of miracles*: The phrase, *to another the working of miracles*, would be more accurately expressed as "the demonstration of mighty powers. Miracles would be descriptive of healing works of the more unusual type. The difference between the gift of healing and the working of miracles is one of degree. These three, faith, healing, and the working of miracles form a connected section by themselves. Obviously they are interrelated.

The gift of prophecy: Those persons who were endowed with the gift of prophecy, the first of another group of gifts, were recipients of that prophetic revelation which yielded insight into the purposes of God, so far as these bear upon the existing state of affairs or indicative future developments. The gift of tongues an their interpretation: Paul treats with caution this peculiar expression of the faith, enthusiasm, and intensity of spiritual emotion in the church. He gives further guidance as to it value to the community and suggests practical tests. Some authorities distinguish the practice of speaking with various kinds of tongues from the activity recorded in the Acts, when after Pentecost the apostles being "filled with the Holy Spirit . . . began to speak in other tongues, as the Spirit gave utterance' (Acts 2:4). Under the stress of spiritual emotion the apostles spoke intelligibly in foreign tongues and were understood by those standing around who spoke the same language. The phrase *kinds of tongues* can better be interpreted as "ecstatic utterances." This is a well-known phenomenon, and has been an accompaniment of all such religious revival movements as were characterized by strong emotions. *To another the interpretation of tongues*: There could have been little guarantee that the interpretation bore any relationship at all to the unintelligible utterance. Yet there can be no doubt that these ecstatic utterances were treasured by the early church as signifying the presence of the Spirit in the midst of the believers. Ecstatic utterances were probably regarded as a kind of divine frenzy, and therefore of super human origin. The Corinthian Christians seem to have been particularly susceptible to this emotional experience, and seem to have attached such value to it that they ranked it above some of these other gifts of the Spirit listed by the apostle. In essence the gift is not to benefit the individual but the community. The last four gifts belong together, prophecy, the ability to evaluate the prophecy, and interpret the tongues. Paul regards the ability to judge true inspiration as being a work of the Spirit no less than the actual revelations themselves.

"Moreover, brethren, I declare unto you the gospel which I preached unto you, which also ye have received, and wherein ye stand. And if Christ be not risen, then our preaching vain, and your faith is also vain" I Corinthians 14:1 and 14. In the context of this chapter the Apostle Paul addresses an issue whereby some members of the Corinthian Assembly sought gifts as they were something they could compete for in the church. Paul lets them know that it is good for them to desire gift but not to envy other people's gifts. You cannot envy a person's gift and attempt to pray to God to give you a gift just because another person has it. If you desire a gift, pray and ask the Lord honestly to give you that gift because you want to be a blessing in the church or local ministry. You should note that there must be a divine reason for your quest for a gift from God. God mainly wants His gifts to benefit others or the church not you. God will not give you a gift for your own benefit. God's gift is not for any selfish means. God's gift is to be shared with others. by doing so, others will be blessed and brought into the kingdom of God. The gift of God is without repentance. You do not have to prayer harder, fast too much to make God give you a gift. You should be willing and ready to be used in this area and ask the Lord to bless you with the gift so that you can bring glory to His kingdom. Tell Him you want not your will but His to be done in your life. With humbleness and willingness to serve and seek guidance from others gifted in this area, the Lord will bless you with the desires of your heart. Every good and perfect gift comes from above (James 1:17). "Every gift is good, and every present is perfect" (H. Greeven, TZ 14 [1958] 1-13).[117] "What counts of a gift is not its value but the givers intention. The source of all created gifts is God, the creator of the heavenly luminaries, the prime instance of His giving good gifts. Unlike heavenly bodies, whose movements according to time and seasons result in corresponding variations in the light they send forth, their creator is unchanging; therefore, his goodness never diminishes" (The New Jerome Biblical Commentary, 911).[118] Paul tells the Corinthians that as they are zealous about spiritual gifts, they should know that the gift or gifts they seek should be only for the edifying of the church, not themselves.

Commenting on the disposition of genuine leadership, Greeven shares the following:

> Being doers of the word (James 1:19-27). The word in which we were given birth by God must be heard, obstacles must be removed, and the word must be implemented in deed. Verse 19, *be quick to listen, slow to speak, slow to anger.* These three admonitions are of a type that frequently occurs in the OT and respectfully in (James 5:11-13; 1:34-37) also in 1:22-25; 3:13-18; and 1:20 plus 4:1-2, slow to speak: This theme is resumed in 1:26 and developed at length in 3:1-12. Verse 20 The reason is given for the last of the three admonitions of v 19, the righteousness of God: I.e., demanded by God, as in Matt 5:20; 6:33.
>
> Verse 21, receive the implanted word: Gk emphytos, "implanted," normally means "inborn" - a meaning that seems logically inadmissible in the present context. This implantation of the word refers rather to the acceptance of the Christian faith at baptism, including the ethical demands involved. The use of "word" (logos) in 1:18, 21-23 reflects typical NT usage. It is God's saving revelation, foreshadowed in the word given to the prophets and in the word that is a synonym for law (t rã), but fully expressed only in Christ and the gospel. The Precept: Be Doers, Not Mere Hearers (1:22). This verse is an apt summary of the whole letter. It is strikingly similar to Rom 2:13. The general theme of a "religion of deed," so characteristic of James, is prominent in other NT writings. Matt 7:24-27 par.: Luke 8:21;11:28. For OT background, se Deut 4:5-6; 28:13-15; Ezek 33:31-32, deceiving yourselves:

---

[117] Raymond E. Brown, Joseph A. Fitzmyer, Murphy Roland E., The New Jerome Biblical Commentary. Englewood Ckifts: Prentice Hall, Inc., 1990, p 911.

[118] Ibid., 911.

For example of this self-deception, see v 26. Simile of the Mirror (1:23-25). Verse 23, in a mirror: The "word" is like a mirror: by presenting ideal human conduct, it reveals the hearers shortcomings, just as a mirror reveals facil blemishes or untidiness. If the one using the mirror forgets what has been seen, one will fail to remedy the situation - one will not be a "doer." Verse 25, once again James introduces a theme ("law") that will also recur later in a lengthy treatment in 2:8-12 and in a brief mention in 4:11. Perfect law of liberty: Because of the close connection of this verse with the preceding, the "law" (as in 2:8-12; 4:11) is to be identified with the "word" of the preceding verses. James lacks Paul's distinction between the law and the gospel, showing rather an affinity to the spirit of Matt 5:17-19 as specified in the Sermon on the Mount. That he does not refer simply to the Old Law seems indicated by the qualifications "perfect" and "of liberty" (see 2:12), as well as by the absence in the letter of any emphasis on the fulfillment of ritual prescriptions. In fact, James manifests no rigid legalism of the type attributed to "James the Just" by later tradition (Greeven, 1958).

Greeven did a spectacular job expounding on three outstanding attributes of a leader as described in the book of James 1:19-21. A leader has to be *a good listener*, one who makes sound decisions under pressure. Listening keenly to others educates one on a variety of things one may have no prior knowledge of. Just by listening, a leader is able to thoroughly analyze a situation or person and be able to render good judgments. Solomon was one of the world's wisest men who ever lived. From day one of his assuming leadership of Israel, he had a council comprising the elders of Israel from whom he sought advice. The Lord chooses the young because they are strong and zealous but chooses the elders because they are wise. A young leader who keeps in his company the elders and experienced will certainly become successful. One of the many encounters of Solomon that comes to mind was when he had to render a judgment between two ladies who were fighting over a baby. Before rendering judgment, Solomon allows both ladies to speak individually. After he listens to both ladies, he gets to know whose child it is from the testimonies of each lady but to solidify his observation, he decides to pragmatically engage both ladies into a contest for the child in a non-traditional manner. Solomon requests that the child should be killed, and right away, the lady who did not own the child agrees for the child to be killed. Solomon then tells her that the child is not hers but the other lady's. Therefore, the child was given to its mother (I King 3). Even Queen Sheba was one of those great admirers in attendance at this occasion.

SUMMARY

While addressing a company of Jews and Gentiles in the church of Ephesus, the apostle Pau admonishes them of their role in the church, and having them understand that their calling or spiritual status in the church or community was not something they merited, rather it was bestowed upon them by the grace of God through Christ. "Paul's ministry in the gospel was not self-chosen, but was the gift of God's grace: its efficacy was dependent not on his own natural capacities, but on the working of God's power (TIB, 668 - 69).[119] *When the call is a general summons to repentance and salvation, every Israelite or Christian is viewed as its recipient and hence Israel and the church are collectively designated God's "called" or "elect" (Isaiah 41:9; Hebrews 3:1).* To accomplish this mission, the Lord has blessed the church with diverse kinds of gifts so that individuals can be used for this purpose (Ephesians 4:11-12). The call of God has no mandatory obligations attached to it but the appointment of man does. God's calling is not based on a merit system, favoritism, nepotism, social status, or fame. No matter who you are or where you are when the Lord decides to use you for His purpose, you will be used. You do not necessarily have to be biblically astute or theologically inclined, when God selects you for the job, you will get it because God says so. God gives out different gifts for the functioning of different offices in the church, all for the spiritual well-being of the body of Christ. Irrespective of one's gift, no one's gift is better or important than the other. Every gift is as important as the other. Humility does not mean disparaging ourselves or thinking we are worse than anyone else and that we all need God. We have to make this sober estimate in accordance with the faith God has given us. There are varieties of gifts but the same Spirit who gives them "for the common good" (I Corinthians 14:4, 7). A *measure of faith* is a charismatic power apportioned to the faithful by God. The different gifts of grace that Christians receive from the Spirit as a result of faith are destined for the benefit of the whole body. Each member must realize the social the social character of the God-given talent and make use of them for the common good without envy or jealousy of the gifts given to other members. Diversity, not uniformity, is the mark of God's handiwork. God's gift is not for any selfish means. God's gift is to be shared with others. by doing so, others will be blessed and brought into the kingdom of God.

ASSESSMENT

1. The efficacy of Paul's ministry depended on what?

2. Why did God bless the church with divers kinds of gifts?

3. What is the difference between the call of God and the appointment of man?

---

[119] George Arthur Buttrick et al, The interpreter's Bible: The Holy Scriptures in the King James and Revised Standard Versions with General Articles and Introduction, Exegesis, Exposition for Each Book of the Bible, Volume X. Nashville, 1953.

4. Is there a hierarchy of gifts in terms of preference and eminence?

5. What is your take on the "measure of faith?"

PERSPECTIVES

The Theory of essentialism (the practice of regarding something as having innate existence or universal reality) as graphed by Plato suggests that all living things or constituents that share the same essence (natural kind) are imperfect. Plato believes in an ideal world that is perfect, eternal, and unchanging which exits apart from the physical world, a world that is imperfect, temporal, and unchanging. Explaining the Great Chain of Being, Aristotle believes that the attributes of one kind of organism can impact and interact better with the attributes of other organisms within its proximity then organisms adjacent to it (*Continuity*). Aristotle argues that the world of organisms created by a benevolent God can have no gaps but inclusive of other organisms of similar characterization (*Plentitude*). Aristoltle and other philosophers assume that God is self-sufficient and perfect but believe that to a lesser or greater degree, God's creatures must lack divine perfection and fall out of line into a single identifiable class apart from the rest of other organisms (*Unilinear gradation*). The French anthropologist and scientist Georges Cuvier tries to rebuttal the "Great Chain of Being" theory by asserting that the continuity and hierarchy of life is a fallacy. He believes that God periodically replaces old organisms with new ones. In proving his idea, he uses the event of the flood in the days of Noah to be the ideal way God replenish his universe or creation. The term used by Cuvier is *Catastrophism*. Making mockery of the catastrophists were the uniformitarians who disagree with catastrophism. They profess of a harmonious integration of nature as essence of God's creativity but disagree that a benevolent God would use natural disasters or catastropies to change the world (Uniformitarianism).

What is your reponse to the aforementioned schools of thought, as presented by Robert H. Lavenda & Emily A. Schultz, heretical, apologetic, or liberalistic? Could you scripturally support your position?

CHAPTER ELEVEN

GREEK ETYMA

Advance—Prokoptō (πρκόπτω) to make progress

Bestow—Didōmi (δίδωμι) to give

Humble—Tapeinos (ταπεινός) of low degree, humble in spirit; Tapeinophrōn (ταπεινόΦρων) humble-minded; Tapeinoō (ταπεινόω) to make low, abasing, to be abased; Tapeinophrosunē (ταπεινοΦροσύνη) lowness of mind

Soldier—Stratiōtēs (στρατυώτης) metaphorically, one who endures hardship for the cause of Christ

Trust—Pepoithēsis (πεποίθησις) confidence; Pisteuō (πιστεύω) entrust

Work—Ergasia (έργασία) to perform, deeds

LEADERSHIP IN MINISTRY

The faith of the head is faith that is dead; the faith of the heart is better in part; but the faith of the hand is the faith that will stand (Anonymous)

He that has lost faith, what has he left to live on (Publilius Syrus: Sentetiae)?

Being *slow to speak* is a quality all leaders must embrace. Mealy mouth leaders get themselves into a lot of trouble because they do not know how to discipline themselves to speak only when it is appropriate. Many organizations suffer great losses from these leaders who do not think before they speak. Not only do they not think before they speak, they inquisitively want to snooze in everyone's business and want to befriend everybody. These leaders are very loquacious. They are busybodies if you will. Because of their immature behavior, their organizations suffer greatly. A leader should know how to carry himself or herself, be cognizant of the company he or she is a part of; not to disassociate oneself from some people but to be mindful of your leadership role. As a leader you have to be careful about the things you say when you are around certain people. The manner of your speaking amongst your buddies should be different when you are among your colleagues. Although your colleagues comprise some of your buddies, all your colleagues are not your buddies. The word "colleague" is a professional term for "associate." There are different types of people in a professional setting. Therefore, one must be mindful. Competition and greed are the cardinal components of a professional environment; nothing personal it is all professional. This is a world where one has to watch his or her back if you will. Before opening one's mouth to speak, as a leader, people expect your speech to be authoritative and sound, therefore they attentively listen to you for knowledge and guidance. As a leader your communicating must be organized, your thoughts must be well put together. Before you speak, you must analyze the matter at hand and speak to inform.

Leadership breeds discipleship. Great leaders were once great followers. In the follower category, this is an area where a person has to strive hard to gain ranks or prove himself or herself. A lot of patience and dedication have to be a part of a follower's lifestyle. A great follower is one who works honestly. This person neither works to gain favor nor compare his or her share of work with others. After going through the stringent path of being a follower, assuming the role of leadership becomes a merited post. The follower and leader paradigm parallels that of the scripture, James 1:22, which admonishes believers to be doers of the word and not hearers only. As a doer of the word, a leader has to be *slow to anger*. It is normal to get mad. As humans we do get mad. It is an inevitable circumstance. However, the Bible says that if we got angry we should not let the sun go down on our wrath *paraphrased* (Ephesians 4:26). In other words, being that you are a leader, you have to set an example for your followers, therefore when you get angry, settle your differences with whom you have a dispute. Do not keep grudge in your heart against anybody, even your wife or husband. Sound judgment cannot be made when you are angry. Your constant behavioral demeanor of anger will drive your followers away from you. If you realize that you have a temperamental problem, seek professional help and pray for God to do something about it. Sooner or later, your behavior becomes equivalent to an addiction which could lead to the demise of your leadership. As a leader over others, you have to utilize a lot of patience. You cannot get mad at everything and cannot be too sensitive to everything. You must exercise acute discretion. Situational ethics should be applied in every situation. Every situation warrants a different type of approach and so must your judgment be at all times. "Wherefore I was made a minister, according to the gift of the grace of God given unto me by the effectual working of his power" Ephesians 3:7. Paul emphasizes on the importance of knowing your calling. You must know whether or not the Lord has called your to teach. You cannot force yourself in the position when you know that the Lord did not call you. You must have the conviction and passion to serve willingly and diligently in this area. You must know that God has chosen you for this task to lead and bring others to Christ. Paul speaks with confidence and humility to let other lay-members in the church of Ephesus who aspired to be ministers and teachers know that he did not make himself a minister, rather, he was made a minister according to the gift of the grace of God given to him. Paul's emphasis is on the gift of the grace of God. Paul wants you to know that neither you nor anybody can make you a teacher except Christ, who by His grace is able to effect this power in you.

"Therefore, the prisoner of the Lord, beseech you that you walk worthy of the vocation wherewith ye are called, with all lowliness and meekness, with longsuffering, forbearing one another in love; endeavoring to keep the unity of the Spirit in the bond of peace. There is one body, and one Spirit, even as ye are called in one hope of your calling" Ephesians 4:1-4. The Apostle Paul alludes to the character of one who is called to teach. In verse one he says he is a prisoner of the Lord. Paul is saying one has to subject himself or herself to the discipline and correction of the Lord. One has to be spiritually institutionalized to the confines and dictate of the Lord. In verse one, the Apostle also urges the gifted teacher to "walk worthy of the vocation wherewith ye are called." The word "worthy" is a strong one. Paul is saying that you have to respect your office or role as a teacher. You should maintain the standards God wants you to maintain as not just a professional but as a special ambassador for Christ. In this role, you have to love what you do and do it well. Cherish it dearly and abstain from anything that shall tarnish your character and profession. You have to walk circumspectly because you are a specialist hired by God to carry out a special task. As a special representative for Christ, your role is to teach fervently and diligently for the purpose of bringing harmony amongst the saints or people of God.

"Neglect not the gift that is in thee, which was given thee by prophecy, with the laying on of the hands of the presbytery" I Timothy 4:14. The Lord can use veterans in the ministry as appointers or recognizes of talent when they see one in the church.

Samuel, a little boy, in Eli's care in the temple heard a voice and asked Eli whether he called him, Eli knew then that God was about to do something great in the life of Samuel. Eli did not discourage Samuel, but told him to go back and wait patiently. Eli told him that the next time he hears the voice, he should say "speak Lord for thy servant heareth" (I Samuel 3:9). Eli had to provide spiritual guidance to Samuel. After the Lord called Samuel 3 times, the scriptures says then Eli "perceived that the Lord had called the child" (I Samuel 3:8). Interestingly, when the Lord decides to give you His gift to carry out a particular task, it is for a genuine reason. You should know that the Lord does not go around selecting everybody for His mission, He selects only a few. Therefore, you must realize that you are very special and privileged to be chosen by the Lord. Not only does the Lord see you as a vessel for only teaching. He sees that you are skillful and useful in other areas that make you just right for the job. Samuel was chosen because he was in favor with both God and men (I Samuel 2:26). Samuel was good at interacting with people. He was adept in public relations but drew the line distinctly regarding the things of God. The people respected him as a person and servant of God. He was a perfect selection. Also the time was right because there was an urgent need. Shame was being brought upon the Priesthood and the temple by the sons of Eli, the priest. Therefore, the Lord had to do something about it. Eli was also old and was not that efficient anymore. You are chosen by God because there is a need, you can make a difference, the image of Christ and Christianity is at stake, leadership in Christendom is slacking and aging, and you have the skills to effect change. Suggested references: II Timothy 1:6; II Corinthians 1:11.

"Every good gift and every perfect gift is from above, and cometh down from the Father of lights, with whom is no variableness, neither shadow of turning" (James 1:17). God has chosen you to be a light to others. He wants to use you to lead others out of darkness into His marvelous light. The light that He puts inside of you will be able to bring witness Christ through you. This same light God gives you can be transferred to those you interact with. You are the light of the world. God does not change. He is the same yesterday, today, and forever. Because he does not change, His character, method or stature does not change. As a gifted person for Christ, God wants you to not compromise your faith or spirituality for anything else. God chose you to be a leader to lead without leniency. There should be no sign of regrets, excuses or sarrows for taking on the task the Lord has designated for you to undertake.

"As every man hath received the gift, even so minister the same one to another, as good stewards of the manifold grace of God" (I Peter 4:10). God gives us His gift not to possess it as our own but to share it with others. Unlike a tangible gift that you could keep to beautify your home or yourself, God's gift is an intangible that you must share with others to bring beauty to Him and His work. By sharing the intangible, the tangible is produced. The big difference between the tangible and intangible gift is that the intangible can beautify both the intangible and tangible but the tangible gift can only beautify the tangible. I will prefer having the intangible than the tangible. You are called to the role of stewardship. A steward is one who is hired to supervise or manage the affairs of a place or thing. God has called you to supervise and manage the gift He has given you, and also to be able to oversee the effectiveness ot the teaching ministry in the church. By ministering one to another, you are sharing God's gift and helping others to know the truth and grow stronger in the church. A good stewardship will impact the church or ministry greatly, but remember it has to be done with humility and passion. My personal beatitude is "he or she who desires to be a leader must be willing to be a follower." Your gift will compliment your personality, experience, and skills. The context of this of this scripture is where Paul is addressing the issue of being gifted to be single or married. The apostle wishes that everyone could take their gift seriously and passionately. Paul was not only a gifted teacher or preacher, he was a single man also. He allowed the Lord to use his unmarried state to be a viable means by which he could effectively utilize his other gifts to the glory of God. Had it not been for the commitment and sacrifice of Paul, you would not have been fortunate to have many of these powerful epistles today. Before David became the leader of people, he was a leader of sheep. Before David got the confidence that he could destroy Goliath, he destroyed a lion and bear, and before he became king of Israel, he already knew that God anointed him through the prophet Samuel that he will be king of Israel one day. David knew that one day he would be king but did not know when. God had to test his patience, endurance, and will.

"A wicked man taketh a gift out of the bossom to pervert the ways of judgment" (Proverbs 17:23). God's gift is not to be used as a weapon against others. God's gift is not for you but for those around you. You are to release and/ or share God's gift with others to perfect and edify the church. God did not give you a gift just to sit on it and decide not to help others who are deficient in that area. You should not be mean to others when they come around you. You have to share it. God's gift is not a trophy or achievement for you to possess. You compete to get a trophy and work hard to achieve something but for the gift of God, no competition or hard work is required. The gift of God is free. Therefore you must reciprocate its value with others. Freely you receive it so freely you should share it. There are no attachments or rewards concerning the gift of God. "A man's gift maketh room for him, and bringeth him before great men" (Proverbs 18:16). When you begin to cherish your gift and do as the Lord requires of you, great things will happen. The Lord will begin to bless you and perform wonders in your life. As the scripture says, "seek ye first the kingdom of God and His righteousness and all these things shall be added unto you (Matthew 6:33). As you commit to using your gift to the glory of God with all your might before the eyes of many shall the Lord exalt you. Recommended scripture reference is Proverbs 17:8.

Your gift is subject to you. You have the power to nurture your gift and make it work for you. A position does not make the person, it is the person who makes the position. Much of what one does in a leadership role depends solely on who he is and what he is made up of. Not everyone has what it takes to teach but the few who find themselves in these front-line positions have to either have the natural gift to do so or have the know-how. In great leadership and stewardship the one attribute that stands out and distinguishes a person from others is his *charisma*. The Webster collegiate dictionary defines charisma as being *a personal magic power of leadership arousing special popular loyalty*. It is interesting to note that hidden in the inner part of charisma is the personality or character of the person. These are traits that define who he is and represent his identity to the outside world. One who really has a gift in a particular area ought to be given the privilege and support to function in that area because ninety nine percent of the times those who are employed or allowed to function in their area of specialty happen to have excellent results. There will always be a difference between one who is gifted and the other who is not. In the short run, the latter will possibly work hard to project a good image in that area but not for long because when things began to get unfavorable and uncomfortable, it is then at this time his true colors will surface. Most of the times, it is only those with the talent who can really survive the hardship. They are the ones who can always shine in the midst of difficulties. It is the character of the person that sticks out all the time in reality when everything else seems to be incompatible. Jerry Stuberfield, author of *The Effective Minister of Education* shares with us some interesting qualities of those remarkable educators. These are phenomenal characteristics, some of which I am going to address.

The first of those is *integrity*. Jerry Stubblefield defines integrity as *honesty* and *single-mindedness* in knowing where one is going in using the ethical means required to enable one to get there.[120] Whether one is appointed or called to fill a teaching position, integrity should be of primary concern. It is integrity that gives the teacher a sense of control and responsibility. *Good people skills* is another attribute a personal character reveals of a good teacher. A sensitive and empathetic teacher will always have an outstanding result working with others because he knows how to connect to people and puts himself in their shoes.

Sensitivity happens to be a great factor of concern amongst people, most especially in the church where we have people of diverse cultural, ethnic, social, and religious backgrounds. In the early church days of the bible, this was an issue of concern in Jerusalem where gentile Christians found it uncomfortable among their Jewish brethren because the Jews tried to impose Judaism upon them. Some Jewish Christians found it impossible for a gentile to fully serve God because of their paganistic background. Paul and the other apostles had to address this issue with great concern. This was an issue involving people who were all part of the body of Christ, a sanctified body of believers who were called and set aside to represent Christ's on earth as witnesses to God's deity but yet they could not love each other unconditionally.

---

[120] Jerry M. Stuberfield, *The Effective Minister of Education* Nashville: Broadman & Holman Publishers, 1993.

There were lots of schisms among the early believers due to misconceptions about the new covenant church, morality, marriage, leadership, among others. However, Paul explains to them what the new covenant church was a body of Christ where there was no distinction between bond or free, Jews or gentiles. They are all saved by the grace of Christ and have become united as one people. This issue today exists in our modern day churches including the body of believers. There are people in the midst from different backgrounds who hold different political and the like views. Of course, sometimes those in leadership may view or judge things differently from the majority. In a situation like this, it will be very difficult for anyone to know whether this person is acting out of ignorance or out of his intent. Nevertheless, as a Christian, there should be no excuse for one to behave uncommonly among his fellow believers.

Believers are to all be in one mind as the scripture says. The mind of Christ should be the mind that all believers must have. In fact, the natural law tells us that ignorance to the law is inexcusable. Even just by looking at the stars and the universe, the moon, and other things around us, one could see the evidence attesting the witness of God. We are inexcusable to the knowledge and things of God. The Bible also gives the believers more insight about the things of God. It is imperative that believers search the scripture daily to understand and know the things of God. Being a people's person warrants one to be concerned about both the spiritual and in most instances the natural affairs of those he interacts with. The apostle James inquires about who a truly religious person is among the brethren. James says that true religion is not caring for oneself and only obeying a part of the law. If one defines himself as truly religious, he has to obey the perfect law of liberty which pertains to obeying the scriptures fully in its context and doing what it teaches as following the example of Christ and the apostles. James talks about the destitute amongst the believers, how could the church as a spiritual entity neglect its concern about the natural well-being of the widows and those in need (James 1:27). This conclusively defines the role of a Christian educator as being one who although is called or hired to teach, must also show concern about the needs of those he administers to. When people begin to sense the manifestation of the true quality of stewardship, they will then be open to learn and cooperate with their leaders.

Professionalism is the required standard society demands today and teaching is no exception to the rule. Teaching requires more skills. We are living in a competitive society that demands the best out of you as a teacher. Employers go out looking for teachers who may not have only taken up teacher's training courses but have also been trained in other areas and have a professional background. The occupancy of some roles in the church has to comply with the laws of the land. In coping with the current trend of society, sometimes it becomes rewarding for a local church to build its administration with the right and qualified individuals required by law to perform certain tasks. For instance, if a church wanted to operate a daycare center, it must have the right certification and trainers the law requires to run such a facility. Also, a church that wishes to run a secular school must have the certification and trained teachers prescribed by the law to operate such institution. When a church tries to fulfill its professional role by maintaining certain standards that coincide with the status code of the land, then it can be known that this church is very much concerned about not only the spiritual, but the natural well-being of its people as well. A professional environment always projects a better image of prestige and integrity. Whether in the church or a corporation, a high standard reflects an image of awe for the entity that utilizes it. It is in the milieu of professionalism that skills, techniques and knowledge at advanced levels are practically materialized, therefore, that makes it imperative that the hired or called educator be a professional as well.

Thorough *preparation* is mandatory for you who aspire professionalism. God Himself admonishes us to study to show ourselves approved unto Him, a workman needs not to be ashamed rightly dividing the word of truth (II Timothy 3:15). There happens to be a sluggish spirit among believers when it comes to self-preparation for the ministry. Some have this notion that the spirit will always speak for them when they get up to speak or minister. That is true but by the same token, if there were nothing in-store in one's mental cabinet upon which the spirit could refresh itself and bring rescue to one's memory, then nothing would be manifested. I am not belittling the spirit in terms of limiting it of not being able to reveal supernatural knowledge. That is beside the point. Many Christians today deliberately refuse to commit themselves to thorough preparation for the ministry. Some rather pick up the Bible every Sunday to preach without even preparing at home than to enroll in some Bible school for some training. A behavior like this is very depreciating to the ministry. God is the God of wisdom and knowledge. He gives understanding to us as a treasure for His work. The scripture says that if anyone lacks wisdom he should ask of the Lord who will give it out freely (James 1:5). Also the scripture says that in Him (Christ) dwells the treasures of knowledge and understanding (Colossians 2:3). I do not think God would encourage believers to disdain from learning only because they feel that it is not necessary for the ministry. I have come across lots of ministers who do not value proper training for the ministry. Some even try to justify their position by making reference to Peter and the other disciples who were uneducated men but yet were used mightily by God. That is right, God uses anybody irrespective of the person's qualifications and background. By the same token, there will always be some basic training requirement to fulfill in anticipating being successful in the ministry. If it is not from being theoretically inclined, it could be from sitting under the leadership of someone with experience for spiritual nurturing. The Apostle Paul was an example of this, after his conversion, he had to serve under Gamaliel for proper training for the ministry despite his secular knowledge and skills. The disciples themselves did not become great overnight, they had to sit under Jesus for proper training. Also, the church has to live up to the style and standards of its age and time; like David who utilized his artistic talent to accommodate the age of arts and poetry in his time.

David used his talent to bring beauty to God and his people. We are in the millennium era, a time of information and technology, a time when knowledge is advancing at an unprecedented rate. I am not saying that the church has to let the times dictate its existence, but that the church has to be aware of the environment that circumvents it.

Teaching is a volatile position. It demands flexibility, dexterity, firmness and commitment. This is a multiple role playing position. As a teacher, you should be able and ready to take on challenging roles if the situation warrants that. You should be able run the administrative department of a church and a Christian school. Also with the proper training, you could capably run the administration of a secular institution. The only difference between the two is that one is Christian-oriented and the other is not. But it does not matter. With the proper training, you are qualified to hold any administrative position. Apart from being an administrator, you could teach secular education. You could also preach and serve as an advisor or an evangelist and could even be ordained as a minister. Not forgetting to mention, you could also pastor a church.

Moreover, the success of a good teacher will have to do with his capability of being a great *planner*. Proper planning is the key to proper management. One who spends much time on planning will spend less time in delivering. The hardest part in undertaking a task is planning. Good planning makes the job easier. One of the factors that helps one overcome failures and defeats is *planning*. I have realized in many instances that adequate planning helps one to be in control of oneself and is able to self-consciously be on top of everything he does. With the right planning, a public speaker gains relaxation and confidence in delivering his speech, delivering only because he has made it of necessity to do his homework before doing the job. Planning is the substitute to the real task, it is the pre-task to the task if you will. It is the practice, analysis, and forecast to the task ahead. It is in one's comfort zone, at home or private study where he could meditate on ways of tackling the pending agenda. A good planner is a good manager of time. He should be able to utilize time efficiently as possible. As the saying goes, *time waits for no man*. In other words, this adage is saying that we all have to either move ahead or along with time.

Those who are not on top of things find themselves lagging behind time. Effectiveness and efficiency depend on the willingness for any one person to undergo the challenge of what it takes to get the job done. Knowing how to use time wisely will enable the planner to accomplish a host of things that ordinarily would have been impossible to undertake without some expertise. Before a planner undertakes a project, he will first assess the project by applying either an inductive or deductive approach whichever will be appropriate to get the job done; where some observation and experimentation, including some testing will take place. Upon taking a studious approach, the planner in no time will be abreast of his target. He will know what his goals are and how he could achieve them, and also how much time it would take to achieve that which he anticipates. It is a fact that improper planning brings improper results. Without indulging oneself to planning in advance, one may attain such results as overwhelming or insufficient or inadequate. Adequate planning will earn adequate results but it entails a lot of dedication and assiduity on the part of the planner.

A teacher must be able to train and motivate his people in order for them to be capacitated to serve and work effectively. An equipper is responsible to provide the basic training necessary to enable the least member of his group to be competent and ready to fulfill the same role as another minister of education tomorrow. That should be the intent of the minister of education, he should ask for God's guidance in enabling him to effect some values in those with whom he interacts so that tomorrow those identical values will surface as a memoir of his accomplishments as an equipper. His today's teaching and leadership should reflect on some values for tomorrow. In other words, he should have the mind set of acknowledging that the quality of what he is doing today will be judged by what those he is leading today will project of him tomorrow, or when he is gone. He is not only to be concerned about how well he is doing his job but rather concerned about how receptive people would be to his work. As an enabler, he serves as an encourager to his people. He is there to assist them the best way possible to be able to strive for success, that is, to thrive and achieve that which they aspire. Many times people struggle in finding the right path to achieve their goals. It is then at this juncture the minister of education comes in to provide all the moral and spiritual support needed to help these struggling people achieve their goals. Because he has the professional experience, the people he is leading are depending on him one hundred percent to share his experience and expertise with them. As an encourager, he is to be there to help others know how to distinguish the pros from the cons and how to maximize on their strengths and minimize on their weaknesses. To have this accomplished it takes only the advice of an expert. The Bible lays strong emphasis on the importance of believers assembling together, how profiting it is to the body. "Not forsaking the assembling of ourselves together, as the manner of some is; but exhorting one another: and so much the more, as ye see the day approaching" (Hebrews 10:25). This text reveals that growth in its vast perspective is dependent on the concerted involvement of each believer in the body. The uniqueness of each person is fed into the body as others learn and intake the thoughts and experience others provide. It is from the testimonies of those who have experienced certain heights and depths in the ministry are others nurtured to grow. As an enabler, the minister of education is both sharing his spiritual testimony as well as his professional experience with his brethren for growth and maturity.

A delegator is one who unselfishly shares his responsibility with others in order to accomplish a task. Sometimes a leader may find it burdensome to ask other people to help out with some of the workload. Those leaders who are caught up in such web may find themselves doing more harm than good, not only to themselves but to the body and those who they are leading. The amount of tasks one man may accomplish in eight hours will be nonequivalent to the result that would be obtained from the involvement of two or more persons in the same number of hours. Economics let us know that *division of labor* enables a wholesome of task to be accomplished efficiently in no time. Division of labor refers to having the job broken down into various parts delegating a certain number of people to individual parts for completion. Conclusively, it appears that the time it would take to complete such task together as a group or team would be less as compared to what the outcome would be if one person tried to do the job. The Christian educator has to be a delegator. He must share openly his task with others and also show others how to pass on such a spirit of delegation. Being a team player is the name of the game. One must know how to use others in obtaining his goals not as an individual but as a body or group. His intent must be to succeed, and this success will be possible by the joint effort of his brethren. This lesson of delegation was a great one Moses learned while in the wilderness with the children of Israel. Moses got burdened with the responsibility of leading and controlling the children of Israel. I believe this was a frustrating situation for him but it was not until his father-in-law, Jethro stopped by to admonish him to entrust some of his duties to the elders of the tribes. With that advice, Moses realized the relief. He realized that had he known before, he would not have gone through a lot of the struggle he went through in the past. I guess Moses was thankful to Jethro for this assistance. The role of Jethro was a great insight to Moses. He taught Moses something that Moses cherished for a long time.

Like Jethro, so is it in many cases as a Christian educator, the rest of the world per se depends on the experiential input of the Christian educator to set the track of guidance in the midst of confusion and disorganization.

"If any man desires to be first, the same shall be last of all, and servant of all (Mark 9:35). This is a great lesson of leadership or supervision given by Jesus to His disciples. This was a statement that came about following a dispute the disciples were having amongst themselves about who among them would be the greatest in the kingdom with Jesus. I assume that because John found himself much closer to Jesus all the time, he just felt that spiritual merit was earned in that way as well. But Jesus replied in the above verse to impart some spiritual knowledge to His disciples. At this scenery, there were two levels of comprehension in play. One was of the natural and the other the spiritual. Jesus' disciples were focused on the natural or earthly level of reasoning while Jesus as always was relating to the spiritual. The disciples were taking the current relationship they had with Jesus to be merits earned for further position with Jesus in eternity. But the Lord had to tell them it was too early for such thought to come about because much of what it takes to gain eternal rewards was more than the current relationship with Him on earth. In other words, Jesus was telling them that there was more to a good discipleship than being concerned about one's rank in eternity. Discipleship was the focal point. It was the example of the type of earthly role one must play that would lead him on to being a candidate for an eternal position with the Lord. This discipleship was one that reflected humility. Jesus was telling His disciples that position or leadership should not so much be based on one's ambition for authority or power but rather, on the merits of how much of a servant duty one displays. The role of supervision is to oversee others in making sure that a required task is done in a timely fashion. Supervision does not mean that one has the power to disrespect his subordinates or use force to accomplish a task, because in so doing, lots of problems eventually will come about which would lead to the demise of such affairs. The perfect supervisor is the one who knows how to communicate and fulfill his role with his coworkers with ease and simplicity. Knowing how to talk to others when they are stressed out or so frustrated at work is the best way of accomplishing something. *Soft answer turneth away wrath* (Proverbs 15:1). It is that motivational and soft talking that will drive people to work a little harder. The role of supervision fosters one of servitude and role-modeling. The Christian educator is to conduct himself as a servant and be an example to those he is interacting with.

The Christian educator is an evaluator. He is to assess the magnitude of the feedback people are getting from his training. There could be an application of various methods through which he would be able to find out whether his effort is being in vain or not. Testing is widely an acceptable method of evaluation. The trainees could undergo a written testing method (an essay or true or false), an internship method or working with a mentor, or a project developing testing method. The trainees could also conduct or undergo a survey screening evaluation on subjects including themselves to compare their findings. Evaluation is necessary because it is the only way the minister of education is be able to determine the level of progress of his people. Evaluation determines the level of growth attained in the training process. It is important that evaluation covers all areas of importance, including the age levels or groups, the performance of each participant, the feedback attained by each individual, and the physical and over all natural benefits each received under his leadership.

"And He give some, apostles; and some, prophets; and some evangelists; and some, pastors and teachers; for the perfecting of the saints, for the work of the ministry, for the edifying of the body of Christ" (Ephesians 4:11-12). The Lord wants faithful men who are able to teach (II Timothy 2:2) According to the webster collegiate dictionary, *Theology* is the study of God and His relation to the world. In the passage above, we can place the minister of education in the role of a teacher. He is mentioned as being included in God's plan to bring edification to the body of Christ. However, although he perfectly fits the category of a teacher, he is not limited in being an evangelist, preacher, pastor or an apostle. There is nothing that I know of scripturally that forbids a minister of education from being able to preach or pastor a church. God's gifts are without repentance and anyone can get it from Him. God freely gives His gifts to anyone who asks for it without any natural obligations. What I mean is that ones' gift is not based on one's good works. It is something that the Lord gives out freely without any merits or tied-in obligation. It is possible for a teacher or any believer to pray and ask God to bless him with more than one gift. A teacher or an evangelist could also become a pastor. But in spite of it all, technically speaking, there are little distinctions of role playing in these categories but with God all things are possible.

God can allow anyone to feasibly serve in more than one capacity. Let us take Paul for an example, not only was he a capable teacher and writer, he also was an evangelist, a missionary, pastor and an apostle. And in each of these roles he served efficiently. If Apostle Paul could do it, it is also possible for anyone today in the ministry. It only takes commitment on the part of the recipient provided he is willing to sacrifice himself for the service of the Lord. I perceive theology and Christian education to be inseparable courses of study that inter-relate both to things pertaining to God and Christianity, but the both have the same goal which is to impart spiritual truth. A Christian educator could be referred to as a theologian, likewise the opposite.

The office of a minister of education is one of a divine calling. This is an office designed by God to serve in one of the many capacities of other gifts to bring profitability and edification to the body of Christ. The diversified role of the minister of education allows him to fill in other areas of the body where a need may be. Because the role of the educator is one of a spiritual nature, it is important that the educator takes his position seriously and conduct himself in a spiritual manner. There is no way a minister of education could isolate himself and his duties from spirituality. The only way he can succeed in his ministry is to follow the footsteps of Jesus Himself. Any office that relates to the body of Christ is spiritual in nature. Fulfilling such role requires a spiritual approach. Except the educator acknowledges God in all his ways, he will find it difficult in being effective. The Bible says that in all our ways we should acknowledge Him and He will direct our path (Proverbs 3:5).

A teacher should be a role model for those he comes in contact with. The role he plays is a spiritual one. At all times he should be mindful that he represents God and His values before those he works for and with. This means that he has to lay down a paradigm for others to follow after. However, despite his spiritual role, he needs not to forget also his responsibility to his family and others. In all that a believer does, among his priorities he should have an hierarchy that places God first, his family next, followed by his church, and then his community. The leadership that one upholds is to serve as a guide in the quest for guidance by many. Because this leadership role is terrestrial in nature and not a celestial, all of the concerns of the terrestrial are of a paramount importance, which include the meeting of the natural needs. As placed in the role of leadership, one is watched closely and scrupulously by others. One as a leader has to be careful about his role because the enemy is out there to criticize his leadership as a means of destroying him. The minister's home should be one of a good example to defend the ministry he promotes. Factually, the home is where an individual begins his ministry. The Bible affirms this as saying that whoever desires an office of a bishop ought to be a good keeper of his home (I Timothy 3:1-4). *Bishop* in the passage represents the place of leadership. In other words, the office that ones seeks does not have to only be that of a bishop before being subject to the scripture, it is any official role in the church.

One who aspires to leadership must first submit himself to the rule of another, that is, to discipline and work on himself. Maturity first has to be attained before trying to lead others. Of course, this does mean that no one could lead without being taught or lead. One hundred percent of the time great leadership depends on the role of a thorough and disciplined person, one who is spiritually mature and has a heart to care for others. Leadership is not only leading but caring as well, therefore, good leaders have to watch out about their nature of empathy and sympathy. How a hired or called educator relates to the people he interacts with will very well speaks volumes about who he is and what he is about. Apostle James says that believers should remember to practice what they believe by being doers of the word and not hearers only (James 1:22).

SUMMARY

A leader should know how to carry himself or herself, be cognizant of the company he or she is a part of; not to disassociate oneself from some people but to be mindful of your leadership role. Leadership breeds discipleship. Great leaders were once great followers. God has chosen you to be a light to others. He wants to use you to lead others out of darkness into His marvelous light. Professionalism is the required standard society demands today and teaching is no exception to the rule. Teaching requires more skills. Thorough *preparation* is mandatory for you who aspire professionalism. God Himself admonishes us to study to show ourselves approved unto Him, a workman needs not to be ashamed rightly dividing the word of truth (II Timothy 3:15). Teaching is a volatile position. It demands flexibility, dexterity, firmness and commitment. Moreover, the success of a good teacher will have to do with his capability of being a great *planner*. Proper planning is the key to proper management. A delegator is one who unselfishly shares his responsibility with others in order to accomplish a task. A teacher should be a role model for those he comes in contact with. The role he plays is a spiritual one. At all times he should be mindful that he represents God and His values before those he works for and with. The leadership that one upholds is to serve as a guide in the quest for guidance by many. Because this leadership role is terrestrial in nature and not a celestial, all of the concerns of the terrestrial are of a paramount importance, which include the meeting of the natural needs.

ASSESSMENT

1. What is required of a leader?

2. What is noted of great leaders?

3. In terms of discipleship, how is a leader viewed.

4. Is professionalism necessarily required in church leadership, why or why not?

5. What role does a leader play in the church?

PERSPECTIVES

With much of his time at Harvard University and Union Theological Seminary, Paul Tillich tries to define "faith" through Philosophy and theology. He views faith as an "ultimate human concern." He believes faith is the most centered act of the human mind. In his words, "faith is a total and centered act of personal self, the act of unconditional infinite and ultimate concern" (Alston, 481-484).[121] Drawing an inference from Emil Brunner, Alston shares these few thoughts, "Neither can there be philosophy of religion in the strict sense of the term in the realm of Christian Theology, for . . . theology has to do not with religion but with revelation" (Alston, 422).[122]

What is your reponse to the aforementioned schools of thought, heretical, apologetic, or liberalistic? Could you scripturally support your position?

---

[121] William P. Alston, Religious Belief and Philosophical Thought: Readings in the Philosophy of Religion. New York: Harcourt, Brace & World, Inc., 1963.

[122] Ibid., 422.

CHAPTER TWELVE

Greek etyma

Abase—Tapenoō (ταπεινόω) signifies to make low, bringing low, to bring to an humble condtion, to humble oneself.

Ability, able (N)—Dunamis (δύναμις) power and ability as residing in a person, power in action as performing miracles. Dunamai (V) (δύναμαι) to have power; Hikanoō, corresponding to the adjective hikanos, signifies to make competent, to qualify, to make sufficient; Echō (ἔχω) your ability, being able, to have the means of

Access—Prosagōgē (προσαγωγή) bringing into the presence of, denotes the freedom to enter through the assistance or favor of another.

Witness—Martus or Martur (μάρτυς) martyr, one who bears witness by his death, of those who witness for Christ by their death, Those whose lives and actions testify to the woth and effect of faith and whose faith received witness in Scripture.

GOD'S OVERVIEW OF YOUR GIFT/ CALLING

Faith is to believe on the word of God, what we do not see, and its reward is to see and enjoy what we believe (St. Augustine)

Ephesians 4:4-6
KJV

4 There is one body, and one Spirit, even as ye are called in one hope of your calling;

NASB

4 There is one body and one Spirit, just as also you were called in one hope of your calling;

The focus of Paul's message is "unity." Paul perhaps senses the misunderstanding and misconception of the saints at Ephesus regarding the operation of the various gifts in the church. Some felt that all these gifts were not needed in the church anyway because they could bring about disharmony instead of unity. Others thought that their gifts entitled them to automatically assume leadership in the church above their pastors or leaders in their communities. God's gift is not to divide but unite. Paul believes some saints were accustomed to the way society operated and they thought that division could easily occur in the church with all these offices being in operation. Some also professed that they did not know why these gifts were provided by God to the community, perhaps, some at least felt that they must have been important, as others perhaps might have thought that disunity and confusion will prevail in the midst of all these gifts being operated in the church, and they did not need all this in the community. God is not an author of confusion. He will not be a part of anything that confuses His creatures or creation (see I Corinthians 14:33

Therefore, Paul is trying to educate the saints on "grace or the new covenant" through Christ. He tells them that under the new covenant grace, love, and humility are interrelated characteristics that interact or saturate together and co-exist. The church is built on Christ, and no one else. When we talk about Christ, love is incorporated with him as a sacrifice for humanity's redemption. It was grace that brought Christ down to save the world, and He humbled himself to carryout this mission. Therefore, under grace love is present as well as humility. Paul tells the saints that when they express love one to another, especially to Christ and have passion for their respective gifts, unity will abound. I do not think any reference of the apostle was made to the history of the "Tower of Babel" in the Old Testament where with unity or one language the people decided to build a tower to heaven and the Lord confounded their language, and scattered them abroad (cf. Genesis 11:1-9). That entire scenario has no relationship to what Paul is addressing in Ephesus. Factually, the act of the people of Babel was a rebellious one; they decided to even make a name for themselves, i.e., they took God out of the picture. However, I may divert and pose an interpolation of this subject relating to the preceding verse in the Old Testament. A spiritual lesson can be learned here; physically in unity, a community could not stand but spiritually it can. In the Old Testament the spirit of God was not dwelling in the people, rather it was dwelling with them. So, I could say that the confounding of their language by God did bring about permanent separation and division at the time due to the absence of the spirit among them less much to say in them.

The Bible says "God scattered them abroad from thence upon the face of the earth" (cf. v 8). This means that God placed a barrier between Him and them, which shows the distancing of Himself from these people. Therefore, I can say that under grace with the presence of the Spirit of God in the believers, although their native tongues may be different, they can still work together in unity. However, if Paul thought that some of these Jewish scholars might have relayed that idea to others about Babel, then he was doing his best to erase that off their minds and let them know that under grace the Law and everything else has changed. In Grace God is dealing with humanity differently, in order for God to established a continued fellowship with humanity, He must unite humanity. It is through grace and Calvary this unity is being established. Therefore, Paul explains to the believers that they are all one in Christ, grace unites us as one body through Christ. With the Spirit of Christ in them and upon them they can work in harmony. They have only one mission or hope of their calling, and that is to please God and work diligently for the Kingdom of God.

Exegesis of Ernest Best on Ephesians 4:4

"One body" is referred to the church, not the physical body of Christ or the Eucharistic image of Christ. The Spirit is associated with the body, not in anthropological terms but spiritually divine terms. The church is called to "hope." Now hope is a part of their inheritance. "Hope" is not the feeling of hopefulness but is the content of their hope (res sperata) which is consistent with the connection of the Spirit whose first-fruits they have already received (The International Critical Commentary, 367-368).[123]

---

[123] Ernest Best, A Critical and Exegetical Commentary on Ephesians. Edinburg: T & T Clark, 1998.

Exegesis from the Anchor Bible on Ephesians 4:4

"Hope" signifies the substance of hope rather than just the psychic disposition of hopefulness. The unity of the church is not constituted by something underneath or inside the church or her several members. Rather, it is eschatological: the reason for the church's hope for unity, and for commitment to unity is "deposited in heaven" [(Colossians 1:5) The Anchor Bible, 429].[124]

Exegeses of Kuhn and Other Exegetes

Ephesians 4:4-6

The unity of the new humanity created in Christ (2:14-16) is exemplified by the church's unity, fostered by the virtues that make life in common a reality: humility, gentleness, patience, and forbearance. The inspiration for the passage is Col 3:12-15. Verses 4, *one body*: The mention of being called in one body in Col 3:15 leads to a seven-part statement of the pervasiveness of the unity that must characterize Christian life. Verse 5, *one Lord*: Cf. I Cor 8:6. This is particularly important because of the Gentile background of the readers and because of the author's emphasis on the subjection of all the heavenly powers of Christ (1:20-20). *One faith, one baptism*: Unity in faith may be regarded in this letter as unity of belief. It denotes the teachings to which all members of the church subscribe. As institutional Christianity emerges in the post-apostolic period, faith becomes the acceptance of an authoritative apostolic tradition (see 2:20), which can be distinguished from the false doctrine (4:14). The reference to unity in baptism is fitting here within the ecclesiological perspective of Ephesians (Pauline Theology, 82:125-26).[125]The new life to which Christians are called in the church (4:1) is entered into at baptism, the formal initiation into the body (cf. Col 2:9-12). Verse 6, *above all . . . through all . . .* and *in all*: A statement of monotheism (cf. Deut 6:4; Rom 3:30; I Cor 8:5-6) culminates the series.

The transcendence and all-pervasiveness of God are described by the fourfold repitition of *panta*, "all."

The unity of the Spirit in the bond of peace is the O.T. creed in N.T. language. One . . . One . . . One . . . - The word is repeated seven times, each time attached to a noun: body . . . Spirit . . . hope . . . Lord . . . faith . . . baptism . . . God. As the Christian churches of the twentieth century wrestle against unity, these verses can be a charter and a guide. Our century is being called, so it plainly appears, to great unifying

---

[124] Joseph A. Fitzmyer, The Anchor Bible: Romans, A New Translation with Introduction and Commentary. New York: Doubleday, 1993.

[125] Raymond E. Brown, Joseph A. Fitzmyer, Roland E. Murphy, The New Jerome Biblical Commentary. Englewood Ckifts: Prentice Hall, Inc., 1990, p 889.

adventures. The sevenfold formula relates the unity of the church to the unity of Christ and God. It has a background in formulas framed by Hellenstic Judaism to link in a similar way the unity of people, temple, and law with the unity of God. The simple formula of the Shema, "hear, O Israel: the Lord our God, the Lord is one" (Deut 6:4). This was the point of departure for a number of more elaborate affirmations. In Zech. 14:9, an oracle belonging to the Greek period, it is declared that the unity of God must issue in the unity of religion: The Lord shall be King over all the earth: in that day shall there be one Lord, and his name one." Josephus, in a great apologia for Judaism, affirms that "there is but one temple of the one God (for the like is ever dear to all), common to all as God is common to all" (Agains Apion II. 193) Philo holds that "since God is one, there should be only one temple" (On Special Laws I. 67); and the Apocalypse of Baruch (tr. Charles), in affirming the claims of Judaism against Christianity, proudly claims, "we are all one celebrated people, who have received one law from One." More directly, however, certain Pauline formulations link the unity of Christ as the one lord of Christian worship, with the unity of God (I Cor. 8:6, "For us there is one God, the Father . . . and one Lord, Jesus Christ . . . "); there is also a clear dependence on the language of I Cor. 12:12-13. The greater elaboration of the formula and the rhetorical structure are probably due to pagan literary influence; Stoicism especially delighted in the creation of multiple expressions of the unity of all aspects of life, arguing from the unity of the Cosmo to the unity of God, of Being, of Law, of Logos, and of Truth (as in a sentence from Marcus Aurelius, cited by Dibelius, *ad loc.*). In the unstable fissaparous society of the Roman Empire the quest for a principle of unity was pursued with a truly desperate earnestness on all levels, theoretical and practical alike. Unlike the pagan philosophies, however, the Christian teaching did not proceed from an unsubstantial faith in the unity of the cosmos to an inference of the unity of God; on the contrary, it started from the conviction that God is one, and made all other aspects of unity, present and prospective, to rest upon the foundation of the unity of God.

The church is one in body and in spirit and in the goal on which its hope is set because it owes allegiance to one Lord and worships one God. Its unity is of the same order as the unity of Christ and of God; as there cannot be other gods or other lords, so there cannot be other churches.

Exegesis of Origen on Ephesians 4:3

Endeavoring to keep the unity of the Spirit in the bond of peace. KJV

Origen points out the consequences of negativity being reaped in the absence of true unity in the church or Christian community: He who has been perfected in the same mind and in the same judgment (I Corinthians 1:10) of the truth and of the truth and of the *logos* and of wisdom with his neighbor preserves the unity of the Spirit. But we dissect it into many parts whenever we do not all speak the *same thing*, and for this reason there are schisms among us (I Corinthians 1:10) and we are not eager to preserve the unity of the Spirit. Even though God gives diversities of gifts, He nevertheless, preserves the same Spirit, and even though diversities of ministries are given, He, nevertheless, maintains the same Lord, and even though diversities of activities are given, nevertheless the same God who works all things in all continues [(I Corinthians 12:4-6) Origen and Jerome on Ephesians, 166]. The usage of *logos* and *same think* in the passage refers contextually to the unity of the spoken word, message, thought, or thing which exemplifies an agreement in perspective of the believers and the Christian community.

Exegesis of Jerome on Ephesians 4:3-4

Endeavoring to keep the unity of the Spirit in the bond of peace.
There is one body, and one Spirit, even as ye are called in one hope of your calling; KJV

It is rightly said to the Ephesians who have already attained the unity of the Holy Spirit, diligently to keep the unity of the Spirit in the bond of peace. For on who has something is admonished to be diligent to keep it but one who does not have it is ordered to be zealous that he may be able to have it. For whenever we do not all speak the same thing and one says, I am of Paul, I of Apollos, I of Cephas (I Corithians 1:12), we divide the unity of the Spirit and tear it into parts and members. Let no one immediately object. How then, are there divers graces and various gifts when the unity of the Spirit is to be guarded? There are, indeed, various gifts, but the same Spirit; and diverse ministries but the same God who works all things in all [(I Corinthians 12:5) Origen and Jerome on Ephesians, 167].[126] Both Origen and Jerome emphasize on the importance of unity in the church amidst diversity. Diversity, not in terms of chaos or schisms, rather, in terms of various gifts and ministries being functional within the same Christian community or the church. However, should division surface among the believers in the church due to a power struggle or fame, the Spirit of unity will not exist. Therefore, God will not be in the midst because God is not the author of confusion.

Tyndale New Testament Commentaries on Ephesians 4:3-6

The exegetical features of the scholars in Tyndale's commentaries elaborated on how the church can maintain unity in the midst of diversity. The commentators view that it is necessary for the church to learn how to function together in the body of Christ. In verse three, some have taken the unity of the Spirit here to mean the spiritual

---

[126] Ronald E. Heinne, The Commentaries of Origen and Jerome on St Paul's Epistle to the Ephesians. Oxford: Oxford University Press, 2002.

unity of the church in the sense that human spirits are linked together wherever men and women are found sharing things that they have in Christ. Paul views the unity as the gift of God which was made possible by the cross of Christ (2:14), and is made effective by the working of the Spirit of God, not man.

Human beings cannot themselves create it; it is given to them, but their responsibility is to keep it, to guard it in the face of many attempts from within and without the church to take it away, Christians are to be eager to maintain the unity. The Greek participle *spoudazontes* coveys the idea of zealous effort and care (cf. I Thessalonians 2:17; II Timothy 2:15; II Peter 1:10, 15; 3:14). In verse four the apostle is aware of temperament and strife amongst the believers and the diverse racial and social backgrounds from which they have come into the Christian church; but would have the saints even more aware of the spiritual realities that now unite them and that should completely transcend their differences. Paul emphasizes on the equal shares of both Jews and Gentiles of grace. It is the privilege of grace that brings about a commonality of unity by the Spirit and the body of Christ, the church. The corporate unity of the church is not a desirable end, but a datum to which the behavior of its members must conform. They are brought together to be one body in Christ. There is an allegiance and affirmation to the unity of the Spirit, as Lordship, and Creator (TNTC, 119-121).[127]

Diversity in Unity (Ephesians 4:7-16)

No one has all the gifts; and also it is true that no member of the body is without some spiritual task and spiritual gift for it. To each, not only ministers or leaders, such grace is given *according to the measure of Christ's gifts*. Concerning spiritual gifts, the gifts are the members of the church. To Christ, 'To Christ', says Calvin, 'we owe it that we have ministers of the gospel.' The church may appoint people to different work and functions, but unless they have the gifts of the Spirit, and therefore are themselves the gifts of Christ to His church, their appointment is valueless. The expression also 'serves well to remind ministers that the gifts of the Spirit are not for the enrichment of oneself but for the enrichment of the church' (Allan). Linked together (by the same article in Greek) are *pastors* and *teachers*. Pastors and teachers were gifted to be responsible for the day-to-day building up of the local church.

Apostles and evangelists have a special task of planting or establishing churches. Prophets bring in a particular from God to address a situation. The pastors are to feed the flock with spiritual food and see to it that they are protected from spiritual danger. The [Greek *pros*] *equip the saints for* [Gk. *eis*] the work of ministry, for [Gk.

---

[127] F. F. Bruce, Tyndale New Testament Commentaries, Revised Edition. The Letter of Paul to the Romans: An Introduction and Commentary. Leicester: Inter-Varsity Press, 1988.

eis] *building up the body of Christ*. The ministry of the church is given to it to equip the saints. The Greek word *energeia* is what the apostle uses to mean *working properly* as a whole united in Christ. Each part, in its place and according to its need, must have this functioning that is made possible by the energizing of God in the whole (TNTC, 122-133).[128]

Exegesis on James 1:17

James 1:17

17 Every good and every perfect gift is from above, and cometh down from the Father of lights, with whom is no veriableness, neither shadow of turning.

The above verse shows that there may be other gifts that may not be classified as "good" and "perfect." Of course these types of endowments may not be from the "Father of lights," perhaps from the "father of darkness" I supposed, Satan. There are many talented and gifted people in the world who devote their loyalty to the work of the devil. I am not talking about non-Christian professionals or scientists. There are people out there who deliberately work in opposition to the creativity of God and campaign to bring destruction against the establishments of God. These are people who one could deem to be disciples of the anti-christ if you will. However, getting to the point, promotion, position, or endowment only from above is genuine and guranteed (see Psalm 75:6). It is God who can put one up and bring one down. A "good" and "perfect" gift is one that originates from God, the "Father of lights." This is a gift that is perfectly designed for the beneficiary or recipient to carryout a specific task in a needed setting.

The gift is just right and suits the occasion for where it is intended. This type of gift, if you will, may have a permanent bearing on you provided you nurture it and utilize it diligently, it may somewhat tend to be a part of your life. Having it as a part of your life, enables you to be blessed continuously by God. Your gift will make room for you (cf. Proverbs 18:16). Just like how the verse alludes to the constancy of God's character as saying that there is no "variableness" or "shadow of turning" in God. God expects the same constancy of unchangeableness in character from you, the recipient of His divine gift. Passion and diligence must be a part of the recipient's life. God gives an individual a gift because there is a need for its usage in the community, and the person must perform and be not like the prophet Jonah who changed course with God. God will not give one a gift just because He feels like doing it, there must be a purpose for that gift being issued.

---

[128] F. F. Bruce, Tyndale New Testament Commentaries, Revised Edition.The Letter of Paul to the Romans: An Introduction and Commentary. Leicester: Inter-Varsity Press, 1988.

Exegesis of H. Greeven

James 1:17

"Every gift is good and every present is perfect." What counts is the gift not its value but the giver's intention. A deeper meaning is added, explaining the source of all created goodness: Every gift comes from above. *Father of lights*: The expression seems intended to refer to God as creator of the heavenly luminaries, the prime instance of his giving good gifts. Unlike heavenly bodies whose movements according to times and seasons result in corresponding variations in the light they send forth, their creator is unchanging; therefore, His goodness diminishes not.

In I Corinthians 14:1 and 12, there were some church members in Corinth who did not understand that the gift given to someone by God was for a divine reason. Some of the members were literally trying to compare gifts amongst themselves for spiritual gifts. In fact, Paul told them that these were spiritual gifts designed to accomplish a spiritual mission which was to bring spiritual growth and edification to the church. In other words, Paul is saying although it is good to desire spiritual gifts from God, one should know that the approach and concept surrounding this cause is one of love and compassion, not lust and competition. God usually uses a person as a vessel to help carry out His divine cause. Not because one is used as a vessel by God means that person should carry a chip on the shoulder as being special and different from the rest of the people in the church. It is an individual gift for a collective cause, that is to bring edification to the church, not self. I Corinthians 12:31 shares more light on this thought. *Various Greek terms, such as "ta pneumatika," which emphasizes the spiritual origin of the gifts (pneuma means "spirit"; I Corinthians 14:1), and more often, "ta charismata," which emphasizes that the gifts are bestowed as an act of divine grace "charis" means "grace"; Romans 12:6* (HarperCollins Bible Dictionary, 1062). Achtemeir and his co-writers say that there is a distinction between "the fruit of the Spirit," which all believers have to display without any variations (Galatians 5:22 - 23) but the gifts of the Spirit do show variations from one believer to another (I Peter 4:10; Romans 12:6; I Corinthians 12:4-11).

There are four separate listings of the Spirit's gifts (Romans 12:6-8; I Corinthians 12:8-10; 12:28; 12:29-30), but since no two of the lists are identical it seems clear that no one list is intended to be definitive. The various gifts may be grouped under three general headings: The *gifts of utterance* include *prophecy* (Romans 12:6; I Corinthians 12:10, 28; I Corinthians 12:8; 14:6), with which the ability to distinguish between false true and false prophecy is closely associated (I Corinthians 12:10; 14:29 and I Thessalonians 5:19-21; *instructions* (Romans 12:7; I Corinthians 12:28; I Corinthians 14:6); *speaking in tongues* (I Corinthians 12:10, 28; 14:1-19); and ability to interpret speaking in tongues (I Corinthians 12:10, 30; 14:5, 13). The *gifts of practical ministry* are caring for the needy (Romans 12:7-8): *serving, encouraging* (TEV), contributing, *performing acts of mercy* and perhaps giving aid (I Corinthians 12:28; helping); and *administration* (I Corinthians 12:28 perhaps giving aid in Romans 12:8). *Healing* (I Corinthians 12:9, 28) and *performing miracles* (I Corinthians 12:10, 28 are *gifts of wonder working faith*, this "faith" (I Corinthians 12:9; 13:2) being distinguished from the faith "reckoned as righteousness" (Romans 4:5) of which Paul usually writes. The *gifts of apostleship*, ranked first in I Corinthians 12:28, is active in all three ways: in the ministry of the word (e.g., I Corinthians 1:17; 4:17), in pastoral care (e.g., Romans 15:25-29; Philemon), and in the working of miracles (e.g., II Corinthians 12:12; Galatians 3:5). It is notable, however, that the lists in Ephesians 4:11 and I Peter 4:10-11 include only gifts of intelligible utterances and of practical ministry; there are no references to speaking in tongues and miracle working.

"Now there are diversities of gifts, but the same spirit" (I Corinthians 12:4). Paul contextually illustrates that God allows different gifts in the church for a reason. Paul says that although there are different gifts in the church, this should not project any though of division being instituted in the church. God's gift is not to bring division in the church but rather His gifts are to be used as a synergy whereby the talents of many are brought together for the common good, which is to bring unity in the church and strengthen the work of the church. Paul emphasizes that diversity strengthens the church. Having different gifts in the church is excellent because it shares that it is the beauty of God to have these various gifts working under the same spirit with the same mission, and that is to bring more souls to Christ. Romans 12:6 shares more light on this concept, I advise you to read it.

"For the gifts and calling of God are without repentance" (Romans 11:29). Paul emphasizes how God has a way of having His mission get accomplished. He uses anyone to carry out His mission. There are no pre-requisites or corerequisites required by God before He uses anyone. Factually, God uses not only people to carryout His work, He uses animals and other things. He used a dumb Moses to deliver the Children of Israel, He used harlot Rahab in the lineage of Jesus Christ, He used a donkey to speak to a prophet, and even a whale to chastise His deserted prophet, Jonah. Therefore, the Apostle Paul is saying that one does not have to be a theologian or do anything in order for God to use him or her. The gift of God comes the way of grace through the cross not of works. Paul emphatically says that the calling and gifts of God are without repentance. Suggested readings are Ephesians 4:7, 8-13; 3:7.

"For every high priest is ordained to offer gifts and sacrifices: wherefore it is of necessity that this man have somewhat also to offer" (Hebrew 8:3) The writer of the book of Hebrew is acknowledging the role of the priesthood in the plan of God. The scripture says that the redeemed of God or believers are of a royal priesthood. A priesthood not after the similitude of what took place in the old Testament but one after manner of Christ. And because of rebirth through Christ, believers become a member of the royal priesthood of God. But believers are not made part of the priesthood just for the name of it. There are duties that priests are assigned to carryout. The scripture says that Christ brought believers out of darkness into His marvelous light to show forth His praise (I Peter 2:9). The act of praising God is expressing the awesomeness of God, witnessing about His power, attesting to His existence, sharing His love, and reaching out to the world. Although the pattern of the priestly order in the Old Testament was a shadow of a better covenant through the blood of Christ, I would like to illustrate the significance of the role of the priest in the plan of God. The priests were the chosen ones of God for a designated purpose. Although the tribe of Levi was the selected tribe from which the priests came from, not all Levites were called into the priesthood.

Therefore, those who were designated or chosen by God were unique. Let us look at some comparisons of the priestly order in the Bible; 1. In the selection process God was the selector and His judgment was based on a lot of things about the person He chose. Some of the attributes of the prospective priest or candidate were trust, obedience, faith, and commitment. "Trust," the person selected must have realized that God can count on him to carryout His work. This person has total dependency and reliance on God; "obedience," this person becomes willing to listen and do what God wants him to do; "faith," this person believes that he does not have to have a second thought about his calling because he knows that God will take care of his family; "commitment," it is the resilience and hard working attitude, willingness, and humility God sees in this person that makes Him select this person for the priesthood. 2. Holiness was the premise of God's selection. God largely speaks of Holiness. Factually God is a representation of holiness. Therefore His affiliates or appointees have to be of that nature. God declares that we have to be holy for He is holy. God will select a person who is capable of a holy lifestyle. Even an expert animal trainer knows that a grown mature animal out of the wild is untamable. A trainer will always work with an animal that is tamable. This is an example of how God is particular about the ones He chooses. Many are called but few are chosen (Matthew 20:16; 22:14). 3. Consecration, God selects someone who will not be too preoccupied with himself or other things other than godly things. This person must be willing to always live a consecrated life before God. In the Old Testament, the way God helped these priests to be daily consecrated was to have them purify their hearts as they came before the Lord. The cleaning of their body signified sanctification before God, the indispensible requisites for God's holy office whether garment or dress worn by the priest and God's anointing upon the priest as he performs his duties. The main color of the dress was white which symbolized "glory" and "holiness." The coat that covered the entire body symbolized spiritual integrity, blamelessness and righteousness in which the idea of blessedness and life are realized. It is God's purpose that his chosen one walks worthy of the vocation he has been called onto, one should live an exemplary life, maintain spiritual integrity as he or she performs God's duty, and uphold righteousness.

It is God's view that if you can represent Him in the world as He wants you to, many will be drawn to the kingdom of heaven. Selected readings are; Daniel 12:6-7; 10:5; Ezekiel 9:3; 10:2 & 7; Matthew 28:3; Revelation 7:9. As the priests were charged to discharged their duties in accordance to God's precepts and commands, so is it in the dispensation of grace. God wants those who He has set aside to carryout specific missions for Him to be obedient to His word and live it. God has called you to offer your gift or talent and sacrifice or serve with due diligence.

"Jesus answered and said unto her, if thou knowest the gift of God, and who it is that saith to thee, give me to drink thou wouldest have asked of him, and he would have given thee living water" (John 4:10). You need discernment or spiritual guidance as you see yourself in a devoted position for the Lord. Because you are carrying out a spiritual mission, you need spiritual intervention as you move along. You have to pray and ask the Lord to give you wisdom and understanding, and open your mind and give you spiritual insight about the area in which He wants you to perform. You need all the spiritual help you can get because Satan is out there to make sure you do not carryout the Lord's mission. When you are in tune to heaven, that is when you will be able to see God perform through you. Of course, the Samaritan woman could not tell whether or not Jesus was the gift from God to the world because she did not have that spiritual sight. Jesus had to reveal to her some of the things that transpired in her life before she realized that He was a prophet or an unnatural person. God wants you to be able to observe the differences between Holy and unholy and righteousness from unrighteousness. It takes maturity and spiritual adaptation to be able to both apply your human instincts and incorporate the divine knowledge of God. Suggested scriptural references are: I Timothy 4:14 and Ephesians 4:4.

"My people are destroyed for the lack of knowledge" (Hosea 4:6). This was the Lord's message through the prophet Hosea to the Children of Israel for their indulgence in sin and transgression against God and His commandments. God told Hosea to tell Israel that they have refused to continuously maintain His precepts, and that they have deliberately laid aside His laws and have taken unto themselves their own laws; ones that were coded by the heathens. But God reminds them that innocence to the law is no exception. He admonishes them that all who sin or violate His laws will bear the consequences. There is a price that must be paid for the anti-God stance anyone takes in life, and Israel was no exception. The Gentiles or the church today is chosen by God to partake in the commonwealth of Israel.

You were grafted into the divine plans of God therefore you are subject to the commission and commands of God. The emphasis of knowledge is very important to God because it was only knowledge or the willingness to know the things of God that would have kept the children of Israel on course in the precepts of God. God on many occasions had to remind the Children of Israel about their past in order for them to realize from whence they came. Through His prophets, He was able to remind Israel not to forget about the Torah, the law that Moses taught them in the wilderness regarding the deity of God and His principles, this they had to learn from their parents and priests as they grew up. It was knowledge He had designated for Moses to impart to the Priests and all Israel from childhood on through life. In other words, God was instilling some discipline or learning in His people so that their endurance and continuity in Him and His word could be one everlasting and eternal. In fact, God had a better plan for them. It was one that focused on the future of these people, Israel and Him. It all stemmed from the beginning of creation where man fell from God's grace through disobedience, and how later God decided to restore His relationship with mankind by choosing Israel as the means through which the implementation of this spiritual and natural binding can be possible. God's dealing with Israel through Moses, the priests, and the prophets were all geared towards a better hope, a covenant that would bring about a spiritual union that would serve as a nexus between God and humanity. However, in order for all this to be realized, God had to set up a training pattern that would prepare Israel for this future relationship which would eventually end up in a spiritual form. God's role in this covenant with Israel was to fulfill that which He promised, and Israel's role was to be willing to adhere to the teachings and commandments of the Lord. However, somewhere down the line, Israel fell short in maintaining her contractual role by being disobedient to God and His word. God received no repentance or reconciliation from Israel for their actions, so He, in return, chose to discipline them for not keeping up with their commitment.

Today, through the blood of Christ, many have been born into the family of God. It is not Israel anymore, but the people of God. All who accept the terms of God through the Lord Jesus Christ has automatically become a sort of spiritual Israel who must be willing to obey and adhere to the teachings of God. Much of this adherence can only be successfully achieved by continuously growing in the sight of God. Growth depends on knowledge and understanding, and there is no where else the people of God could ever find knowledge and understanding except from God. The Bible says that in Him are hid the treasures of wisdom and knowledge (Colossians 2:3). It takes much wisdom and knowledge from God in order for a child of God to live the required life God wants him to live. But, one must be willing and ready to feed on the type of nurture that is essential for such growth. Just how God designated priests and prophets to teach and lead his people, so has He today. The church today, as the body of Christ, has preachers and teachers who are designated by God to nurture God's people in the way that He intends for them to grow. Interestingly, every believer including those who are designated by God to lead ought to first mature in the precepts of God before being fit to lead others. The church as a body has to live a life similar to what God expected Israel of old to live when they were chosen through Abraham. In carrying out this cause, gifts and talents have been placed amongst the believers in a local assembly by God to perfect the saints. These talents are brought into the church to edify the church. This growth is to bring about and build a joint relationship or fellowship amongst the believers; a kind that would help to continuously hold up the principles and values of God.

The Bible admonishes believers not to forsake the assembling of themselves together as the manner of some is but exhorting one another daily as the day approaches (Hebrews 10:25). The church is on a spiritual pilgrimage, and much of this journey entails spiritual confrontations and temptations. The only way the church could endure such travel is by maturing spiritually, and spiritual growth can only be given by God. It is He who is capable of shaping and molding His children in ways that would make them strong enough to surpass the trials and tribulations this life poses for them. The need for teaching is crucial to the church's prosperity in the Lord. Growth is dependent on faith. The Bible tells us of the importance of faith, as saying that it is the only means by which a believer is able to know and live the word of God. Faith is the means by which one can please the Lord (Hebrews 11:6). The Bible says that faith comes by hearing and hearing by the word of God (Romans 10:17). As one commits his time and effort to knowing the word of God, sooner or later he will begin to experience the build-up presence of the spirit by applying the word in his life. The educational ministry of the church is essential for growth and spiritual maturity. There are lots of things that believers need knowledge for. Knowledge is a light that shines within an individual that enables him to project a light that absorbs darkness to show clear the path that lies ahead. That is why the word of God is to be taught to impart knowledge to the people of God because it is that knowledge that will build up spiritual self-esteem and assurance within the believer to make him confident of his faith.

The teaching church is one that helps its members grow stronger in the Lord by expounding on what faith is, how can one attain it, and how to grow in it. These are three elements I find to be the very foundation that the church's focus should be built on before any other preliminaries. What is Faith? The Bible teaches that faith is the substance of things hoped for, and the evidence of things not seen (Hebrews 11:1). In the entire eleventh chapter of the book of Hebrews, the writer projects an array of faithful hall of famers who walked before God during their tenure of interaction with God. One example is Abraham, who sojourned to a city whose builder and maker was God. In other words, although Abraham did not know where the Lord wanted him to go, he agreed to go under the direction of God. That in essence is a typical example of what faith is. Faith is believing that the impossible is possible. In this position, one has no other choice but to surrender to God's guidance and direction. Anyway, it is the Lord who orders our footsteps, so why should not we depend on His leading? Solomon admonishes us to acknowledge God in all our ways and he will direct our path (Proverbs 3:6). Acknowledgment to God's terms places us in a secured haven of protection and prominence. Faith can only be defined and found when one looks up to the Lord for direction. We are not to lean unto our own understanding but the Lord's because ours is sensual and misleading.

The Apostle Paul puts it this way as saying that the natural man understands not the things of God because they are foolishness unto him. The sensuality of the natural man is that of carnality which is contrary to God. No way could man in his natural state please God. In order for him to please God he must have faith and dwell in the spirit because God is a spirit and they that worship him must worship Him in spirit and in truth. It is by knowing how to live in faith that makes the need for the teaching ministry in the church crucial. However, much of the maturity process could also be learned or taught practically just from the lifestyle of the believers. Traditional teaching in Sunday school and Bible Study sessions are other ways in which maturity can be attained. This type of training and nurturing can be ascertained from no where else but the Bible. There are lots of examples and lessons one can always find in the Bible that can be instrumental in meeting the spiritual needs of the church. No scripture is of private interpretation. The Bible in itself has enough resources to validate its claims.

SUMMARY

The church is built on Christ, and no one else. When we talk about Christ, love is incorporated with him as a sacrifice for humanity's redemption. It was grace that brought him down to save the world, and he humbled himself to carryout this mission. Therefore, under grace love is present as well humility. The Spirit is associated with the body, not in anthropological terms but spiritually divine terms. The church is one in body and in spirit and in the goal on which its hope is set because it owes allegiance to one Lord and worships one God. Its unity is of the same order as the unity of Christ and of God; as there cannot be other gods or other lords, so there cannot be other churches. However, should division surface among the believers in the church due to a power struggle or fame, the Spirit of unity will not exist. The ministry of the church is given to it to equip the saints. Apostles and evangelists have a special task of planting or establishing churches. Prophets bring in a particular from God to address a situation. The pastors are to feed the flock with spiritual food and see to it that they are protected from spiritual danger. Your gift will make room for you (cf. Proverbs 18:16). The gifts of the Spirit do show variations from one believer to another. The gift of God comes the way of grace through the cross not of works, those who were designated or chosen by God were unique. Let us look at some comparisons of the priestly order in the Bible; 1. In the selection process God was the selector and His judgement was based on a lot of things about the person He chose. Some of the attributes of the prospective priest or candidate were trust, obedience, faith, and commitment. Holiness was the premise of God's selection. God largely speaks of Holiness. Factually God is a representation of holiness, therefore His affiliates or appointees have to be of that nature. 3. Consecration, God selects someone who will not be too preoccupied with himself or other things other than godly things. This person must be willing to always live a consecrated life before God. Growth depends on knowledge and understanding, and there is no where else the people of God could ever find knowledge and understanding except from God. The teaching church is one that helps its members grow stronger in the Lord by expounding on what faith is, how can one attain it, and how to grow in it.

ASSESSMENT

1. What key element has a lot to do with Christ's role in humanity's redemption?

2. What is the significance of the ministry of the church?

3. Explain Proverbs 18:16.

4. What is the mission of God's prophets?

5. Compare the priestly order with the role of the ministry in the church.

PERESPECTIVES

The Ontological Argument, the argument regarding the existence of God, states that if the being you think of has every desirable attribute except that of existence, it is not the greatest, or most perfect possible, because a being that exists is both greater and more perfect than one that does not. Therefore, the greatest most perfect possible being must exist.

CHAPTER THIRTEEN

GREEK ETYMA

Afirm—Diabebaioomai (διαβεβαόομαι) to confirm, make sure, to assert strongly.

Deacon—Diakonos (διάκονος) servant, servant of Christ in the work of preaching and teaching, or those who serve in the churches. This word is different in meaning from the Greek word

Knowledge—Gnōsis (γνῶσις) seeking to know, knowing of spiritual truth, subjectively of God's knowledge; Epignōsis (ἐπίγνωσις) discernment, recognition, a greater participation by the knower in the object known.

Mind—Nous (νοῦς) the seat of reflective consciousness, concerning the faculties of perception and understanding, of the mind of God; Ennoia (ἔννοια) an idea, notion, intent

Passion—Pathēma (πάθημα) a passive emotion

EDUCATION MINISTRY

It is faith among men that hold the moral elements of society together, as it is faith in God that binds the world to his throne (William Maxwell Evarts)

That gift of his, from God descended, Ah! Friend, what gift of man does not (Robert Browning: Christmas Eve Canto XVI)?

Christian Education and Theology are inseparable disciplines. They are interrelated, one cannot be taught without the other. Actually, they are dependent on each other for clarity and distinction in terms of pinpointing where an individual stands as a Christian before

God and man. It is very important that a Christian's conduct and attitude be representative of God's image and purpose. Christian Education is a medium of portrayal of a Christ-like life of the believers. Christians are to live the life that Jesus Himself lived when He was down here on earth. The Bible distinctly states that Christians are to always let their little light shine before men in order for the God they serve to be glorified. Wherever the application of Christian Education is apportioned, Theology has to be mentioned because Theology incorporates Christian Education. Theology is the reason why Christian ethics and Christian disciplining are of necessity to the entirety of Christendom. Theology in my own words is the science and study that focuses on the deity and attributes of God and how they relate to man and creation. God is the source of our learning process, there is nothing else we could ever try to teach or do without including God and His study as part of that which we are teaching or learning. Even down to the nitty-gritty of Christian Education, if we tried to separate the two, there would be no spiritual accomplishments at all. We would be left with education alone. Mere education is just vague and empty. In fact, some one said that education without salvation is a damnation to the human soul. In simple terms, we would only be left with secularism without putting God in the picture of our learning. Christian Education is the means by which the church learns how to keep in a holy state as God requires. By so doing, Christ will continue to be in close fellowship with the body

The church's position in the world is to maintain a constancy and consistency in terms of being propagators of the gospel of the Lord Jesus Christ. As every Christian sojourns this spiritual path of the Lord, he is charged to continuously live the life and adorn himself with the word of God as the scripture admonishes him to. The epistle of James encourages every child of God to daily apply the scriptures to his life. James continues to say that it is not only always good for believers to read the scriptures and not live that which they teach. What good it is to read the scripture and not practice what the scriptures teach. James says that if we say we are Christians and yet fail to obey a portion of the scripture, we are guilty of all (James 2:10). It is not easy surviving in this troublesome world as a Christian. That is why the teaching of the practical living and lifestyle of Christ be studied and taught by believers to help the body of Christ continue to be in the right frame of mind. It is said that a concentrated mind is never disturbed. A mind that contemplates Christ will always remain focused on Christ. Believers should let the mind of Christ to always be in them. We are living amidst a world of trials and temptations of all sorts and the only way of survival is for the people of God to be consistent in their walk with the Lord.

The Christian witness has to be one who is equipped with the word of God, doctrinally sound, and spiritually strong to lash out into the stratosphere of a world of taunts to propagate or proclaim his beliefs. Without any conviction for the love of souls and directions from the Lord or proper training, one could not just decide to step out into the unbelieving world to witness. Primarily, witnessing is not something anyone could decide to do in the spur of a moment. One has to first have the conviction to reach out to lost souls and pray to God to lead and guide him to help bring people into the kingdom of God. After one has heard from God and has been given the green light by God, the next step is for that person to prepare himself scripturally and spiritually before taking off on his mission.

One day while getting across one of His parabolic thoughts on the importance of fasting and praying, Jesus' disciples asked Him why they did not fast as the Lord supposes, Jesus told them that because He was with them they did not need to fast and pray but the time will come, He said, when they will have to. At that time, they probably did not get the message. But later on during the Lord's ministry, He brought up that same topic of discussion, but this time it was approaching the time for His departure from among them to return to glory. He told them that they would be left in a world of tribulations, trials, and temptation, and the only way out was through prayer and fasting. In fact, He told them that when He departed they would have to go back to Jerusalem and continue in prayer until they were endued with power from on high. It was the comforter, which was the Holy Ghost; He promised that would come to live in them and guide them into all things. The Apostle Paul explicitly made it clear as saying that we are in a spiritual warfare and this is such a kind that cannot be fought by flesh and blood. Instead, it is one that has to be fought in the spirit. He goes on by naming some tools of preparation believers may need to have in order to survive in this battle: having our loins girth about with truth, the breastplate of righteousness, our feet shod with the preparation of the gospel of peace, taking on the shield of faith, the helmet of salvation, and the sword of the spirit which is the word of God (Ephesians 6: 12-17). In essence, Paul admonishes the believers to put on the whole armor of God, not just some but all. It is a serious matter, not sort of a political campaign, business lobbying or sales canvassing. This has a spiritual concern and is realistic. The devil's world is one of realism, there is a real devil and there are real demons or spirits of darkness that oppose the things and people of God. Witnessing is a challenging task, a very serious one. One time there were some young men in the scripture, the sons of Sceva to be precise, who thought that they could just lay hands over a demoniac and rebuke the evil spirits out like that. But they were ought for something that they would never attempt to do for the rest of their lives. The demons in this man spoke and told them that they knew Jesus and the Apostle Paul but who were they to rebuke them out of their host? Because they had no answer, the spirits got out of the man and got into them. They uncontrollably ran into the streets possessed with the demons they had no authority over. The devil is real, therefore, to be a witness, one must first solidify his spiritual grounds before seeking training for the field.

Now-a-days, due to competition and opposition, much training is needed as one ventures out in the field to witness. With this age and time changing and advancing to new levels of knowledge, it becomes more challenging for those in Christendom aspiring to field witnessing. There is a need for better and proper training for anyone deciding to witness. Proper preparations place the believers in the right position to be ready for any confrontations that they might encounter while out on the field of soul winning. The Bible admonishes believers to always be ready to answer any man who challenges their faith. This situation, the Bible says must be answered with meekness and fear (I Peter 3:15). There are some people out there; instruments of the devil who find pleasure in challenging to the people of God. Some do it for fun and others do it because of curiosity and interest. Most of these people who attack the believers know the Bible very well. Sometimes they pose questions and scenarios that put the Christian witness on the spot. Witnessing is more than just picking up the Bible and deciding to reach out, it takes training and spiritual growth. Planning is essential in the process of training and setting up an administration. For an administration that caters to education, I find it very much in place to engineer an agenda that would meet the needs of the education department and the church.

In order for a church to have a genuine Christian education program, proper planning is needed. God believes in decency and order, therefore, anything we anticipate to do for Him must show some order and decency. Before tackling a project, one must first conduct a research. One has to dig out every piece of information he can ascertain that reflects on the subject matter or that project. If possible, there could be a committee setup where every individual will conduct his search and at a given time the group meets to share and discuss the data uncovered. The public library and the internet are suggestible resources from which most information could be gathered. However, after the search is done, the committee could be broken up into two small groups where one group would go out to conduct an external survey by getting information from other church leaders and Christians within the locale of the church, while the other group continues with assessing the data that was brought in from the research at the same time. When the external surveyors return with their findings, then the entire unit could sit together to compare and contrast the information gathered. After the pros and cons have been tabled, the committee can then focus on monetary costs or means of generating funds to operate such project. The committee will also have to think about allocating space to erect a structure; one that finds the means of meeting local government standards to govern these establishments, including staffing and programs or operating activities; in terms of what they are, how they are going to be instituted, and when are they going to be implemented as planned. When all this is taken care of, then the group can setup the administration by allotting the various offices or departments to operate.

"Line upon line and precept upon precept" are words of the Lord through His prophet regarding order and priority setting (Isaiah 28:10,13). This is an example of how organizing and coordinating departments and offices in the church is important. It is the responsibility of the church's education department to set things orderly and appropriately in the church. The education department is to make sure that the necessary departments that are needed in the church exist to function well. Also, consideration must be measured with regards to church size. In other words, a church of a certain size, let say a small church should have the right number of departments needed to smoothly handle its affairs. Likewise the departments allotted for a larger church should measure up to the needs of its membership. Of course, a small and large church would vary in terms of the number of departments allotted based on the size of their respective congregations. Nevertheless, in either case the church's leadership must be careful to not have more departments than needed because this could be costly and useless. It is the responsibility of church leaders to make sure that the right people are assigned to their respective areas. Staffing is very crucial to the growth aspect of the church. Church leaders have to pray and ask the Lord to reveal or bring the right people to fill the vacancies available to help in carrying out the functions of the church.

Without the guidance of the spirit in the selection process, appointing someone who does not have the spiritual know-how will be detrimental to the prosperity of the church. In this case, sometimes the pastor will have to send out an open invitation to volunteers who would be willing to serve. But as a point of concern, not everyone who comes up as a volunteer should be accepted. There should be a resume check, reference check, and individual church record check. It perhaps should be recommended that most of the volunteers selected should be those who are trained and qualified or have the experience for performing such task with meekness and Godly fear. Once the staffing is in perspective, then the next focus should be on assessing the effectiveness and efficiency of the various departments and their leaders. Where there seems to be some kind of a deficiency, the education committee of which the pastor is a part, would have to find a way of assisting in that area that needs help. However, the committee should be careful how they go about doing this because its action could be interpreted the wrong way by the leader of that area who has the deficiency. The committee's manner of approach should be to motivate and to chastise. Without care, the church might end up losing that person or some of its members who opposed the selection process. That person or those impacted may walk out of the church and never come back. I believe where deficiency is noticeable, additional training or additional staffing together with the leader of said departments ought to be able to work together. By doing this, it is possible that this person will gradually learn some things that he did not know before, and may be able to capitalize on them to improve in the area of his deficiency.

In administering a church educational organization, the leaders have to be precautionary in how they setup their staff and operate their departments because it could be somewhat an existence of vulnerability in losing the point of focus and the church's mission objectives. Every church has to have a mission purpose in mind. It might start from one person, the pastor, who will then reveal his vision for assessment and support. It is sometimes hard to find someone willing to share another person's vision and to work on in seeing it materialize. While getting the message across, there may be some who would envy the visionary for his ambition and refuse to support him. For the few who come around, the pastor or founder should be very careful as he tries to convey his message for support. One thing that pastors must remember is that no one is compelled to work along with him. He is neither to impose any burden on anyone nor force anyone to join him. He should neither get himself indulged in tactics or trickery to entice any one to join the church. As long as he believes that the Lord has called him, with much prayer and proper preparation, the Lord will lead people to come and join him. When the Lord brings people into the church, the pastor should be careful not to drive them out. Sometimes, leaders get too excited when their membership begins to grow. As soon as that begins to happen, leaders are apt to change their mission purpose. At first, their purpose was God-ordained but now they see their membership increasing, so they decide to engineer another purpose which becomes one that is sensual and greed-driven.

When this happens, the pastor has to watch out because the same God who elevated him is able to bring him down. As a pastor begins to sway from his mission purpose, he gives room to Satan to invade his ministry. In fact, it would be an easy takeover by Satan without any hassle. With all the temptation, no one pastor is able to do it all by himself without having God continuously as the nucleus of his ministry. Christ must always be the center of a pastor's mission plan. As a church loses it purpose, secular learning takes dominance, and sooner or later, this organization which once started as a religious entity would end up being a secular one.

Specialized education is necessary provided there is a need. Churches should not get into any extraordinary work or project that would create a lot of constraints on them financially. But if there is an ardent need for such learning to take place, then a church could go ahead and undertake the project. Areas of specialized education could be some of which cater to the needs of disabled members, seniors, pre-school children, and slow-learning students who are members of the local assembly. These are also means by which churches could gain extra membership. A program of this sort would appeal to the entire community and not only church members. This agenda would show that this is a church that cares about the well being of all, not only spiritually but physically as well. This is what James, the writer of the epistle had to say about the perfect law of liberty, this is what he refers to as visiting the sick and the widows, doing justly, and catering to the needs of needy (James 2:12-15). The church has to reach out to all because God does not pick and choose.

An effective and productive administration exists as the result of the competent staff it has to run its affairs. Even from an aggregate perspective, business become successful because of the trained managers that run them. In order for growth to take place, there must be an application of genuine effort on the part of all those who are involved. There must be skills, resources, and dedication exhibited within the milieu of that setting or body. Before a church decides to operate an education department, there must be someone capable to oversee its operations. Many times a task may become difficult to manage because of limited knowledge, limited skills and experience. Nowadays, due to the high pressure of competition in the business world, companies are driven to look for skillful and experienced applicants. The standard that most of the corporate sector lays out today is to look for someone with a college degree. It is believed that training a college graduate would be less hassled than training a high school graduate. However, in some instances, although one may have his degree, some still base their search on experience. Companies in return ask the applicant whether he has any experience. This really becomes heartbreaking to some who have earned their degrees and are in search of jobs. Now they need to have the experience even though they have just graduated college.

The most frequently asked question by these graduates is "how do they expect us to have an experience when we just graduated?" Most employers today prefer hiring someone with experience as opposed to hiring someone with only a college degree. Nevertheless, the degree is a plus to the person's professional profile. Experience is the key. Experience proves that one is exposed to a certain type of job, and that he knows what it takes to get it done. If a church does not have experienced leaders around to run its education department, it could seek help from an outside source to train one or two persons, and later on, these individuals who have been trained can train as many members as necessary who are interested to work in the education department. It is better to have trained than untrained people working. A company sometimes incurs a loss due to unnecessary spending and costs. If checked properly, the financial statements of these companies would show how their operational expenditures exceeded their revenues, and would show that much of the weight was due to inadequate staffing, poor management, and high wages. When there is an inadequacy in leadership, serious consequences are bound to occur. If leadership flawed due to lack of competence, the entire operation will suffer. Therefore, it is very important to have trained leaders and staffers operating the education department in the church. In fact, there should be trained people working in every department of the church.

The critical stage in the life of a believer or convert is the beginning of his life in the church. At this point, even though this person is converted, he constantly goes through a battle of finding his place in the church. He has now become a member of an environment he has never been a part of before. Lots of adjustments have to be made on his part. It is like an infant trying to adapt to its new environment. When going through the stages of growth. A new Christian experiences pressure not only from his "old man" or old ways and habits, but just for taking on a new role, makes one vulnerable to lots of pressure; both internal and external. There are pressures from unsaved parents or homes, also from his peers. With all this happening in the world of this person, the pastor or spiritual leader should be sensitive to the needs of this member and reach out to spiritually shelter him. This person needs a place like the church where he could come to any time and commune with people who have extended their lovely arms as a family. The members of the church should have open arms toward the new converts because if such warmth does not exist in the church, that kind of mean attitude will drive the new Christians away. New Christians need to be fed first with "milk" and then with "meat" or "substance." Much care should be given. Patience and love should always be the twins that shadow the teaching environment of the new Christians. At such a premature stage, proper training is needed because if not, the convert would grow unnourished. The Bible says that we should train up the child in the way he should grow and when he is old he will not depart from it (Proverbs 22:6). A child's behavior is developed from the attitude its environment offers it or exposes it to. Mistakes made during the nurturing of the child are likely registered in the child's memory. To the child, there is no distinction of behaviors. The child cannot determine that certain behavior is wrong or unacceptable, as long as the child sees an adult behavior being displayed a certain way in its environment, it takes it to be acceptable and proper. As in the scenario about the child, so is it with a new Christian, at that stage of development, everything that is taught and practiced by the church would register in the mind of the new Christian as being right. Therefore, the upbringing of a new Christian in the church must be handled properly. Teaching and nurturing should have their foundation basically built upon the scripture.

    A spiritual leader should be concerned about when and how to outreach. This is a critical area in the ministry because the church is reaching out to outsiders and at the same time interacting with other people, some of whom are not Christians or believers. Also, one should take into consideration that this outreach initiative is such that censures satan's kingdom. The unsaved people the church intends to witness to are the devil's own, and satan would not want the church to take any of his followers out of his kingdom. This is an area where much prayer and experience are needed. Those mature believers should be the ones on such a team because the anti-godly forces out there are serious about not surrendering any of their own to the Lord. The pastor would have to get closely involved with the outreach team because this is an important area. This is how members are brought into the church, but it is not that easy to win someone over. The outreach ministry of the church must have a staff of dedicated and trained members who are willing to sacrifice their time and service to witnessing for the Lord.

    There are lots of things involved in witnessing. The trained staffs should know the area the outreach team is going to meet, or if they are not familiar with the area, prior to scheduling the meeting for that site, they could conduct a survey and get information about the area, the residents, the community and the economic clouds that overshadow the area. With this information, the outreach team can know how to organize themselves and know what to expect when they get there.

If there is a need to re-invent the entire education ministry in the church, the leaders can go ahead and do it but they have to be very careful not to completely destroy the ministry's original image. Sometimes, mixing in new wine with the old tends to destroy the flavor of the wine. The wines could both be from the same source but because one is fresher than the other, the taste of both together may be unpleasant. Perhaps, the application of ingredients in the production process might differ from each other. As in the above analogy, so is it in the process of renewing or recreating something that was once established. Caution is very much needed. Renewal is to only refurbish and slightly create; not to totally tear down the old for something new. Before one destroys an existing project, he must realize what the outcome will be. To start something new is not easy a task. One who destroys without any prior knowledge and preparation is headed for a tough start. There is an adage that says it is hard to teach old dogs new tricks. Of course, to a certain extent, I believe that it all depends on whether the "old dogs" are cohesive for change and are ready to see it transpire. On the contrary, if the "old dogs" are rebellious and do not want change, that makes things worse. It is hard for people to easily give up their old ways for something new, but, it also depends on the technique or approach of the architect of change, that is, the soul-winner. If he is one who is aggressively forcing others to accept change, then not only would people be rebellious, many might quit being a part of the group. Should there be a need for renewal, much prayer must be done for God to guide the process. The leaders should be patient and go about witnessing one step at a time.

Whether in a small or large church, the pastor's role in the Christian Education affairs is very important. Although the Bible says a pastor should be apt to teach, even if the pastor realizes that he has a weakness in this area, he still has to be involved. He should not make himself scarce in the affairs of the department. If the pastor is uncomfortable, he could appoint a capable person to work along with him to oversee the work. In doing this, he would gradually learn a whole lot from this person.

Most of the time, the only way the units in the church can function properly is when the presence of the pastor is consistent and his endorsement or approval for a proposal to be carried out is unquestionable. Therefore, a pastor should never avoid being active in the various departments and activities that go on. It has a motivating impact on the members when they find their leader utilizing his leadership role effectively. By the same token, the pastor should also be careful not to over do himself. In the case of a large church, as opposed to a small one, the pastor could sectionalize the education department and appoint trained and dedicated members to assist him in overseeing the work. No group wants to see a burned out leader. Once the leader is not functioning as he should, chaos is soon to occur. It is at this point satan then gets the liberty to creep into the church. Therefore, to avoid losing their church, leaders have to be willing to share their responsibility if they realize that the anticipating task is too much for them alone to handle. Pastors are to do the same. A pastor would not like to see his vision go down the drain as being unheard of without any materialization. If the work is too much, do as Moses father-in-law, Jethro told him to do, to share the responsibility with the able ones.

SUMMARY

The church's position in the world is to maintain a constancy and consistency in terms of being propagators of the gospel of the Lord Jesus Christ. As every Christian sojourns this spiritual path of the Lord, he is charged to continuously live the life and adorn himself with the word of God as the scripture admonishes him to. The Christian witness has to be one who is equipped with the word of God, doctrinally sound, and spiritually strong to lash out into the stratosphere of a world of taunts to propagate or proclaim his beliefs. Without any conviction for the love of souls and directions from the Lord or proper training, one could not just decide to step out into the unbelieving world to witness. Primarily, witnessing is not something anyone could decide to do in the spur of a moment. One has to first have the conviction to reach out to lost souls and pray to God to lead and guide him to help bring people into the kingdom of God. Without the guidance of the spirit in the selection process, appointing someone who does not have the spiritual know-how will be detrimental to the prosperity of the church. A spiritual leader should be concerned about when and how to outreach. This is a critical area in the ministry because the church is reaching out to outsiders and at the same time interacting with other people, some of whom are not Christians or believers. Leaders have to be willing to share their responsibility if they realize that the anticipating task is too much for them alone to handle.

ASSESSMENT

1. How does the church maintain constancy and consistency regarding the kingdom of God?

2. Who is a Christian witness?

3. Why would one need spiritual guidance to witness?

4. Why should a spiritual leader be concerned about when and how to outreach?

5. Is sharing responsibility necessary in ministry, why or why not?

PERSPECTIVE

The Teleological Argument, the argument that the universe exhibits design and purpose: the acorn becomes the oak, the stars move in predictable course, everything seems to be acting out of some purpose or plan (Magee, 57).[129]

---

[129] Bryan Magee, The Story of Philosophy: The Essential Guide to the History of Western Philosophy. London: Dorling Kindersley Publishing, 1998.

CHAPTER FOURTEEN

GREEK ETYMA

Ambassador—(N) Presbeia (πρεσβεία) eldership, denotes experience and maturity.

Apostolē (ἀποστλή) a mission, apostleship

Craft man—Technitēs (τεχνίτης) artisa, maker, innovator; Ergasia (ἐργασία) diligence; dēmiourgos, one who works for the people, whose work stands out in the puplic (dēmos, people, ergon, work).

Doulos, a bondservant, slave. Diakonos revies a servant in relationship to his work, and doulos reviews a servant in relationship to his master.

Praise—Ainos (αινος) only of praise to God; Aineō (αἰνέω) always use of praise to God; Humneō (ὑμνέω) to sing, to laud, sing to the praise of

Prothesis (πρόθεσις) of the purposes of God.

Purpose—Boulēma (βούλημα) to will, a deliberate intention;

THE PURPOSE OF YOUR GIFT

Ephesians 4:11-16

11 And he gave some, apostles; and some prophets; and some, evangelists; and some, pastors and teachers;

12 For the perfecting of the saints, for the work of the ministry, for the edifying of the body of Christ:

13 Till we all come in the unity of the faith, and of the knowledge of the Son of God, unto a perfect man, unto the measure of the stature of fullness of Christ:

14 That we henceforth be no more children, tossed to and fro, and carried about with every wind of doctrine, by the sleight of men, and cunning craftiness, whereby they lie in wait to deceive;

15 But speaking the truth in love, may grow up into him in all things, which is the head, even Christ:

16 From whom the whole body fitly joined together and compacted by that which every joint supplieth, according to the effectual working in the measure of every part, maketh increase of the body unto the edifying of itself in love.

Here, the Apostle Paul is laying out the blueprint if you will of the Christian ministry in the community. Paul is telling his audience that Christ did not come to planet earth just to minister for a few days, die, resurrect, and ascend to heaven. God's purpose for coming into the world in human form was to redeem humanity. In order for this mission to fully be accomplished, He had to get resurrected and ascend to heaven to be able to come back in a non-corporeal form as the Spirit or Comforter to to aid humanity in the process of possibly being eternally redeemed someday form this corruptible sphere. In this process, Christ provides various gifts and allows different ministries to exist within the community to realize this hope of redemption. The apostle goes on to name the various ministries or offices the Christian community should have in order to effectuate the Lord's puepose: *Apostles*, the word apostle is from the Greek word *apostolos* which literally means one sent forth (*apo*, from *stellö*, to send [see John 17:3; Luke 6:13; I Cor. 9:1; Acts 14:4]). In the gospels we see Jesus selecting twelve men to follow Him. After His resurrection, He commissioned these men including Paul to be pillars of the ministry down here on earth. The commission charged to these men was a special one. Today, it provides a spiritual hierarchal autonomy in the church.

These apostles were charged to oversee the work of Christ and make sure that they multiply His work. *Prophets*: prophet originates from the Greek word *prophëtës* which means one who speaks forth or openly proclaims a divine message (see Amos 3:7,8; Numbers 11:17-20; Matthew 5:12; Matt 10:41; Rom. 17:3). In the Old Testament the prophets were used as God's mouthpiece. They spoke to the people on God's behalf. They were mediators between God and the people. Likewise in the New Testament, prophets are designated in the church to reveal any divine message the Lord chooses to channel through specific individuals for the community.

God is certainly a great "economist" if you will. The division of labor is being applied here. Before, in the O.T. God used one person to carryout more than one mission for Him in the community, but in the N.T., it is a different story because of "grace," God decides to spread out His spiritual wealth amongst the believers within the community. Instead of having one person doing more than one work or duty, God decided that He can use more than one person in the community by providing various gifts and offices to operate. Therefore, a prophet in this church age does the same divine speaking for God but this is a specific ministry or office. Nevertheless, in this church age Christ still endows people with more than one gift but the opportunity of having others also used by God is in abundance. In the O.T., a single prophet was gifted as a teacher, preacher, miracle worker, evangelist, and leader. *Evangelists:* Evangelist comes from the Greek word *euangelistës* which means a preacher of the Gospel (see Acts 21:8; II Tim. 4:5 euangelizö, to proclaim glad tidings). An evangelist is one who goes around preaching the gospel message. As opposed to a preacher or pastor, an evangelist is not stationary. This is an office that requires mobility.

The message of an evangelist can be stern or uncomfortable as would be the message of a pastor or stationary preacher. This does not show that a certain group has a compromising message than the other, it is just how God intended it to be. As in the O.T., God's messages through His prophets were designed specifically to suit every location. He appointed prophets who fit the style of the message and the occasion if you will. Jeremiah's approach as a weeping prophet suited the occasion and style of message the Lord intended to be carried out. Isaiah's stern gesture fitted the message and occasion the Lord intended to use him for. God is the chief architect who masterminds His kingdom's work. He knows just what He is doing and knows how to operate and use a prophet suitably for warranted occasions. When a pastor feels like his congregation has become too complacent, he can get an evangelist with the right message from God to help him out. *Pastors:* The word pastor shares the root foundation of the Greek word *poimën* which means tends or herds the flock as a shepherd. The shepherd protects, leads, and instruct or feeds the sheep (cf. Acts 20:28; I peter 5:1,2). This is a delicate position. It entails a lot of responsibilty and accountability. This is a stationary position that last for a very long time if you will. The pastor does not only preach to the members, he teaches them as well. He also makes sure that the members are protected from the infiltrating of false doctrines into the community. While dealing with his community, there will be times when personal care will be warranted by members who the pastor must provide care for. The pastoral position somewhat operates as would a father do for his household but the only difference is that this caring for others is spiritual in essence but although they are to be nurtured to gain spiritual growth, sometimes the natural becomes as important as the spiritual. *Teachers*: The word teacher in Greek, *didaskalos*, correspondingly can be used with the Greek prefix, *kalo* which means good. Therefore, *kalodidaskalos* denotes a teacher of that which is good as opposed to the prefix, pseudo which means false teacher. Of course the community needs teachers of that which is good than false teachers. The apostle Paul was also alluding to the office comprising teachers who teach the truth and impart divine knowledge. This is an office that helps to facilitate the message of the pastor but in a practical and systematic form.

Verssse 12, *for the perfecting of the saints*: The apostle emphatically informing the church that these gifts or offices are needed to benefit everyone in the church. Individually, members will know that they are important in the community in that they are being trusted with a divine position by God. *For the work of the ministry*: Paul is saying that although one is given a gift, it should not be handled as a personal present from God. God gives a gift for the carrying out of His divine work on planet earth. Once it is understood by the majority that the purpose of God's gift is for the benefit of the kingdom of God, than the Gods' misson can take effect. The community can become spiritually nurtured and more established or *edified*.

Verse 13 assures that with comforming to the way in which Christ intended for the gifts to be used, that would suffice the purpose of the church's mission here on earth.

Verse 14, Pauls affirms that so long every offfice is functioning well as Christ intended and everyone is commited to working diligently in his or her respective office, spiritual growth is eminent. When teachers are imparting the truth, pastors preaching the truth and caring for the sheep, a lot can be accomplished. Much knowledge will be attained and the community can flourish well.

Verses 15. The apostle tells the saints not to worry about the false teachers or heretics in the community. They should just teach and preach the truth, and do that which is right. Paul encourages them to serve in love, have love for Christ, the ministry, and the community.

Verse 16. Paul elevates Christ to be an example for them to follow after. Humility is referred to and Christ-likeness is emphasized on. Paul admonishes them that it is only through Christ can they become effective in their ministry. It is Christ through whom the church can survive and proper as one body. Unity is possible only in Christ.

Exegeses from the Interpreter's Bible

Ephesians 4:11-16

Verses 11-12 *The Christian Ministry*: We are familiar with the word ministry and minister in church life. They have come to designate a professional class within the Christian community. Nor was such a ministerial caste absent in N.T. days. The church, as early as the day of Pentecost, had within it the apostolate, a group set apart for specialized functions. The church, both Catholic and Protestant, has had an order of the ministry ever since. To define the meaning and functions of this order, especially after it became solidly institutionalized, has caused the church much agony. Diversiveness in Christendom has been symbolized by nothing so clearly as by differences in the theory of the ministry. Some at least of the sad chapters in Christian history, however, might have been avoided if the original meaning of ministry had been kept in mind. The beautiful phrase of our very passage, *the work of ministry*, has deep significance. A literal translation of the Greek word for ministry is "deaconing," and corresponds to our English word "to serve." "Deaconing" is the normal N.T. word for serving, Jesus once said, "Whosoever will be great among you, shall be ever of you will be the chiefest, shall be servant [lit., "slave"] of all (Mark 10:43-44). It is surely a paradox that the humblest of the professional ministerial orders in Christian history; that of a deacon should carry the functional name which ought to characterize all Christian service. If the later story of the ministry in the church had always been one of true "deaconing," or true "slavery," most of the revolts against ecclesiastical tyranny would never have happened. We are familiar in our day with the "gospel of service." We use the phrase all too freely, and even commercialize it. Think of what the words "service station" mean as we see them on our highways. The concept of service can be degraded by ignoble motive. A satirist once coined the slogan It pays to serve." Indeed, it does. "The children of this world are in their generation wiser than the children of light" Luke 16:8). Despite all vulgarizations, however, mutual service remains as one of the chief marks of Christian community life. The world of commerce has merely been a beneficiary of Christian grace. Fully Christian *work of ministry*, however, seeks no reward except being accepted by God as a "sacrifice of praise and thanksgiving." It is motivated by gratitude. Christian morality could be generally defined as "grateful penitence." It differs in kind from all merit morality. That is why even the highest expressions of secular ethical idealism cannot be equated with Christian love. Paganism produced many noble theoretical philosophies.

But examine the motivations to which they appeal and a great gulf still separates their power from that which lies behind the Christian gospel of service. Non-Christian moral ideals can at best call into play only human strength. They beckon to the pursuit of virtue and even to the achievement of the divine in mortal garments. Non-Christian virtues are very conscious virtues, the result of strenuous striving. God will deal with them in his own way. But the true Christian life is resultant not of striving, though striving is not absent, but of response to an undeserved gift. At it highest it is not even conscious of being good. "When did we see thee hungry and feed thee, or thirst and give thee drink?" (Matt. 25:37). A humility which results from repentance, for example, will be conscious of repentance, not of its accompanying humility. A true lover buying a ring for a loved one is not conscious of virtue of sacrifice. He is conscious only of the unworthiness of the gift. And a true church is a company of true lovers of God in Christ. Response to the gift of forgiveness produces grateful penitence. A new social order, undreamed of in pagan philosophies, is born. Ministry, service, becomes the bond of fellowship. Ministry itself is a gift and not a work looking toward a reward. It is cumulative, *building up the body of Christ.* A true church is today as much a miracle as was the fellowship of Pentecost.

Verse 13 *Unity of the faith:* This phrase has often been misinterpreted in Christian preaching and teaching. It is tempting to make it mean the exclusiveness of orthodoxy, a unity of a fractional group of Christians subscribing to a common formulation of a theological confession. We need not belittle orthodoxy. It means "right belief." Christian faith requires right belief, and even right, not wrong, intellectual formulations of the gospel. Heresy was and is, as our epistle will shortly tell us (vs. 14), a constant danger to the church. *Unity of faith* clearly means here, however, the unity demanded by the faith in Christ. Faith itself is not, first of all, an intellectual assent to an intellectual system. Christianity is not mathematics or a system of philosophy like Platonism. It is not mental gymnastics. Faith, as the Bible understands the concept, is a personal act. It has been well defined as "trust in obedience." The unity of the people of God must consist above all in common trust, common obedience, common listening to the words of the Lord. The specific commands of the Lord, like his gifts, may vary endlessly as they come to Christian individuals or groups. The unity can consist in the shared listening and in the shared trust. As with faith, so with *knowledge of the Son of God,* this too should be thought of in personalized terms. Where can Christ be personally known? Not in systems or formulas, but in the thousands of fellowships were Christ is personally present in the Spirit. *Knowledge of the Son of God* comes in large part through unity itself, through the common life in the body of Christ. The corporate setting of this whole passage is important. Modern individualistic pietism may not find such social knowledge of Christ altogether congenial.

Individualistic interpretations may obscure also the full meaning of the further phrases in this verse, *mature manhood, . . . the stature of the fullness of Christ.* Later passages in our epistle will be addressed to the individual ("every one" of vs. 25 ff.). Here the subject is "we." The apostolic writer is thinking of the church. Every Christian should, of course, be an example of Christ. But can he attain to this high vocation except as he shares in the *fullness of Christ* in the fellowship? The fellowship has powers of Holy Spirit which transcend any individual gifts. The body of Christ can forgive sins. It cab absolve and take a sinner back into fellowship. Let the body of Christ become mature and attain to full stature. The individual Christian will partake of the maturity. The church of Christ in its N.T. grandeur has been obscured in both Catholic and Prostantant history. In Catholicism full Christian stature has been ascribed to the hierarchy or to the monk and the nun; in Protestanism, to the individual. Where in either tradition has the "whole body [of Christ], joined and knit together" (vs.16) received full recognition? The orthodox churches of the East may have preserved this note of the N.T. concept of the *fullness of Christ* better than the West.

Verses 14-15. *Christian maturity:* The virtues of childhood, in contrast with the virtues of maturity, have rarely been better evaluated than in Paul's words to the

Corinthians, "In malice be ye children, but in understanding be men" (I Cor. 14:20). The Christian gospel must be guarded against misinterpretation on two sides. It is not a "professor" religion. The childlike heart is needed for its appreciation. But this does not mean that Christians should cultivate childishness and immaturity. "When I became a man, I put away childish things" (I Corinthians 13:11), says Paul in his chapter on Christian love. The setting of this famous phrase is important. Love demands maturity for its full flowering. Colloquial speech points to a real truth when it calls an untested, merely romantic relationship between man and woman "puppy love." The illusion that Christianity is a religion for children and not for grown men and women is disastrous. It is widespread. A few memories of Sunday school are not enough for the storms of later life. Ignorance of Bible and creed and Christian doctrine-blame worthy ignorance, one may add-exposes thousands of men and women to *every wind of doctrine*, or to the *sleight of men*, or to *cunning craftiness*. The Christian faith is not like a first lesson in geometry, which once learned, can be forgotten or taken for granted. It sometimes looks that way. Boil Christian doctrine down to a few ethical precepts and no great demand for study or understanding appears essential. But the mature Christian needs much more than this. Paul preached a very simple faith has dimensions of height and depth; it is not milk for babes. Paul's epistles are not easy reading. Yet the mature Christians of all the ages, even if they only heard the N.T. in lesson or sermon, have fed their souls on Paul's insights. Christianity, like Judaism, is the religion of a book.

    A Christian without daily, or at least weekly, contract with Holy Scripture, and without continuous growth in understanding of its meaning, will soon find his faith withering away. He will be open to the wiles of error. Our verses, furthermore, envisage Christian maturity in a social sense. The plural "we" is important. The writer thinks of maturity as a mark of unity in the church. We grow into Christ by speaking the truth in love. Individualism and egotism are destroyers of unity. They are signs of childishness. As pure individualists we cannot become full-grown men, but the body of Christ can grow into the "fullness of Christ" (vs. 13). Nothing matures us as Christians so effectively as full sharing in the common life the Christian fellowship. Think of such a concrete ideal as *speaking the truth*. It is easy to "tell the truth." Only in a fellowship of repentance can hearts be open and lips unsealed. Only in a community of forgiveness can envy be exorcised and hatred exposed and transformed. In a society untouched by the grace of forgiving love we do not dare to approach open communion of person with person. A famous "thought" of Pascal reads: "If all men knew what each said of the other, there would not be four friends in the world." A terrifying, even though exaggerated truth! We are accordingly locked up in our separate cells of self-hiding. Only in the church can our mutual sharing of forgiveness transform us corporately into the mature body of Christ. There we can *grow up in every way into him who is the head, into Christ*

    Verse 16. *The church as community*: Modern man has lived under the illusion that to establish community life is relatively easy. Bring people near to each other and the trick is done. Contiguity, annihilation of distance, a seating around a conference table, these themselves will produce brotherliness. Hence our naïve faith in leagues of nations or other unitings in assembly halls, in the telephone or the telegraph or the airplane, as instruments of unity. Experience is teaching us hard lessons. A bringing of people close to each other may mean merely a greater knowledge of mutual faults, or an intolerable clashing of egotisms. Distance, rather than contiguity, may be a preserver of peace. Neighborliness may be helped rather than hindered by a border wall. The appalling rise of divorce statistics casts a lurid light upon the problem of creating communion. Here is a relation buttressed by sexual instinct, custom and law, by vows of "true love," and the memory of romance, yet how easily it turns into bitter hatred and a broken home. Well may we be afraid that our unitings between larger human groupings, between social classes and nations, may produce divorcings in place of households of love. We might conceivably re-enact in the twentieth century the drama of the Tower of Babel. The ancient world was more realistic than the twentieth century. That is why the church appeared to the contemporaries of Paul as a great miracle. To create fellowship is simply not easy. It calls for divine grace. Every man is by nature a little god to himself. This is part of the truth involved in his being created in the image of God, and in the story of the Fall. Unconverted human society resembles a battlefield of rival gods. The establishing of true community between clashingegotisms, as in a marriage, means a resigning of thrones. It involves a dying to self. The N.T. does not hesitate to call it dying. The church is a fellowship of repentant and forgiven sinners. Repentance is equivalent to a kind of dying. "Reckon ye also yourselves," says Paul, "to be dead indeed unto sin, but alive unto God through Jesus Christ our Lord" (Rom. 6:11). A community of the dead and risen-that is the church. Only such a community can speak of true unity only such a fellowship can risk honest togetherness. The church in the story of the Bible stands over against the Tower of Babel. Only such a body, as it *upbuilds itself in love*, can bring true fellowship onto the stage of history. And as the church lives in a world which is attempting uniication on the secular plane, its vocation is breath-taking. It can be the one agent on earth producing tru community. It knows the secret of the true bond between the warring wills of men and of nations, the bond of repentance and forgiveness. It can take into itself the poisons of unredeemed society. It can be the cross-bearer of the world. Corporately, as also by way of each of its members, the church can obey the command of her Lord, "Whosoever will come after me, let him deny himself, and take up his cross, and follow me" (Mark 8:34).

Exegesis on Ephesians 4:4-6 from the Interpreter's Bible

One . . . one . . . one . . . The word is repeated seven times, each time attached to a noun: body . . . Spirit . . . hope . . . Lord . . . faith . . . baptism . . . God. All Christians of whatever name still worship the same God. They unite in confessing Jesus as Lord.

They join in one hope of salvation, and in the vision of the chorus of unity before the throne of Christ in heaven (The Interpreter's Bible, 685).[130]

Exegesis of Ernest Best on Ephesians 4:12-16

Verse 12: The purpose of Christ's gift of office-bearers to the church is to (1) restore, reconcile; (2) reset broken bones; (3) furnish, prepare; (4) train, and discipline. Preferably "equip" could sum up the purpose.

Verse 13: The purpose of Christ's gift of ministers to the church is to prepare all its members to serve. The goal is presented as the end of the journey.

Verse 14: The ministry is given not only to enable the church to grow but also that it would be able to resist any forces that might corrupt or destroy it. Ministers themselves are not the direct agents in this resistance. All believers are summoned to the task; should any fail, unity may become a chaos.

Verse 15: This verse emphasizes on the movement towards maturity. Believers console, strengthen, and correct one another through the gospel and so build up their communities. They can do this in love because their lives were founded and built on "love" (3:17).

Verse 16: The church is to grow from Christ its head and will grow in love (A Critical and Exegetical Commentary on Ephesians 366, 395-409).[131]

Exegesis of S. Wibbing

Ephesians 4:11-16

Verse 11. *He gave apostles*: After a christological interpretation of the Scripture citation, the author adds the ecclesiological dimesion by interpreting the "gifts" of Ps. 68:19 as church offices. First are apostles and prophets, who for the author belong to the past are the foundation of the church (2:20).

---

[130] George Asthur Buttrick, Bowie, Russell Walker, Paul Scherer, John Knox, Terrien, Samuel, The Interpreter's Bible: The Holy Scriptures in the king James and Revised Standard Versions With General Articles and Introduction, Exegesis, Exposition for each Book of the Bible. Nashville: Abingdon Press, 1983.

[131] Ernest Best, A Critical and Exegetical Commentary on Ephesians. Edinburg: T & T Clark, 1998.

They are followed by preachers of the gospel, shepherds, and teachers, which are church offices prominent in the period of the writer. This list of offices is to be distinguished from similar lists in the Pauline letters (Rom 12:6-8; I Cor. 12:8-11,28), which enumerate charisms bestowed on individuals by the Spirit. *Shepherds*: As a title for a church official, "shepherd" (or pastor) is not used elsewhere in the N.T. Allusions to such an office, however, occur in exhortations to church leaders (Acts 20:28; John 21:15-17; I Peter 5:7) to tend the flock and in the image of Jesus as the good shepherd (John 10:11). These offices equip the church for ministry and contribute to the growth of the body.

Verse 13. *To full-grown adulthood*: The emphasis of the Gk *anēr* in this context is not on but adulthood, in contrast to the childhood mentioned in following verse (BAGD 66[2]). This full adulthood is measured in relation to "the stature of the fullness of Christ."

Verse 14. *Every wind of doctrine*: False doctrine poses a threat to the unity in the faith; see comment on 4:5.

Verses 15-16. *Grow up . . . into the head*: The author returns to images first used in 1:23 and 2:20-22, depicting the body as a living organism that has Christ as the source and goal of its growth. *When each part is working properly*: The growth and development of the body depend on each member performing the tasks proper to him or her.

Exegesis of Origen on Ephesians 4:11-16

And he gave some, apostles; and some, prophets, and some, evangelists; and some, pastors and teachers; for the perfecting of the saints, for the work of the ministry, for the edifying of the body of Christ: Till we all come in the unity of the faith, and of the knowledge of the Son of God, unto a perfect man, unto the measure of the stature of the fullness of Christ: That we henceforth be no more children, tossed to and fro, and carried about with every wind of doctrine, by the sleight of men, and cunning craftiness whereby they lie in wait to deceive; But speaking the truth in love, may grow up into him in all things, which is the head, even Christ: From whom the whole body fitly joined together and compacted by that which every joint supplieth, according to the effectual working in the measure of every part. Maketh increase of the body unto the edifying of itself in love. KJV

For since Christ is above all and through all and in all but grace was given to each of the saints according to the measure of the gift of Christ, consequently some are apostles, some are prophets, others evangelists, and after these pastors and finally teachers, If, then, to be teacher is a gift given in accordance with the measure of the gift of Christ, clearly also the pastor who pastors with understanding needs to have a gift to pastor. And how will someone be an evangelist if the feet of his soul, so to speak, are not beautify (Romans 10:15)? God must supply them with beauty that may be so. But a prophet, whom we must consider to have been appointed by God in the church (I Corinthians 12:28), also reproves and judges unbelievers (I Corinthians 14:24), for this is the work of the prophet of the new covenant. Now if these offices can exist continually in the Church, perhaps apostle, too, can be found even now to whom it is given to produce the signs of an apostle (II Corinthians 12:12). Apostles, prophets, and the others are needed for the perfecting of the saints that they may be perfected for the work of the ministry of Christ do that the body of Christ might be built up from living stones (I Peter 2:5) *Origen and Jerome on Ephesians, 174-175.* In response to verses thirteen through fifteen, Origen remarks: One must ask who we all are who will come to the unity of the faith. Is it all mankind in general or we who have been appointed in Christ? It will appear to the first suggestion because the winds of doctrine are many and they buffer all, more or less or, at least, most, and carry them about in the trickery of men, in cunning with the scheming of error. But one must strive to come to the unity of the faith and, in reference to the unity of the faith, to come also to be in the unity of the recognition of the Christ. When this have occurred and we humans have put aside all childishness, we shall be called *perfect*, having fully received the measure of the stature inwardly (Romans 2:29). This measure of the stature is the measure of the fullness of Christ. In response to verse sixteen, Origen sees the whole building up by which the body of Christ is increased through its parts will be completed in mutual love for itself. We understand all rational creatures under the example of one rational animal and whatsoever we may say of its members and parts we know is to be referred to each rational creature. Let us suppose that this animal has been torn apart throughout its limbs, veins, and flesh so that bone does not cling to bone nor is nerve joined to nerve. Let us suppose that the eyes lie apart, the nose lies separately, the hands occupy one place, the feet have been thrown into another, and the remaining members have been scattered and divided among themselves in this way.

Therefore, it will be in the restoration of all things when Christ Jesus, the true physician, shall come to heal the body of the whole church which is now scattered and torn apart (Origen and Jerome on Ephesians, 176-181).[132]

Exegesis of Jerome on Ephesians 4:11-16

And he gave some, apostles; and some, prophets, and some, evangelists; and some, pastors and teachers; for the perfecting of the saints, for the work of the ministry, for the edifying of the body of Christ: Till we all come in the unity of the faith, and of the knowledge of the Son of God, unto a perfect man, unto the measure of the stature of the fullness of Christ: That we henceforth be no more children, tossed to and fro, and carried about with every wind of doctrine, by the sleight of men, and cunning craftiness whereby they lie in wait to deceive; But speaking the truth in love, may grow up into him in all things, which is the head, even Christ: From whom the whole body fitly joined together and compacted by that which every joint supplieth,

---

[132] Ronald E Heine, The Commentaries of Origen and Jerome on St Paul's Epistle to the Ephesians. Oxford: Oxford University Press, 2002.

according to the effectual working in the measure of every part. Maketh increase of the body unto the edifying of itself in love. KJV

God appointed some in the church, first apostles, second prophets, third teachers, then miracles and gifts of healing, helpers, administrators, and various kinds of tongues (I Corinthians 12:28). Christ has given apostles, prophets, evangelists, pastors, and teachers. The prophets are not those who foretell future things such as we read about the Old Testament, but those who reprove and judge the unbelievers and ignorant (such indeed he defines prophets of the New Testament to be in another epistle [cf. I Corinthians 14:24])—evangelists, whose feet are beautiful for announcing peace (Isaiah 52:7; Romans 10:15). I do also think that in the churches today just as prophet and evangelist, as well as pastor and teacher, are found so also an apostle can be found in whom both the signs and proofs of the office of apostle are fulfilled (Origen and Jerome on Ephesians, 175).[133] Jerome's opinion on verses thirteen through fifteen is summed up as follows: We must investigate who the "all" are who come to the unity of the faith. Are saints, or perhaps all who are capable of thought? Now he seems to me to speak of all humans because there are many winds of doctrines and, when the waves have been stirred up by their blowing, humans are carried here and there in uncertain course and manifold error. Whence, we must labor with all zeal to come to the unity of the faith then to have the recognition of Christ in the same unity. Once we possess these things securely and cease to be infants and receive the measure of the inner person which measure is the measure of the fullness of Christ and we obtain the designation "perfect person," the goal, therefore, is that the whole multitude of believers might reach the complete age of the fullness of Christ and by no means be tossed to and fro by dogmas and borne the uncertain sea of faithlessness like infants, while the winds, meaning heresies or the wisdom of this world and diverse systems in contention, blow over them from this side. To verse sixteen, Jerome shares the same thought with Origen that it is Christ who unites the various parts of the church to make it a complete whole. That is, the various gifts or offices in the church can only work in harmony if the saints operate as lifting up Christ instead of themselves. If Christ is exalted, the kingdom of heaven and the ministry shall grow enormously (Origen and Jerome on Ephesians, 175-181).[134]

Exegesis of Wayne A. Gruedem on I Peter 4:10-11

10 As every man hath received the gift, even so minister the same one to another, as good stewards of the manifold grace of God.

---

[133] Ronald E. Heine, The Commentaries of Origen and Jerome on St Paul's Epistle to the Ephesians. Oxford: Oxford University Press, 2002.

[134] Ibid.

11 If any man speak, let him speak as the oracles of Gof; if any man minister, let him do it as of the ability which God giveth: that God in all things may be glorified through Jesus Christ, to whom be praise and dominion for ever and ever. Amen.

Within the fellowship of the church, earnest love for one another will find expression in the use of spiritual gifts, not for self-advancement or to draw attention to ourselves, but for the benefit of others. The expression a gift is indefinite and implies at least one gift but does not mean that each person is entitled to only one gift (cf. I Corinthians 12:31; 14:1, 13, 39). A spiritual gift (charisma, the same word used in I Corinthians 12-14 for spiritual gifts) is any talent or ability which is empowered by the Holy Spirit and able to be used in the ministry of the church. There are five different lists of spiritual gifts in the New Testament (Romans 12:6-8; I Corinthians 12: 7-11; 12:28-30; Ephesians 4:11; I Peter 4:10). Since the lists are all different (no one gift is on every list, and no list includes all the gifts), and since I Corinthians 7:7 indicates two gifts not on any list (marriage and celibacy, which Paul calls charismata), it is legitimate to conclude that they are not exhaustive. Since there are different types within any one gift (people with the gift of evangelism may differ in the kinds of evangelism they do best. Varied (poikilos) means many faceted, having many different aspects or differing kinds. As God's grace is richly varied, so are the gifts flowing from His grace. Good stewards of God's gift will not hide it, but employ it for the benefit of others (cf. the parable of the talents, Matthew 25:14-30; Luke 19:11-27). God's rule for our gifts if that we use them. Whoever speaks include s not just teaching or preaching, but many kinds of gifts involving speech-activity: evangelism, teaching, prophesying, and perhaps singing or sharing words of praise and testimony in the assembled congregation. In all these cases the Christian must do them as one who utters oracles of God, oracles (logia) means "sayings," but especially sayings spoken from God to man (used in Acts 7:38; Romans 3:2).

Yet this does not mean that the words he speaks are God's own words, not of every word spoken during a church meeting. It rather means 'with the seriousness of purpose which one will use if one were speaking God's words.' Whoever renders service should do it to the glorification of God (Tyndale New Testament Commentaries, 174-176).[135]

"Study to shew thyself approved unto God, a workman that needeth not to be ashamed, rightly dividing the word of truth" (II Timothy 2:15). The maximizing of efficiency and effectiveness in any activity requires much discipline; whether cultural, social, religious or secular, there must be a set pattern developed, a kind that builds confidence and assurance in a person, allowing him to bring out his

---

[135] F. F. Bruce, Tyndale New Testament Commentaries, Revised Edition. The Letter of Paul to the Romans: An Introduction and Commentary. Leicester: Inter-Varsity Press, 1988.

best. The Apostle Peter admonishes that being a child of God one should always be ready to give an answer to anyone who asks him about the reason of his hope (I Peter 3:15). Any discipline that promotes cultural values will subject its promoters to full knowledgeability with the nitty-gritty of everything that pertains to that culture in order to have good results. In case of a social setting, every norm and value must be enhanced in the process of educating the public about the type of lifestyle that is required. The religious and secular worlds are no exception to this principle. In fact, a person's affiliation with either of the two obligates him to total commitment and dedication. He is to defend and uphold the values that warrant him to be accepted and recognized as part of that society by his colleagues and others. That may appear as though he took an oath to pledge his allegiance and support to everything that setting or discipline demands. One who aspires to become a religious educator must be willing and ready to sacrifice his time and life to know and do everything that is required to satisfy his position as a bonafide religious educator. In the secular world, those who ambitiously desire to become a teacher must comply with the rules and regulations the *system* lays out for them to follow. It could be a system that demands hard work and commitment and one's willingness to be molded as required in a mandatory manner in order for him to be accepted and recognized as a licensed teacher. The *system* then becomes that guide by which all aspirants and affiliates abide as long as they are a part of it.

Aspirants and affiliates of the Christian ministry must be willing and ready to commit themselves to the rule of Christ if they so desire to instruct others about Him. Nevertheless, without any contradictions, the rule of Christ is the same as the rule of God. "Christ" is the anointed name of Jesus, which distinguishes His power and authority. "…the single usage *Christos* is sometimes used without the article to signify the One who by His Holy Spirit and power indwells believers and molds their character in conformity to His likeness, Romans 8:10; Galatians 2:20. As to the use or absence of the article, the title with the article specifies the Lord Jesus as "the Christ;" the title without the article stresses His character and His relationship with believers" (Vines Expository Dictionary).[136] The anonymous book, Hebrews, reveals Him as the "expressed image of God," One who has the full representation of God. Looking at Him will be looking at the manifestation of God. In fact, Jesus was both God and man when He walked the face of the earth some two thousand years ago. On one occasion, He told His followers that He and His father were one (John 10:30), and said if they have seen Him they have seen the father also (John 14:9).

When Jesus revealed Himself and His ministry to His followers, He said that He came only to fulfill the laws and the prophets. He did not come to add or subtract anything other than that which has already been laid out by God. There is an old

---

[136] W. E. Vine, *Vine's Expository Dictionary of Old and New Testament Words* (Iowa: World Publishers, 1981).

saying that a parent's heart is the child's classroom. Your dreams, your efforts, your examples and loving exhortations set the boundaries for your child's education. "Parents often attach the most importance to higher education, yet elementary school has a far greater impact. Except for family and church, no institution is so influential." It is documented that many U.S. schools are not meeting today's challenge. Surveys and test scores are disheartening. The national Assessment of Educational Progress reports that fewer than one third of fourth graders are "proficient" readers. Nearly 40 percent read below the "basic" level, which means they can barely read at all. One third of high school seniors cannot identify the countries we fought during World War II. Employers complain that many job applicants lack the basic reading and math skills they need to perform the jobs they are seeking. The U.S. has been "reforming" its schools for the better part for two decades. We have tried a hundred different program and a thousand gimmicks. We have poured in countless billions of dollars.

Yet it's clearer than ever that none of these nostrums has worked. Some even have made matters worse. American seniors are among the worst in the industrialized world.

The Preschool Years - "Growth of curiosity": children are born to learn. All healthy infants exhibit an innate desire to investigate in the first weeks and months of life. It is crucial to fan those early sparks of curiosity throughout the preschool years. If they are dampened, a child's academic future is jeopardized. "Development of interest" The interest children find early in life can be powerful predictors of later academic success. "Formation of character" students who have been taught the importance of hard work and responsibility are much more likely to get good grades. "Shaping of Personality" The foundations of an individual's personality are laid early. "Social development" modern psychology says that childhood experiences have an enormous impact on the ability to form close emotional ties with others. "Brain development" A child's brain structure continues to develop after birth. Cells are growing. Microscopic nerve connections are being formed. "Language development" The amount of language learned during the first few years is incredible. By the time a child is three years old, he should be able to understand most of the words he will use in everyday conversation for the rest of his life. Language skills honed in the preschool years have a heavy bearing on whether or not a child gets off to a good start in school. Early Moral Training - "children need to be healthy, rested, and well-nourished" "children come into the world programmed to imitate" - your child is constantly copying what he sees and hears. He takes careful note of your words, behaviors, attitudes, moods, habits, and priorities. He observes how you treat other people, how you spend your time, how you go about your work and meet your obligations. He watches to see what brings a smile to your face, and what makes you bored or angry. All these things are early and powerful lessons. They shape his own behavior and attitudes, including his attitudes about learning. "reading to your child" "Too much TV interferes with learning" "children need practice and routine" "children need to ask lots of questions and get your answers" "little children do not think like you do" "direct experience is critical" "Trial and error are a big part of learning" "play is the business of childhood" "No two children grow exactly in the same way"

The role of God as a teacher is one that reveals Him as being orderly and decent in His ruling, creativity, and dealing with man. As the creator, His framed governance systematically subjects all creatures to His rule. It was His leadership role that disallowed

Lucifer's rebellion from corrupting His rule in heaven. Lucifer's disobedience to the instructions of God resulted in His casting away from heaven. It did not stop there, God had to also chastise Adam and Eve; ones that were made in the likeness of Him and the angels for not following the instructions He laid out for them. As the Master teacher, God first instructed Adam and Eve of things they could do and not do, and He also told them of the consequences that would follow if those instructions were not adhered to. Man being in the image of God had dominion over the things of the earth. Man served as an adjunct teacher to God. It was just what God intended for man to be, a *full representation* of Him on earth, but man failed. Like Lucifer, man failed to comply with the teachings and commands of God, therefore he was removed from the garden of Eden and physically punished by God for his disobedience. There was always a sort of punishment for the ones who transgressed and disobeyed God. When Cain killed his brother, Abel, God cursed him of becoming a vagabond through out his life (Genesis 4:12). It has always been God's intention to pass on His instructions to designated individuals who could then serve as a medium through whom others could be reached. Noah, in his time was an instrument used by God to communicate His instructions to his people. When God was about to bring judgment upon the earth with a flood, He used Noah to instruct his people about the coming wrath, and to warn them about their transgressions and disobedience. In like manner, Abraham was used by God to witness to his people and teach his people more about Him. In fact, Abram, as he was called, got into a contract with God assuring God of his willingness and readiness to represent God amongst his people. And because of his faithfulness, God changed his name to Abraham which means *father of a multitude*. Abraham imparted to his household and people the nurture and spiritual discipline he experienced from God. In Genesis chapter twenty-two we see a clear example of a humble and disciplined son, Isaac, who being the object of a burnt sacrifice did not resist but faithfully submitted himself to his father believing that his dad knew what would be best for him. He asked his father where the lamb was, he could see the fire and the wood but where was the lamb for the burnt offering (Genesis 22:7)? In response, his father said that the Lord will provide. It was the teaching of *faith* passed on to Abraham from God that Abraham in return taught his son Isaac. Isaac's father's teachings molded him to be a lad of faith, and one of obedience and submission.

Another character example of a good father who instilled good values in his children was Job. Job was a God-fearing man who lived a devotional and faithful life before God. He played the role of a father, priest and God's representative in teaching and upholding the values of God. His household was a part of his devotional life. I guess it was why satan became jealous and envious of Job because of Job's faithfulness to God. Satan decided to bring Job to the lord for evaluation. At the end of the ordeal, God was proud of Job because he withstood the test and taught a lesson of faith, patience, endurance and longsuffering to his wife and friends. Another Character that was used by God greatly to carry and implement the message of deliverance to his people was Moses. Moses became a deliverer to the people of God. He used his secular and divine skills to deliver and lead the people of God from bondage. Moses taught and made sure that the Israelites kept the laws and commandments of God sacredly. God instructed him to communicate to his people ways in which He wanted them to live by giving Moses some laws and principles for the Israelites to observe and obey. These laws were the groundwork towards a pattern of spiritual disciplining God was developing for His people. When God made a promise to Abraham, He said that because of Abraham's faithfulness, many nations of the earth would be blessed through him. When the angel of the Lord met Jacob on his way to meet his brother, Esau, Jacob asked for a blessing. His desperation extended to his disallowing the angel to leave without blessing him. The Bible says that he wrestled with the angel until the angel touched the hallow of his thigh making it to come out of joint (Genesis 32:25). Because of his courage and perseverance, the angel said that his name was going to be changed to "Israel," a name by which a chosen people of God would be called on earth. It was the plan of God to use a group of people as a *repository* to represent Him and His values amongst all peoples of the earth. God's plan in preserving the Israelites for His intended purpose was to nurture them through his laws and ordinances. Moses became very instrumental in carrying out this task for God. Apart from the Ten Commandments, there were other laws the Israelites were to be governed by. They were to observe these laws in order to live up to the anticipated standard of God. These laws were to shape their lifestyle and personality. The scope of God's plan for Israel was not only for the present but the future as well. The gap of disfellowship that existed between God and man due to Adam's transgression had separated man entirely from God's fellowship. But a merciful God still desired man's companionship, therefore, this time He decided to first nurture and discipline man before re-embracing him into His fellowship. This was why God had to designate people like Moses and Joshua to serve that purpose of teaching and guiding the children of Israel in the way of the Lord with total adherence to the laws and precepts of God.

Because of God's intended purpose of embracing humanity back into His fellowship, He this time, had a plan of dealing with man on a divine basis as a means of cleansing and sanctifying man prior to accepting him into His fellowship. The purpose of God's eternal plan for man was to work on the mortal part of man in preparation for immortality; the carnal part to be replaced with the Holy Spirit, and to educate man from the natural to understanding the supernatural things of God. St. Thomas Aquinas better defines the role of God and His dealing with man as saying, "the reason and nature of man in the integrity and autonomy of its specific constitution; to defend the human in man without isolating it from God." The tabernacle worship was one way of teaching and nurturing His people in the way of spirituality. The tabernacle, a sanctuary built in the wilderness, was to host the presence of God in fellowship with His people. Every element of the tabernacle was a type of a better and eternal covenant that God had planned for His people. The tabernacle was where the Ark of the Covenant that had the mercy seat which typified the divine presence of God stood. The people of God were to pay special homage and reverence whenever they came in the presence of the Lord. The prophet Habakkuk better expresses this as saying, "the Lord is in His holy temple let all the earth keep silence before Him" (Habakkuk 2:20). It was in the Lord's presence His people were to learn how to worship. The rituals and ceremonies that were carried out in observance of the various festivals were ways that the people of God were taught to pay reverence to God.

The elderly in eastern cultures always give wise instructions to the young. They unselfishly share their life's experience with the youth as a means of helping the youth live a better and smarter life. The wisest man history brings out who ruled as a king at a young age, Solomon, although got his wisdom from above, it was the elders in his chambers who served as his advisers that helped him gain maturity to rule his people. There were also other young rulers of Israel and Judah who became great men in knowledge and leadership because of the counsel of great teachers who taught them both how to rule and to live. Josiah, at age eight succeeded his father's throne, and with the help of the elders, he ruled well (II Kings 21:26;22:1). Solomon shares his wisdom with the world by writing great instructional words such as the *Proverbs, Ecclesiastes, and Song of Solomon* to all who desire wisdom. He dramatized his wit by the way he ruled and imparted instructions via poems and songs. Apart from Solomon's example, there were many more. It has always been customary that Jewish rulers have wise men in their advisory chambers to assist the kings with decision making. In fact, it was the advice of great wise men that a king's rulership depended on to survive. Bad advisory counsel produces bad leadership and vice versa. It was the aiding counsel of Daniel that elevated him to higher ranks in Babylon. Another example of a wise man's help was Joseph, Jacob's son, who interpreted pharaoh's dream, and instructed him of the Lord's plan and the future of Egypt. The prophets of old were used as a mouthpiece for God. They were used as a mediator between God and His people. On many occasions God had to have the prophets instruct the people on things pertaining to Him. The prophets instructed men as they themselves were instructed by God. God had the prophets in the midst of the people purposely to guide them in the way of the Lord. The prophets were to cry out, spare not, lift up their voices like a trumpet, and show the people their transgression and sins (Isaiah 58:1). Even in exile, God still did not neglect His people. Exile was a turning point and also a lesson of chastisement for the children of Israel. It was God's way of chastising them for not obeying Him and keeping up with his precepts. God wanted them to be in full adherence to His commands. Therefore, just being in exile was a great lesson for the children of Israel. However, God did not neglect them. He sent along as captives some prophets. God wanted these prophets to encourage and teach these people in the things pertaining to Him. The prophets were there to make sure that God's people did not deter from Him, and also to make sure that they did not get corrupted with heathenism.

SUMMARY

Christ provides various gifts and allows different ministries to exist within the community to realize this hope of redemption. : *Apostles*, the word apostle is from the Greek word *apostolos* which literally mean one sent forth (*apo*, from *stellö*, to send [see John 17:3; Luke 6:13; I Cor. 9:1; Acts 14:4]). *Prophets*: prophet originates from the Greek word *prophëtës* which means one who speaks forth or openly proclaims a divine message (see Amos 3:7,8; Numbers 11:17-20; Matthew 5:12; Matt 10:41; Rom. 17:3). Nevertheless, in this church age Christ still endows people with more than one gift but the opportunity of having others also used by God is in abundance. *Teachers*: The word teacher in Greek, *didaskalos*, correspondingly can be use with the Greek prefix, *kalo* which means good. Therefore, *kalodidaskalos* denotes a teacher of that which is good as opposed to the prefix, pseudo which means false teacher. *Evangelists:* Evangelist comes from the Greek word *euangelistës* which means a preacher of the Gospel (see Acts 21:8; II Tim. 4:5 euangelizö, to proclaim glad tidings). An evangelist is one who goes around preaching the gospel me Diversiveness in Christendom has been symbolized by nothing so clearly as by differences in the theory of the ministry. As opposed to a preacher or pastor, an evangelist is not stationary. A literal translation of the Greek word for ministry is "deaconing," and corresponds to our English word "to serve." "Deaconing" is the normal N.T. word for serving, Jesus once said, "Whosoever will be great among you, shall be ever of you will be the chiefest, shall be servant [lit., "slave"] of all (Mark 10:43-44). Ministry itself is a gift and not a work looking toward a reward. It is cumulative, *building up the body of Christ.* Faith itself is not, first of all, an intellectual assent to an intellectual system. Christianity is not mathematics or a system of philosophy like Platonism. It is not mental gymnastics. Faith, as the Bible understands the concept, is a personal act. It has been well defined as "trust in obedience." The unity of the people of God must consist above all in common trust, common obedience, common listening to the words of the Lord. A spiritual gift (charisma, the same word used in I Corinthians 12-14 for spiritual gifts) is any talent or ability which is empowered by the Holy Spirit and able to be used in the ministry of the church.

ASSESSMENT

1. Why Christ provides various gifts and allows different ministries to exist?

2. Who is an Apostle?

3. Who is a Prophet?

4. Who is an Evangelist?

5. Who is a teacher?

PERSPECTIVES

Merriam-Webster's Collegiate Dictionary defines "virtue" as conformity to a standard of rights, valor, or potency. Ayn Rand philosophically defines "virtue" as allegiance to existence; it consists of man recognizing facts and then acting accordingly. "In a primacy-of-consciousness philosophy, virtue consists of allegiance to the ruling consciousness, such as God and society" (Peikoff, 250).[137] Ayn Rand views virtue in six ways: independence; one's acceptance of the responsibility of forming one's own judgments and of living by the works of one's own mind…, integrity; loyalty in action to one's convictions and values, honesty; the refusal to fake reality, that is, to pretend that facts are other than they are, justice; the virtue of judging men's character and conduct objectively and of acting accordingly, granting to each man that which he deserves, productiveness; the process of creating material goods or services. Such creation is a necessity of human survival, and pride; the commitment to achieve one's own perfection (Objectivism: The Philosophy of Ayn Rand, 251-303).[138]

---

[137] Leonard Peikoff, Objectivism: The Philosophy of Ayn Rand. New York, Penguin Books, 1991.

[138] Ibid., 251-303.

CHAPTER FIFTEEN

GREEK ETYMA

Benefit—Euergesia (εύεργεσία) good work

Distribute—Diadidōmi (διαδιδωμι) to give through (dia, through, didōmi, to give), as from one to another; koinōneō, to share in common with, fellowship

Preach—Kērusso (κηρύσσω) to be herald, to preach; **Parrhēsiazomai** (παρρησιάζομαι) to preach boldly

Salvation—Sōtēria (σωτηρία) deliverance, preservationinclusively to sum up all the blessings bestowed by god on men in Christ through the Holy Spirit

Vessel—Skeuos (σκεύος) household stuff, for the service of God, a chosen vessel, vessel of honor,

The Premise of Your Gift/ Calling

Faith is in the spiritual realm while money is in the commercial realm (Anonymous)

Faith does nothing alone, nothing of itself, but everything under God, by God through God (William Stoughton)

Exegesis of William Temple on John 4:10

10 Jesus said answered and said unto her, if thou knewest the gift of God, and who it is that saith to thee, give me to drink; thou wouldest have asked of him, and he would have given thee living water.

In the aforementioned verse Jesus confronts a Samaritan woman at the well and asks her for water to drink but she clings on to traditionalism and questions Jesus' approach and request. She lets Jesus know that the Jesus' approach is against the laws of the Jews and Samaritans. The Jews were forbidden to communicate with the Samaritans. The Jews had rejected the Samaritan hundreds of years as an impure race. According to Jewish history the Samaritans were Jewish captives by Assyria who were somewhat indoctrinated by Jeroboam to worship his golden calves. Although the Samaritans were believed to comprise the ten tribes of the children of Israel and had the Pentateuch with them, their style and way of worship on Mt Gerizim was different from that of the Levitical Order set up by God for the Children of Israel. This was why the rest of Israel renounced any association with this group of Israelites in the region of Samaria. For years this division had been going on. Therefore Jesus came by way of Samaria that day to put and end to a traditional and historical divide that existed among the Jews in Samaria and the Jews in Judea or Jerusalem. Jesus reveals His redemptive plan to the lady at the well but she could not understand it. He tries to tell her that He represents a new covenant that makes Mt. Gerizim and Mt. Sinai of no significance in his plan. His New Covenant is not about Samaria or Jerusalem but for all of humanity, both Jews and non-Jews. Jesus tells her the history of Israel and Samaria in a nutshell by saying that the well she came to draw water from was Jacob's well, which was a gift to all of Israel. Therefore, He has come to carry on this legacy but in a different manner. Christ tells her not only is He the long awaited gift that Jacob and the prophets anticipated seeing, He has also a gift He could give her that transcends that of the literal water she came to drink to quench her thirst. Jesus reveals the "living water" in reference to the indwelling of the Spirit which will give her life of a Spiritual nature and life eternal as well. William Temple shares his views as follows: The gift of God cannot be received to be merely enjoyed. It must always be shared. Its very nature involves that; for it is Himself, His own Spirit, the Spirit of love.

To receive that does not mean to enjoy the knowledge that God love us. It means that His active love is present in our hearts; and if so, it must go out to others (Reading in St John's Gospel, 60-61).[139] Wahlde concurs with Temple in his analysis that the "living water" was symbolic of the gift of the "Holy Spirit" Christ promises to give to the Samaritan woman if she asked for it (The Signs Material In John, 85).[140]

"Now concerning spiritual gifts, brethren, I would not have you ignorant…Now there are diversities of gifts, but the same spirit. And there are differences of administrations, but the same Lord. And there are diversities of operations, but it is the same God which worketh all in all…But all these worketh that one and the selfsame Spirit, dividing to every man severally as he will" (I Corinthians 12: 1,4,5,6,11). The entire twelfth chapter addresses the gifts of the spirit in length. The circumvention of heresies, egocentrism, and pagan conceptualism around the church moved Paul to render a pristine explanation about the manner in which God intends for the church, a divine entity, to function. Paul reminds the believers in Corinth that they cannot compete amongst themselves for the gifts of God in the church the way the world competes for a prize. This way of competing becomes detrimental to the unity of the church. God is not the author of confusion. If the church were the imprint of God, as the chief imprinter, then the church allow Him to put things in proper perspective.

God wants His church to operate in a united form to implement a diverse agenda but to accomplish a common good, that is, to benefit the assembly or believers. In verse 12 of the twelfth chapter, the Pauline Theologian tries to draw a parellelism between the diversitative perception of society and that of the church. He notes that his idea of diversity in the church only relates to the different offices that members could function in within the decorum of unity under the guidance of the Spirit as opposed to the uncontrollable and unguided diversity that exist in society. Paul's mirroring of the division that is in society is being referenced to the situation in Galatia (Galatians 3:28). Paul had to let the saints in Galatia know that the covenantal provisioning of Christ gives no room to social sectionalism. Under Christ, there is no Jews or Gentiles, black or white. Racism should not even be an issue.

Under Christ the believers become one family. Therefore, God made provisions for this diverse group of individuals to be able to work efficiently as brothers and sisters to profit the kingdom of God. Paul equates the functioning of the church to that of an organism. Cells, the unit structures of living things are grouped into units as tissues to carryout a particular function, and these same tissues are grouped together as organs to better function on a larger scale as they are also grouped together in an organized

---

[139] William Temple, Readings in St. John's Gospel. London: Macmillan & Co. Ltd.,1963.
[140] Ibid., 85.

form to make sure that the organs, tissues and or cells work in a systematic form. Not one cell, tissue, organ, or system can willfully decide to sabotage the functioning of the human body for personal reasons if you will. However, in society, it is common to find saboteurs every where. For individual reasons, people willfully can decide to erupt a process, organization or anything. Murphy O'Connor's concept of unity as he addresses the matter, views things as thus:

> In verse 12, many members: Diversity is rooted in unity. The different members all share a common existence. Christ: as in I Cor. 6:15, the name is predicated of the community. Verse 13, one Spirit to drink: The fact that the verb *potizen* is a or, militates against a reference to the eucharist (I Corinthians3:6-8). The Spirit is within the church (I Corinthians 3:16; 6:19). Verse 14, one member: In context this is the key statement. Just as the human body needs different members (vv 14-20), so the church needs diversity of spiritual gifts, and each one makes a specific contribution. Verse 21, do not need you: The perspective changes slightly. Now the point is that members need each other. Verses 23 through 25, in terms of clothing, the genitals receive more attention than ears or nose. The instinct of modesty reveals the divine plan to ensure that the eyes (for example) should not command all consideration. Verse 27, taken singly: The precise force of the *ek merous* is unclear. Collectively the Corinthians are the body, but individually they are its members (cf. Romans 12:5). Verses 28 through 30, Paul makes the application of v 14 to spiritual gifts. 28. The first three gifts set off from the others by being numbered and personalized, constitute the fundamental threefold ministry of the word by which the church is founded and built upon. Teachers: Their role may have differed from that of prophets by being exercised outside the framework of the liturgical assembly, Romans 12:6-7 (O'Connor, 1976).

All through Paul's ministry he had to address the matter of unity in the church amidst the operations of diverse gifts. This was a very befuddling matter amongst the saints not only in Rome or Corinth but in Ephesus and other churches in Asia Manor. Church leaders had a problem in trying to explain the concept of "divers kinds of gifts" to operate in the spirit on "unity" in the church. Many perceived it to be an impossible phenomenon. Even today, the post-Apostolic era, many church leaders in this century doubt the possibility of these gifts being in existence. In Ephesians chapter 4:1-16, Paul addresses this matter seriously. A the beginning of the exhortatory section in verse one through six, the image of Paul, the prisoner in the Lord, is again invoked to confer his authority upon the exhortations. The unity of the new humanity created in Christ (2:14-16) is exemplified by the church's unity, fostered by the virtues that make life in common a reality: humility, gentleness, patience, and forbearance. The inspiration for the passage is Col 3:1-15. Verses four to six, *one body*: The mention of being called in one body in Col 3:15 leads to a seven-part statement of the pervasiveness of the unity that must characterize a Christian life. In verse five, one Lord: Cf. I Cor 8:6, is important because of the Gentile background of the readers and because of the author's stress on the subjection of all the heavenly powers to Christ (1:20-22). *One faith, one baptism*: Unity In faith may be regarded in this letter as unity of belief. It denotes the teachings to which all members of the church subscribe. As institutional Christianity emerges in the post-Apostolic period, faith becomes the acceptance of an authoritative apostolic tradition (2:20), which can be distinguished from false doctrine (4:14). The reference to unity in baptism is fitting here within the ecclesiological perspective of Ephesians. The Unity of the body in vv 3-6 provides the setting for the discussion of the diversity of church offices. Verse thirteen, every wind of doctrine: False doctrine poses a threat to the unity of the church and the various offices in the church make the church equipped for ministry and contribute to the growth of the body.

But the manifestation of the Spirit is given to every man to profit withal. The apostle Paul informs believers in Christ that they should seek to know and understand the things of God. We should take advantage of the spiritual treasures the Lord has to freely give to anyone who makes himself or herself available. Paul wants the saints to know that they can ask the lord to bless them spiritually, and He will but one must have faith in God and believe that his or her sufficiency is in God I Corinthians 12:1. As the Nehemiah says, "the joy of the Lord is our strength" (Nehemiah 8:10). Believers have to know that as children of God, they are entitled to the many gifts that heaven has to offer. No one should feel left out or underprivileged when it comes to the benefits of God. The scripture says no man understands the things of God but the spirit (I Corinthians 2:10-12). One has to commune with God in the spirit in order to know and understand the ways of God. The Bible says the natural man cannot understand the things of God because they label the things of God as foolishness. Obviously, that would be the best expected of a natural man who is shy pf spiritual enlightenment. Except the Lord build the house they labor in vain that build it (Psalm 127:1). The purpose of God's gift to the church is to have the church as a unified body of believers purposely chosen by God to be a spiritual repository to exemplify the knowledge of God on planet earth. The church is to show that it is a unique entity, although of a terrestrial construct, purposely is of a celestial design which is divine. Unlike how the world struggles or battles to maintain a balance of power and a sense of orderliness, the church exemplifies that amidst its many talents or diversities, the spirit of God brings calm and order amongst the believers. There are many offices but one office that whose spirit unity is brought among the believers to enhance growth and spirituality (I Corinthians 12:4). God's gift to the church is to edify the church (I Corinthians 14:12). The kingdom of God has an urgency.

There is a shortage of capable people in the church to expand the church. God is recruiting people to help expand His work. God is raising up capable men and women to be a Daniel, Elijah, Moses, or Deborah to keep the church firm on its foundation, not to have the church built on a sand as the scripture alludes to the foolish man but to have the church built on a sure foundation or rock as the wise man did according to the Bible (Matthew 7:26). Read Romans 1:11. The purpose of God's gift to the church is to teach and enlighten believers. Not to only reach out to the unsaved but to make sure that they cannot fall away from the truth (Hebrews 6:4- 15). God is assuring that the only way believers can individually and collectively maintain firmness and be blessed is by being obedient to God's word, diligent in or walk with God, and faith in your stewardship. It is very important that ministry workers be familiar with the Bible. As ministry workers, the Bible stands as the only authority or tool that the ministry is dependent on, therefore we have to be on the alert, Apostle Timothy admonishes us to study to show ourselves approved unto God, a workman that needs not be ashamed rightly dividing the word of truth (Timothy 2:15). As laborers in the Lord's vineyard, we should be able to apply and utilize the Bible skillfully to our advantage because it is the only resource we shall continuously access for the ministry. And it is the only weapon we can use to our defense in times of trials and temptation.

The Psalmist David's application of the scripture as his guide is recorded as follows: "thy word have I hid in mine heart, that I might not sin against thee" (Psalm 119:11). David was a great *workman* who took advantage of studying God's word. He studied it and knew it so well that whenever he was in a situation, there was a portion of the God's word applicable to sustain him. He took God's word to be a lamp unto his feet and a light unto his path (Psalm 119:105). David relied on God's word for direction and instruction. By the same token, it was David again who said that the steps of a good man are ordered by the Lord (Psalm37:23). David depended on the Lord for guidance. He delighted himself in the way of the Lord. The scripture was the basis of everything he did. David is a good example of how ministry workers should practically study and use the word of God and depend on it at all times and for everything. On the other end of scriptural usage, the apostle Paul warns us to put on the whole armor of God in order for us to be able to stand against the wiles of the devil (Ephesians 6:11). He goes on to say that we should put on the breastplate of righteousness, the sword of the spirit which is the word of God, the helmet of salvation and have our feet shod with the preparation of the gospel of peace (Ephesians 6:14-16). The purpose of God's gift to the individual or the church is to use it not quench it (II Timothy 1:6-7). You should not let self or Satan stop you from sharing God's gift with others. The gift is God's not yours to keep or treasure. Just like how a banker would tell you that your bank card is a privileged card service because your account can be closed at anytime and the plastic card could be taken from you because it is their property, it is just how the gift situation is. God's gift to you or the church is a privileged service, if unused or misused could cause one to lose it. God wants you to bear fruits or utilize your gift to its full potential (Phillipians 4:17). As believers, studying the scriptures is needed as a means of equipping us for our journey with the Lord and the ministry. We study the scriptures because we want to be prepared for the ministry. We want to be prepared so that in the event we are challenged, tempted, or tried, we could know how to respond or react. "...Rightly dividing the word of truth..." warrants one to have a wealth of knowledge of the scripture to know how to teach and apply it contextually. Whenever the scripture is taught or interpreted out of context, it becomes faulty and misconstruing. We do not have to add or personally express what we suppose the scripture is saying. God does not need man's wit to interpret the scripture. The scripture interprets and explains itself. The Bible says, "no scripture is of private interpretation" (II Peter 1:20).

Among Richard Warran's twelve proven bible study methods, I selected a few that I found very important and interesting.[141] The *Devotional method* should be one of necessity for every child of God. The devotional method prepares and puts one in the mood to study the scripture, after which other approaches could be used and applied. I find the *verse by verse analysis* to be very useful in a group or home Bible study session where each individual has a chance to participate. The *Thematic, Biographical and Book Background methods* could resultfully be used within the *Synthetic Bible study* while the *Topical, Word study, Chapter analysis, and Book survey methods* could strongly fit in with the *Analytical Bible study* category. In most instances, the *Synthetic study* is very concise in presentation and the *Analytical* is more detail-built.

Preparing to Deliver

What chance would I have of hitting the target if I didn't ? Very little. Aims and objectives: the 1st thing to ask you, Why are you teaching? What are your motives for teaching? Many times a Sunday school may not ssee his or her rewards in their life time. If you are looking for great monetary gain, you may not. What are you trying to accomplish for teaching? Some people objective is to keep their students quiet. Some teachers' objective is to keep the students busy. These are inadequate reasons. Other teachers want to get through the time frame. Some want to keep the kids from fighting. There should be some real reasons. Teaching without aims is like a man who starts out on a vacation without knowing where he is going. Going to vacation, you must have a plan or preparation, and know what to carry and how much to carry. Aimless teaching is poor teaching. There must be clarity. Some purposes: **1.** A teaching needs to see through his own activity and probable activity of the students.

Teaching should involve a change. **2.** To provide continuity, to avoid rambling, to distinguish minor and major points. If you know why you are going, it will help you select your teaching materials, methods and activities. One must develop have some skills, practice. **3.** Aimed objectives provide a basic for measurement and progress. **4.** Helps the students to develop or set learning aims for themselves. **5.** Aims inspire the

---

[141] Richard Warren, The Purpose—Driven Church: Growth Without Compromising Your Message and Mission. Grand Rapids: Zondervan, 1995.

teaching. Long range aims: If you can achieve your aims, you certain aim should be to have your students to get save. Growth should be another long range aim. Fulfillment, that they may fulfill Gods' will in their lives. We do not want Sunday school held just for knowledge or attendance purposes. II Timothy 3:17. To help you determine aims in each lesson, these questions are important: 1. At the end of each lesson, what do I want my student to know as the result of it? 2. What do I want my students to feel, what convictions, what strong feeling I want them to have or experience from the lesson? 3. What do I want my students to do? Not to be a hearer of the word but a doer. The greatest weakness in teaching is aimless teaching. The student won't know what they supposed to know, feel, or do if you do not know either. When you know what you want to achieve, then drive for it. How do you determine your lesson? You must know the specific needs of your students. You are to discipline, correct bad behaviors, and teach good manners or etiquette. Good observation around the kids and their environment can help. Also prayer can help give you spiritual insights. Luke 10: 29-37: Lesson: Who is your neighbor? The person who lives next door? Anyone who you comes in contact with is your neighbor, does not have to be of the same race, nationality, creed, ethnicity, When we someone in need we should teach or apply compassion. What do you need to do? If you are on your way to church and you saw someone in an accident, what will you do? Qualities of a good lesson: You have brief enough, specific enough to meet the needs, has to be clear, practical enough to be achieved. Example, you want your students to memorize the entire bible. This is not practical, possible, or necessary. If you had an aim or objective to achieve, you may have to use different methods in order to have every student archive. Every student may not be able to grasp the lesson the same way.

Before entering the classroom, the teacher should have studied and prepared a lesson plan. Being prepared is always good for the teacher because this will help make him more relaxed and confident in himself and his plan. A teacher should do his best by working hard in preparing a good lesson plan for his class. Great feedbacks are only possible from great planning. In constructing the lesson plan, the teacher must first focus on the learning level of his learners, second, gather all relevant resources and information, and third, pray that the Lord opens the hearts and minds of his learners to be ready to accept and receive God's word. This is one thing that makes the Christian Educator different from the secular educator, The secular educator depends only on his knowledge and intelligence but the Christian educator applies his knowledge with great dependence on God as the knowledge giver. The Apostle Paul says that it is only God who gives the increase (I Corinthians 3: 6-7). We as humans can do but so much. When we realize that we can go no further, it is that time that we ask the Lord to take over. A good learning formula for a Christian student should be to always study first and then pray that the Lord helps him in retaining that which he has studied. A Christian teacher should do the same thing. He should use all necessary resources and materials needed to accomplish his teaching goal, and then prays that the Lord makes the students receptive. Because the *goal* of a lesson plan is of outmost importance, the teacher should make sure that his instructional objective be accomplishable and simple. A complex instructional objective may cripple the students' learning and hamper the teacher also from being clear and timely with his lesson. The instructional target must be in the interest of the learners. Based on the students' level of comprehension, the teacher should use activities that will reflect just what the learners would be attracted to because it would be terribly incompatible and incomprehensible if the teacher used advanced activities which are above the learners' level of comprehension or if he uses less challenging activities which are below the learners' comprehension level. Whichever way, there must be a balanced appropriation. Much can satisfactorily be accomplished if the right learning activities are used. In so doing, the teacher could avoid an embarrassment on himself and the learner. A student could get embarrassed when asked to perform a certain task or asked a certain question about something that he has no knowledge of. An embarrassment of this sort does nothing else but makes the teacher's plan for that day uninteresting. Any feedback following this foul behavior on the part of the teacher would reap only negative results. A disciplined teacher will always want to work closely with his learners. He will want to follow the curriculum set up by the administration and also want to evaluate the learners' potential to see whether there could be some compatibility or not.

The most critical age group among all other groups that demand careful attention is the preschooler. This is the group where feedback is more of a silent type then being verbal, meaning that this is a group where communication is not fluently effective as one would find in other groups. Of course, this does not mean that preschoolers are not responsive. It is just that they respond at a slower pace than would other older age groups, but their senses pick up things very quickly. They are very sensitive to their environment. Their observation level is very high. They are curious about a lot of things around them. This is how they learn and respond. Preschoolers imitate other people who interact with them in their environment. They are like a "walking tape recorder" that records everything that happens around them. I guess Jesus' disciples may have wondered why the children of Jesus' day were not afraid of the crowd, and why the children acted so concerned as everyone else around Jesus. The little ones were curious and wanted to be a part of what was going on. I guess some of them persisted and pushed their way through as they were being pushed back by the disciples. I agree with the findings of search institute that much attention is not given to the curriculum of preschoolers, and less effort is made to include them in God's salvation plan. I watch sometimes how when an altar call is made by a minister after the sermon is preached, among those responding would be some little children but the ministers only touch the head of the children without uttering a word of prayer. But for an adult, they spend ten to fifteen minutes praying. I do understand that the adults are given more attention because of the contribution they could make if they got saved or because they are older. Nevertheless, the children could also need salvation or deliverance from sickness or problems like the adults. Perhaps, if the children were honestly prayed for by the preacher, they could get some deliverance. Although in some instances the children may not know what their spiritual needs are, it is not our place to decide who deserves prayer and who does not or who could get delivered and who could not. God is no respecter of persons (Acts 10:34; James 2:1) God uses anybody and anything to reflect His glory and purpose. In fact, David could be a clear example for us to look at. Jesse, David's father did not expect his youngest son to be anointed as king of Israel but it did happen. It is about time that we do away with outward appearance judgmentalism and let the Lord be the judge, and be in charge of the decision making. Little Samuel, Hannah's son, in Eli's temple is another example of how the Lord chooses young people at times to carry out His work. The Lord even told the prophet Jeremiah that before Jeremiah was born he knew him and chose him to be a spokesperson for Him (Jeremiah 1:5). I concur with Jean Piaget's psychological findings of preschoolers from birth to adulthood. Piaget's six stages of information processing of preschoolers are interestingly reasonable.[142] The first stage, *senses*, is the beginning point of information processing. This reflects the response behavior of a preschooler to his environment. *Curiosity*, Piaget's second stage is when preschoolers begin to explore new things. *Relationship*, the third stage is when values and actions are learned and practiced. The fourth stage, *Repetition*, is when memorization takes course. The fifth stage, *play and limitation*, is the period of creativity for the preschoolers. This also is the time preschoolers practically exhibit behaviors they learned from adults. The last stage of Piaget's observation, *Doing*, is when preschoolers begin to develop self-dependency in some chores that they observe an adult do around them.

They are anxious to put on their own socks and clothes, or flip the pages of a book, try to read without wanting help even though they may not be able to read. They would prefer feeding themselves when parents attempt to feed them. The teaching curriculum for preschoolers could be one comprising symbols and pictures incorporated with songs. Much repetition is needed in order for them to take in some information. At this stage of development, the parents play a major role in their preschoolers' lives. With care and concern, the parents will successfully impact on the preschooler's life. This is when the Christian parents make sure that the family devotions are held consistently. The child gets to know the difference between the Bible and other books, he gets to learn how to pray and how to sing. And as times go by, the child takes the initiative of reminding the parents about devotion when it is time to go to bed, and about prayer at the table for dinner. Although very immature in terms of sensormotor skills, a preschooler would at times correct his parents if they were doing something different from what they taught him or if his parents forgot to do certain things that they normally do when he is around them.

---

[142] Daryl Elgridge, The Teaching Ministry of the Church: Integrating Biblical Truth With Contemporary Application. Nashville: Broadman & Holdman Publishers, 1995.

Pre-kindergarteners' mental ability is not too strong, they like to challenge themselves. With this kind of energy-pact orientation, they could learn a lot. A teacher who is sensitive to the needs of this group could use activities and teaching methods that will make learning effective. It is known that this group enjoys activities such as drama and stage-performances, therefore employing a curriculum that is built around activities relative to drama and recitation, singing, and storytelling will be very effective. Children in this age group would be interested in knowing about baptism and salvation. Bible stories written on their level will aid them in getting great insight on the scriptures. Bible Videos are also another effective way this age group can learn about God and His word. DVDs, our latest technological development, are all instruments through which Christian learning can be made simple for this age group. These tools are attractive to this group of learners. Much attention is drawn when these young learners are watching videos, digital video dics or the like. Also, using coloring books that have pictures of the cross and other Bible characters will impact the learning process. However, parents and teachers must guide them in selecting the right colors for coloring these pictures. Colors also have a way of reflecting the reality of the story in the minds of the young students. This is an age group of mental sharpness. The average mental level of this group is developed to the extent of being capable of learning and assimilating almost anything. Their curiosity drives them to taking on unique challenges. They sometimes believe that they are smarter than everyone else. With this group, a teacher could use activities that reflect both the knowledge and comprehension skills. An effective and productive lesson plan should have more activities of the knowledge skill and not too much of the comprehension. It is not that these *third and fourth graders* are not mentally developed to being able to think creatively, rather, it is because a teacher would not want to overwhelm these learners with too much at once. These learners at this age are capable of reciting prayers, memorizing verses from the Bible and thinking constructively in terms of understanding what a teacher would mean if he were to prove or disprove a phenomenon. They could understand who God is, why did Jesus die on the cross, what baptism is, why are they to get baptized and so on. These learners are capable of responding positively to any advanced level of learning. Applications that are used for a junior high level can be of less challenge to this group.

Unlike the third and fourth graders, the fifth and sixth grade learners possess developed psychomotor skills. They learn by hands-on very quickly. Many at this age begin the developing of their artistic ability. They can formulate concepts and ideals. They become self-dependent and engage themselves in activities modeling the role of responsibility, which of course make them vulnerable to peer- influences. Much learning could be accomplished by this group if teachers implemented group activities whereby taking turns each learner can learn the role of leadership for his group. Constant role playing of group activities would have a great impact on this group. What the teacher should not do is to neither put a learner on the spot nor embarrass him in front of his peers. This could cause a serious emotional problem for the embarrassed learner. Because of this group's level of sensitivity, aggression and anger are characteristics that are easily displayed as a means of defense. A trainer should be very careful not to allow scorning, teasing, joking or ridiculing of learners among themselves in the event a learner did not respond to a question appropriately. Much praise should be given to learners even if they were wrong. For inadequate responses and behavior, a soft and tender reaction from the teacher to the situation will be very good. Because these learners are apt to understand right from wrong and the consequences that proceed after a wrong or right behavior, the teacher does not have to use aggression or the means of force to discipline or correct a learner. Sometimes a one-on-one situation could preferably be the absolute resultful gesture by any one teacher

The younger youth capitalize on the behavior and characteristics expected of the fifth and sixth grade age group. They share the same attributes but the younger group develops a little maturity in activities and responses. Most of the behaviors displayed by the younger youth are ones they have learned from home and school. Sometimes unfortunately, behaviors learned at school out-weight the ones learned at home. This is bad because all the things learned at school do not come directly from the teacher or by way of the classroom. Peer pressure also contributes to some behaviors learned at school. In most instances when we have greater influence from peer pressure than basic class room training, it becomes dangerous. Of course, there are some good things children can learn from each other but most of it is not proper in perspective. Younger youth are very intuitive and innovative. They are of a greater challenge to their teachers. Their curiosity leads to asking a lot of "why" questions. They are apt to determine whether an answer is satisfactory or not, therefore a teacher must try to be as honest as he can in responding to any questions asked by this age group. Even parents as well have to be honest with their youngsters. A lesson plan that is built around *case studying, brainstorming, problem solving and researching* will be appealing to this group. Competition is apparent in this group. Learners like to compete amongst themselves. Teachers should give learners enough space and resources in allowing them to explore their world of discovery. Their involvement in the children's choir and other activities that promote leadership and challenge will be a plus to their learning.

To teach adults is not too much of a problem in terms of getting results or feedback as opposed to preschooler and other younger groups. These are matured individuals who have the capability to access and evaluate teaching methods that are posed before them prior to deciding which one to assimilate and which one to trash out. Unlike the adult group, younger groups do not have the mental maturity in most cases to think abstractly but because the adult group has gone through many developmental stages of life, they are able to control their response factor based on their experiences. In the *continuum model of lifelong learning*, I believe adult learning contains the blending of the *objective, subjective and relational modes. As* long as a person continues to live, these three modes are going to continually be a part of his learning process, although, there may be brief moments of reflecting a little more of one mode than the other. However, eventually the person's response level will go back to the blending stage of utilizing all three modes. I believe each mode depends on the other to make a perfect whole. With this age group, Benjamin Bloom's three domain of learning could all be applied successfully to the lesson plan designed for adults.

The Curriculum

Curriculum materials must be compatible with the learners' ability to assimilate without any problems. A curriculum must generally meet the age groups' level. More importantly, A church curriculum must be built around the doctrinal principles of that church. It would look confusing and somewhat misleading a situation to have a church using a curriculum that teaches views that are different from its beliefs and doctrine. Also the teachers of that church must honor the views of that organization for which they work and be loyal to their jobs and the ones they are responsible to teach. In some cases, it would be wrong for an organization's leadership to compel all its teachers to be a part of them before serving as a staffer. I believe that if the leadership of this organization worked closely with these teachers, the Lord could make them accept membership and get converted as well. However, it would be in the organization's good interest to encourage and support its members to sharing their career with their own organization instead of using an outsider. My example of the non-member staffer as an exception reflects only in the event where this person happens to be a trained and certified teacher who is part of a staff that functions in a secular unit which is an entity of the church. For example, an elementary or junior high school runs by a church organization or a parochial school. Perhaps the church may not have members of its own who are qualified to teach, therefore, in order to meet the educational standard within that locale, the church must employ certified teachers to teach. It would be a different matter if it were only a situation involving a Sunday School. If that were the case, then under no circumstance should a pastor allow a non-believer or non-member to conduct a bible class because a teacher has to believe in what he teaches and live it as well.

Learning Objectives

Advantageously, it benefits both the teacher and pupils to harbor teaching in an environment of objectivity. The implementation of learning goals helps a teacher or trainer find it much easier to plan and teach. Great planning is a product of great organizing. And one who is well organized makes a great planner. It should be the concern of every teacher or trainer to be a good planner. The role of teaching is one that sets precedence for others to follow. It provides a pathway for leadership and serves as a guide to others. Much discipline is required in order for one to be successful. Learning goals are very crucial in teaching and training. They serve as the blueprint to the structure the trainer intends to build in the mind of his trainees. Proper planning brings about good results; that which a teacher ascertains only if he properly prepares himself and his lesson. A key element in structuring a resourceful planning is an "objective" or "goal." A teacher or trainer must have an objective or goal in his planning. He must know the purpose of his teaching, what he hopes to accomplish and how he is going to accomplish it, he must know how long it takes to accomplish it, and what is the best possible way of accomplishing it with ease and simplicity.

Unit one concentrates on the first step in successful teaching, the *learning goal*.[141] The learning goal helps one to focus precisely on his lesson plan, so that he can be very effective in teaching within the limits of the plan. This type of disciplined behavior on the part of the teacher is what the author calls a *fence*, a learning goal built around the plan to enable the teacher not to rumble off course or get out of context. A learning goal directs one fully in all activities and resources confined within a designed parameter of the lesson plan which helps make the entire process of learning complete with clarity and good comprehension. These activities are indicators that are compatibly used in lesson planning to help strengthen a primary learning outcome. Utilizing the kinds of learning activities that would give better results is very important, that is why a teacher must try to be as broad as he can and simple in his teaching. By being *broad*, one is forced to use all the resources needed, and the simplest method necessary to serve the intended purpose of capturing the minds of the learners. The application of resources and methodologies benefit both the pupils and the teacher. They help the teacher work smoothly from an organized system that makes his job easier. Goal planning is essential in everything we do, even in life today, one must have a purpose in life. A person must think in terms of knowing where he is from and where he is going, and what he intends to achieve in order to not stumble in life when situations arise. It is not that the goal-oriented ones are better off in life than the non-goal oriented ones. It is just that with a goal-oriented person, his response and way of handling a situation would be better than that of the other. A goal-oriented person's approach to a given situation is different from that of a non-goal oriented person. Apparently, from the goal-oriented person's perspective, a situation could be solvable due to life's experiences and advanced preparations, but that would not be the case with the one who is non-goal oriented. The former lives his life expecting the odds, and prepares himself to deal with them as opposed to the latter.

A great planner will be very effective not only because he knows the subject matter and the pupils' needs but because he is *goal-direct*. He will always be able to get his plan across with ease in a timely fashion. "The road to good education is easier than we sometimes realize. A trip to the supermarket, a picnic in the woods or a visit to the airport can open a child's eyes."[142] Nancy Larric means that education can be taught anywhere and at anytime. Parents could seize any moment in or out of the house to teach their children.

It should be the intent of a planner or teacher to get a positive result from his planning or teaching. A good feedback lets the teacher know that the application or method used was very successful and resultful. This unit focuses on the means by which a teacher could know whether his teaching is effective or not. A disciplined teacher is always anxious to get a good feedback from his students because he realizes that tomorrow's bliss of excellence of any one of his students will be a crown of great pride for him. Therefore, applying the best teaching approach and tools would bring about a great pay-back. However, instead of concentrating only on how well the students are doing, the teacher should be aware that he himself is being evaluated by the type of method used. Whatsoever output the pupils produce would reflect on the kind of training and trainer they received. As it is said in the Bible, "a good father makes a glad son," so would it be with a good teacher who does his best in doing his job well. He knows that the reward of his teaching could only mean so much to him if his students achieved the maximum level of achievement and performance as expected. Accomplishing this task of excellence on the part of the teacher warrants self-evaluation also so that the teacher recognizes the kind of feedback that is being projected from the actions and reactions of himself and his students, and the kind of responses he gets from his students. Much of measuring progress is made possible by rating the performance of each student based on the materials presented. Rating requires a certain standard by which the teacher could know the average performance of each of his students. There must be a specific requirement or criterion met to validate a student's eligibility for promotion or not, but a lot of this could work out cohesively if the teacher provided the opportunity to grant each student the privilege to maximize his performance level. With adequate circumstantial academic background profile of each student provided, I believe it would be enough to justify the outcome of the teacher's evaluation. The *goal-indicator* describes the type of action the teacher wants his students to demonstrate as a sign to indicate whether the students are learning something or not. It is from the indicator the teacher bases his test on, and also from the activities provided to the students. The activities are aimed at making sure that these objectives are met by the students. The activities help bring out the output of each student to the teacher. The teacher is able to recognize the slower students from the students that are progressing at a faster pace.

The key to proper planning is to have a *goal-indicator* in one's plan because it is from the goal-indicator a planner would know where he is heading with his plan. It is the *goal-indicator statement* that lays out objectively the expectations of the planner and the learner. For instance, the planner must specifically spell out what he intends to get across and what he expects the learners to do in receiving what he has to offer, and how he or the learner could know that something has been accomplished. Usually a goal-indicator statement of the lesson may state what the planner expects the learner to exhibit. It could be certain educational results, such as the learner demonstrating a certain drill or reciting a poem, or identifying something as being given by the planner as a measuring rod to prove that something was accomplished. This unit concentrates particularly on ways of designing learning activities to get results. The goal of a teacher is to formulate a lesson plan that would be easy and simple for the pupils to grasp. In doing this, the teacher must familiarize himself with the learning potential of each of his students. He must know the learning strengths of his students, knowing this he would be able to put together a plan that matches on average the entire class. By knowing his students, the teacher is able to use the kinds of activities that would match each student. These activities are then regulated by certain standards that would help make the learning process simple. The application of principles is useful in drawing specifics on the primary learning outcome to make the lesson plan as clear as possible, whereby, if any exercise is to be done, the students would find it less difficult in completing the task or assignment. Principles practically describe the learning outcome, and practically exhibit the kind of activity that is applicable in the process.

The purpose of learning is to gain knowledge, to understand it and to know how to apply it appropriately. The purpose of a teacher is to see how well he could provide the resources for attaining knowledge and how well he could enhance the level of that knowledge attained by the pupils. There have to be stages of development or growth in everything we do today. In life there are stages of development, and so it is in other situations and encounters we face each day. As in these cases, so is it in learning or teaching. First, the teacher must be prepared to create an environment in which his students would get to know the existence of elevation in gaining knowledge and some of the incentives that follow as one continues to excel in knowledge. Once there is an awareness the teacher then must develop a suitable plan that would shelter such atmosphere of acceptance on the part of the students. It then becomes the teacher's responsibility to present materials and activities that would support his objective. Because much of the students' behaviors change is initiated by the teaching environment, it then becomes the responsibility of the teacher to make sure that he develops that pattern of motivation and aspiration in each of his students. Sometimes it is not possible to have all one hundred percent of the students transformed, but regardless, it should be the primary objective of the teacher to impact almost one hundred percent of the class with his lesson plan. It is incumbent upon a teacher to be ethical and principled in his career. He should be apt to sense the responding level of his students and know what percentage of his class is picking up what he is teaching, and the percentage that is not picking-up. He should know the trend of the class, whether the majority of the students require advanced treatment or a minority requires the normal level of training. He also should know the learning strength of each of his students. There could be some that are slow in learning but show good sign of managing advanced treatment. Knowing the learning strength of the students would be very helpful in figuring out the level of ability a student has and can carry. That is why it is good that an institution develops levels and categories of training for students to determine the intelligence quotient of each student. By so doing, good students would not be hampered, and the institution's administration would not run into complications in maintaining a staff capable of meeting the needs of each student on an efficient and timely basis. The levels of activities instituted are necessary within a given training unit, and the using of indicators is very helpful in determining the actual performance of each student

After knowledge is attained, it must be exercised or utilized. An attained knowledge that is not used becomes stagnant and ineffective and eventually fades away. When knowledge is explored or experimented, it advances from one level to another. This is a time when avenues of creativity and innovation begin to surface. *Understanding* is a factor behind creativity on what is given to be an astronomical exponential level. This unit deals with the three levels of learning in the area of *understanding* which are categorically advanced. A Planner using these levels of learning must design them specifically to suit the class for which the plan is being prepared. If not, his effort becomes useless because he designed a plan that is below the standard of the class. For instance, a supposedly advanced class that is tested only on *knowledge level* would find the lesson too easy or less challenging. It would only be a waste of time for the students as well as the teacher. The students must learn how to *interpret* ideas by breaking them down into parts. Perhaps, in the process of simplifying complex problems, new thoughts could be discovered. *Analyzation* is a great way of exercising one's mind in finding out how things are organized. Another exploratory level of understanding is *synthesis,* that is, a level at which pupils are able to utilize their thoughts in a more mature fashion. They are able to take the missing pieces of a puzzle and put them back together. Sometimes, though, in the process of doing this, the puzzle could picture a brand new concept that had not been discovered before. Students become brighter in *understanding* after they have learned how to *analyze* and *synthesize.* Their evaluation of things is based on the *knowledge* they have acquired and the *understanding* they possess to know how to *analyze* and *synthesize* things.

Knowledge is like a valued commodity on the market that one cannot afford to do without. Having it enables one to have better incentives to survive the economy that he faces, and that without it the chance of survival becomes bleak. Knowledge is essential in the world in which we live. It opens avenues of opportunity, serves as a gateway to success, and almost tends to be lifeless without it. Because of the valued labeling of knowledge in this age and time, it becomes imperative that everyone takes advantage of it in order to succeed. *Knowledge* is that level of achievement that places one on the pinnacle of acceptability by others in his society. It provides him a room to harbor in and a safe haven to keep apart from the rest of the illiterate world. Humanity exists because of *knowledge,* knowledge is part of what and how we think and how we do things. Learners must place a great value on learning, and so must the teacher. The students must be taught that the continued process of learning is a building block of one's future that is solely predicated on *knowledge.* The students must be aware that there are stages of learning and levels of knowledge that every pursuer must come across. A teacher who is teaching for *knowledge* should use all the tools and materials available to implicitly instill the values required into the minds of the pupils.

The principles listed by this unit are useful tools in having much of this accomplished: *Using learning activities that call for active responses.* The key to this scenario is getting the students to be a part of what goes on in the classroom. The concern of the teacher should be that everyone participates. The teacher must create the opportunity of motivating the students to give some feedback. *Provide activities in which learner uses more than one sense simultaneously.* The teacher must make the lesson interesting and appealing to the students, so that students become eager to forego the challenges that are attached to the level of knowledge that needs to be attained. This is when the pupils get to think and write at the same time. *Provide activities using advanced organizers.* This is another level of knowledge or learning when the students are individually able to exercise their memory and at the same time realize the importance of using it. This is when the pupil finds the lesson motivating and challenging, and decides to be the best student in the class by going ahead of the class. *Provide learning with immediate knowledge of results.* With such enthusiasm, the teacher should add more fuel to the flame of the pupil's zeal by making the pupils feel good about their hard work, class activities, and performance. The teacher must always let the pupils know how well they do in their work. *Involve numerous and varied activities.* The lesson becomes more interesting and challenging when the teacher includes in his plan numerous and varied activities in order to improve the students learning. Different kinds of activities help expose the pupils to various challenges and levels of learning. *Involve novel activities.* The best principle of all is to have students perform live a subject matter or lesson in a drama or play. Games are also a helpful way of novelty through which the goal of the lesson can be met without any difficulty. One is apt to retain knowledge longer when he participates or dramatizes what is to be learned.

Knowledge alone by itself would have less of a value without *understanding*. In learning or training, *understanding* is a key. It is *understanding* not knowledge that is the medium through which the goal of a lesson is met. Most of the time, the recalling of facts is there but teachers and trainers prefer having the involvement of students in activities that would exemplify facts literally. A teacher should employ guidelines that would help in designing adequate lesson plans for understanding. Pupils must be able to expand on the facts or knowledge they know. They must be able to see the picture the facts represent and be able to objectively accept the truths of the facts. And in their own thoughts and ideas, they should be able to relate the facts into something most common to them by translating the facts in their terms, and interpreting the facts the way they see them. As pupils move on from one level to another, they confront challenges, and their only way out is to have a remedy to withstand or overcome these challenges. In a given confrontation, the pupils must be able to subdue the situation by applying any of the best approaches he knows. Sometimes not every approach would seem to be good, there would be times when one approach may produce positive results while another negative. Before applying any techniques to quell a situation, the pupils must be able to make the right judgment. They must first be able to define the problem and *analyze* it before solving it, in so doing they come out with good results. Sometimes in the process of *analyzing* a situation it is expedient that the students know how to *synthesize* a concept before implementing it. Students must learn how to brainstorm their thoughts and implement an idea that would be extraordinary to the subject matter. The implementation of creativity could be something that all would prefer as acceptable. Of course, much of the *synthesizing* would end up being evaluated or screened in the students' mind on standards they know to be appropriate and on procedures they have been taught to be the right approach to the situation. When pupils reach this level of concluding what is good and not good, what is ethical and not ethical, what is procedural and not procedural, or what makes sense and what does not make sense, we say they have learned and experienced great thoughts and understanding that fashion them to respond like this. Activities provided by the teacher guide the students in knowing how to translate ideas, how to compare and contrast between words and phrases, how to develop ideas that best describe a concept as they picture it from their perspective, and how the implementing of these ideas in a fashion that gives them a more practical understanding, is as helpful as anything else.

One of the challenges a teacher faces is trying to change the attitudes and values of his students. Sometimes the attitudes and values of teenagers may not be as difficult to change as would the values and attitudes of adults. The values and attitudes of most young people are not as matured as adults. Young people are vulnerable to being influenced by their immediate environment. Even though attitudes and values go far beyond the classroom, teaching can still impact them. With the proper usage and application of guidelines or principles of learning, it is possible for designed activities to have a positive effect on the students. Obviously, in order for this scenario to work, by the same token, the teacher must have the right attitude also towards his students. It takes one attitude to change another attitude, be it good or bad. Attitudes could also have genetic connection. It is probable that a child's attitude could develop from his parents' genes. Although much of the child's values and attitude could be attributable to his up-bringing environment, other natural causes could also have something to do with it. While applying the principles of learning, much passion should be displayed by the teacher. With patience, the teacher will learn to work along with the students and with passion he will be able to understand the emotions of the students. *Arranging for learners to observe leaders and peers;* this is one of the best ways young people learn by observing others around them. A leader in this case could make a good leadership by being a good example. *Arranging for learners to read or hear about persons who exemplify good attitude:* Consistent reading about great heroes and heroines would have an impact on the pupils' attitudes and values. *Exposing learners to authoritative sources: Knowledge, Understanding and Skills* are guided by modeling after one's admirer. People also imitate others in areas of their specialty. *Help learners identify and specify attitude and learn what the attitude mean:* It is good for a trainer to encourage learners to study certain attitudes and understand why others behave as they behave because some people take on certain attitudes just for the fun of it and because of stereotypical reasons. Therefore, by educating them things might change. *Provide ways for learners to have meaningful emotional experiences:* Sometimes it would take an emotional experience to break down a student who has a stuck up attitude. He acts as though nothing on earth could ever change him.

There could be certain reasons why people behave a certain way, therefore if one could find a means of finding the soft spot on this person's emotion, it would be very impacting. *Lead learners to a positive action:* Because learners are apt to imitate and model after other people, it is always good to keep a positive atmosphere around them. *Provide opportunities for learners to analyze their own values:* It is always good to give the learners adequate room for privacy in order for him to undergo self-purging. It is not good to use force towards anyone, one has to respect the pupils' liberty and not infringe on it. *Provide ways for learners to reflect on life experiences in the light of the truth:* "You should know the truth, and the truth shall make you free" John 8:32. If a learner is respected and told that he has great values and if determined, he could capitalize on his admirer's work, I believe the learner will go for it. *Arrange for learners to share their insights with others in a climate of freedom:* Freedom brings about relaxation and self-comfort. In such atmosphere, it is possible to get the best out of a person. Teachers should learn how to deal with situations pressure-free, not to be too pushy. When people are given respect and dignity, then are they able to let go some of their personal feelings. At this point, sharing would be very helpful.

There comes a time in a learner's life when he has to practically utilize all the theoretical knowledge, understanding, and skills he has. His practical behavior is shaped by the principles and ethics that govern the types of training he receives. Sometimes, apart from the understanding and skills the learner has, there would be instances when he has to make decisions or react to situations differently from the way he has been trained. As this occurs, the learner gains an experience, and develops a change of attitude that would react to a given situation in a matured fashion. For instance, a learner's attitude begins to shape up at the *first level* of attitudinal learning when he then acknowledges the existence of something, and tries to adapt it. This new information gives the learner's attitude a different reflection. At the *second level,* the learner decides within himself that the object or subject confronted is something that is appealing, and he begins to think whether to accept the idea or not. Before the learner decides to commit himself to accepting that object or subject matter, he will place a value on it. Placing a value on that thing, person, or place would be a sign of trust, surety and commitment between both the learner and the teacher. The learner then contemplates the pros and cons of the matter at hand and tries to figure out how beneficial the lesson being taught is. The duty of the teacher is to design activities that would bring to light the significance of the lesson and how useful it is. Pupils look for many motivating factors in and out of the class room, therefore the teacher must be aware of the pupils' interest by making sure that these plans and activities are motivating. Every now and then pupils experience difficulties in trying to make a decision, most especially, the right decision. At times pupils are baffled with choosing from their list of ideas the appropriate one that would help them out perfectly. The *organization level* of training is when the learner shows his maturity by applying as many values as he can to a give situation. The learner would always use that which eventually registers as part of him. He develops a life-style that is characterized by his beliefs and what he stands for.

Within the class, it is possible to find few students who are very quick when it comes to psychomotor skills. Likewise there are students who have similar intensity when it comes to perceptual skills. Nevertheless, it is incumbent upon the teacher to help train the percentage of those students who have less psychomotor skills to develop them, and those students with less perceptual skills to learn them. No matter what type of activities involved, the teacher's job is to professionally be able to create and develop in the students the kind of training or skills they need. It makes sense to say that for a lesson that requires much perceptual skills, almost one hundred percent of the teacher's lesson plan must comprise activities that are perceptual, and a lesson that is aimed at influencing psychomotor skills should contain activities to a higher degree than anything else. However, both skills could be used in a given scenario, but I believe that when it comes to categorical training skills like *psychomotor* and *perceptual,* one must objectively use a higher percentage of activities relative to the type of skills involved. It happens that this unit treats a lesson on developing motor skills. In accomplishing his goal as a teacher, one must use activities that center around psychomotor skill. The simplest possible way to meet the goal for this type of skill would warrant a trainer to use hands-on activities, such as students learning mechanical skills to physically touch the engine or parts of the machine to know its components, functions, and design, or for students learning music, the physical holding and playing of the keyboard, guitar and other musical instruments including knowing the various musical notes, chords, beats, and understand what a melody is and what lyrics are. The teacher could also use visuals, such as films, charts or videos and pictures or even apply novelty in the learning process. One should not totally rule out the application of perceptual tools. They all could play a vital role in making the lesson simple and comprehensible. In terms of learning indicators, the teacher should mostly use psychomotor applications to evaluate the students' level of achievement. These should be indicators of the same techniques used in the lesson. The pupils should be able to recognize the parts of an engine and know how they function. Likewise, the students of music must be able to identify parts of the instrument learned, its components, and know the various notes and keys.

There is an adage that says, "practice makes perfect." By constantly doing something over and over again, one becomes good at it. The five steps or levels of developing motor skills are very unique in helping a trainer or teacher get his objective across. The first step of *perception* is when the pupils are aware of the task before them that need to be accomplished. It could be a lesson plan that requires the students to learn how to play a certain kind of sport, let say basketball, or a plan that is centered around having the students learn how to build something. The level of perception is when a student gets himself aware through the senses the kind of energy that would be exerted to doing this activity. He would observe the various movements of the person performing the act and at the same time familiarize himself with the rules of the game, provided the task pertains to learning a particular sport. The second level, *set*, is when the student becomes aware of the kind of energy he has to use in playing the sport and decides within himself that he "can do it." This is the time when one affixes himself for the challenge and convinces himself that he is able to perform. The third level, *guided responses* is when the teacher or trainer steps in and decides to familiarize the pupil with the "ins" and "outs" of the game. It becomes the trainer's job of making sure that the rules of the game are explained thoroughly to the pupils. He should make sure that the object of the game is explained, and he must let the pupils know what must be done in order for them to become more competitive, and what to do if their opponents are more aggressive or more competitive than them. After all this session of advice and explanation has taken place, the level of "mechanism" comes in when the pupils realize that playing the game would require some physical fitness and some practice. They must realize that they have to focus on practice and self-discipline as the way to good performance. Pupils then learn that they could train themselves at all times even during the absence of the trainer in order to be in good shape for that sport. After constantly practicing, a habit develops. The individuals then eventually find passion in the sport, and make the sport a part of them. Performance of the *complex overt response* becomes possible after the learner has discovered tricks or techniques that help him perform competitively well. He learns how to perform differently from the average person and learns how to play with a certain style that would single him out as a different athlete. As the learners begin to become more competitive, they reach the stage when they could perform a task with no problems at anytime, with great accuracy. For instance, with athletes who compete for the Olympics, they become exceptionally good to the extent that no one locally could ever outplay them. Because of the athletes' hardworking habits in that sport, their skill becomes "supernormal" if you will. Their techniques become unbeatable and matchless.

The purpose of teaching is to impart knowledge; knowledge that could be useful and beneficial to the one to whom it has been imparted. It is the teacher's desire to instruct a person or group of people who are willing to receive and accept that which is taught including the teacher himself who is doing the teaching. The "willingness" of a person eager to learn is what a teacher feeds on to achieve his goal. From the teacher's perspective, the learner must be able to prove that he has acquired knowledge and can retain it. Therefore, in making sure that the learner has learned something, the teacher would have to evaluate the learner based on the indicators of the lesson and the level of knowledge attained or taught. It is important that test materials indicate the type of response the lesson's indicator projects. It is not good for a test to have questions that are different from what has been taught, that confuses the learner and make responding difficult. Also, teachers should let testing materials be subject related.

Teaching one thing and testing in another area other than that which was taught is inappropriate and unethical. Teachers should not get in the habit of trying to confuse the students or make things complicated. Although an exam is sometimes longer than an ordinary quiz or class work, it does not have to contain instructions and concepts that are not related to the topic discussed in class. It would be a different story if the students were tested generally as in testing their aptitude, but that is not the case, when it comes to evaluating a class on lessons that were previously taught, I believe that it would be ethical to have tests cover only the lesson discussed. Lastly, the test should reflect the same level of learning the indicator calls for. Sometimes, students sit long before a test trying to figure out whether the teacher meant that they should list something or explain it. Perhaps, the students were only trained to analyze something but on the test the teacher wants them to synthesize, the students definitely would have a problem figuring out how to answer the question. Testing is just an evaluation in proving that the students acquired something but not to fail the students or make the students look like dummies. Teaching becomes worthless when teachers behave like this.

The intent of all teachers in both the secular and non-secular arenas should be to teach to get something accomplished. The entirety of the teaching profession circumvents this goal of getting satisfactory results for the time and effort allotted to get the job done. However, in both areas, that is, the secular and non-secular, there may be a slight difference due to their respective values and beliefs. But they both have one thing in common which is to accomplish their task by aiming at the same primary goal of seeking to get some kind of reception from the pupils they try to teach. This should be the purpose of teaching, which is to seek a better means for imparting knowledge to the illiterate, wisdom to the unwise, and understanding to the ignoramus. But in the process of instilling wisdom, knowledge, and understanding, one should be very cautious and conscientious about how he goes about with the application, because it is through the technique applied one is able to get something accomplished. Long before the birth of Christ, the scriptures pointed out this rule of objectivity by God through the prophets. God has always been the greatest disciplinarian the universe has ever portrayed. In the book of Isaiah, God instructs His prophet that He never teaches in vain, i.e., without accomplishing anything. Therefore, He does not expect His prophets and teachers to teach without seeking better results. In Isaiah 55:11, the Lord says, "so shall my word be that goeth out of my mouth: it shall not return unto me void, but it shall accomplish that which I please, and it shall prosper in the thing whereto I sent it." In the preceding verse, the Lord is laying out a paradigm for His prophets by saying that whenever they instruct, they should be purposeful in attaining a response from those to whom they speak. The primary objective should be to save and deliver people from their state of misery and confusion into deliverance and blessing. But in spite of it all, the primary goal is to get some feedback from the audience. It then features the question, how will His prophets be able to ascertain such goal; the solution which God Himself has? God intends for His prophets to utilize the application that best suits the aim of accomplishing this goal of knowledge that could be none other than the divine application which He Himself imposes to be followed and exemplified as His divine guidance. Unlike secular teaching, this is the utmost distinction that differentiates Christian teaching or Christian Education from all other areas of teaching. Christian trainers use as their primary guide, a purpose of God or the spirit being the focal point of their teaching which is saturated in all applications or techniques used in the process of teaching.

Christian Trainers are to be adept at knowing how and when to apply the word of God to suit their training occasions. They are to have an in-depth knowledge of the word of God which is the only source of their goals and strength. Like the Carpenter and Mason, a Christian Educator has to always have the Bible as a basic tool to all his teaching and training. The Bible is the final authority a Christian has to refer to for guidance and knowledge in the things pertaining to spiritual growth and nurturing. It is clearly shown in the Bible how the treasures of knowledge and wisdom are found no where else but hidden right in the Lord (Colossians 2:3). Also James, the writer of the epistle of James lets us know that man's source of wisdom can only be obtained through God and no one else (James 1:5).

The Bible as a tool for the Christian educator, must be well mastered in order for it to practically serve as a forte in Christian ethics and training. *Better Bible Knowledge* is very needful in Christian education. Despite all the other psychological and social implications and applications in the process of training, the Bible should always serve as the foundation.

A Christian Trainer has the responsibility to make sure that he imparts knowledge in the most proper fashion there is. It is a duty he commits himself to before the eyes of God, he must do justly to the ones he teaches and be loyal to the God who he serves. God has laid much emphasis on believers being astute in the word. God, on one occasion told his prophet that His people are destroyed due to the lack of knowledge. Knowledge pertaining to the life and ways of God can be ascertained from no where else but the Bible. The believers must devote their time in studying and reading the word. It is the word that would guide and lead anyone who commits himself to reading it. David says that it is the word that serves as a lamp to guide his steps as he walks and a light to show him the way. When Jesus came down from the mount after fasting for forty days and nights, it was His defense on the word that defeated the devil. The believers are to learn how to live by the word and not bread alone. Above all our needs, the spiritual need counts the most. It is the spirit not the flesh that communes with the spirit of God to be sensitive and matured. That parental environment becomes one of exposure that would help shape the life of that child. As the child begins to grow, it copies and practices everything that it sees going on around it. At the exposure stage, the child is very observant, if you will, the child becomes a living and walking tape recorder and camera. The child records everything he hears and imitates everything he sees moving about around him. Not only in early childhood we find that going on, teenagers including adults also learn from exposure. In other words, all of us learn from exposure. In fact, this is how our experience is developed, it is developed from what we see around us, and the things we counteract and interact with. The reactions we recognize and realize from these interactions are than registered in our characteristics which we decide to either use acceptably or not. The lessons we notice from these interactions are then assimilated as experiences we have encountered. The teacher of the Bible has to expose his pupils to the ethical and principal features of Christian living in order for them to know which conduct is acceptable and which one is not. I may advice that in this stage of exposure, *visual aids* should be used to tell stories and give examples of biblical characters and the life they live as being Christ-like and acceptable. Perhaps, preferentially, the lives of living believers within that vicinity could practically be the best exposure the pupils could get as a living example of how God wants His children to live.

Repetition, the second step is a vigorous level during which learning in childhood begins to pick up. I had this experience with my three-year old daughter who currently attends pre-kindergarten. She was given a recitation to say for their Christmas program. When I looked at the recitation and realized that it was too difficult for a three and a half-year old child, I decided to take it back to the school and question the teacher about it but then a second thought came to me. I however took it as a challenge, and decided to work with my daughter to learn it before the week of the program. One part of my mind was telling me that this would be impossible for her to learn, and the other part was telling me that with much effort the mission could be accomplished. So, what I did was to write down the recitation on pieces of post-it pad sheets and placed them at key places in the home including one on my dashboard in the car. I told her mother to have one with her all the time so that she could be able to recite the recitation to our daughter at all times. While taking our daughter to school every morning, I repeatedly recited the recitation out loud and asked her to repeat after me. I also sang it at times just to help her pick up the words. I made sure that her mother recited it to her when she picked her up from school in the car and also when she got home. To our amazement, in less than three weeks she could clearly recite the recitation. I am a witness that *repetition* does work. It is an effective tool in the process of learning, teachers should frequently use it. Repetition could be sung or even played as a game among the pupils in the classroom.

Understanding, the third step is essential in the process of learning because it is the medium by which the teacher will be able to measure the learning level of his pupils. It is very important to note that a lesson taught must be one worth understanding. It is possible for someone to take in thoughts without proper understanding but such in-taking is not guaranteed to last for long because it is only taken in through the short-term memory which does not store memories permanently or for a long period of time. Only when knowledge is properly learned with understanding will it have some permanent long-lasting value for the learner. Take for an example, memorization is an example of short-term memory learning. A person could memorize an entire book of the Bible but would still not understand that which he has memorized. Only a learning or lesson that is assimilated with understanding is durable because one would mix such understanding with meaning and substance which will eventually bring about interest in the process of learning.

One of the factors that presents a purview of certainty for dynamic teaching results is *attitude*. Attitude plays a major role in the process of teaching and learning. Both the teacher and students have to reflect an image of delight and warmth. With such display of warmth and delight, we then would have a pleasant environment where learners are willing to learn and a teacher is pleased to teach because of the joy it brings for him to instruct others. A teacher with the wrong attitude could cause a stymie in the teaching-learning process. The students become very sensitive when they sense the unfriendly disposition of their teacher. A teacher who presents a mean image drives his students away from coming over for help. It also causes the students to lose interest in the learning process. Students like to have a teacher who is friendly because that teacher could very well be a counselor to them in lots of ways. A friendly teacher sometimes could help a student with domestic problems to be able to overcome them. A teacher has to focus not only on the material he is teaching, rather on the needs of the students he is teaching. Sometimes a student may be going through something at home that is distracting his commitment to learning, and could decide to seek help by choosing to ask a pertinent question in class as being the only available opportunity to get some indirect advice. A teacher may notice this to be time consuming, but he should not shun the student because this may be a life saving situation. Teachers must always try to carry the right attitude to the classroom. Likewise the students have to know that they have to be respectful and obedient in the classroom as being the only way they could ever learn anything.

Being to the point in our conversations, negotiations, discussions, speeches, and lessons is very important, if not we may lose the attention of the ones we are trying to interact with. Good preparation is one way one could find help in being specific. A teacher must always have a lesson plan before going to teach, and the lesson plan should contain an aim that is needful, short, and simple to grasp. The teacher should have his objective concisely structured to accommodate the time allotted for the class period. With such short and sweet objective, the learning process will be meaningful and effective. Sometimes, it is a lot of fun with the students. Any lesson that is attractive to the students will always gain the attention of the students. The students will be willing to sit attentively and learn with fun. Inspiration, charisma, and the like are attributes that are attained from proper planning and teaching. Being right to the point alleviates boredom. Especially, in this age of impatient-youthful gesticulation, it becomes imperative that teachers apply techniques that will make their lesson interesting. At the verge of boredom, lots of thoughts run across the pupils' minds. Some of the students would contemplate recess or lunch, and others would have their thoughts wandering in the world of adventure while the lesson is going on.

There are times a teacher has to let his class know that certain materials need close attention before they can be assimilated. The teacher is left with the responsibility to instill seriousness to the students if that is what it would take for them to learn the lesson. As the Poet Solomon puts it, there is a time for every purpose under the heaven (Ecclesiastes 3:10). It should be the initiative of the teacher to let the students know that certain lessons require more effort and hard work on their part in order for them to learn. Certain lessons require different levels of approach. These lessons should not methodologically be applied as would other lessons be. These are lessons that require more attention and commitment from both the teacher and the students. It is the teacher's job to make such difficult lesson as simple as possible, and it is the responsibility of the students to work a little harder than normal to grasp the lesson. Purposeful Bible study is needed in Christian training because it is by this type of training the pupils become walking and living bibles. It is always good for a teacher to prepare in advance for the unexpected just in case time does not allow the entire lesson to be fully covered. Preparing for the unknown should not be ruled out from the teacher's lesson plan. There could arise instances during the class session when issues of concern could be brought up by one of the students that might take up almost the entire class period. In this case, a teacher should ask the Lord for guidance in handling the situation because it could mean a whole lot to the students. If a teacher is too quick to react in trying to only concentrate on covering his lesson plan for that period and not open to discuss in length any topic that might hinder him for covering his lesson, he would be doing much harm than good to his students. He would be acting arrogantly and unfairly to the ones he says he has been called to teach and lead. A teacher must be willing to accept those times when students will interrupt the class with issues that sometimes may or may not be related to the topic of discussion. Nevertheless, the teacher has to be professional and loving enough to not desist from going into depth with such issues. He should sincerely do his best to iron out those issues as clearly as possible to satisfy the curiosity of the class. However, the teacher must know where the lesson ended prior to the raised issues in order for him to know where to begin at the next class session in case he runs out of time. Securing carry-over is very important because a teacher could easily skip a valuable lesson or topic that needs to be covered. The teacher does not have to worry about not being able to complete his plan for the semester as planned if he were to drift off tract by addressing issues of diverse kinds that are posed by his students. This is what makes teaching phenomenal, that is, by enlightening the minds of the students not only on the fixed lesson plan or subject, rather, it is by the entertaining of concerns that makes teaching interesting to the students.

I concur with the findings of the various survey results regarding the trend of limited bible knowledge in Christendom from my research. During the tenure of my service as a Sunday school superintendent, I began to realize that the attendance at Sunday school had been very low. In fact, most adults think that Sunday school is only for the little ones. The majority of the devoted Christian adults today are more concerned about getting to church on time than to Sunday school. I discovered that most adults believe that they know more Bible, therefore, it is only their children who need to be taught because it is the little ones with the deficiency not them. Some adults choose not to go to Sunday school because of their narrowed view that Sunday school comprises only children, they feel that it would be embarrassing for them to sit in the midst of these children just to learn some bible stories. A lot of adults out there who pay no time to visit a Sunday school session have such erroneous views about Sunday school. They sometimes live with this mislead concept all their lives without coming to the realization that Sunday school is not what they think it is. It is pathetic to note that today there are lots of things in our lives that we desist transforming from just because of what someone told us about that thing. We do not try to research for ourselves to verify the validity of the conclusion we claim, rather, we just refused to do otherwise. It is a shame because with this kind of narrow-mindedness, we do ourselves much harm, we shut the doors of knowledge which might eventually bring about liberation to our world. The reason why such deficiency exists among church-going adults is that they believe the church service will be the proper setting where much biblical knowledge can be attained. I am afraid to say that this concept is misleading and vague because in a church service, little is taught from the pulpit in terms of considering the basic rudiments of teaching. The pastor only preaches from the pulpit. There is no question and answer section, and there is no time allotted for group discussions or a forum type display. It is in Sunday school where a lot is learned, questions are asked randomly, answers and assignments are given, and much time is allotted for general discussions. According to a Christian survey, less than 50% of adult Christians had limited bible knowledge. Even when the survey was extended to few Bible Seminaries and Colleges, they found out that less than 75% of bible students could actually display in-depth knowledge of the Bible. Because most of Christendom today only read their bibles on Sundays at church services and not regularly, it is not strange to note that there is a deficiency and that the rate is overwhelming. As for the Seminaries and Bible Colleges, I believe because some are taking theology to be tantamount to other professions, the bible is being studied with less interest. If we in Christendom wish to dominate or win the world before Christ comes, then it is about time that we go back to reviewing our bible lessons from bible schools, having family devotions two or three times a day, and having family being encouraged to attend Sunday school consistently.

"For when for the time ye ought to be teachers, ye have need that one teach you again which be the first principles of the oracles of God; and are become such as have need of milk and not strong meat" (Hebrews 5:12). Contextually, the anonymous writer of the book is admonishing the Hebrew Christians that there are basically two stages in a believer's life. He has to first go through the primary stage, which characterizes him as a *babe in Christ,* and the secondary stage, the *mature stage.* Every Christian experiences these two stages in his walk with the Lord. The primary stage is that stage when the Christian is just born into the kingdom of God as being a new convert and needs much guidance from the elders and those who have been around longer. The secondary stage, which comprises maturity, is that stage all Christian continues to grow in unto an infinite state. This stage entails much endurance, patience, long-suffering, persistence, and passion. This is the one stage that one does not outgrow, it leads on to eternity or death. But in every Christian's life, he must endure some kind of teaching and guidance in order to be able to mature in the Lord. Before one reaches the secondary stage, much growth is needed in the primary stage and one must be willing to go through this nurturing process. In fact, reaching the secondary stage does not mean that nurturing ends at this point. If you will, this level of secondary elevation is just a promotion but contains tougher confrontations ahead. Nevertheless, the only difference is that, now at the secondary stage, one is mature enough not to give up fighting but to continue fighting for his convictions. As in the above-cited scenario, so is it in Christian administration, the teachers themselves who teach have to be supervised or taught as well. There has to be some order because God is one of decency and order. In fact, admitting anyone to teach or explore the liberty of others in terms of saturating their views is very critical. In a situation like this, the ones being taught are vulnerable to anything. Therefore, it is expedient that teachers themselves be supervised and evaluated. As humans, teachers are susceptible to human frailties. Therefore, by getting supervision that might help overcome some of the human weaknesses will be very helpful. As far as evaluation is concerned, the process is there to keep the teacher on tract, and to make sure that the teacher behaves properly and professionally.

The role of the teacher in the lives of the students who he teaches is very crucial. It is natural that the students are prone to copy the behavior and characteristics of their teacher. That teacher could be a role model after whom the students could follow. Because of this opportunity, it is important that the teacher represents a good and godly conduct that would be rewarding to the pupils he trains. Except adult or intelligent young adults, sometimes the most vulnerable ones are younger students who are less matured in making prudent decisions and assessment on opinions and views. In line of eradicating this disadvantageous position, the administration has to intervene in making sure that it has the right person in the classroom teaching.

It is incumbent on all who aspire to teach to have some semblance to the soul not only to himself but to the ones in front of whom he stands to train. Every believer once saved, is been designated by God to be a Numerous times we have heard on the news how students are being molested and abused by their teachers, and how parish priests sexually abuse young boys in their schools. Who could have known, perhaps before these news broke out to the public, these abuses had been going on long before and these children or victims had been terrified and horrified to keep quiet; not disclosing this to anybody including their parents. Who knows at this moment how many youngsters are being continually abused by some teacher or so-called mentor who preys on these defenseless youths who have no means of fighting back. They could either be intimidated from telling anybody or bribed to keep quite. These criminal acts are going on not only in public schools but Christian schools as well. The teachers' administration board must follow the normal procedures the law requires in hiring a teacher to teach. Proper evaluation must be done followed by periodic examining. The behavior of the teachers has to be in check and the students and administrative board have to both evaluate their teachers. Teachers should not be made to think that they are not to answer to anybody and that their actions are unquestionable. Some teachers impress the students to think that they are above the law, and that they do not have to answer to anyone for their actions. Many students believe them and become reluctant to say something about their teacher's bad behavior. A god-fearing teacher will always place himself in the role of a servant to faithfully serve the students who he teaches. He will try to do nothing to hurt the feelings of his students, and he will allow nothing to stampede the learning process. His concern is to make a difference in the lives of all his students. In accomplishing this task, this godly teacher will be willing to improve in areas of incompetence because of the love he has for the profession and the ones he teaches. witness to others regarding his rebirth experience. One really does not need any kind of in-depth biblical training to explain to someone how he feels with Christ being on the inside of him. For instance, on the day of Pentecost Peter had not felt anything like the way he felt when he got baptized with the spirit, but he was able through the unction of the spirit to explain to the bystanders what they felt on the inside. According to Peter, it was an experience inexplicable and incomprehensible.

After interpreting the scriptures and revealing the prophetic nature of the occasion, many believed and were added to the church. In fact, this is how the body of believers grows. It depends on the testimonies of others that bring life and resuscitation to the body. The scriptures encourage believers to worry not over what they are to say when placed on the spot of expressing their relationship with the Lord because the spirit of truth will teach them and bring all things to their remembrance. Nevertheless, this does not mean that believers should pay no mind of studying the scripture, I believe this is referring to an event where one without any pre-knowledge has been confronted with a situation to which he has to give an answer. This does not mean that a Christian ought not to be concerned about learning the scripture, it is not the case. The Bible lets us know that believers are to study to show themselves approved unto God (II Timothy :15). Peter also admonishes the believers to be ready always to give an answer to anyone who asks them about their faith, therefore, this does not exempt a believer from being studious in the word. Every believer is responsible to study the scriptures and know them well because much of it depends on their witnessing and defense in the times of trials and temptations. Like every other believer, so is the teacher, he must study the scripture and seek the spirit's unction in his study. As it is normally said, it is the anointing that makes the difference and breaks the yoke. Being a teacher, places a lot of burden on the person because he has to know his stuff very well because not only is he studying for himself, he is also studying to impart knowledge to others. He must master his material so well and use all the tools he would need to make his job simple and comprehensible.

SUMMARY

The gift of God cannot be received to be merely enjoyed. It must always be shared. Its very nature involves that; for it is Himself, His own Spirit, the Spirit of love. To receive that does not mean to enjoy the knowledge that God love us. It means that His active love is present in our hearts; and if so, it must go out to others. The purpose of God's gift to the church is to have the church as a unified body of believers purposely chosen by God to be a spiritual repository to examplify the knowledge of God on planet earth. The church is to show that it is a unique entity, although of a terestial construct, purposely is of a celestial design which is divine. The purpose of God's gift to the church is to teach and elighten believers. Not to only reach out to the unsaved but to make sure that they cannot fall away from the truth (Hebrews 6:4- 15). God is assuring that the only way believers can individually and collectively maintain firmness and be blessed is by being obedient to God's word, diligent in or walk with God, and faith in your stewardship. God's gift to you or the church is a privileged service, if unused or misused could cause one to lose it. God wants you to bear fruits or utilize your gift to its full potential (Phillipians 4:17). Above all our needs, the spiritual need counts the most. It is the spirit not the flesh that communes with the spirit of God.

ASSESSMENT

1. Why the gift of God cannot be merely enjoyed?

2. What is the purpose of God's gift to the church?

3. How is the church a unique entity?

4. How is God's gift a priviledged service to the church or saint?

5. Is one's gift destined, definite, or eternal? Explain.

PERSPECTIVES

The Cosmological Argument, the argument that the universe's being here at all means that someone must have created it, it cannot just have come into existence all by itself (Magee, 57).[143]

---

[143] Bryan Magee, The Story of Philosophy: The Essential Guide to the History of Western Philosophy. London: Dorling Kindersley Publishing, 1998.

CHAPTER SIXTEEN

GREEK ETYMA

Active—Energēs (ἐνεργής) effectual

Accomplish—Pleroō (πληρόω) to fulfil, to carry out; Plēthō (πλήθω) to accomplish

Commission—Parathēkē (παραθήκη) a deposit with, a deposit with Christ as committing oneself to His service and will

Christians—Christianos (χριστανός) followers of Christ, as acclaimed by the Romans.

Doctrine—Didachē (διδαχή) teaching, instruction; Didaskalia (διδαςκαλία) that which is taught; didachē is used only twice in the Pastorial Epistles, II Timothy 4:2; Titus 1:9

Light—Phōs (Φώς) to give light, used in scripture as the glory of God's dwelling place, God as the illuminator of his people, the illuminating power of the scriptures Jesu as the illuminator of men

THE EXTENT OF YOUR GIFT/ CALLING

Faith is kept alive in us, and gathers strength, more from practice than from speculations (Joseph Addism: The Spectator)

Matthew 28:19

"Go ye therefore, and teach all nations…"

Mark 16:15

"Go ye into all the world, and preach the gospel to every creature."

Acts 1:8

"But ye shall receive power, after that the Holy Ghost is come upon you: and ye shall be witnesses unto me both in Jerusalem, and in all Judæ'a, and in Samaria, and unto the uttermost part of the earth."

There are no limits to our commission or ministry. The church and believers are commissioned to spread the Good News of Christ to every creature and nation. Of course, the word "creature" may pose an extreme compelling but it does not include animals or animated features. The Greek word *zöon* which relates to a living being (zōĕ, life), refers to *animal* or *beast* from the English translation. However the Greek word *ktisis* although signifies the act of creating, does refer to mankind in general as the creatures of God's creative act in Mark 16:15. Now with that clarification we can note that Jesus was referring to humanity when the word creature was used. Although it might have a strong connotation to it, in fact, that shows how serious and imperative the mission is for us. No place or no one should be excused for not being privileged to hear the gospel message. God is making the gospel message expandable through out the world and rules out all dispensability.

Factually, even without our witness, the creatures, fowls of the air, and everything that creeps and lives on planet earth does live under the orders of God as evidence of God's providence. They are aware of him being their creator and they honor Him. Of course, Christ does not want us to spend much of our time to communicate God's saving plan to the animals or animated creatures. Nevertheless, if you communicate very well with animals, you are an exception. There should be no excuse whatsoever for any of mankind to not have the gospel message. This is a compelling universal commission Gods wants the church and believers to fulfill, and He has engineered ways to easily make our mission possible and successful but we need to apply ourselves. The psalmist David declares: "The heavens declare the glory of God; and the firmament sheweth his handiwork. Day unto day uttereth speech, and night unto night sheweth knowledge. There is no speech nor language where there voice is not heard. There line is gone out through all the earth, and their words to the end of the world" Psalm 19:1-4. The Lord has already removed all obstacles and has made clear the pathway for us to spread the Good News. Illustratively, in the rural area of a less developed nation or third-world country, one of the African or Latin American belts, where modern technology is somewhat not popular and affordable, in order to make a passage or path to travel on in the village, the path-maker uses a cutlass or machete to cut through the bushes to make a fine path to travel on. Believers however do not have to worry about the obstacles that might befall them and impede their mission or journey because Christ has already cleared the pathway and has removed the obstacles for them. This He did on Calvary. The only requirement for service is a willing heart and readied mind. The church's and believers' mission is both internal and external, both intra-witnessing as well as inter-witnessing, and demands an introversive interaction as well as extroversive. That shows that this commission covers the whole nine yards of the ministry. One can minister to one-self to make sure that one is on one accord with the commissioner. One is responsible to be a living testimony to his fellow believers and others, one is obliged to spread the word to one's neighbors, friends, workmates, associates and the like, whenever the opportunity arises, one should seize the opportunity to be a witness for the Lord at anytime and anywhere. There is no limit, nothing territorial and nothing circumstantial.

God has called us to be *witnesses*. A witness can only report on what he has seen and heard. Acts 22:15 (Ananias speaking to Paul: "for thou shalt be his witness unto all men of what thou has seen and heard." What you and I have seen and heard becomes our personal experience. It becomes our *personal testimony*. One is very comfortable in telling his personal testimony. The belief that one develops in one's testimony is wrapped up in one's conviction and confidence. It is this conviction that can penetrate hearts and make something happen. This definitely is what Christ wants from His witness, to believe in Christ, have faith in Christ, to have a conviction for the message one preaches and teaches, and expects divine intervention which likely brings positive results. When Peter and John were going to the temple in Jerusalem to pray and they met the lame man at the temple's gate, they could spare some change but they felt that it would not have sufficed the situation, therefore they decided to turn it over to the commissioner for divine intervention to make this man's situation be completely taken care of. They believed that coins or change would serve a *temporal* cause but a divine intervention would serve a *permanent* one. Therefore in faith and conviction, they told the man that they could not spare silver or gold but give him what they had instead, they called on *the name of Jesus* and *commanded Christ to intervene and make the supernatural happen*. This act of divine intervention did not only change the entire being of the lame man, it also increased the faith of Peter and John seeing that this was the first post-Pentecost miracle performed in the history of the church, and to their account. Even when the leaders of the town came to threaten them about persecution and or imprisonment, the more Peter and John began to preach by boldly telling the Jewish rulers, "for we cannot but speak the things which we have seen and heard" Acts 4:20. Conviction increases one's faith and destroys fear.

Christ gives not His witness the spirit of fear but of love power and of a sound mind (II Timothy 1:7). Christ's witness will always be ready for the mission because one can rest assured that the Lord will bring fear in subjection to his Spirit and guarantee a secured mission for His witness. Once fear is out, faith comes in. Faith is the only witnessing element that can penetrate and destroy the enemy's territory. Faith can change the devil's mind and turn the devil's no into a yes. *Intra-personally*, a witness must be on terms with God. He or she must be prayerful and committed to the work of the Lord. If there should be anything that could be a hindrance to the ministry, the witness must take that situation to the alter and leave it there. Be like the song of the psalmist that says *search me Lord if you find anything in me that should not be, take it out and strengthen me because I want to be right and want to be made whole.* Of course, this song relates to the Psalmist David asking the Lord to search him and create in him a clean heart (Psalm 51). *Interpersonally*, any opportunity the witness has to interact with someone, that occasion must be seized to share your testimony and be a witness. An *introversive witnessing* may be local in one's community or church as opposed to an *extroversive witnessing* which has to do with reaching out to others out of your comfort zone.

Reaching out to other communities and spreading the Good News. People can argue with you over the scripture, and choose not to believe what the WORD of GOD says, but they cannot argue against what you personally have experienced. John 9:24-25 "Then again called they the man that was blind, and said unto him, give God the praise: we know that this man is a sinner. He answered and said, whether he be a sinner or not, I know not: one thing I know, that, whereas I was blind, now I see." Sharing what God has done for you is one of the most exciting and effective methods of soul winning, when it is done as it should be, with a HOLY K. I. S. S. (Keep it silent & spoken). Primarily, our silent witness is expressed in the scripture: I Thessalonians 1:5-8: "For our gospel came not unto you in word only, but also in power, and in the holy ghost, and in much assurance; as ye know what manner of men we were among you for your sake. And ye became followers of us, and of affliction, with joy of the Holy Ghost: so that ye were ensamples to all that believe in Macedonia and Achaia. For from you sounded out the word of the Lord not only in Macedonia and Achaia, but also in every place your faith to God- ward is spread abroad; so that we need not to speak anything." Your life is the only Bible some people read. II Corinthians 3:2-3: "Ye are epistle written in our hearts, known and read of all men: Forasmuch as ye are manifestly declared to be the epistle of Christ ministered by us, written not with ink, but with the spirit of the living God; not in tables of stone, but in fleshly table of the heart." People read us at *Home, work, church,* and *at all times.* We affect them by *how we look, where we go, what we say,* and *what we do.*

Secondarily, our witness is spoken as expressed in the scripture: "But ye shall receive power, after that the Holy Ghost is come upon you: and ye shall be witness unto me both in Jerusalem, and in all Judaea, and in Samaria, and unto the uttermost part of the earth." We are called to be witnesses not Jurors, lawyers, judges, or defendants. Your testimony is powerful because it is *captivating, inoffensive, enticing, stirring, convincing,* and *indisputable.* Just tell them what you have seen and heard: Acts 4:20: "For we cannot but speak the things which we have seen and heard." Acts 22:15: "For thou shalt be His witness unto all men of what thou hast seen and heard."

As part of being a true disciple and a proponent for kingdom evangelism to foster change and growth, one must be prone to reaching out and willing to share one's gifts with others in the community. One's God-given gift must be exhibited in a priceless and passion manner or in love. This particular type of love is not a mere relationship that exists between a man and a woman. This particular type of love transcends the mundane sphere of its etymological context in definition. It is a love that is originates from the celestial sphere with a divine connotation in describing its entirety. This is an *agapē* love which by definition means *God's love.* This is a sacrificial type of love, one that money cannot by. It was this same love that made God to robe Himself in human flesh to bring redemption to dying humanity. God did not bargain with humanity in His planning to redeem humanity. He did it because He wanted to restore a divine relationship with man once again that was lost due to man's transgressions. Therefore, when God gives His gift to you He primarily is concerned about establishing a kingdom relationship as opposed to an individual relationship. It is not that God does not have you in mind, rather, He has a macrocosmic picture in mind, which is to use you as an instrument to bring more into the kingdom. But the only way you could effectively carry out this mission is by doing things God's way. The outmost approach you could use that typically represents God is by using your gift in love. Romans 12:9 says, "let love be without dissimulation," i.e., love should be without false appearance or pretense. Your love should be real and radiant. You must detest evil and love to do good for the sake of Christ and the gospel. You must serve and work with passion, diligence, show hospitality, be prayerful, be motivating, concerned about the welfares of others, empathetic, and help others learn to wholly depend on God for their needs and protection. It is when you display the aforementioned attributes in sincerity before the manifestation of Spirit will take effect. You cannot partially carryout your mission and expect God to fully manifest Himself in your work, you must obey and fulfill the mission as God recommends in order to get God's approval.

Exegesis on Romans 12:9-21

Romans 12:9 - 21

9 Let love be without dissimulation. Abhor that which is evil; cleave to that which is good.

10 Be kindly affectioned one to another with brotherly love; in honor preferring one another.

11 Not slothful in business; fervent in spirit; serving the Lord.;

12 Rejoicing in hope; patient in tribulation; continuing instant in prayer;

13 Distributing to the necessity of saints; given to hospitality.

14 Bless them which persecute you; bless, and curse not.

15 Rejoice with them that do not rejoice, and weep with them that weep.

16 Be of the same mind one toward another. Mind not. Mind not high things, but condescend to men of low estate. Be not wise in your own conceits.

17 Recompense to no man evil for evil. Provide things honest in the sight of all men.

18 If possible, as much as lieth in you, live peaceably with all men.

19 Dearly beloved, avenge not yourselves, but rather give place unto wrath: for it is written, vengeance is mine; I will repay, saith the Lord.

20 Therefore if thine enemy hunger, feed him; if he thirs, give him drink: For in so doing thou shalt heap coals of fire on his head.

21 Be not overcome of evil, but overcome evil with good.

    In gaining profitability in their ministries, the apostle Paul tries to instill maturity and spiritual discipline in the believers at Rome. From his experience as a missionary and one who has interacted with lots of people of all social strata, Paul offers some advice to these saints as they approach the world to minister. In this section of his epistle, the apostle lays a lot of emphasis on "love." Love is being singled out as key to good ministrying. Great lessons are to be learned from the few verses on "love."

Verse 9. A true servant of God needs to let the light inside of him or her shine at all times. Love should surface at all times, not in pretense. In ministry or the church, the children of God, especially leaders have to be an example to others. The community is looking up to them for guidance. One must be able to distinguish oneself from the ones that corrupt the things of God and be able to support and be a part of the company that promotes the things and people of God. Bad crowds do corrupt good manners. Therefore, choosing that which brings glory to the kingdom of God is worthy than anything else.

Verse 10 Respect for one another is not only required in a civilized culture, it is also required in the culture of Christendom. In fact, this is an ethical standard spelled out in the Bible as was practiced and encouraged by the early church leaders. However, Paul is telling these saints to show love to each other as Christ loves the church. The author is laying emphasis on the "agape" type of love not just the display of natural affection. Respect and regards for the ministry and others are two crucial requirements in ministry work.

Verse 11. Paul tells them not to take their position or appointment by God lightly. They should, if you will, treat the duty of the Lord with due diligence. "Slothfulness" in the verse alludes to "spiritual apathy or inactivity." The word also means to be "slow or lazy." God does not give us His gift to sit on it, He wants us to use it to the best of our ability, to His glory. It is not whether we feel like it or not. We have to do it because the Lord wants us to do it. God wants us to be zealous about our ministry and His work than we would for ourselves or others. Not mere enthusiasm, rather, God intends for us to incorporate our eagerness with the Spirit which entails much praying and fasting.

Verse 12. The writer encourages the believers not to ever feel like their work is in vain or that they will profit nothing for their service to God. He says they should be hopeful and be glad in their service for great will be their reward one day. The present may seem dim but their future will be brighter in God. Therefore, they should work with all their might to the glory of God in their ministry. In spite of the trials and tribulations, with patience and longsuffering they shall overcome. No suffering of the present can be compared to what the Lord has for us in glory (see Rom. 8:18).

Verse 13. The saints are to share and use their gifts to benefit the community. They should know that the gifts God gave them are not theirs personally, rather, it is for the edification of the members and the church. Therefore, they should share their blessings with others and be more receptive and not pompous to others.

Verse 14 The lesson of true discipleship is passed on to these believers. Paul lets them know that not everybody in the community will be receptive and support of their work, however, they have to love those who may not appreciate their presence and bless them as well. They should pray for God to save them and deliver them from that seed of bitterness that dwells in them. Jesus teaches this doctrine of forgiveness, so we all have to in the ministry of Christ (cf. Lk. 6:24).

Verse 15. The act of a spiritual warrior is required in the ministry. You, although conquerous, have to be empathetic with others. You have to be merciful to others, and show them that you care about not only their spiritual well-being but their physical well-being as well.

Verse 16. Paul continues to touch on the word "empathy." He wants a servant of God to not think too highly of the gift or position the Lord gives him or her. This gift is not for personal beautification. Rather, it is for the beautification of others and the church other than oneself. This kind of mentality of knowing that you are a servant to serve, not to boss others will pretty much put you on a good course with God. The spirit of humility will enable you to accomplish a lot in your ministry. You have to love and not be judgmental and condemning to others. The mind of Christ must be in you (see Phil. 2:5 [Jer. 45:5]). Being all things to all men, is a good approach to soul winning (cf. I Cor. 9:22).

Verse 17 Living an exemplified life is very crucial to one's ministry. Your leadership does impact the community. If you become one of those who only speaks the word and does not live it, you will end up being alone in your ministry. The community seeks leaders who can give them some sense of direction and good leadership. The community expects you to be an example to them. You have to be a light to guide them out of their paths of darkness. Honesty is required in the ministry. People will trust you and be willing to forgive you if you were honest to them. If you try to conceal and hide anything from the community, when God brings it to light, that will be the end of your ministry. The community will rescind your leadership. Because the ministry belongs to God, let God be your defender for everything. Let the Lord fight your battle. This battle is not yours but the Lord's. He called you therefore He will protect you. All this comes in the package of your commissioning by God, it is a divine guarantee.

Verse 18. Paul tells the believers to learn to live peacefully with others, even if that person tended to hate them. This is a genuine Christ-like attribute that all believers must display without any hesitation. This should be part of their repertoire if you will.

Verse 19. "pay backs" or "grudge" should not be mentioned or displayed by any believer. The only gesture should be love and a forgiving spirit. Believers are not to hold things against others in the community. Believers are representatives of Christ. They have to behave like Christ. A leader who gets too sensitive to things that happen around him or her to the extent that decisions are instantly made without any thorough investigation, has a problem and needs to address it before it gets worse. If one decides to lead others whereas one's emotions need to be worked on, it becomes a serious matter. Not only spiritually dangerous, it is dangerous naturally as well. One who aspires leadership role must be self-disciplined. Temperament and other attributes should be well under control because one will be severely tested. Remember, in this work, not one's work but God's, one has to lay everything at the cross, be forgiving, have patience, and let God fight for him or her.

Verse 20. The attitude of a child of God is to love the enemy and pray for deliverance for the enemy. God does not want us to get personal or suggestive when it comes to deciding the fate of our enemies. Leave it to the Lord, He will take care of your battle for you (cf. II Chr. 20:15).

Verse 21. It is love that will project a Christ-like behavior in you. Once you display love, evil will disappear. God requires a good a reputable behavior from you as you represent Him here on earth and minister for Him in the community.

Exegesis of David K. Bernard

Romans 12:9-21

Exegete Bernard lays out 21 principles of love from chapter twelve commencing from the ninth verse:

Verse 9. (1) Manifest love (agape) unfeigned, undisguised, without deceit, with sincerity. (2) hate evil things. This is part of divine love: "You who love the LORD, hate evil!" (Psalm 97:10). (3) Clasp, cling to hold on tightly to good things.

Verse 10. (4) Be tenderly affectionate to fellow Christians in brotherly love (*philadelphia*). (5) Honor one another above yourselves. Show respect and honor for each other rather than seeking honor for yourselves. "In lowliness of mind let each esteem others better than himself" (Philippians 2:3).

Verse 11. (6) Be not lazy in what you do-be diligent. The KJV uses the word "business," not in the sense of an economic venture but in the original sense of "busyness." (7) Be zealous, be on fire in spirit. The Greek word literally means "boiling." (8) Serve the Lord. Be His bond-slave in all these things.

Verse 12. (9) In your hope be joyful. (10) Be patient in trials and afflictions. (These two points are reminiscent of 5:1-5). (11) Be faithful and persistent in prayer. Maintain the habit of prayer and always be ready to pray.

Verse 13. (12) Contribute to needy saints. As in 1:7 and through out the New Testament, the word *saints* refers to all born again persons. (13) make a practice of hospitality. The Greek verb literally means "to pursue" hospitality. The Greek noun for hospitality is literally "strange-loving" (*philoxenia*).

Verse 14. (14) Pray for blessings upon your persecutors; do not curse them. To curse means "to call down judgment upon, to invoke evil upon, to denounce violently." This verse is no doubt based on Christ's words: "bless those who curse you, and pray for those who spitefully use you" (Luke 6:28).

Verse 15. (15) Share in the joy or sorow of others. Show genuine interest, concern, and compassion. More than showing sympathy, develop the capacity for empathy-participating in the feelings and thoughts of others.

Verse 16. (16) Live in harmony with one another; be of one mind. (17) Do not be haughty or too ambitious and do not be overly impressed by great and powerful things, but rather associate with people of low position. This last clause could be applied to things instead of people, meaning to accommodate to humble ways or, as an NIV footnote says, "willing to do menial work." The KJV uses the word *condescend*, but in modern usage that word connotes a patronizing, superior attitude, which is emphatically not what this verse teaches. (18) Do not be wise in your own eyes. Do not be vain or conceited. This is apparently a quotation of Proverbs 3:7a. Paul used the same language in Romans 11:25.

Verse 17. (19) Do not repay any man evil for evil. This follows Christ's teachings not to resist evil, to turn the other cheek, to love our enemies, to do good to those who hate us, and so on (Matthew 5:38-48). (20) Always be careful to do what is good and right in the sight of everyone. "See that your public behavior is above criticism" (Phillis). This is a reference to Proverbs 3:4, particularly in the Septuagint. Not only should our honesty be known to God, it should be evident to all men (II Corinthisn 8:21). Our lives, including business and church dealings,should be transparently honest. We should avoid even the appearance of evil or impropriety (I Thessalonians 5:22).

Verse 18. (21) If possible, as far as it depends on you, live at peace with everyone. By saying "if possible," Paul recognized that we cannot control the thoughts or actions of others. For two parties to be at peace, both must have the proper attitude. We cannot dictate the attitudes of others, but for our part we can refuse to retaliate, react violently, hold grudges, or be unfriendly.

Verse 19. (22) Do not take revenge. Instead, let wrath take its course without your participation. Some interpret this to mean we should let the opther party vent his rage. more probably it means to let God's wrath (divine judgment) take its course. In other words, wee should not take matters in our hands, but turn them over to God and let Him impose any judgment He deems necessary. This meaning is apparent from Paul's supporting scriptural quotation from Deuteronomy 32:35, in which God promises to punish all evil Himself and asserts His exclusive prerogative to do so. This does not mean we should actively desire God's vengeance to satisfy our personal feelings, but our attitude should be: If any vengeance is due, let God send it and not us.

Verse 20. In further support of this, verse 210 quotes Proverbs 25:21-22, which teaches us to give food and drink to enemies in need. In doing so, we will heap coals of fire upon their heads. This last statement is obscure and has been the source of much speculation. Some interpret the coals as a symbol of damnation, as in Psalm 140:10. By assisting our enemy, then, we increase his guilt and therefore his punishment. To view this as advice on a permissible way to inflict greater punishment on one's enemy, however, violates the teaching of these verses. Identifying the coals with punishment has some merit if we don not see this verse as referring to our motives but only to the result of our enemy's action. I other words, we genuinely help our enemy out of noble motives, but in the end God will punish the enemy for refusing our overtures of friendship. Some have ingeniously proposed that his verse refers to the eastern practice of carrying things on one's head. If someone's fire went out, a friend or neighbor would give him coals to relight his fire, heaping them in a pan on his head. In this case, the verse says that feeding one's enemy is like giving him coals for his fire. Probably the best interpretation is to see coals as symbolic of shame. By assisting one's enemy, we will provoke him to a sense of shame. His face will become hot and red as if coals were poured on his head. This may lead him to repentance and reconciliation, whereas if we had repaid evil for evil he would have remained a bitter enemy. In making this connection some commentators have pointed to a ancient Egyptian custom of expressing penitence by publicly carrying a pan of coals on the head. Regardless of the precise significance of the coals, the passage clearly teaches us not to desire or seek revenge. The only "retaliation" or "vengeance" we are allowed is to do good to our enemy out of a sincere desire to help him and to become his friend.

Verse 21. (23) Do not let evil overcome you, but overcome evil with good. This final admonition summarizes well the specific teachings of verse 17:20, but it also serves as a fitting conclusion to the entire passage. In the final analysis, Christian living means to conquer evil with good. Through divine love, we can defeat and overwhelm the forces of evil with the superior forces of truth and righteousness.

Exegesis of F. F. Bruce

Romans 12:9-21

Verse 9. *Let love be genuine.* Greek *anypokritos*, lit. 'without hyprocrisy' (NEB 'in all sincerity').

Verse 10. *Outdo one another in showing honour.* Cf. Philippians 2:3, 'count others better than yourselves': also Ephesians 5:21, 'be subject to one another out of reverence for Christ.'

Verses 11-13. *Be aglow with the Spirit.* The same Greek expression is used in Acts 18:25 of Apollos ('fervent in spirit'); whatever the force of 'spirit' may be there, here the reference is ost probably to Holy Spirit. *Serve the Lord.* NEB margin 'meet the demands of the hour' represents an inferior Western reading which replaced the dative *kyriö* ('Lord') by *kairö* ('time', 'opportunity').

Verse 14. *Bless those who persecute you; bless and do not curse them.* Cf. luke 6:28, 'bless those who curse you, pray for those who abuse you.' in the present passage there is some ancient evidence for the omission of 'you' after 'persecute'; in that case Christians may be exhorted to call down blessings on persecutors, whether they themselves are the victims of the persecution or not. For Paul's own practice in this regard cf. I Corinthians 4:12b-13a; Acts 28:19b.

Verse 15. *Rejoice with those who rejoice, weep with those who weep.* This is no Stoic teaching, according to which an impassive detachment was essential to the good life; it is consistent, however, with the way of Christ.

Verse 16. *Live in harmony with one another.* Cf.15:5-6; see also Philippians 2:2-5, where the injunction to be 'of the same mind' (not the same thing as 'seeing eye to eve') is followed by a statement of the only in which this possible in a Christian context: 'Have this mind among yourselves, which is yours in Christ Jesus.' *Do not be haughty.* Cf. verse 3; also 11:20, 'do not become proud.' Associate with the lowly. Or (taking the adjective *tapeinois* as neuter, not masculine) 'give yourselves to humble tasks' (mg.). Never be conceited. As in 11:25 above, this is a quotation from Proverbs 3:7a.

Verses 17-18. *Repay no one evil for evil.* For the Christian principle of non-retaliation see Matthew 5:38-48. (Cf. I Thes. 5:15; I Pet. 3:9). *Take thought for what is noble in the sight of all.* 'Let your aims be such as all men count honorable' (NEB). A quotation from Proverbs 3:4 (LXX).

Verse 19. *Leave it to the wrath of God.* The genitive 'of God' is implied, but not expressed in the Greek text (cf. 5:9). Make room, the injunction means, for the law of divine retribution to operate whether now or 'on the day of wrath' (2:5). '*Vengeance is mine, I will repay.*' A quotation from the Song of Moses: '*Vengeance is mine, and recompense*' (Dt. 32:35, MT; LXX has 'in the day of vengeance I will repay'). The present form of the text, found also in Hebrews 10:30, appears in the Aramatic Targums and was probably current in a Greek version not now extant. The point of the quotation here is that, since vengeance and requital are God's prerogative, their exercise should be left to Him. So in the Qumran community private vengeance was forbidden on the ground that, according to Nahum 1:2, it is God alone who 'takes vengeance on his adversaries and keeps wrath for his enemies.'

Verse 20. 'If your enemy s hungry, feed him; if thirsty, give him drink; for by so doing you will heap burning coals upon his head.' A quotation from Proverbs 25:21-22; Paul omits the concluding clause: 'and the Lord will reward you.' The original force of the admonition may have been: 'Treat your enemy kindly, for that will increase his guilt; you will thus ensure for him a more terrible judgment, and for yourself a better reward - from God.' Another view is that the proverb refers to an Egyptian ritual in which a man testified publicly to his penitence by carrying a pan of burning charcoal around on his head. I any case, by placing the proverb in this context and omitting the last clause, Paul gives it a nobler meaning: 'Treat your enemy kindly, for that may make him ashamed and lead to his repentance.' In other words, the best way to get rid of an enemy is to turn him into a friend, and so *overcome evil with good* (verse 21).

Verse 21. The series of short clauses which now comes to an end may have been given this form so as to serve as an easily memorized catechesis. Cf. I Thessalonians 5:14-22.

Exegesis of Robert B. Hughes

I Corinthians 14:12

"Even so ye, forasmuch as ye are zealous of spiritual *gifts*, seek that ye may excel to the edifying of the church."

In essence, the issue at hand in the church at Corinth relating to spiritual gifts as being spelt out by the Apostle Paul in this letter, according to Hughes, was *self-edification* versus *church edification*. According to Hughes Paul is encouraging the Corinthians to let their zeal for spiritual gifts direct them toward an equal zeal for edification, which is *edification of the church* (Everyman's Bible Commentary: First Corinthians, 129, 131).[144] The question in mind is what is the intent of one's zeal as one desires spiritual gifts or a spiritual gift? Meritocracy I belief has no reckoning in this regard because such order of recognition or acceptance does not happen to be a prerequisite in the providential entity of God. In this matter, I am afraid providence will accept wholeheartedly the willingness and humility of one to allow the giver of all gifts, God, that is, to give as He pleases whereby instead of propping up individuality or individualism, collectivity or communalism would surface as the divine agendum for God's assembly.

"Neglect not the gift that is in thee, which was given theee by prophecy with the laying on of the hands of the presbytery" (I Timothy 4:14). The Apostle Paul is admonishing his son in the gospel, Timothy not to take for granted the gift the Lord passes on to him through the laying on of hands by the presbytery. The OT has many examples of how the Lord used prophets, kings, and other leaders to pass on gifts to others. The Lord does honor the passing on of blessings to others in His economic. Every good and perfect gift come from above. Therefore, when the Lord designate a leader to pass on a portion of his gift to you, you should honor it and know that God approves it.

Just to name a few, Elijah passed on his mantle to Elisha (II King 2:12-14), The Lord took a portion of Moses gift and passed it on to selected elders in Israel (Exodus 18:25), Isaac passed on the blessing intended for Esau to Jacob (Genesis 27:27-29), and the Lord send Samuel to anoint David as a future leader of Israel (I Samuel 16:13). Paul admonishes Timothy to make use of the gift the Lord has given him to the best of his ability. It is not given to him to posses but to share with others to benefit the church or community. Contextually, in chapter four of the first letter to Timothy, Paul was warning about False teachers who came into the community to teach their philosophies and tried to mixed Christianity with their philosophy. Paul tells Timothy to rebuke and reject these so-called refined gospel lessons or heresies that were being taught by zealous philosophers or heretics. Who else should be responsible for the success of his son other than a father? Paul as encourages Timothy to not overlook himself or let anyone undermine him. He said Timothy should let know one despise his youth. Paul lets him know that his role as a leader puts him in charge of the community. He is to cater to the spiritual well being of both old ("elders or older men" *presbyteroi*) and the young ("younger men" *neōterous*). The God-parent

---

[144] Robert B. Hughes, Everyman's Bible Commentary: First Corinthians. Chicago: Moody Press, 1985.

of the young pastor, admonishes his son in the gospel that he should compete with the false teachers, he should just teach and preach the truth. J. Meier further gives his exegesis on the situation of false teaching in Timothy's community as such:

> On 6:3-10, much of the language of this section, is stock invective drawn from polemic of philosophers against their opponents. As in the Platonic dialogues, these latter are regularly depicted as "sophists" who teach for pay and seek to please rather than to present the truth. Several words recall 1:3-4, *the healthy words*: On the application of health/sickness imagery - note also v 4 - to teaching Titus 1:13; 2:1. *Having understood nothing*: In the philosophical tradition *epistēmē* is the highest form of knowledge, knowledge of the truth itself. The false teachers lack this altogether. Cf. Titus 1:1. Verse six, *piety that encompasses self-sufficiency is a matter of great profit*: The sophositlike false teachers, who teach a so-called piety to acquire monetary profits. They lack they lack the philosophical virtue of *autarkeia*, "self-sufficiency," i.e., contentment with the goods they have, and so do not obtain true(i.e., spiritual) profit.

You are to not neglect the gift of God. It is given for a mission and God is entrusting you to accomplish that mission. He could use no one else but chose you because there was none like you. However, you should not think that if you refused the mission God's work will not be done. In no time God could extend this blessing from you to someone else if you do not want to honor his purpose. God provides many gifts in the church to bring about a holistic growth. As every man hath received the gift, even so minister the same one to another, as good stewards of the manifold grace of God. If any man speaks, let him speak as the oracles of God; if any man ministers, let him do it as of the ability which God giveth: that God in all things may be glorified through Jesus Christ, to whom be praise and dominion for ever and ever. Amen. The elders which are among you I exhort, who am also an elder and a witness of the suffering of Christ, and also a partaker of the glory that shall be revealed: Feed the flock of God which is among you, taking the oversight thereof, not by constraint, but willingly; not for filthy lucre, but of a ready mind (I Peter 4:10-11; 5:1-2). The preceding verse is admonishing teachers as well as preachers to communicate the gospel in their communities (I Thessalonians 2:13; II Corinthians 5:20). Raymond Brown explains that the exhortation to elders and faithful in chapter five of I Peter in addition to 2:13-3:7 reveals a relatively underdeveloped church structure. Elders, the office of pastoral leadership was taken from contemporary Judaism. Fellow elder: is a term coined by the author to indicate solidarity between apostle and elders, like Paul's "fellow workers" (Romans 16:3,9,21; Philippians 24; Colossians 4:11; II Corinthians 8:23. Witness refers to one who testifies, not necessarily "eyewitness" (Luke 24:28; Acts 1:8; 22:15,20; Revelation 2:13;17:6). Tend the flock of God: The picture of an ideal teacher or pastor (John 21:15-17; Acts 20:28; Ephesians 4:11). There is a gift

Teaching and Understanding Pneumatology & Spiritual Gifts   245

that specifically enhances doctrine, reproof, correction, and instruction. According the scripture, these individual gifts are in place to enable the saint to be perfect and thoroughly furnished or well seasoned in the precepts of God and the ministry (II Timothy 3:15-16).

In view of the hierarchy of gifts, many scholars of the Bible looked at I Corinthians chapter 13 where love is specified as the greatest gift to be not a coherent part of the diverse kinds of gifts specified in I Corinthians chapters twelve and Romans Chapter twelve. E.L. Titus says that at first sight, chapter 13 appears to break the connection between chapters 12 and 14. Hence, it has been considered (a) a non-Pauline interpolation (E. L. Titus, JBR 27[1959] 299-302)[145]; (b) a misplaced part of one of the letters combined into I Cor (W. Schenk, ZNW 60 [1969] 219-43)[146]; (c) a text composed for another occasion and inserted here by Paul (Barrett, Conzelmann). According to R. Kieffer, the three statements of the other scholars are all constructed on the same model. In each case the conditional *protasis* contains an allusion to a charism mentioned in chapter 12, tongues (v 1 and 12:280 prophecy (v 2 and 12:10, 28), knowledge (v 2 and 12:8), faith (v 2 and 12:9), helping (v 3 and 12:28). There is a progression from the lowest gift, tongues (14:6-12), via the intellectual gifts and miracle working faith, to act of supreme devotion benefiting others. Verse 2, *I am nothing*: Only by loving does the Christian exist authentically (1:30). Verse 3, *to be burned*: The reading *kauthēsomai* is to be preferred to *kauchēsōmai* ((R. Kieffer, NTS 22 [1975-76] 95-97).[147] Commenting also on chapter 13 of I Corinthians, on verses 4 through 13, E. Miguens says that rather than defined love Paul personifies it in verses 4 through 7. The 15 verbs all involve another person and were chosen in order to highlight virtues neglected by the Corinthians. The strong were no "patient and kind" (8:1-13). The sexual ascetics tended to "insist on their own way" (7:1-40). The community "rejoiced at wrong" (5:1-8). Verses 8-13, Paul contrasts the present ("now") in which the Corinthians overvalue spiritual gifts with a future ("then") in which they will give supreme importance to the essential virtues of faith, hope, and love (E. Miguens, CBQ 37 [1975] 76-97).[148] Verse 10, *when maturity comes, immaturity will be abolished*: This interpretation of the *to telerion*—to *ek merous* contrast is recommended by the following verse. Paul considered the Corinthians childish (3:1, 14:20) and desired them to be "mature" (14:20) Verse 12, *to see face to face*. The metaphor says no more than *epignōsomai*, "I shall really know," and is used in the OT to express the quality of Moses' knowledge of God (Exodus 33:11; Numbers 12:8; Deut 34:10) in this present life. There is no reference to the beatific vision. *As I have been known* 8:3; Gal 4:9; Rom 8:29.

---

[145]   Raymond E. Brown, Joseph A. Fritzmyer, Roland E. Murphy, The New Jerome Biblical Commentary. Englewood Ckifts: Prentice Hall, Inc., 1990.
[146]   Ibid., 810.
[147]   Ibid., 810.
[148]   Ibid., 811

Verse 13, Faith and hope are incompatible with the beautific vision, but with love are essential to Christian life, I Thess 1:3; II Thess 1:3-4; Col 1:4-5 (The HarperCollins Bible Dictionary, 811).[149] Your gift as a teacher pretty much does a great 3:1work in the church than any other gifts. Although all the other gifts are needed, it is your responsibility to educate the saints on the purpose and usage of these gifts. Illustratively, a saint may have the gift of prophecy but may not know how to use his or her gift. This saint with the gift of prophecy must be taught to know that the gift is subject to him or her. Likewise, in the case of having another saint with the gift of interpretation, this saint must know when is appropriate to interpret a prophecy in order for confusion not to be in the midst or interruption in the church service and mixed feelings amongst the saints. There are times when the Lord will reveal a message to one who is gifted in prophecy for a member of the church. The gifted prophet should know whether or not that is a personal message that must be told privately or openly in the church. Sometimes with a matured attitude, that person will know the appropriate time or manner to to reveal the message without creating a problem.

Elaborating on the gifts of tongues and prophecy, R. H. Gundry decides to record straight from his perspective on the interpolation of the idea of the gift of prophecy being more important than tongues (I Cor 14:1-2):

> Paul's criticism of tongues indicates that the Corinthians attached undue importance to this gift. The mysterious babble of unintelligible sounds was seen as the clearest sign of possession by the Spirit and so offered enhanced social prestige. The latent individualism is rough out by Paul's assessment in terms of utility to the community, which he highlights by contrasting tongues with prophecy.
>
> Verse 1, *eagerly desire*: There is a certain realism in the hint that believers tend to get the gift they want. Verse 2, *tongue*: though audible, glossolalia is intelligible only to God, the author of the gift, and so is quite different from the foreign languages of Acts 2:4-11 (R. H. Gundry, JTS 17[1966] 299-307).[150]

Giving more views to these concepts on prophecy and tongues, A. C Thiseselton adds the following: Verse 3, *prophesies*: Prophecy is defined by its effect on the community. Revelation in the sense of a new insight into the mystery of salvation is

---

[149] Paul J. Achtemeier, Roger S. Boraas, Michael Fishbane, Pheme Perkins, and William O. Walker, The HaperCollins Bible Dictionary. San Francisco: Harper Collins Publishers, 1996.

[150] Raymond E. Brown, Joseph A. Fitzmyer, Roland E. Murphy, The New Jerome Biblical Commentary. Englewood Ckifts: Prentice Hall, Inc., 1990, p. 811.

actualized in pastoral guidance and instruction I Thess 5:19-21; Rom 12:6. Verse 5, *unless the latter can put it into words*: In this case there is no difference between glossolalia and prophecy; v 13 and vv 27-28. Verses 6 through 12, Paul uses three arguments to prove that sound without intelligibility contributes nothing: his own ministry (v 6); musical instruments (vv7-8); and foreign languages (vv 10-11). Verse 11, *I shall be a foreigner to the speaker*: Yet in the community of faith the other should be a brother (8:11-12)! Glossolalia breaks the unity of the community. "Foreigner" translates *babaros*, "barbarian." Verses 13 through 19, tongues can make a contribution to the community provided they are accompanied by the exercise of the mind, which makes them intelligible. Verse 13, *he who speaks in a tongue should pray for the power to produce articulate speech*: There is no gift of "interpretation" given to others distinct from the speakers in tongues. The latter should aspire to a further gift that would make their inchoate experience of God intelligible (A. C. Theiselton, JTS 30 [1979] 15-36).[151] B. C Johanson also gives his input on the same matter emphasizing on a couple of verses of the same chapter and book: Verse 14, *my spirit*: The holy Spirit active in the person as a gift and working through psychological channels distinct from the rational *mind*. Verse 15, The inarticulate activity of the Spirit should overflow into the mind and become intelligible, *sing with the mind* Col 3:16. Verse 16, *if you bless*: God is praised in "thanksgiving" (eucharistia) for his grace, e.g., II Corin 1:3-4; 2:14, *the one who has the status of an outsider*: A believer confused about what is going on or a non-Christian.

Verses 20 through 25, having dealt with the intracommunal dimension of glossolalia, Paul now turns to its relationship to the apostolate of the community. Verse 21, Paul cites Isaiah 28:11-12 in translation close to that of Aquila. Since the Israelite will not listen to the prophets, he threatens them with "the terrible gibberish of foreign invaders" (Robertson—Plummer), which they cannot understand. Verse 22, Paul places an inference from the citation in the mouth of an imaginary opponent, who claims that if glossolalia (in contrast to prophecy) is ineffective within the church, its purpose must be to serve as an apologetic sign to those without (B. C. Johanson, NTS 25 [1978-79] 180-203).[152] In verse 23 Paul resumes his argument and contradicts his interlocutor. *Outsiders or unbelievers*: The two terms refer to the objective (outsider) and the subjective (unbelieving) aspects of the same group; the order is reversed in the next verse. *You are raving*: A judgement that would put Christianity on the same level as the ecstatic pagan mystery cults. Verses 20 through 25, the mutual concern expressed in edification, encouragement, and consolation (14:3) is so obviously good and so evidently at variance with the self-centeredness of the "world" that the outsider is effectively challenged to perceive the active presence of God in the

---

[151] Ibid.
[152] Raymond E. Brown, Joseph A. Fitzmyer, Roland E. Murphy, The New Jerome Biblical Commentary. Englewood Ckifts: Prentice Hall, Inc., 1990, p. 811.

community. Liturgical assemblies that were disorderly or too long would not build up the community. Paul, in consequence, has to discount the view that possession of a gift entitled one to impose oneself on a meeting (HCBD, 811).[153]

Spiritual growth is possible through thorough teaching in the church. Preaching is right but it is only sound teaching that can keep the church strong and faithful. Not proffering that preaching is not gift, of course it is but after the preaching, teaching has to follow to bring clarity and understanding. The apostle Paul was a man of humility although endowed with great wisdom. On occasions Paul thanked the saints of local assemblies for their prayers in his accomplishments. Paul realizes that being one in the body of Christ, one's accomplishment is the accomplishment of all. Whenever Paul went on a missionary journey and got a blessed and glorious result whereby many got saved and delivered by the spirit, he shared his testimony with the local members and let them rejoice unto God for what has happened. He always let them know that it was not of human power or intuition but by the grace of God souls were saved.

This is an attitude you must have. When you see that the Lord is using you greatly whereby many are being blessed under your ministry, you should be careful not to take God's glory. The Lord's glory shall no one take. If you want to continue being blessed than do not show off or make others think that you are indispensable to God's work. When you start to feel that way, you should go to the altar because you are heading in the wrong direction and will soon fall and lose your gift. Be careful because when you lose your gift, you may or may not have another chance to regain it. The apostle wants love to be the center of our work in the ministry. We should love our gift and work diligently with others in perfecting God's gift in us. Suggested references: II Corinthians 1:11-15 and I Corinthian 13:1-6. "To the weak became I as weak, that I might gain the weak: I am made all things to all men, that I might by all means save some" (I Corinthians 9:22). These are the words of Apostle Paul sharing his commitment and sacrifice in the ministry for the sake of the gospel. It is the same Paul who says that for him to live is Christ and to die is gain (Philippians 1:21). From the two passages read, we can picture a believer in the Lord whose belief has motivated him to go the last mile just to accomplish Christ. In other words, he realizes that anything he accomplishes, is not by any human power but the Lord's, therefore, any soul that is won to the Lord is won not because of his witnessing but because of God whose directing made it possible for him to come in contact with that person. As humble as Paul was, he did not allow anything to stand in the way of the Lord's glory. He attributed all his accomplishments to the power of God. Paul found the key in true discipleship, it was not one of just pointing and showing others the direction to take and not being involved himself, instead, he was living an exemplified life to bring glory to Christ and the gospel. Paul's life became a living testimony of his

---

[153] Paul J. Achtemeier, Roger S. Boraas, Michael Fishbane, Pheme Perkins, and William O. Walker, The HaperCollins Bible Dictionary. San Francisco: Harper Collins Publishers, 1996.

loyalty to Christ and the gospel. He dedicated himself to a belief and ministry that he found to be the whole truth for dying humanity. Because of his love, he was willing to sacrifice himself to help others come to the true knowledge of the gospel of the Lord Jesus Christ. The only way Paul saw that such witnessing could be effective was for him to be all things to his fellowmen in order to win them to Christ. That is the true precedence set up by the Apostle for all believers today. Paul's lesson of good discipleship was for others to share the burden and pain of the ones around them who are lost in Christ. There is no other way to succeed in doing such witnessing if one is not willing to go through what it takes to lead someone through the gospel. It takes self-sacrifice. The apostle Paul has laid the road map for all believers to navigate from. "Life in the New Testament times was mobile. The impression one gets in reading the epistles is that of incessant travel" (Albert Bailey, Daily Life in Bible Times).[154] Albert is attesting to the fact that mobility is an effective means through which knowledge can be spread. There are many homeless, runaways, and juvenile delinquent children on the streets who could be delivered if witnessed to.

"And he said unto the, go ye into all the world, and preach the gospel to very creature. He that believeth and is baptized shall be saved; but he that believeth not shall be damned. And these signs shall follow them that believe, in my name shall they cast out devils; they shall speak with new tongues; they shall take up serpents; and if they drink any deadly thing, it shall not hurt them; they shall lay hands on the sick, and they shall recover" (Mark 16:15-18). The problem is not a lack of power. The problem today, as in the days of the disciples, is simply a lack of faith. Believers should be ready to do whatsoever is necessary, including hearing the word (Romans 10:17), praying, and fasting, in order to build their faith to the point of laying aside all unbelief. Unbelief is the only thing standing in the way of the supernatural for Spirit-filled believers. In his last words to his disciples, Jesu said, "But ye shall receive power, after that the Holy Ghost is come upon you: and ye shall be witnesses unto me . . ." (Acts 1:8). The word "witness" has a two-fold significance. First, a witness is one who sees something happen. Then, because of what he has seen, he is a witness when he tells what he saw. The implication of Jesus' statement is that, after receiving the Holy Ghost, believers have the power resident within them to see Jesus at work in a supernatural way, and as a result of what they see, they will tell others of his miraculous power. If you have received the baptism of the Holy Ghost with the initial evidence of speaking with other tongues, you have within you the power to cast out devils and heal the sick. The only thing which can prevent you from doing these things is unbelief. So put your skepticism aside and begin to believe God for the "impossible!" As you sit through these classes, don't try psychoanalyze every person being prayed for, or the person doing the praying. If the word of knowledge is in operation, do not ask yourself, "does he really know what he is talking about?" In other words, do

---

[154] Albert Edward Bailey, *Daily Life in Bible Times*. New York: Charles Scribner's Sons, 1943.

not try to explain away and rationalize the move of the Holy Spirit. Just release your faith and let God do what He will. You will find that God will do much more for and through those who have simple childlike faith than those who are always questioning and trying to explain away His work

Practical Observations on the Operation of the Gifts

Many Spirit-filled believers are reluctant to enter into an active operation of any spiritual gift, for they do not want to make a mistake. They want to be sure their operation of any spiritual gift is done perfectly, from the very first. This attitude will most certainly prevent one from ever entering into the operation of the gifts of the Spirit, for it fails to realize that the spiritual gifts work through frail human vessels which are prone to, indeed which are certain to, make mistakes and errors.

Believers learn to operate in the realm of the gifts of the Spirit more perfectly as they do it. This is not to say that a person can learn to use a spiritual gift by natural ability; but a person can learn more perfectly how to yield to the Spirit, how to be led by the Spirit, and how to discern what the Spirit is saying. In fact, a part of learning these things is making mistakes, for a person who makes a mistake learns how the Spirit does not lead or work. There is no need to fear that God will be angry with any believer who sincerely desires, and in good faith attempts, to be used in spiritual gifts. Instead, God will reward the faith of any person who attempts to yield to God in this area. Like a toddler learning to walk, the believer must learn to more perfectly exercise the spiritual gifts. When he stumbles, God will pick him up and send him on his way again. His weak attempts do not displease God; it pleases the Lord to see His children attempting to walk in His Spirit. When a person believes the Holy Spirit is moving on him to operate in some gift, it is important that he responds immediately, within the boundaries of decency and order (I Corinthians 14:40). The more he hesitates, the more unlikely he will be ever to move, for the natural mind will begin to supply many reasons why the prompting could not be of God. Pride will enter in, the fear of being embarrassed. "What if I am wrong?" The procrastinator will wonder. The more quickly a person responds to the leading of the Spirit, the more frequently the Holy Ghost will move on him, and he will probably not that the operation of the gifts will increase in significance. For her, like in every other spiritual area, those who are found faithful in few things will be rewarded with authority over many things.

However, while a person should respond immediately to the moving of the Spirit, it is also important not to rush. It is impossible to rush the Holy Ghost. The person who does this will soon move into the area of the flesh. The best policy is to relax and not to be distracted. There is great value in keeping one's open while one ministers to others. Nothing in the Scripture suggests that the gifts should operate with the eyes closed. A person who keeps his eyes open and who asks the recipient of the ministry to look on him as he ministers, will be able to observe the effect of the ministry and of the Holy Spirit on the person to whom he is ministering. Indeed, just as did Peter and John in Acts 3, it is good to have the recipient "look on." Much can be discerned by looking into the eyes of the person receiving ministry. Is he receiving it in faith? Is he skeptical? The light of the body is the eye, Jesus said, and much of the inner man is communicated through the eye gate. Those who have experience the operation of the gifts of the Spirit in their ministries over a period of time have observed that the Holy Ghost prompts or leads often three basic ways.

A Revelation May be Seen

This can occur in a variety of ways. The person operating in the gifts of the Spirit may "see" something in the Spirit. If he is to give a prophecy or an interpretation to a message in tongues, he may "see" the words he is to speak, as if printed on a scroll or on a page from a book, or in any number of other ways. If he is operating in the discerning of spirits, he may "see" an unclean spirit, perhaps in the shape of an ugly creature, sitting on a person's shoulder or elsewhere. If he is to operate in the gifts of healings, he may "see" the diseased part of the body, perhaps like a dark area over the diseased area. If he is to operate in the word of knowledge, he may "see" the person to whom he is ministering in a certain situation, or involved in a specific act, or in a certain place. The word of knowledge may take the form of describing what is seen. This is certainly not an exhaustive description, but this will help to show a general way in which the Holy Spirit often gives revelations.

A Revelation May be Heard

In the same way a person may "see" something in the realm of the Spirit, he may "hear" it. This may take the form of an audible voice, but it is probably more usually an "inner" voice. That is, words or thoughts may come unbidden into a person's mind to give him ministry direction. If he is to operate in a word of knowledge, a name, or a place, or other information may just suddenly appear in his mind. If this occurs, it is best to act on it immediately. As that information is given, the Holy Spirit may supply additional information. A person will never know for sure if the information is of God until he actually steps out by faith to act on it. If he feels uncertain enough, he may want to say something like this: "I may be wrong, but it seems to me that the Lord is saying . . ." If it is of God, it will be confirmed. If not, nothing is lost, and a lesson is learned. If a person is to give a prophecy or a message in tongues or an interpretation of a message in tongues, he may "hear" the words, either audible or mentally. If he is to minister healing, the names of diseases may suddenly come to mind. There is no doubt an infinite variety of ways in which the Holy Spirit can cause a person to "hear" His voice, but the more readily the recipient responds to these messages, the more clearly and easily he will be able to distinguish the voice of the Spirit.

The Revelation to Occur May be Felt

This seems to occur most commonly when ministering the gifts of healings. The person ministering may "feel" the pain of the individual to whom he is ministering. This may enable him to pinpoint the location and nature of the ailment, which will tend to build faith in the sick person. Or when ministering to someone under great depression, the person ministering may suddenly, unexplainably, feel depressed. The person ministering should not be quick to accept any physical symptom as his own; they may very well be the Holy Spirit's way of giving him information about the person to whom he is ministering.

The Four-Pronged Key to Success in Ministry

To Timothy, Paul said "till I come, give attendance to reading, to exhortation, to doctrine. Neglect not the gift that is in thee, which was given thee by prophecy, with the laying on of the hands of the presbytery: meditate upon these things; give thyself wholly to them; that thy profiting may appear to all" (Timothy 4:13-15).

A careful examination of this passage will show that Paul encouraged Timothy in the following areas:

Reading

Reading is extremely important, for it fills our minds with information, understanding, and challenge. If we hope to operate in the gifts of the Spirit, it is essential that we guard our reading carefully. The first thing we should read is the Bible itself. Next, we should read material that is faith building and encouraging. We should be hesitant to read anything which casts doubt on the supernatural or which explains away the operation of the gifts of the Spirit.

Exhortation

The word "exhortation" speaks basically of "encouragement." The minister should give himself to exhorting, or encouraging others, daily (Hebrews 3:13). This should be the main thrust of ministry.

Teaching

A bishop must be "apt to teach" (Timothy 3:2). What is the difference between preaching and teaching? Someone suggested that preaching is proclaiming, while teaching is explaining. This is probably a fairly accurate description. In order to teach, one must first study. In this, he is to be concerned about being approved of God (II Timothy 2:15).

Exercising one's Spiritual gift.

Paul told Timothy not to neglect the gift that was in him. This indicates that Timothy was to use this gift as he was led by the Spirit of God. We would do well to heed the same counsel. A neglect of the gift within us will surely limit our ministry, just as would a neglect of reading, exhortation, or teaching (doctrine). Speaking of these four things, Paul said "meditate upon these things; give thyself wholly to them; that thy profiting may appear to all: (Timothy 4"15). If a person will meditate (think deeply upon) his reading, exhortation, doctrine (teaching) and the exercise of his spiritual gift, if he will give himself wholly to these things, the spiritual success of his ministry will be evident.

Discipling entails caring and loving those to whom we witness and when we come in contact with. Discipling entails empathy and sympathy towards the conditions of the ones we attempt to reach out to for Christ. Disciples in Christ should not forget to take to memory and heart the passage of Apostle James which admonishes believers to not only reach out to cure the spiritual but also the natural state of the needy (James 2:15-16). Because this mission of the kingdom is one of a spiritual nature, it is impossible for one to rely on his own wit and intuition to win someone over to Christ. This is an entity that involves the spirit, it only takes the spirit and guidance of God to save and deliver people. Psychology will in no way do the work of the Lord. Who are we to think that God needs our intuition to bring people into His kingdom? God does not need our help. The only thing He requires of us is to obey Him and do things according to His leading and guidance. These days, we see many of these man-made approaches coming from the pulpit as an attempt to add to their membership. They are less concerned about the spiritual health of the person, rather, they engineer scams and schemes to entice people to bring in their wealth to the church. Where is the spirit of God? Where is the leading of God? Where is Christ in the process? Questions without adequate answers. Some, if asked may try to justify their position. That is just what many are doing today, they have become very defensive in taking the scripture to support their personal interest. Nevertheless, in the midst of it all, only that which we do for Christ will last. Everything else will fail and get disbanded but only that which the Lord Himself establishes will endure. The Bible says except the Lord built the house, they labor in vain that built it (Psalm 127:1). Because the local assemblage is an establishment of God, man by himself cannot run it. For those who think that their adept knowledge of the mind can heap up treasures for themselves, they have to think twice. They may try all they can but it will be to no avail.

SUMMARY

There are no limits to our commission or ministry. The church and believers are commissioned to spread the Good News of Christ to every creature and nation. One should cease the opportunity to be a witness for the Lord at anytime and anywhere. There is no limit, nothing territorial and nothing circumstantial. God has called us to be *witnesses*. A witness can only report on what he has seen and heard. Acts 22:15 (Ananias speaking to Paul: "for thou shalt be his witness unto all men of what thou has seen and heard." What you and I have seen and heard, becomes our personal experience. It becomes our *personal testimony*. God wants us to be zealous about our ministry and His work than we would for ourselves or others. Not mere enthusiasm, rather, God intends for us to incorporate our eagerness with the Spirit which entails much praying and fasting. The community seeks leaders who can give them some sense of direction and good leadership. The community expects you to be an example for them. One who aspires leadership must be self-disciplined. God provides many gifts in the church to bring about a holistic growth. You are to not neglect the gift of God. It is given for a mission and God is entrusting you to accomplish that mission. He could use no one else but chose you because there was none like you. Spiritual growth is possible through thorough teaching in the church. Preaching is right but it is only sound teaching that can keep the church strong and faithful. A revelation may be seen; the person operating in the gifts of the Spirit may "see" something in the Spirit. A revelation may be heard. In the same way a person may "see" something in the realm of the Spirit, he may "hear" it. This may take the form of an audible voice, but it is probably more usually an "inner" voice. A revelation may be felt; the person ministering may "feel" the pain of the individual to whom he is ministering. This may enable him to pinpoint the location and nature of the ailment, which will tend to build faith in the sick person.

ASSESSMENT

1. How is the commissioning role of the church not territorial or circumstantial?

2. What is expected of a witness?

3. What are some of the expectations of the community in a leader?

4. Why should one neglect his or her gift?

5. What are some manifestations of a revelation?

PERSPECTIVES

Friedrich Nietzsche sees man as a "demoniacal individualist run by the will to power." John Dewey views man as a "piece of flux (material) run by the expediency of the moment." Sigmun Freud speaks of man as an "excrement-molding pervert . . ." Ayn Rand views man as a volitional, self-made being of a self-made soul"(Peikoff, 200-202).[155]

What views could you share in reponse to the aforementioned thoughts about "man" as presented by Dr. Peikoff, heretical, apologetic, or liberalistic? Could you scripturally support your position?

---

[155] Leonard Peikoff, Objectivism: The Philosophy of Ayn Rand. New York, Penguine Books, 1991.

ESSENTIAL VOCABULARY

Antilegomena Certain books of the New Testament which were for a time not universally received, but which are now considered canonical: Hebrews, James, Jude, II Peter, II and III, John, and Revelation.

Atheism The belief that God does not exist.

Biblical Inerrency Biblical truths, the trueness of the scripture.

Biblical Liberalism The intermixing of Biblical truths with idealism.

Big Bang Theory A theory in Astronomy (study of objects and matter outside of the earth's atmosphere) that the universe originated billions of years ago in an explosion from a single point of nearly infinite energy density.

Cosmic Existence Extraterrestrial existence; a vastness of the universe in contrast to the earth.

Cosmogony The theory of the origin of the universe.

Cosmos Universal orderliness.

Conspicuous Obvious to the eyes and minds.

Deduce To infer from a general principle.

Deftly Characterized by skills.

Devoid Without the usual backing.

Dialectic Reasoning Intellectual dialogue or investigation.

Teaching and Understanding Pneumatology & Spiritual Gifts 257

Dichotomy contradictory with two different views.

Dissent Without assent, difference in opinion or views regarding religious, political, cultural, and social issues.

Dissenter One who does not assent conventionally to mainstream views, has different religious, political, social, and cultural views.

Egalitarianism A belief in human equality with respect to social, political, rights, and privileges; a philosophy that advocates ideological inequalities.

Eisegesis The interpretation of a text by reading into one's own ideas.

Emperical Theology Emphasizes that method is an outcome of content. Emperical methods are the means to justification, correction, and revision.

Enlightment Rationalism Extreme rationalixzation of the scripture reflecting traditional views and modern perceptions.

Esotericism Knowledge restricted to a small group; secret knowledge.

Exegesis Explanation or interpreting the scripture.

Exegete One who explains or interprets the scripture.

Existentialism Analyzing ones's existence in the universe, and how one should respond responsibly to one's free will and actions without preguidance or knowledge of knowing what is right or wrong.

Experientialism Emperical principles and procedures psychologically based on external and internal facts.

Extraterresterial Occurance outside of the earth or atmosphere.

Evangelical Rationalism Emphasizes that method is an outcome of content. Emperical methods are the means to justification, correction, and revision.

Facticity The state or quality of being the fact.

Feminist Theology Theology emphasizing on the social equality of the sexes.

Fideism Faith that preceeds the intellect.

Fount Source

Fundamentalism Believe in the virgin birth, the resurrection, the atonement, and the second coming of Christ.

Gnosticism The belief that God is alien to this world, yet a spirit and good.

Heresy A religious belief opposed to the commonly accepted as part of the faith.

Heretic Noncoformist, one who dissents from the common belief, faith, or ideology.

Hermeneutic Principles used to interpret the scripture or a text.

Homiletics The art of preaching.

Homologoumena The collection of books from the New Testament recognized from the earlier periods of the Christian church as authoritative and canonical.

Indefectibilty Flawless, excusable, capable of being right, or fautless.

Inerrency Facticity.

Infallibility The scripture is incapable of deception or leading one astray.

Ideologue An idealist with inhibited views that are not prudently practical or situationally effective.

Illuminism Enlightened, unsually given an extraordinary perception.

Liberation Theology A theology that addresses social, political, and cultural issues.

Locus The center of activity

Medieval Scholasticism Medieval or Middle Age thinking that gives mixed views about Christianity.

Monophysite Means Christ has a single inseperable nature as divine and human.

Montanism A 2nd century view that Christ's promise of the comforter was not fulfilled in the upper room on Pentecost.

Mundane Characteristic of the world

Narrative Theology A religious belief that the scripture is an historical account of the Hebrews and God's dealing with man.

Noethically Based on the intellect

Obscurantism Withholding knowledge from the general public.

Pietism Spiritualism, non-intellectualism, uplifting gospel message, non-controversialism.

Polemicism Conroversial, disputable, aggression.

Premevalistic Waste or "darkness" Preexistence from the beginning.

Premordialism Earliest form of growth.

Process Theology The acknowledgement that contemporary understanding of God and God's expression through creation, including human beings, is always in "process" and never complete.

Propositional Truth Truth that can be doubted, debated, believed or not believed.

Protestant liberalism Emphasizes on ethics and humanism over doctrine.

Pseudepigrapha Texts written between 200 B.C. and 200 A.D. that are falsely ascribed as being canonical.

Rationalistic Orthodoxy A dogma or doctrine based on human intelligence and human way of thinking.

Self-Condescensionalism Self-patronizing, pietism, self-inferiorism.

Static Little change, on and off, back and forth

Subjectivism A belief that one's idea is the ultimate criterion of the good and right.

Systematic Theology Views on Christianity based on present day setting.

Terrestrial Realting to the earth.

Transcendency The doctrine that states God exists in the real beyond or apart from the universe, nature, and that the universe depends on God.

BIBLIOGRAPHY

Achemeier, Paul J., Romans: Interpretation, A Bible Commentary for Teaching and Preaching. Atlanta: John Knox Press, 1985.

Achtemeier, Paul J., Boraas, Roger S., Fishbane, michael, Perkins, Pheme, and Walker, William O., The haperCollins Bible Dictionary. San Francisco: Harper Collins Publishers, 1996.

Alston, William P., Religious Belief and Philosophical Thought: Readings in the Philosophy of Religion. New York: Harcourt, Brace & World, Inc., 1963.

Anderson, Neil T., *Helping Others Find Freedom in Christ: Connecting People to God Through Discipleship counseling*. Ventura: Regal Books, 1995.

Anyon, Jean, Ghetto Schooling: *A political Economy of urban Educational Reform*. New York: Teachers College Press, 1997.

Armstrong, Herbert W., *The Incredible Human Potential*. New York: Everest Publishers, 1978.

Arnold, Clinton E., Ephesians, Power and Magic: The Concept of Power in Ephesians in Light of its Historical Setting. Cambridge: Cambridge University Press, 1989.

Bailey, Albert Edward, *Daily Life in Bible Times*. New York: Charles Scribner's Sons, 1943.

Bailey, Becker A., PhD., *Easy to Love Difficult to Discipline*. New York: William Morrow and Company, 2000.

Baird, William, The Corinthian Church: A Biblical Approach to the Urban Culture. New York: Abingdon Press, 1964.

Barclay, William, The Promise of the Spirit. Philadelphia: The Westminster Press, 1960.

Barth, Markus, The Anchor Bible, Ephesians. New York: Doubleday, 1960.

Bartlett, David, Romans. Louisville: Westminster John Knox Press, 1995.

Bauckham, Richard, Wisdom of James, Disciple of Jesus the Sage. New York: Routledge, 1999.

Becker, Gaven De, *Protecting the gift: Keeping children and teenagers safe and parents sane.* New York, The Dial Press, 1999.

Bengel, John Albert, Bengel's New Testament Commentary. Grand Rapids: Kregel Publications, 1981.

Bennett, William J, Finn, Chester E. Jr. & Cribb, John T. E. Jr., *The Educated Child : A parent's guide from preschool through eighth grade.* New York, The Free Press, 1999.

Benso, Silvia and Schroeder, Brian, Contemporary Italian Philosophy: Crossing the Borders of Ethics, Politics, and Religion, New York:State university of New York Press, 2007

Berkhof, Hendrikus, The Doctrine of the Holy Spirit: The Annie Kinkead Warfield Lectures, 1963-1964. Richmond: John Knox Press, 1967.

Bernard, David K., The Message of Romans. Hazelwood: World Aflame Press, 1987.

Berryman, Phillip, *Liberation Theology: Essential Facts about the Revolutionary Religions Movement in Latin America and beyond.* Philadelphia: Temple University Press, 1987.

Best, Ernest, A Critical and Exegetical Commentary on Ephesians. Edinburg: T & T Clark, 1998.

Black, Matthew, New Century Bible Commentary. Grand Rapids: William B. Eerdmanns Publishing Company, 1975.

Blum, Laurie, *Free Monney for Day Care.* New York: Simmon & Schuster, 1992.

Bray, Gerald and Oden, Thomas C., Ancient Christian Commentary on Scripture: New Testament VII 1-2 Corinthians. Downers Grove: InterVarsity Press, 1999.

Brosend II, William F., James and Jude. Cambridge: Cambridge University Press, 2004.

Brown, Raymond E., Fitzmyer, Joseph A., Murphy Roland E., The New Jerome Biblical Commentary. Englewood Ckifts: Prentice Hall, Inc., 1990.

Bruce, F. F., Tyndale New Testament Commentaries, Revised Edition. The Letter of Paul to the Romans: An Introduction and Commentary. Leicester: Inter-Varsity Press, 1988.

Bryan, Christopher, A Preface to Romans: Notes on the Epistle in Its Literary and Cultural Setting. Oxford: Oxford University Press, 2000.

Buchamann, Christina and Spiegel, Celina, *Out of the Garden*. New York: Fawcett Columbine, 1994.

Buttrick, George Arthur et al, The interpreter's Bible: The Holy Scriptures in the King James and Revised Standard Versions with General Articles and Introduction, Exegesis, Exposition for Each Book of the Bible, Volume X. Nashville, 1953.

Calao, Flora and Hosansky, Tamar, *Your Children Should Know*. New York: The Bobbs-Merrill Company, Inc, 1983.

Calvin, John, Commentaries on The Epistles of Paul to the Galatians and Ephesians. Grand Rapids: Baker Book House, 1981.

Caplan, Frank, *The First 12 months of Life: Your Baby's Growth Month by Month*. New York: Grosset & Dunlap, 1993.

Cetron, Marvin and Gayle, Margaret, *Educational Renaissance: our schools at the turn of the twenty-first century*. New York: St. Martin's Press.

Chai, Winberg and Chai, Ch'u, *The Sacred Books of Confucius and Other Confucian Classics*. New York: University Books, 1965.

Chapman, Geoffrey, The Word and the Spirit. San Francisco: Harper & Row Publishers, 1984.

Chester, Andrew and Martin, Ralph P., The Theology of The Letters of James, peter, and Jude. Cambridge: Cambridge University Press, 1994.

Collinson, Diané, Fifty Major Philosophers: A Refrence Guide. London: Routledge, 1987.

Cooper, John Charles, The Spiritual Presence in the Theology of Paul Tillich. Macon: Mercer University Press, 1997.

Conner, Walter Thomas, The Work of the Holy Spirit. Nashville: Broadman Press, 1940.

Corford, F. M., *From Religion to Philosophy*. New York: Harper & Row, 1957.

Cranfield, C. E. B., A Critical and Exegetical Commentary in the Epistle to the Romans. Edinburgh: T & T Clark, 1979.

Cremin, Lawrence A., *The Republic and The School Horace Mann on the Education of Free Men*. New York: Columbia University, 1965.

Crim, Keith, Bailey, Lloyd Richard, Furnish, Victor Paul, Bucke, Emory Stevens, The Interpreter's Dictionary of the Bible: An Illustrated Encyclopedia. Nashville: Abington Press, 1991

Daniel-Pops, Henri, *Israel and the Ancient World*. New York: Image Books, 1964.

De Bruyn, Theodore, Pelagius's Commentary on St Paul's Epistle to the Romans. Oxford, Clarendon press, 1993.

Edge, Findley B., *Teaching for Better Results*. Broadman & Holman Publishers, 1995.

Eldridge, Daryl, The Teaching Ministry of the Church: Integrating Biblical Truth With Contemporary Application. Nashville: Broadman & Holdman Publishers, 1995.

Epiphanins, William A. M., *The Wisdom of Confucius*. New York: Wings Books, 1995.

Estenson, Paul S. and Peterson, Wallace C., *Income, Employment, and Economic Growth* (New York: W.W. Norton & Company, 1995).

F., William and Walter, James Arthur, The Anchor Bible: I Corinthians: A New Testament Translation. Garden City: Doubleday & Company, Inc., 1976.

Fee, Gordon D., The First Epistle to the Corinthians. Grand Rapids: William B. Eerdmann Publishing Company, 1987.

Fiero, Gloria K., *The European Renaissance, the Reformation, and Global Encounter* (London: McGraw Hill, 1998.

Findlay, G. G., The Epistle to the Ephesians. London: A. C. Armstrong and son, 1903.

Fitsmyer, Joseph A., The Anchor Bible: Romans, A New Translation with Introduction and Commentary. New York: Doubleday, 1993.

Flew, Anthony, God and Philosophy: Philosophy at Work. London: Hutchinson of London, 1966.

Foreman, Kenneth J., The Layman's Bible Commentary: The Letter of Paul to the Romans. Richmond: John Knox Press, 1961.

Foulkes, Francis, The Letter of Paul To The Ephesians: An introduction to Commentary. Grand Rapids: William B. Erdmans Publishing Company, 1989.

Furnish, Victor Paul, New Testament Theology: The Theology of the First Letter to the Corinthians. Cambridge: Cambridge University Church, 1999.

Garfield, S. L. and Bergin, A. E., *Handbook of Psychotherapy and Behavior Change* (3rd ed., 1996).

Gay, Kathlyn, *Church and State: Government and Religion in the United States* (Illinois: Monmeyer Press, 1992.

Grob, G. N., *Mental Illness and American Society*, 1875-1940 (1983); Brown, P., *Mental*

Groppe, Elizabeth Teresa, Yves Congar's Theology of the Holy Spirit. Oxford: Oxford University Press, 2004.

Grudem, Wayne A., The First Epistle of Peter: An Introduction and Commentary. Grand Rapids: Inter-Varsity Press, 1988.

Guerra, Anthony J, Romans and the Apologetic Tradition: The Purpose, Genre and Audience of Paul's Letter. Cambridge: Cambridge University Press, 1995.

Guthrie, Donald, The Pastoral Epistles: An Introduction and Commentary. Grand Rapids: William B. Eerdmans Publishing Company, 1990.

Haberer, Jack, Living the Presence of the Holy Spirit. Louisville, Geneva Press, 2001.

Hadden, Jeffrey K., *The Gathering Storm in the Churches*. New York: Anchor Books, 1970.

Harman, David, *Illiteracy: A National Dilemma.* New York: Cambridge, 1987.

Harvey, Cox, *Religion in the Secular City: Toward a Postmodern Theology.* New York: Simon & Schuster, 1984.

Health Care and Social Policy (1985); Richardson, T., *The Century of the Child* (1989); Torrey, E. F., *Nowhere to Go* (1992).

Heine, Ronald E, The Commentaries of Origen and Jerome on St Paul's Epistle to the Ephesians. Oxford: Oxford University Press, 2002.

Helminiak, Daniel A., PhD., *What the Bible Says about Homosexuality.* San Francisco: Alamo Square Press, 1994.

Hendry, George, The Holy Spirit in Christian Theology. Philadelphia: The Westminster Press, 1952.

Heron, Alasdair C., The Holy Spirit. Philadelphia: The Westminster Press, 1983.

Holloway, Paul A., Consolation in Philippians: Philosophical Sources and Rhetorical Strategy. Cambridge: Cambridge University Press, 2001.

Holt, Rinehart and Winston, *You shall be as Gods: A Radical Interpretation of the Old Testament and its Tradition.* London: Soncino Press, 1949.

Horngren, Charles T., Harrison, Walter T., Jr., Bamber, Linda Smith. *Accounting.* New Jersey: Prentice-Hall, 1992.

Horsley, Richard, New Testament Commentary: I Corinthians. Nashville: Abingdon Press, 1998.

Hughes, Philip Edgcumbe, A Commentary on the Epistle to the Hebrews. Grand Rapids: William B. Eerdmans Publishing Company, 1977.

Hughes, Robert B., Everyman's Bible Commentary: First Corinthians. Chicago: Moody Press, 1985.

Hunt, Allen Rhea, The Inspired Body: Paul, the Corinthians, and Divine Inspiration. Macon: Mercer University Press, 1996.

Hurst, L. D., The Epistle to the Hebrews:Its Background of Thought. Cambridge: Cambridge University Press, 1990.

James, E. O. *Jerusalem:A History*. Edited by J. Boudet. New York: Published by G. P. Putnam's Son, 1967.

Johnson, Joan J., *Kids Without Homes*. New York: Franklin Watts Publishers, 1991.

Kärkkäinen, Veli-Matti, Pneumatology: The Holy Spirit in Ecumenical, International and Contextual Perspective. Grand Rapids: Baker Academic, 2002.

Kistemaker, Simon J., New Testament Commentary: Exposition of the 1st Epistle to the Corinthians. Grand Rapids: BakerBooks, 1993.

Landreth, Harry and Colander, David C. *History of Economic Thought*. 3rd ed. Princeton: Houghton Mifflin Company, 1994.

Larric, Nancy, *A Parent's Guide to Children's Education*. Canada: A Trident Press, 1996.

Larsen, Elaine. *Israel*. Printed by Elliot Brothers & Yeoman Ltd, Liverpool L24 9 JL for the Publishers B. T. Batsford Ltd, 1976.

Lavenda, Robert H. and Schultz, Emily A., Anthropology: What Doest it Mean to Be Human? Oxford: Oxford University Press, 2008.

Lawson, Michael S and Choun, Robert J. Jr., *Directing Christian Education: The Challenging Role of The Christian Education Specialist*. Chicago: Moody Publishers, 1992.

Leftwich, Howard D., Keys, Bernard, Goad, William P. *The Executive Simulation*. Iowa: Kendall/Hunt Publishing Company, 1994.

Lenski, R. C. H., The Interpretation of the Epistle to the Hebrews and of the Epistle of James. Columbus: Wartburg Press, 1946.

Lindars, Barnabas, The Theology of the Letter to the Hebrews. Cambridge: Cambridge University Press, 1991.

Lipman, Eugene J., The Mishnah: Oral Teachings of Judaism, New York: W. W. Norton & Company, Inc., 1970.

Livingstone, E. A. *The Oxford Dictionary of the Christian Church*. Edited by F. L. Cross. London: Oxford University Press, 1997.

Maclaren, Alexander, Expositions of Holy Scripture: Romans. Grand Rapids: Baker Book House.

MacDonald, Margaret, Colossians and Ephesians. Collegeville: The Liturgical Press, 2000.

McGovern, C. M., *Masters of Madness: Social origins of the American Psychiatric Profession* (1985).

Magee, Bryan, The Story of Philosophy: The Essential Guide to the History of Western Philosophy. London: Dorling Kindersley Publishing, 1998.

Malony, H. Newton and Lovekin, A. Adams, Glossolalia: Behavioral Science Perspectives on Speaking in Tongues. Oxford: Oxford University Press, 1985.

Martin, Dale B, The Corinthian Body. New Haven: Yale University Press, 1995.

Martin, Ralph P., The Epistle of Paul to the Philippians: An Introduction and Commentary. Grand Rapids: Wiliam B. Eerdmans Publishing Company, 1987.

Mead, Frank S., The Encyclopedia of Religious Quotations. Westwood: Fleming H. Revxell Company

Melanchthon, Philipp, Annotations on First Corinthians. Milwaukee: Marquette University Press, 1995.

Mills, Watson E., A Theological Exegetical Approach to Glossolalia. Lanham: University Press, 1985.

Mills, Watson E. et al, Mercer Commentary on the Bible. Macon: Mercer University Press, 1995.

Moltmann, Jürgen, The Source of life: The Holy Spirit and the Theology of Life. Minneapolis: SCM Press, Ltd., 1997.

Moo, Douglass J., Romans: The NIV Application Commentary, from Biblical Test . . . to Contemporary Life. Grand Rapids: Zondervan, 2000.

Moule, Handley C. G., The Epistle of St. Paul to the Romans. London: A. C. Armstrong and Son, 1903.

Mounce, Robert H. et al, The New American Commentary. Broadman & Holman Publishers, 1995.

Murphy, Joseph M., *Working the Spirit*. Boston: Beacon Press, 1994.

Nee, Watchman, Spiritual Authority. New York: Christian Fellowship Publishers, Inc., 1972.

Oakes, Peter, Philippians: From People to Letter. Cambridge: Cambridge University Press, 2001.

O'Brien Steinfels, Margaret, *Who's Minding the Children?* New York: Simon and Schuster, 1973.

Ostriker, Alicia Suskin, *The Nakedness of the Fathers*. New Jersey: Rutgers University Press, 1994.

Pegis, Anton C., *The Wisdom of Catholicism*. Canada: Random house, 1949.

Peikoff, Leonard, Objectivism: The Philosophy of Ayn Rand. New York, Penguine Books, 1991.

Penner, Todd C., The Epistle of James and Eschatology: Re-reading an Ancient Christian Letter. Sheffield: Sheffield Academic Press Ltd, 1996.

Perkins, Dwight H., Radelet, Stevens, Snodgrass, Donald R., Gillis, Malcom, and Roemer, Micael, Economics of Development. 5th edition (New York: Norton, 2001).

Perkins, Pheme, Abindon New Testament Commentaries. Nashville: Abingdon Press, 1997.

Peterman, G. W., Paul's Gift From Philippi: Conventions of Gift-Exchange and Christian Given. Cambridge: Cambridge University Press 1997.

Pfeiffer, Charles F. et al, The Wycliffe Bible Commentary. Chicago: Moody Press, 1962.

Pollock, David R. *Business Management In The Local Church*. Chicago, Illinois: Moody Press, 1996.

Powers, Bruce P., editor. Christian Education Handbook. Nashville: Broadman & Holman Publishers, 1996.

Price, Susan et al, *The Working Parents Help Book*. Princeton: Peterson's Press, 1994.

Prior, David, The Message of I Corinthians: Life in the Local Church. Downers Grove: InterVarsity Press, 1985.

Raju, P. T., *Idealists Thought of India*. Cambridge: The Harvard University Press, 1953.

Robertson, A. T., The Divinity of Christ: In the Gospel of John. Nashville, Broadman Press, 1976.

Royster, Dmitri, The Epistle to The Hebrews: A Commentary. Crestwood: St. Vladmir's Seminary Press, 2003.

Ruppel-Shell, Ellen, *A Year in the Life of a Day Care Center.* Boston: Little, Brown, and Company, 1992.

Sergiovanni, Thomas J., Leadership for the schoolhouse: How is it different? Why is it important, San Francisco: Jossey-Bass Inc., Publishers, 1996.

Shawchuck, Norman and Heuser, Roger, *Managing the Congregation* (Nashville: Abington Press, 1993).

Smith, D. moody, The Theology of the Gospel of John. Cambridge: Cambridge University Press, 1995.

Stavsky, Lois and Mozeson, I.E., *The Place I Call Home: Voices and Faces of Homeless Teens.* New York: Shapolsky Publishers, 1990.

Steelsmith, Shari, *How to Start a Home-based Day Care Business.* 2nd ed. Connecticut: The Globe Pequote Press, 1997.

Stokes, Philip, Philosophy: 100 Essential Thinkers. New York: Enchanted Lion Books, 2003.

Stott, John R. W., The Message of Ephesians: God's New Society. Downers Grove: Inter-varsity Press, 1979.

Stowers, Stanley K, A Rereading of Romans: Justice, Jews, and Gentiles. New Have: Yale University Press, 1994.

Stubblefield, Jerry M., *The Effective Minister of Education* Nashville: Broadman & Holman Publishers, 1993.

Taylor, C.C.W, Hare, R.M, and Barnes, Jonathan, Greek Philosophers: Socrates, Plato, and Aristotle. Oxford, Oxford University Press, 1999.

Temple, William, Readings in St. John's Gospel. London: Macmillan & Co. Ltd.,1963.

The Columbia Electronic Encyclopedia, 2000, Columbia Press.

Thiselton, Anthony S, The First Epistle to the Corinthians: A Commentary on the Greek Text. Grand Rapids: William B. Eerdmans Publishing Company, 2000.

Thompson, Frank Charles, The Thompson Chain-Reference Bible, 5th improved ed. Indianapolis: B. B. Kirkbride Bible Co., Inc., 1988.

Tomilinson, Gerald, Treasury of Religious Quotations. Englewood Cliffs: Prentice Hall, 1991.

Turecki, Stanley and Wernick, Sarah, *The Emotional Problems of Normal Children*. New York: Bantam Books, 1994.

Unger, Merrill F., *The New Unger's Bible Dictionary*. Chicago: Moody Press, 1988.

Vine, W. E., *Vine's Expository Dictionary of Old and New Testament Words* (Iowa: World Publishers, 1981).

Wade, Theodore E. and others, The Home School Manual: plans, pointers, reasons, and resources. 6th edition (Brigdeman: Gazelle Publications, 1995).

Wahlde, Urban C Von, The Earliest Version of John's Gospel: Recovering the Gospel of Signs. Wilmington: Michael Glazier, 1989.

Warren, Richard, The Purpose—driven Church: Growth Without Compromising Your Message and Mission. Grand Rapids: Zondervan, 1995.

Welker, Michael, God the Spirit. Minneapolis: Fortress Press, 1994.

Wilkinson, Bruce H. *The Seven Laws of The Learner.* Oregon: Multnomah Press, 1992.

Wood, Leon J. *A Survey of Israel*. Revised by David O'Brien. Grand Rapids, Michigan: Zondervan Publishing House, 1986.

Yocom, Rena and Barr, and William R., The Church in the Movement of the Spirit. Grand Rapids: William Eerdmans Publishing Company, 1994.

Zimmerman, Thomas E, Carlson, G. Raymond, Bicket, Zenas J., And He Gave Pastors. Sprinfield: Gospel Publishing House, 1995.

QUOTATIONS

A contended Spirit is the sweetness of existence (Anonymous)

Spirit is immortal Truth; matter is mortal error (Mary Baker Eddy)

In this world there are two forces: the sword and spirit. The Spirit has always conquered the sword (Napoleon Bonaparte)

The Spirit indeed is willing but the flesh is weak (NT: Mtt 26:41)

It is the Spirit that quickeneth (NT: John 6:63

Not of the letter, but of the Spirit: for the letter killeth, but the spirit giveth life (NT: II Cor. 3:6)

The Spirit of man is the candle of the Lord (OT: Pr. 20:27)

He that hath no rule over his own spirit is like a city that is broken down, and without walls (OT: Pr 23:28).

He who is small in faith will never be great in anything but failure (Anonymous)

Without faith a man can do nothing, but faith can stifle all science (Henri Fréderick Amiel: journal)

For what is faith unless it is to believe what you do not see (St. Augustine).

There never was found in any age of the world, either philosophy, or sect, or law, or discipline which did so highly exalt the public good as the Christian faith (Sir Francis Bacon)

Faith is a higher faculty than reason (Philip James Bailey: Festus)

Live by faith until you have faith (Peter Boehler to John Wesley)

Teaching and Understanding Pneumatology & Spiritual Gifts

Faith is the daring of the soul to go further than it can see (William Newton Clarke)

All work that worth anything is done in faith (Albert Schweitzer)

These are no tricks in plain and simple faith (William Shakespeare)

Faith is the force of life (Leo Tolstory: My Confessions)

The man without faith is a walking corpse (Pope Xystus I: The Ring)

Give to the world the best you have and the best will come back to you (Anonymous)

Faith is the union of God with the soul (St. John of the Cross)

Faith needs her daily bread (Dinah Maria Mulock Craik: Fortune's Marriage)

Faith is dead to doubt, dumb to discouragement, blind to impossibilities (The Defender)

Religion is a life. Faith is only the fuse (Anonymous)

Faith is not a sense, nor sight, nor reason, but taking God at His word (Arthur Benoni Evans)

Faith must have adequate evidence, else it is mere superstition (Archibald Alexander)

Workless faith God never rewards, faithless work God never rewards (D. L. Hood)

Faith will beget in us three things: Vision, Venture, and Victory (George W. Riclout)

Faith is saying "Amen" to God (Merv Rosell)

APPENDIX A

THE ORIGIN AND GROWTH OF THE ENGLISH BIBLE

Original Manuscripts 1500 BC-100 AD

Massoretic Text 100 B.C.

Samaritan Pentateuch 400 B.C.

Aramaic Targums 400 B.C.

Septuagint 300 B.C.

Early Copies

Codex Alexandrinus 425 AD

Codex Vaticanus 340 AD

Codex Sinaiticus 330 AD

Other Ancient Copies

Codex Ephraem 300-400 AD

Codex Bezae 300-400 AD

Codex I 400 AD

Codex W 400 AD

Codex Claromontanus 500 AD

Codex Laudianus 585 AD

Codex Regius 700 AD

Minuscule Manuscripts

Minuscule 565 800 AD

Minuscule 1739 900 AD

Minuscule 1and 2 1100 AD

Minuscule 13 1300 AD

Minuscule 61 1400 AD

Ancient Versions

Syriac Versions

The Diatessaron 140 AD

The Old Syriac 400 AD

The Curetonian Syriac 400 AD

The Sinaitic Syriac 400 AD

The Peshitta 400 AD

Vulgate 400 AD

Coptic Versions

The Sahidic 300 AD

The Bohairic 400 AD

Modern Translations

Wycliffe 1380

Tyndale 1525

Coverdale 1535

Matthews 1537

Great 1539

Geneva 1560

Bishops 1568

King James 1611

Revised Version 1881

American Standard 1901

Revised Standard Version 1952

Berkeley 1959

Amplified 1965

JB 1966

New English Bible 1970

New American Standard Bible 1971

Living Bible 1971

TEV 1976

The Good News Bible 1976

New International Version 1976

New King James Version 1982

APPENDIX B

The Seven Churches of Asia Minor

- **Ephesus,** the orthodox church (Revelation 2:1-7).

- **Smyrna**, the poor-rich church (Revelation 2:8-11).

- **Pergamos**, the church with bad surroundings (Revelation 2:12-17).

- **Thyatira,** the church of the evil prophetess (Revelation 2:18-29).

- **Sardis**, the dying church (Revelation 3:1-6).

- **Philadelphia**, the weak but loyal church (Revelation 3:7-13).

- **Laodocea**, the rich-poor church (Revelation 3:14-32).

APPENDIX C

Hall of Famers in the History of the Church

AUGUSTINE born in Tagaste (Soul Ahras), Algeria, North Africa, form 354-430 A D. His mother, Monica was a devout Christian. He schooled in Carthage (coastal area of Tunisia, North Africa). He was later sent to Rome were he studied the Scriptures and Philosophy. He was a pagan intellectual. He became mixed into Manicheism (pegan belief in the scientific explanation of nature). After many prayers by his mother and friends he got converted to Christianity. Later he became a Bishop of Hippo and apologist, who opposed heresies. He wrote many Christian literatures and apologies.

CYPRIAN born in North Africa, around the third century, was a wealthy and distinguished pagan intellectual, orator, and writer. He got converted to Christianity and was baptized. He became Bishop of Carthage (Tunisia), North Africa in 249 A D. On September 14, 258 A D, he was later arested from being a Christian apologist, and imprisoned to die by the sword.

TERTULLIAN born in Carthage (Tunisia), North Africa in 160 A D. He was a prolific Christian author. He was first to write Christian Latin literature. He was a notable apologist who wrote extensively against heresies. He studied law and practiced in Rome. He was a great student of philosophy and history. He died around 220 A D.

ORIGEN (185-254) born in Alexandria, Egypt, he studied Greek philosophy. He was a writer and famous teacher. He was a student of Clement of Alexandria. He is noted to be by far the greatest scholar the church had produced. He wrote many large and learned books. He wrote commentaries on all books of the Bible. He was a Christian apologist, who later became bisop of Caesarea.

ATHANASIUS believed to be a native of Alexandria in Egypt travelled and studied the Bible in Libya an Egypt respectively. At the Council of Nicaea in 325 A D, he answered the question whether Christ, the Son, was truly and fully God as the Father. Athanasius informed his confused fellow Christians that Christ was the very God. He was a smart Christian apologist. His life spanned from 293-373 A D.

CLEMENT OF ALEXANDRIA born in Athens, Greece but spent much of his days in Africa due to persecution of the believers. He was a teacher and apologist. He did a lot of writings to lead the church to a better understanding of the person of Christ.

JOSEPHUS born in 37 A D, alsp known as Yosef Ben Matityahu, when naturalized to Roman citizenship, his name was Titus Flavius Josyphus. He was a first century Jewish historian and apologist of a priestly and royal ancestry who survived and recorded the destruction in Jerusalem in AD 70. His work gave an important insight into first century Judaism.

THEOPHILUS OF ALEXANDRIA was a bishop of Alexandria, Egypt. He was one of the greatest preachers of the church.

JUSTIN MARTYR (100-166 A D) wrote bodly and very ably as an apologist in defense on the Christians. He was a philosopher. His outstanding work on the "logos" attracted many contemporary Christian scholars of his time. He wrote voluminously against heresies.

IGNATIUS (67-110 A D), was a native of Antioch. He wrote series of letters which have been preserved as an example of early Christian theology. He is believed to be a follower of the Apostle John. He became the third bishop of Antioch.

POLYCARP (69-155 A D) was a second century bishop of Smyrna. He died a martyr when he was stabbed after the attempt to burn him at the stake failed. He was arrested and charged for being a Christian. When told to benounce Christ and save his life, Polycarp replied, "eighty and six years have I served Him, and He has done me no wrong; how can I blaspheme Him, my King, who has saved me? I am a Christian." He was a bold Christian apologist.

APPENDIX D

Biblical Civilizations

The three categories of civilization within the span of two thousand years each: 1) Civilization from Genesis chapters 1 through 11. God is dealing with the human race from creation to Noah. 2) Civilization from Genesis chapter 12 through Malachi. God is dealing with the human family from Abraham to Christ. 3) Civilization from Acts through Revelation. God is dealing with the church from Pentecost to the Rapture. Etnically, to divide the Bible according to race or people or group; 3 groups of people: Jews, Gentiles, and the Church.

The First Civilization, first 2000 years

The antediluvian cultures comprised people living before the flood: Adam, agriculture was the main scale of this civilization. Some tended animals and were herdsmen. Cain, agriculture, mucis, arts, and architecture were part of this civilization. Seth, farming, great field workers, and botany were importatent elements of this civilization.

The dulivian cultures comprised Noah, architecturing, arts, and farming were their forte. Shem, Ham, and Jappeth dealt with agriculturing, architecturing, arts, and trading.

God divided the human race at Bable. Shem's race inhabited the lands of Assyria north of the Tigris and **Asia**; Ham's race inhabited **Africa** and **Arabia/ Middle East**; Jappeth's race settled in Europe.

About 3000 B.C. civilization began in Egypt, the mother of modern invention, the cradle of civilization where an irrigation system, modernized agriculturing, dams for electricity, arts, architecturing, the invention of the papyrus and hieroglyphics.

The Second Civilization, second 2000 years

This began with the call of Abraham by God between 1900 through 1930 B.C. from the Ur of the Chaldeans which is south of Bagdad in Iraq. This was an Indo-European civilization in the 1900s B.C. Moses was born around 1520 B.C. Between 1440 to 1400 B.C. God called Moses to go and deliver His people from the Egyptian captivity. There was the birth of the Grecian culture or civilization around 470 to 332 B.C. Socrates, Plato, Aristotle, Hippocrates (Greek father of medicine), Herodotus (Greek historian), Pythagoras, Euclid, and Archimedes (Greek Mathematicians). The Arts and Sciences were born. Around 356 to 323 B. C. Alexander the Great took center stage. The Hellenistic culture in language, Architecturing, communications, and writing were in effect. Roman civilization existed between 437 to 264 B.C. The Old Testament was translated in Alexandria Egypt from Hebrew to Greek called the "Septuagint." In 27 B.C. the Roman Empire was established. Christ was born in about 4 B.C. Roma civilization advanced into the 4th century A.D.

The Third Civilization, third 2000 years

The church was born at 33 A.D. Around 313 A.D. various church councils were held to discuss issues relating to the scriptures: 1. Council at Jerusalem, salvation being extended to the gentiles; 2. Council at Nicaea, Christ is God in 325 A.D.; Council at Constantinople, The Holy Sprit is God? Held in 381 A.D.; Council at Ephesus, human beings totally depressed in 431 A.D.; Council of Chalcedon, Christ both man and God in 451 A.D. Jerome, educated in Romes, lived as a monk, lived in Bethlehem around 400 A.D. translated the Old Testament from Hebrew to Latin called the "Latin Vulgate." Augustine, born in North Africa, lived between 342 and 430 A.D. is credited for Catholicism. His mother, Monica, an educated Christian, sent him to Rome to learn, became a great Christian writer, became Bishop of Hippo. Tertullian, another North African born, studied law and practiced in Rome, became a Presbyter of Carthage in North Africa. He was a philosopher and teacher.

APPENDIX E

Canonical Historiography

The Bible is composed of documents which are not written long ago but have been transmitted and preserved through years by writings. Some early writings proffer that the bible is a very old book although not the oldest in the world. Recent discoveries show that writing was a well-established method in many countries long before the beginning of the Hebrew nation on the land of Palestine. Egypt and Mesopotamia were ancient cultures that did a lot of writing. Hieroglyphics or hieroglyphs were Egyptian forms of writing of picture based on a complicated system of consonants. About 1750 B.C. Egypt and Mesopotamia in the area of Syria or Palestine, some Semitic persona developed the alphabet. From this alphabet, al other alphabeths derived. An example of the alphabetic script on the so-called proto-Semetic inscriptions found in 1500 B.C. at the original site of Mt. Sinai. Moses was born in 1520 B.C. and called by God before 1440-1400 B.C.

Written Materials

Stone was the first material used for writing. Egypt, Mesopotamia, Babylonia were regions that used stone. Babylon legal and religious laws were written on stones. Humurabi in 1750 B.C. displayed 250 laws of Baybalonia well-known king. Earliest ebrew writings were on stone, such as theGezer Calender and Siloam inscription (700 B.C. relating to King Hezekiel in 2 Kings 50:50—Chronicles 32:30 mentioned an S-Shaped tunnel dug. Hebre alphabet is dated from 925 B.C. another well-known inscription was the Moabite inscription in a stone Aramic Text. *Clay* was another ancient material used for writing. These writings were in the Cuneiform (wedge-shape) form. The other earliest material used was *wood* in a wax-like form. *Metal* was also used in the forms of gold, silver, copper, and bronze. Roman soldiers used bronze tablets for diplomas. *Ostraca* or *ostracon* which was the combination of clay and shells, *potshed* and *shells* were used in 1100 B.C. through 750 B.C. *Papyrus* was another material used which was lighter and flexible. Paper was made from the papyrus plant. Leather and parchment both are animal skins but leather is tanner and processed with chemicals as parchment in stretched and dried on a frame from small animals such as sheer and goats. *Vellum* (veal of animal skin) used interchangeably with parchment. Veal, made of fine calf skin was also used but parchment was widely used in both the Old Testament and New Testament times. For many centuries the form of ancient books were *rolls* and *scrows*. Later the *codex* was invented. It was convenient, could be folded, and were sheets.

Languages of the Bible

Hebrew was the official language in the state of Isreal. Aramic was spoken in Syria and other Middle Eastern countries. Greek was highly spoken as an international language. All books of theOld Teastament at this time were written in Hebrew, Hebrew comprise diverse languages called Semitic, which was the prototype of Aramaic, Syriac, Arabic, Akkadian (Assyrian and or Babylonian). After the exile in 500 B.C., Aramiaic became the official language of Palestine. Jesus spoke Aramaic. Example "Abba" "Eloi, Eloi." Greek was a first century official language as English is today.

Manuscripts of the New Testament

Manuscript is anything writted by hand. The New Testament manuscripts are of two types: 1. *Uncilas*, written in capital letters and 2. *Cursives* or *Minuscules*, written in small letters. There are ove 5,300 New Testament manuscripts. A large portion of the New Testament was minuscules or cursives. Uncila scripts amounted to 650. Uncial dated and cursives dated from the 9th through the 16th century. Uncials are written with spaces or punctuations. Out of the 650 manuscripts 95 papari and more than 270 lectionaries (liturgical readings or texts).

Important Uncials

Valuable uncials were dated from the 2nd through the 4th century. They were about 50. Our oldest vellum manuscripts with the Old Testament complete and New Testament almost complete with pages missing.

NOTES

INTRODUCTION

1. William Barclay, The Promise of the Spirit. Philadelphia: The Westminster Press, 1960.

2. George Hendry, The Holy Spirit in Christian Theology. Philadelphia: The Westminster Press, 1952.

3. Hendrikus Berkhof, The Doctrine of the Holy Spirit: The Annie Kinkead Warfield Lectures, 1963-1964. Richmond: John Knox Press, 1967.

4. Rena Yocom and Barr, and William R., The Church in the Movement of the Spirit. Grand Rapids: William Eerdmans Publishing Company, 1994.

5. Jack Haberer, Living the Presence of the Holy Spirit. Louisville, Geneva Press, 2001.

6. Thomas E. Zimmerman, Carlson, G. Raymond, Bicket, Zenas J., And He Gave Pastors. Sprinfield: Gospel Publishing House, 1995.

7. Watchman Nee, Spiritual Authority. New York: Christian Fellowship Publishers, Inc., 1972.

8. Paul J. Achtemeire, The HarperCollins Bible Dictionary. San Francisco: Harper Collins Publishers, 1996

9. Alasdair C. Heron, The Holy Spirit. Philadelphia: The Westminster Press, 1983.

10. Paul J. Achtemeire, The HarperCollins Bible Dictionary. San Francisco: Harper Collins Publishers, 1996

CHAPTER 1

1. Veli-Matti Kärkkäinen, Pneumatology: The Holy Spirit in Ecumenical, International and Contextual Perspective. Grand Rapids: Baker Academic, 2002.

2. Ibid., 12.

3. Ibid., 17.

4. Veli-Matti Kärkkäinen, Pneumatology: The Holy Spirit in Ecumenical, International and Contextual Perspective. Grand Rapids: Baker Academic, 2002.

5. Ibid., 15.

6. Veli-Matti Kärkkäinen, Pneumatology: The Holy Spirit in Ecumenical, International and Contextual Perspective. Grand Rapids: Baker Academic, 2002.

7. John Charles Cooper, The Spiritual Presence in the Theology of Paul Tillich. Macon: Mercer University Press, 1997.

8. Elizabeth Teresa Groppe, Yves Congar's Theology of the Holy Spirit. Oxford: Oxford University Press, 2004.

9. Chapman, Geoffrey, The World and the Spirit. San Francisco: Harper & Row Publishers, 1984.

10. Michael Welker, God the Spirit. Minneapolis: Fortress Press, 1994.

11. Veli-Matti Kärkkäinen, Pneumatology: The Holy Spirit in Ecumenical, International and Contextual Perspective. Grand Rapids: Baker Academic, 2002.

12. Veli-Matti Kärkkäinen, Pneumatology: The Holy Spirit in Ecumenical, International and Contextual Perspective. Grand Rapids: Baker Academic, 2002.

13. Veli-Matti Kärkkäinen, Pneumatology: The Holy Spirit in Ecumenical, International and Contextual Perspective. Grand Rapids: Baker Academic, 2002.

14. Peikoff, Leonard, Objectivism: The Philosophy of Ayn Rand. New York, Penguine Books, 1991.

CHAPTER 2

1. Barnabas Lindars, The Theology of the Letter to the Hebrews. Cambridge: Cambridge University Press, 1991.

2. Philip Edgcumbe Hughes, A Commentary on the Epistle to the Hebrews. Grand Rapids: William B. Eerdmans Publishing Company, 1977.

3. C. E. B. Cranfield, A Critical and Exegetical Commentary in the Epistle to the Romans. Edinburgh: T & T Clark, 1979.

4. John Calvin, Commentaries on The Epistles of Paul to the Galatians and Ephesians. Grand Rapids: Baker Book House, 1981.

5. Robert H. Mounce et al, The New American Commentary. Broadman & Holman Publishers, 1995.

6. Matthew Black, Peake's Commentary on the Bible. London, Routledge, 1962.

7. Charles F. Pfeiffer et al, The Wycliffe Bible Commentary. Chicago: Moody Press, 1962.

8. Charles F. Pfeiffer et al, The Wycliffe Bible Commentary. Chicago: Moody Press, 1962.

CHAPTER 3

1. David Prior, The Message of I Corinthians: Life in the Local Church. Downers Grove: InterVarsity Press, 1985.

2. Gerald Bray and Thomas C. Oden, Ancient Christian Commentary on Scripture: New Testament VII 1-2 Corinthians. Downers Grove: InterVarsity Press, 1999. 452 Notes

3. Walter Thomas Conner, The Work of the Holy Spirit. Nashville: Broadman Press, 1940.

4. Gordon D. Fee, The First Epistle to the Corinthians. Grand Rapids: William B. Eerdmann Publishing Company, 1987.

5. Leonard Peikoff, Objectivism: The Philosophy of Ayn Rand. New York, Penguine Books, 1991.

CHAPTER 4

1. *The Nine Gifts of the Spirit* and their usage in the Ministry of Jesus and the Early Church are compilations of Daniel L. Segraves, *Introduction To Signs and Wonders: A Guide to the Supernatural Realm,* Christian Life College, United Pentecostal Church, Inc., Stockton, California.

2. Philip Stokes, Philosophy: 100 Essential Thinkers. New York: Enchanted Lion Books, 2003.

CHAPTER 5

1. Allen Rhea Hunt, The Inspired Body: Paul, the Corinthians, and Divine Inspiration. Macon: Mercer University Press, 1996.

2. Simon J. Kistemaker, New Testament Commentary: Exposition of the 1st Epistle to the Corinthians. Grand Rapids: BakerBooks, 1993.

3. Philipp Melanchthon, Annotations on First Corinthians. Milwaukee: Marquette University Press, 1995.

4. Victor Paul Furnish, New Testament Theology: The Theology of the First Letter to the Corinthians. Cambridge: Cambridge University Church, 1999.

5. Victor Paul Furnish, New Testament Theology: The Theology of the First Letter to the Corinthians. Cambridge: Cambridge University Church, 1999.

6. Dale B Martin, The Corinthian Body. New Haven: Yale University Press, 1995.

7. Ibid., 5.

8. Dale B Martin, The Corinthian Body. New Haven: Yale University Press, 1995.

9. Anthony S Thiselton, The First Epistle to the Corinthians: A Commentary on the Greek Text. Grand Rapids: William B. Eerdmans Publishing Company, 2000.

10. Ibid., 928.

11. Ibid., 928.

12. Anthony S Thiselton, The First Epistle to the Corinthians: A Commentary on the Greek Text. Grand Rapids: William B. Eerdmans Publishing Company, 2000.

13. Ibid., 937.

14. Anthony S Thiselton, The First Epistle to the Corinthians: A Commentary on the Greek Text. Grand Rapids: William B. Eerdmans Publishing Company, 2000.

15. Anthony S Thiselton, The First Epistle to the Corinthians: A Commentary on the Greek Text. Grand Rapids: William B. Eerdmans Publishing Company, 2000.

16. Ibid., 186-87.

17. Anthony S Thiselton, The First Epistle to the Corinthians: A Commentary on the Greek Text. Grand Rapids: William B. Eerdmans Publishing Company, 2000.

18. Philip Stokes, Philosophy: 100 Essential Thinkers. New York: Enchanted Lion Books, 2003.

19. Ibid., 37

CHAPTER 6

1. Anthony S Thiselton, The First Epistle to the Corinthians: A Commentary on the Greek Text. Grand Rapids: William B. Eerdmans Publishing Company, 2000.

2. Ibid., 945.

3. Ibid., 945.

4. Anthony S Thiselton, The First Epistle to the Corinthians: A Commentary on the Greek Text. Grand Rapids: William B. Eerdmans Publishing Company, 2000.

5. Ibid., 948.

6. Anthony S Thiselton, The First Epistle to the Corinthians: A Commentary on the Greek Text. Grand Rapids: William B. Eerdmans Publishing Company, 2000.

7. Ibid., 956.

8. Anthony S Thiselton, The First Epistle to the Corinthians: A Commentary on the Greek Text. Grand Rapids: William B. Eerdmans Publishing Company, 2000.

9. Anthony S Thiselton, The First Epistle to the Corinthians: A Commentary on the Greek Text. Grand Rapids: William B. Eerdmans Publishing Company, 2000.

10. Anthony S Thiselton, The First Epistle to the Corinthians: A Commentary on the Greek Text. Grand Rapids: William B. Eerdmans Publishing Company, 2000.

11. Anthony S Thiselton, The First Epistle to the Corinthians: A Commentary on the Greek Text. Grand Rapids: William B. Eerdmans Publishing Company, 2000.

12. Anthony S Thiselton, The First Epistle to the Corinthians: A Commentary on the Greek Text. Grand Rapids: William B. Eerdmans Publishing Company, 2000.

13. Ibid., 968.

14. Anthony S Thiselton, The First Epistle to the Corinthians: A Commentary on the Greek Text. Grand Rapids: William B. Eerdmans Publishing Company, 2000.

15. Ibid., 971.

16. Anthony S Thiselton, The First Epistle to the Corinthians: A Commentary on the Greek Text. Grand Rapids: William B. Eerdmans Publishing Company, 2000.

17. Philip stokes, Philosophy: 100 Essential Thinkers. New York: Enchanted Lion Books, 2003.

18. Ibid., 47.

19. Ibid., 49.

CHAPTER 7

1. Anthony S. Thiselton, The First Epistle to the Corinthians: A Commentary on the Greek Text. Grand Rapids: William B. Eerdmans Publishing Company, 2000.

2. Anthony S. Thiselton, The First Epistle to the Corinthians: A Commentary on the Greek Text. Grand Rapids: William B. Eerdmans Publishing Company, 2000.

3. Malony, H. Newton, Lovekin, A. Adams, Glossolalia. Oxford: Oxford University Press, 1985.

4. Ibid., 1907.

5. H. Newton Malony and A. Adams lovekin, Glossolalia: Behavioral Science Perspectives on Speaking in Tongues. Oxford: Oxford University Press, 1985.

6. Ibid.,

7. Watson E. Mills, A Theological/ Exegetical Approach to Glossolalia. New York: University Press, 1985.

8. H. Newton Malony and A. Adams Lovekin, Glossolalia: Behavioral Science Perspectives on Speaking in Tongues. Oxford: Oxford University Press, 1985.

9. Ibid.,

10. Ibid.,

11. Watson E. Mills, A Theological/ Exegetical Approach to Glossolalia. New York: University Press, 1985.

12. Ibid.,

13. Ibid.,

14. Ibid.,

15. H. Newton Malony and A. Adams Lovekin, Glossolalia: Behavioral Science Perspectives on Speaking in Tongues. Oxford: Oxford University Press, 1985.

16. Robert H Lavenda. and Emily A. Shultz, Anthropology: What Doest it Mean to Be Human? Oxford: Oxford University Press, 2008.

CHAPTER 8

1. Stanley K Stowers, A Rereading of Romans: Justice, Jews, and Gentiles. New Have: Yale University Press, 1994.

2. Margaret McDonald, Colossians and Ephesians. Collegeville: The Liturgical Press, 2000.

3. John R. W. Stott, The Message of Ephesians: God's New Society. Downers Grove: Inter-varsity Press, 1979.

4. William F. and James Arthur Walter, The Anchor Bible: I Corinthians: A New Testament Translation. Garden City: Doubleday & Company, Inc., 1976.

5. Markus Barth, The Anchor Bible, Ephesians. New York: Doubleday, 1960.

6. John Calvin, Commentaries on The Epistles of Paul to the Galatians and Ephesians. Grand Rapids: Baker Book House, 1981.

7. John Calvin, Commentaries on The Epistles of Paul to the Galatians and Ephesians. Grand Rapids: Baker Book House, 1981.

8. Philip Stokes, Philosophy: 100 Essential Thinkers. New York: Enchanted Lion Books, 2003.

9. Ibid., 77.

10. Ibid., 79.

CHAPTER 9

1. *The four-fold Ministry; the Biblical nature of God's leader as an Eagle, Ox, Lion, and Man; Personal Tesimony* (vocal and visual), *Dynamics of "Oikos Ministry," The Power of Agape*, and the various methods and tools for the soul winner. The work in it entirety was compiled by John E. Putnam, Dynamics of Soul Winning, Christian Life College, Stockton, California. Credence to Gene Edwards, *How To have A SoulWinning Church*.

2. Philip Stokes, Philosophy: 100 Essential Thinkers. New York: Enchanted Lion Books, 2003.

3. Ibid., 95.

4. Ibid., 99.

CHAPTER 10

1. George Asthur Buttrick, Bowie, Walter Russell, Paul Scherer, John Knox, Samuel Terrien, The Interpreter's Bible: The Holy Scriptures in the king James and Revised Standard Versions With General Articles and Introduction, Exegesis, Exposition for each Book of the Bible. Nashville: Abingdon Press, 1983.

2. Christopher Bryan, A Preface to Romans: Notes on the Epistle in Its Literary and Cultural Setting. Oxford: Oxford University Press, 2000.

3. De Bruyn, Theodore, Pelagius's Commentary on St Paul's Epistle to the Romans. Oxford, Clarendon press, 1993.

4. Theodore De Bruyn, Pelagius's Commentary on St Paul's Epistle to the Romans. Oxford, Clarendon press, 1993.

5. Matthew Black, Peake's Commentary on the Bible. London, Routledge, 1962.

6. Raymond E. Brown, Fitzmyer, Joseph A., Murphy Roland E., The New Jerome Biblical Commentary. Englewood Ckifts: Prentice Hall, Inc., 1990, p 863

7. Ibid., 863.

8. William F. and Walter, Arthur Walter, The Anchor Bible: I Corinthians: A New Testament Translation. Garden City: Doubleday & Company, Inc., 1976.

9. Alexander Maclaren, Expositions of Holy Scripture. Grand Rapids: Baker Book House

10. Raymond E. Brown, Joseph A. Fitzmyer, Murphy Roland E., The New Jerome Biblical Commentary. Englewood Ckifts: Prentice Hall, Inc., 1990, p 863.

11. Raymond E. Brown, Joseph A. Fitzmyer, Murphy Roland E., The New Jerome Biblical Commentary. Englewood Ckifts: Prentice Hall, Inc., 1990, p 911.

12. Ibid., 911.

13. George Arthur Buttrick et al, The interpreter's Bible: The Holy Scriptures in the King James and Revised Standard Versions with General Articles and Introduction, Exegesis, Exposition for Each Book of the Bible, Volume X. Nashville, 1953.

CHAPTER 11

1. Jerry M. Stuberfield, *The Effective Minister of Education* Nashville: Broadman & Holman Publishers, 1993.

2. William P. Alston, Religious Belief and Philosophical Thought: Readings in the Philosophy of Religion. New York: Harcourt, Brace & World, Inc., 1963.

3. Ibid., 422.

CHAPYER 12

1. Ernest Best, A Critical and Exegetical Commentary on Ephesians. Edinburg: T & T Clark, 1998.

2. Joseph A. Fitzmyer, The Anchor Bible: Romans, A New Translation with Introduction and Commentary. New York: Doubleday, 1993.

3. Raymond E. Brown, Joseph A. Fitzmyer, Roland E. Murphy, The New Jerome Biblical Commentary. Englewood Ckifts: Prentice Hall, Inc., 1990, p 889.

4. Ronald E. Heinne, The Commentaries of Origen and Jerome on St Paul's Epistle to the Ephesians. Oxford: Oxford University Press, 2002.

5. F. F. Bruce, Tyndale New Testament Commentaries, Revised Edition. The Letter of Paul to the Romans: An Introduction and Commentary. Leicester: Inter-Varsity Press, 1988.

6. F. F. Bruce, Tyndale New Testament Commentaries, Revised Edition. The Letter of Paul to the Romans: An Introduction and Commentary. Leicester: Inter-Varsity Press, 1988.

CHAPTER 13

1. Bryan Magee, The Story of Philosophy: The Essential Guide to the History of Western Philosophy. London: Dorling Kindersley Publishing, 1998.

CHAPTER 14

1. George Asthur Buttrick, Bowie, Russell Walker, Paul Scherer, John Knox, Terrien, Samuel, The Interpreter's Bible: The Holy Scriptures in the king James and Revised Standard Versions With General Articles and Introduction, Exegesis, Exposition for each Book of the Bible. Nashville: Abingdon Press, 1983.

2. Ernest Best, A Critical and Exegetical Commentary on Ephesians. Edinburg: T & T Clark, 1998.

3. Ronald E Heine, The Commentaries of Origen and Jerome on St Paul's Epistle to the Ephesians. Oxford: Oxford University Press, 2002.

4. Ronald E. Heine, The Commentaries of Origen and Jerome on St Paul's Epistle to the Ephesians. Oxford: Oxford University Press, 2002.

5. Ronald E. Heine, The Commentaries of Origen and Jerome on St Paul's Epistle to the Ephesians. Oxford: Oxford University Press, 2002.

6. F. F. Bruce, Tyndale New Testament Commentaries, Revised Edition. The Letter of Paul to the Romans: An Introduction and Commentary. Leicester: Inter-Varsity Press, 1988.

7. W. E. Vine, *Vine's Expository Dictionary of Old and New Testament Words* (Iowa: World Publishers, 1981).

8. Leonard Peikoff, Objectivism: The Philosophy of Ayn Rand. New York, Penguin Books, 1991.

9. Ibid., 251-303.

CHAPTER 15

1. William Temple, Readings in St. John's Gospel. London: Macmillan & Co. Ltd.,1963.

2. Ibid., 85.

3. Daryl Elgridge, The Teaching Ministry of the Church: Integrating Biblical Truth With Contemporary Application. Nashville: Broadman & Holdman Publishers, 1995

4. Bryan Magee, The Story of Philosophy: The Essential Guide to the History of Western Philosophy. London: Dorling Kindersley Publishing, 1998.

CHAPTER 16

1. Robert B. Hughes, Everyman's Bible Commentary: First Corinthians. Chicago: Moody Press, 1985.

2. Raymond E. Brown, Joseph A. Fritzmyer, Roland E. Murphy, The New Jerome Biblical Commentary. Englewood Ckifts: Prentice Hall, Inc., 1990.

3. Ibid., 810.

4. Ibid., 810.

5. Ibid., 811.

6. Paul J. Achtemeier, Roger S. Boraas, Michael Fishbane, Pheme Perkins, and William O. Walker, The HaperCollins Bible Dictionary. San Francisco: Harper Collins Publishers, 1996.

7. Raymond E. Brown, Joseph A. Fitzmyer, Roland E. Murphy, The New Jerome Biblical Commentary. Englewood Ckifts: Prentice Hall, Inc., 1990, p. 811.

8. Raymond E. Brown, Joseph A. Fitzmyer, Roland E. Murphy, The New Jerome Biblical Commentary. Englewood Ckifts: Prentice Hall, Inc., 1990, p. 811.

9. Ibid., 811.

10. Paul J. Achtemeier, Roger S. Boraas, Michael Fishbane, Pheme Perkins, and William O. Walker, The HaperCollins Bible Dictionary. San Francisco: Harper Collins Publishers, 1996.

11. Albert Edward Bailey, *Daily Life in Bible Times*. New York: Charles Scribner's Sons, 1943.

12. Leonard Peikoff, Objectivism: The Philosophy of Ayn Rand. New York, Penguine Books, 1991.

13. Exegesis by David K. Bernard, The Message of Romans. Hazelwood: World Aflame Press, 1987.

14. Exegesis by F. F. Bruce, Tyndale New Testament Commentaries, Revised Edition. The Letter of Paul to the Romans: An Introduction and Commentary. Leicester: Inter-Varsity Press, 1988.

15. Exegesis by Robert B. Hughes, Everyman's Bible Commentary: First Corinthians. Chicago: Moody Press, 1985.

NAME INDEX

Aaron 16, 104

Achtemeier, Paul J 17,18

Alland 94

Alexander of Hales 74

Alexander the Great 27

Alston, William P. 152

Ambrose 41

Ambrosiaster 40, 41

Anselm of Cantebury 70

Anselm of Cantebury 70

Anselm of Laon 70

Aquinas, Thomas 70, 77, 86, 102, 196

Aristotle 52, 70, 79,137

Arminius, Jacobus 92

Assyrians 27

Athanasius 20

Augustine 23, 40, 41, 77, 78, 88

Aurelius, Marcus 88

Babylonians 27

Bacon, Roger 70

Bailey, Albert E. 249

Barclay, William 14

Barkeley, George 115

Barr 15

Barth, Markus 100, 101

Basil 20, 40

Benedict de Spinoza 102

Bengel 75, 77

Berkhof, Hendrikus 15

Bernard, David K. 124, 239

Bernard of Clairvaux 70

Best, Ernest 90, 155, 188, 239

Bishop of Cloyne 115

Bittlinger 81

Black, Matthew 34, 127

Boethins 70, 88.

Browning, Robert 170

Brown, Raymond 127

Bruce, F. F. 129, 159, 192, 241

Bryan, Christopher 125

Buchsel, J. W. 81

Butltmann, Rudolf 23, 125

Buttrick, George Athur 118

Calvin, John 33, 86, 88, 101

Chapman, Geoffrey 24

Chrysostom 40, 41, 76, 77, 85, 86, 125

Clement of Alexandria 76

Collyer, Robert 98

Conner, Welter T. 42

Cooper, John Charles 24

Conzelmann 75, 81, 87

Cranfield, C. E. B. 32

Cyril of Alexandria 20

Cyril of Jerusalem 20, 40, 41

Davis, James 77, 78

De Lille, Alain 70

Dryer, Elizabeth 20

Dunn 76

E., Murphy R. 128

Eldridge, Daryl 209

Ellis, E. 130

Erasmus, Desiderius 102

Evarts, William M. 170

F., William 128

Fee, Gordon D. 42, 45, 81

Fitzmyer, Joseph A. 127

Forbes, Christopher 86

Forsyth, Peter T 67

Estius 86

Furnish, Victor P. 71, 72

Gee, Donald 82

Greeven 134

Groppe, Elizabeth T. 24

Gundry, Robert 86

Haberer, Jack 15

Harrington 74, 75

Hart 94

Heinne, Ronald E. 158

Hildegard of Binger 70

Hine 94

Hobbes, Thomas 52

Hugh of St. Victor 70

Hughes, Robert H. 243

Hughes, Philip E. 32

Hugo, Victor 52

Hunt, Allen 67, 79, 78

Jerome 41, 99, 157, 190

Jewett, Robert 84, 126

Joachim of Fiore 70

Johnstonin, Robin 92

Jung, Carl 91

Kant 52

Kärkkäinen, Veli-Matti 20, 21, 22, 23

Kildahl, J. P. 90

Kistemaker, Simon J. 68, 69

Kuhn 156

Lategan 74, 75

Leibniz, Gottfried W. 115

Lichtenberg, George C. 67

Lindras, Barnabas 32

Lombard, Peter 70, 91

Lovekin, A. Adams 91

Lovenda, Robert 95, 96, 137

Luther, Martin 70

Macchia, F. D. 90

MacDonald, Margaret 99

Mackie 91

Maclarey, Alexander 129

Magee, Bryan 179, 229

Malebranche, Nicolas 102

Mahony, H. Newton 91, 94

Martin, Dale 73, 74

Melanchthon, Philipp 69, 70, 71

Milk, Watson E. 92

Moltmann, Jurgen 25

Mounce, Robert 34

Muller, Ulrich 84

Nietzche, Friedrich 255

Oden, Thomas C. 42

Origen 86, 98, 157, 189, 190

Ozman, Agnes 93

Parham, Charles 93

Paveisky, 94

Peake 34

Peikoff, Leonard 29, 30, 36

Philo 65, 95

Pinnock, Clark 25

Plato 70, 137

Prior, David 40

Rahner, Karl 23

Ramsay 93

Rand, Ayn 29, 30, 199

Ribourg, E. 32

Sachs, John 22, 23

Saint Dominic 70

Schlick, Moritz 115

Sherill 93

Shultz, A 95, 96, 137

Smith, Helen 91

St. Anselm 88

Stokes, Philip 65, 79, 88

Stott, John R. W. 100

Stuberfield, Jerry M. 143

Sunden 94

Temple, William 201

Tertullian 76, 87

Theodore, DeBryan 126, 127

Theodoret of Cyr 41, 86

Thiselton, Anthony S. 75, 76, 77, 78, 82, 86

Virgil 86, 90

Walter, Arthur 128

Warren, Richard 206

Whitman, Walt 98

Woodbridge, Fredrick J. 81

Wycliffe, John 70

Yeo, Khiok-Khing 77

Yocom, Rena 15

Zodhiates 75, 76

Zwaanstra 93

GENERAL INDEX

A

A Gift of Grace 14

A word of knowledge 39, 55

Abase 153

Ability 153

Able 153

Absolute 29

Access 153

Accomplish 231

Active 231

Acknowledge 31

Act 17

Adorn 97

Administrators 39

Advance 138

Affirm 169

Air 26

Ambassador 180

Angels 104

Another 31

Antilegomena 256

Apologetes 97, 98

Apologies 31

Apology 32, 33, 34, 35

Apostolē 180

Apostles 38, 39, 41, 44, 103

Apt to teach 104

Aristonian realism 36

Atheism 256

B

Bearer of life 27

Benefit 318

Benevolence 31

Bestow 138

Biblical inerrancy 256

Biblical liberation 256

Big Bang Theory 256

Birth 13

Bishop 13

Body 13, 95

Bless 97

Blow 26

Breath 13

Breathing 27

C

Call 103

Catastrophism 137

Charisma 14

Charismata 14

Charismatic 21

C

Christ 103

Christian community 20

Christian maturity 185

Christians 231

Christology 72

Church edification 243

Cinderella of Theology 21

Clothe 26

Comforter 19

Commission 231

Communal discernment 23

Communalism 243

Complimentary gifts 15

Confirmation 58

Conflict dualism 95

Conservative Evangelicals 256

Conspicuous 257

Conviction 56

Cosmic Existence 256

Cosmogony 256

C

Cosmos 256

Craft man 180

Creation 30

Cosmological Argument 230

D

Deacon 169

Deduce 257

Deftly 257 95

Dependency syndrome 90

Determinism 95

Devoid 257

Dialectic reason 257

Dichotomy 257

Discerning 80

Discerning of Spirits 39, 43

Dissent 257

Dissenter 257

Distribute 200

Divine gift 16

D

Divinity 20

Divine revelations 36

Divine Spirit 26

Divine wisdom 76

Doctrine 231

Dualism

E

Ecclesiology 72

Ecstatic utterances 36

Ecstasy 99

Edification 116

Effective deeds of power 82

Egalitarianism 257

Eisegesis 257

Emperical Theory 257

Enlightment rationalism 256

Epicureans 16, 73

Epistemology 36

Equip 39

E

Escathology 72

Esotericsm 258

Essentialism 137

Evangelist 182

Evangelical rationalism 256

Exegesis 40, 43, 256

Exegete 256

Exegetes 97, 98, 258

Existentialism 258

Experientialism 258

Extra Sensory 36

Extraterresterial 258

F

Facticity 258

Faith 13, 39, 41, 43

F

Faithful 37

Father of Lights 161

Fellowship 116

Feminist Theology 258

Feudalism 21

Fideism 256

Flesh 26

Foreign Language 90

Fount 256

Fulfill 116

Fulness of Christ 185

Fundamentalism 259

G

Gift 53

Gifts 14, 34, 41, 43

Gift of administration 44

Gift of faith 39

H

Heal 80

Hellenistic culture 27

Heresy 89, 259

Heretic 259

Gifts of faith 41

Gift of grace 14

Gifts of grace 14

Gift of healing 43

Gifts of healing 35, 39, 41, 43

Glossolalia 90, 91, 92

Gnosticism 259

God's gifts 35

God the Spirit 25

Good people skills 143

Gospel 103

Grace 35, 37

Grace gifts 35

Gratuity 14

Grecian civilization 26

Grow 116

Hermeneutic 259

Holy 80

Holy Ghost 28

Holy Spirit 15, 20, 26, 33, 39

Homiletics 259

Homologoumena 259

Humble 138

Human spirit 47

I

Idealism 95

Ideologue 259

Illuminism 260

Indefectibilty 259

L

Leadership 138

Leading 125

Liberality 125

Liberation pneumatology 20

Inerrency 259

Infallibility 259

Inspired 43

Instruct 34

Intellectual power 76

Intent 80

Intepret 43, 66

Interpretation 35, 36, 43

Interpretation of tongues 43

Intrinsicists 36

Liberation Theology 260

Life 19

Life-Breath 28

Life force 27

Light 21, 231

Likeness 19

Locus 260

Love 116

K

Knowledge 40, 43, 169

M

Manifest 89

Materialism 95

Matter 95

Marxism 21

Measure of faith 127

Medieval Christian Theology 70

Medieval mystics and Souls 76

Medieval Scholasticism 260

N

Narrative Theology 260

Noethically 260

Nomalism 36

Message 19

Messenger 53

Merciful helper 131

Metaphysics 29

Mind 95, 169

Minister 103

Ministerial leadership 15

Monophysite 260

Montanism 260

Moral teaching 35

Motivational gifts 46

Mundane 260

Mysteries 43

O

Obedient 70

Objectivism 30, 317

Obscurantism 418

Office 70

One baptism 246

One body 151, 246

One faith 246

Ontological Argument 270

Orthodoxy 119

P

Passion 169

Pastor 15, 80

Paraklētos 19

Pauline Theology 90

Pentecostal 21

Pentecostalism 21

Pietism 260

Pneumatology 20, 24

Pneumatological renaissance 20, 28

Propositional Truth 261

Prothesis 180

Protestant Liberalism 261

Peudepigrapha 261

Psychē 73

Philosophy 89

Planner 146

Platonic realism 36

Plentitude 137

Pneuma 13, 23, 24, 26, 27, 28

Polemicism 260

Praise 180

Preach 200

Preacher 66

Premordialism 261

Preparation 58

Process Theology 261

Prophecy 41, 43, 50, 69

Prophet 38, 41, 44, 66

Purpose 180

R

Rationalistic Orthodoxy 419

Realism 1

Reality 30

Revelation 148

Right 8

Ruach 22, 27, 28

Ruling 194

S

Salvation 200

Sanctification 72, 89

Scholasticism 70

Self-condescensionalism 261

Self-edification 243

Servant of God 17

Shepherd 37

Soldier 138

Son of man 105

Soteriology 72

Soul 95

Static 261

Stoics 16

Subjectivism 261

Sixth sense 36

Speaking in Tongues 35

Spirit 17, 26, 28, 35, 37, 95

Spirit-filled 21

Spirit of Christ 17

Spirit of God 26

Spiritual gifts 15, 17, 28

Spirit of Grace 33

Spirit of Jesus 17

Spirit of Life 25

Spirit-inspired 50

Spirit people 44

Spirits 39

Spiritual Calisthenics 107

Supernatural power 27

Systematic Theology 24, 261

T

Tabernacle 19

Talent 13

Teach 15, 37

Teacher 13

Teachers 16, 38, 44

Teaching 15, 16, 34

Teleological Argument 179

Telos 79

Terrestrial 262

The church as a community 186

The four-fold ministry 103

The Holy Spirit 15, 17

Translate 97

Trust 138

Truth 21, 31, 185

U

Understanding 13

Unilinear gradation 137

Unintelligible 90, 91

Unintelligible utterances 91

Unity of the faith 185

Useful 53

The Spirit of His Son 17

The working of miracles 41, 43, 50

Theological discipline 20

Theology 20

To another 83

To blow 26

Tongue 19, 89

Tongues 35, 36, 41, 43, 44, 50

Transcendency 262

Utter 89

Utterance 31

Utterance of Knowledge 39, 41

Utterance of Wisdom 39

V

Vessel 200

Virtue 199

W

Wind 26

Wind of Doctrine 185

Wisdom 31, 40, 43, 55

Witness 153

Word 66

Word of Wisdom 55

Work 138

Working of faith 162

Worship 97, 110

The geographical extent of the orient and occident is a validation of the cultural and ideological differences that have existed with constancies between the two hemispheres throughout the ions of time. Ideological pluralism has been the common practice of the inhabitants of both spheres but with unique manifestations. Christianity along with other religions are warmly embraced and pragmatically characterized by the orientals and occidentals with reserved peculiarities. Oriental Christians viewed pneumatology as being a significant particle of their theological and liturgical lives, while Occidental Christians see Christology as the primal substance in Christianity. Although both groups have a history of singling out this distinction, over the years, theologians and theology have helped both sides understand the importance of both pneumatology and Christology in Christianity. It is concertedly understood that neither of the two can be studied or taught without the other. Their inseparable existence makes Christianity a complete whole.

The author's exploration and literary expedition through myriad of sources allow him to compile data relevant to understanding the importance of the Holy Ghost and Spiritual gifts within the Christian community. Whether a secular or non-secular intellectual, you will find the information in this book to be rewarding, resourceful and informative. You will come across comments from some of humanity's and Christendom's finest and brightest academics in an eclectic form. Join the author now on his literary expedition. Welcome!

Elijah E. Dunbar earned his Bachelor of Arts degree in Economics from Kean University of Union, New Jersey. He is a graduate of Maranatha Bible College of Tubmanburg, Liberia, West Africa, an alumnus of Christian Life College of Stockton, California, earned his Master's and Doctorate in Christian Education from Freedom Bible College & Seminary, and served as dean of True Vine School of Biblical Studies where he taught several courses. He is also a certified Secondary Social Studies/ U. S. History teacher and candidate for a Master of Arts degree in teaching at the University of North Carolina at Charlotte. He is the author of ***Christian Education in The Millennium: A 21st Century Focus*** (Author House, 2004), ***Effective Counseling: A Contemporary Guide For Troubled Teens and Their Families*** (Morris Publishing, 2005), including other published and non-published works. He is also the inventor of the ***Educational Game, "Worldly-Wise"*** with a concentration in Mathematics, the Sciences, Social Studies, World History, and current events for elementary, middle grade and secondary learners. He is currently working on a few secular textbooks to publish.

Printed in the USA
CPSIA information can be obtained
at www.ICGtesting.com
LVHW022333180424
777863LV00028B/188